COMMUNICATION, NEW MEDIA AND EVERYDAY LIFE

COMMUNICATION, NEW MEDIA AND EVERYDAY LIFE

tony **CHALKLEY**   adam **BROWN**   toija **CINQUE**   brad **WARREN**   mitchell **HOBBS**   mark **FINN**

OXFORD
UNIVERSITY PRESS
AUSTRALIA & NEW ZEALAND

OXFORD
UNIVERSITY PRESS

Oxford University Press is a department of the University of Oxford.

It furthers the University's objective of excellence in research, scholarship, and education by publishing worldwide. Oxford is a registered trademark of Oxford University Press in the UK and in certain other countries.

Published in Australia by
Oxford University Press
253 Normanby Road, South Melbourne, Victoria 3205, Australia

National Library of Australia Cataloguing-in-Publication data

Tony Chalkley … [et al.]
Communication, new media and everyday life

9780195572322 (pbk.)

Includes bibliographical references and index.
Communication–Textbooks.
Mass media.
Chalkley, Tony.

302.23

Edited by John Mahony
Text design by Kerri Wilson
Typeset by diacriTech
Indexed by Russell Brooks
Printed by Sheck Wah Tong Printing Press Ltd

CONTENTS

PART 2 CONTENT AND CULTURE

10 Ideology and Meaning in Film: Life in Surround Sound

Adam Brown

11 Organisational/Professional Communication: Modelling the World of Work

Tony Chalkley

12 Values, Ideals and Power in the Brave New Digital World

Toija Cinque

13 Constructed Reality: What's 'Real' Nowadays?

Brad Warren

LIST OF FIGURES

GUIDED TOUR

Family X
This fictionalised family helps bring to life the often complex concepts and theories to be discussed.

What you will learn from this chapter
Outlines the key concepts and themes of the chapter.

CHAPTER 2 WHAT EXACTLY IS MEDIA AND WHAT IS 'NEW' IN NEW MEDIA? « 9

content and program schedules, with resulting economic, social and political implications. These events have led to technical, regulatory and conceptual transformations.

The wider use of broadband services including the internet (via the personal computer/television as one unit), together with video services via mobile telephony, has regulators such as the Australian Communications and Media Authority (ACMA) reconsidering the definition of media markets due to these evolving technologies. The new media services, providing a diverse array of media forms and content choices, place demands on traditional media, requiring it to be more informative and competitive. According to Nielsen Online, Australian internet use has taken over television viewing for the first time (Nielsen Online, 2008: 1). A Cisco commissioned study found similar results reporting that where an average of 14 hours was spent viewing television, 22 hours were spent on the internet (Hendry, 2008). Many theorists are predicting that traditional broadcasting is on the way down (Levinson, 2009; Tapscott, 2009). We should, however, be cautious in anticipating the 'death of broadcasting' (to use Given's 1998 turn of phrase) because the introduction of radio did not see the complete demise of print, nor television the demise of radio. How traditional media industries respond to the new media environment will be an ongoing process as technology and audience expectations continue to change. An interesting point is that much of what is considered 'new media' is no longer new, so it is reasonable to question what happens to the old new media, a point taken up later in this chapter.

Have you watched 3DTV? Does it revolutionise the televisual experience or is it just bad for your optical health (note that it does come with health warnings)?

What exactly is 'media' and what does it mean to us?

The traditional media forms of the press and, later, broadcasting were originally meant to be independent institutions that could empower the people of liberal democracies (see Alexander, 1981). There is a well-established political imperative to the function of the media in its role as the 'fourth estate' (discussed further in Chapter 3). This is an accountability function—that is, the media acts as a 'watchdog' and is used to keep the public informed about what politicians are doing on their behalf or important events or issues that should be raised publicly, for example. This important role dates back to the eighteenth and nineteenth centuries in liberal democracies (for print because broadcasting as we know it was not yet invented) and was performed by journalists in the public interest (the first estate being God, the second the Crown, and the third the government) (Schultz, 1998: 48). For more than two centuries the traditional media forms have been largely defined by geography and limited by political and cultural boundaries. New digital technologies and the increasing array and distribution of ideas, choice and opportunities facilitate innovative methods of communication through the spheres of finance, economy, government, work, health, entertainment and leisure. All this has meant massive change for the traditional media.

Mass media: media for a large group of individuals engaging in similar activities, such as watching a particular television show during prime time (7pm to 9pm) or reading the Saturday edition of a newspaper.

While print media forms such as newspapers, magazines and books have existed for centuries, the term **mass media** gained widespread use in the 1920s with the creation of nationwide radio networks such as the ABC in Australia. It was then used with reference to the later introduction of television. Essentially, it is media for a large group of individuals engaging in similar activities. The various **media industries** are involved in developing, producing and disseminating content through a wide variety of formats including the press, electronic publishing, telecommunications, radio, music, cinema and television.

Media industries: Media industries are involved in developing, producing and disseminating content through a wide variesty of formats including the press, electronic publishing, telecommunications, radio, music, cinema and television.

Using a different term, McQuail (2005: 81) describes the media as an institution (or institutions) that have the central aim to produce and distribute *knowledge* in the widest sense of the word. And that such knowledge 'enables us to make some sense of our experience of the social world, even if

Side bars
Contain definitions of key concepts that are introduced in the text. They also contain short reflections and activities.

Summary
Highlights the key points covered in the chapter.

Further reading
Lists of references used to inform the writer and develop the structure of the chapter.

Weblinks
Lists of interesting websites for you to follow.

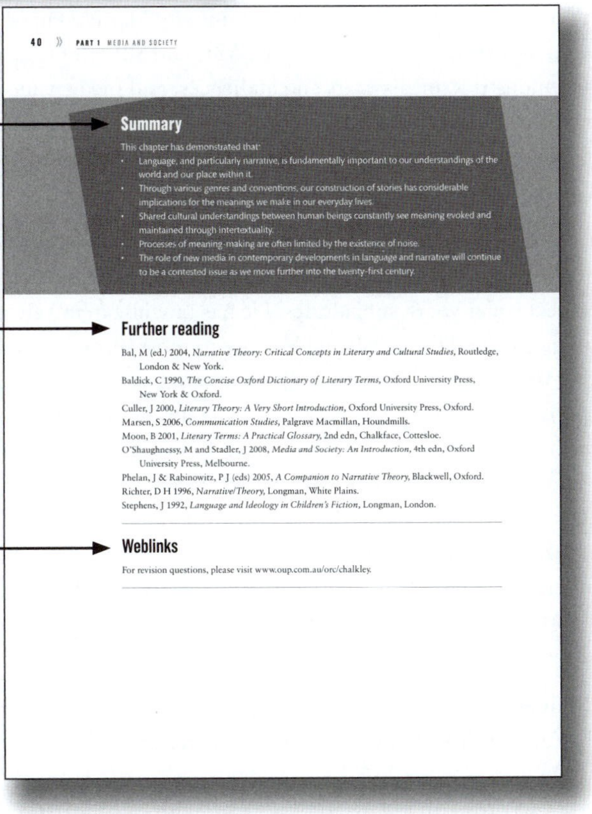
40 » PART 1 MEDIA AND SOCIETY

Summary

This chapter has demonstrated that:

- Language, and particularly narrative, is fundamentally important to our understandings of the world and our place within it.
- Through various genres and conventions, our construction of stories has considerable implications for the meanings we make in our everyday lives.
- Shared cultural understandings between human beings constantly see meaning evoked and maintained through intertextuality.
- Processes of meaning-making are often limited by the existence of noise.
- The role of new media in contemporary developments in language and narrative will continue to be a contested issue as we move further into the twenty-first century.

Further reading

Bal, M (ed.) 2004, *Narrative Theory: Critical Concepts in Literary and Cultural Studies*, Routledge, London & New York.
Baldick, C 1990, *The Concise Oxford Dictionary of Literary Terms*, Oxford University Press, New York & Oxford.
Culler, J 2000, *Literary Theory: A Very Short Introduction*, Oxford University Press, Oxford.
Marsen, S 2006, *Communication Studies*, Palgrave Macmillan, Houndmills.
Moon, B 2001, *Literary Terms: A Practical Glossary*, 2nd edn, Chalkface, Cottesloe.
O'Shaughnessy, M and Stadler, J 2008, *Media and Society: An Introduction*, 4th edn, Oxford University Press, Melbourne.
Phelan, J & Rabinowitz, P J (eds) 2005, *A Companion to Narrative Theory*, Blackwell, Oxford.
Richter, D H 1996, *Narrative/Theory*, Longman, White Plains.
Stephens, J 1992, *Language and Ideology in Children's Fiction*, Longman, London.

Weblinks

For revision questions, please visit www.oup.com.au/orc/chalkley.

ABOUT THE AUTHORS

Tony Chalkley's research, irrespective of how it starts, always seems to bring him back to communication studies, be it in schools, teams, factories, government departments or online social worlds. Working as an organisational ethnographer (while undertaking a PhD) he noticed that most people wanted to talk about 'communication' and, more than anything else, they wanted to talk about what happens when it goes wrong. This simple discovery, teamed with an awareness of the power of new media, led to an interest in finding out more about 'the future of communication'. Some of the early discoveries about the nature of 'futuristic communication' you will find here, in this book. On a personal note, Tony is the father of five children, the owner of two dogs and, despite his dislike of egg, the proud keeper of a number of scruffy chickens.

Dr Adam Brown is a lecturer in Media, Communication and Public Relations at Deakin University. He holds a PhD in Cultural Studies, focusing on representations of the Holocaust in different media. His thesis, *Representation and Judgement: 'Privileged' Jews in Holocaust Writing and Film*, received the Isi Leibler Prize for the best contribution to advancing knowledge of racial, religious or ethnic prejudice in any time or place. Adam also works as a volunteer at the Jewish Holocaust Centre in Melbourne, where he has initiated the digitisation, indexing and cataloguing of the centre's survivor videotestimony collection. He is currently working on research in the areas of children's television, new media in museums and Holocaust film. Adam has a small, fluffy dog. Her name is Tiffany.

Dr Toija Cinque is a lecturer in the Media and Communication program in the School of Communication and Creative Arts at Deakin University. Her PhD in Media and Communications was a study of the Public Interest Obligations of the ABC and SBS. Her teaching areas include communications institutions and industries, media texts and audiences, and the new media. Toija supervises postgraduate students in media and communication. Her research interests focus on communications and media policy, new media, public broadcasting, digital television, internet use and regulation, digital democracy, and globalisation.

Dr Brad Warren holds a PhD in Sociology from Deakin University, as well as a Diploma of Education from the University of Melbourne. His doctoral thesis was a reassessment of the body of theory pertaining to spectacular youth subcultures. He has taught extensively in both the secondary and tertiary sectors, including Media, IT, English and History to most secondary year levels in Perth, Sydney and Melbourne. For the last five years, he has taught a range of subjects in the Media and Communication and Sociology areas at Deakin University, as well as supervising theses at Honours and PhD levels. Current research interests include youth cultures, the effects of new media on literacy, and literacy standards generally, and he has published on all of these topics. In recent years, Brad has specialised in the teaching of research methods, both qualitative and quantitative, including statistics, and is firmly convinced that the latter doesn't have to be boring. In 2000 and 2003, Brad taught English at universities in Guangzhou in China, at both undergraduate and postgraduate levels. Other interests include reading, cooking and student welfare, not necessarily in that order. He thinks marriage is a wonderful institution, having done it twice.

Dr Mitchell John Hobbs is a Conjoint Lecturer in Sociology and Anthropology at the University of Newcastle, New South Wales, where he regularly teaches subjects concerned with the media and communication. He completed his undergraduate education in Sociology, Political Science and Psychology at La Trobe University and received his doctorate in Sociology and Anthropology from the University of Newcastle in 2010. His research and publications are concerned with media institutions and their political, social and cultural ramifications.

Dr Mark Finn is a Senior Lecturer in Media and Communications at the Swinburne University of Technology in Melbourne. He has published widely on various aspects of new media, including the historical development of electronic commerce and the social implications of mobile computing technologies. For the past five years he has been specialising in the social and cultural dimensions of computer games, and was a key contributor to a recently published anthology of papers focusing on the *Grand Theft Auto* series of games. His most recent work examines the way new communications technologies are combining aspects of real and virtual spaces through applications such as augmented reality and other location-based services.

ACKNOWLEDGMENTS

The authors and the publisher wish to acknowledge the following sources and thank the copyright holders for reproduction of their material:

Jürgen Habermas, translated by Thomas Burger, The Structural Transformation of the Public Sphere, © MIT, The MIT Press, p. 2, p. 23; © Telegraph Media Group Limited 2009, pp. 38, 39; The Geelong Advertiser Group, p. 127; How I became a Foursquare cyberstalker, Leo Hickman, 23 July 2010 © Guardian News and Media Ltd 2010; With kind permission from Springer Science + Business Media: Journal of Business Ethics, Digital Piracy: Factors that influence attitude toward behaviour, volume 63, 2006, Sulaiman Al-Rafee p. 196; Hall, S (1980) 'Encoding/Decoding', in S Hall, D Hobson, A Lowe and P Willis (eds), Culture, Media, Language. Working Papers in Cultural Studies, 1972–79, Hutchinson, London, pp. 128–38, pp. 224, 225.

Every effort has been made to trace the original source of copyright material in this book. The publisher will be pleased to hear from copyright holders to rectify any errors or omissions.

ONLINE RESOURCE CENTRE

Find out more about the online resources accompanying this book by scanning this QR code with the camera on your mobile phone. Scanning the code will take you to the book's website. You will need to download and install a code reader (available for free online) to scan the code. (Note: Internet download costs may be charged by your mobile phone provider.)

Alternatively, visit the website at <www.oup.com.au/orc/chalkley>.

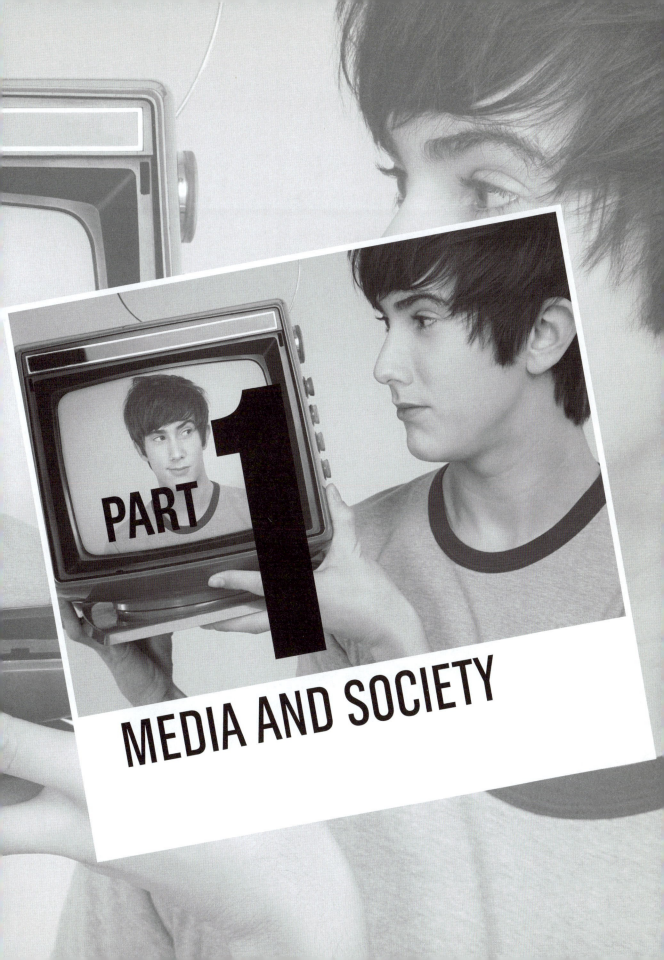

PART **1**

MEDIA AND SOCIETY

chapter 1

Introduction

Tony Chalkley

The first thing you should do after purchasing this book is return to the cover and cross the word 'new' out of the title. You might well ask (perfectly reasonably, because books cost money and you have just defaced this one) why we have included the word 'new' if it is unwanted, redundant, and now crossed out. The reason is simple: the word 'new' serves as a reminder. 'New' reminds the reader that even though we live in a world of rapid redundancy and disposability, a place where 'new' very quickly becomes 'old', we have to remember that, at some stage, all this common technology—things like social software, online shopping and other stuff—was 'new' and revolutionary. So, maybe don't cross out 'new', but instead occasionally pretend it's not there!

With this in mind, this book assumes that 'new media' is no longer external to everyday life; it's not something we artificially apply to our actions, friendships and communication. It is now embedded into most things we do, converged into our communication as much as the old-fashioned acts of speaking, writing, reading and communicating with those around us. New media *is* communication.

The aim of this book is to use stories to describe and explain the journey from 'new media in communication' to 'new media is communication'. Some of these tales are dark, dystopian accounts of bullying, theft and misery. Some stories are of bright new connections, happiness and joy. But all these stories have one thing in common: they are underpinned by theory, and it is theory that helps us understand what the stories are trying to tell us (and vice versa). There is a simple way to appreciate how these stories are told, reproduced and organised, and it's the metaphor of how sand is layered on the beach as sediment. The process of 'sedimentation' is the way in which we, over time, structure our ideas and construct reality by progressively layering our concerns and issues by sedimenting a different set of understandings over preceding ones (Tolbert & Zucker, 1997). Think of the stories in this text as the most recent layer of sediment, with many layers below and many more to come. Many other coastal phenomena also work with this 'sand and beach metaphor'; think of how wind storms whip one layer away, swiftly replacing it with another; how human impact can rapidly transform (or deform) the beach; and how, if we dig down in the sand, we expose the many layers below. It's the same for communication.

The book is organised into three different parts (you might even think of them as sedimented levels). The first, **Part 1: Media and Society**, introduces the reader to the building blocks of communication: its basic tools, devices and approaches. Here you will read about narrative, meaning and subtext, non-verbal communication, gendered communication, semiotics and the theories of postmodernity.

The second, **Part 2: Content and Culture**, takes the ideas and concepts in the first part and applies them to the things we might call 'new' media. Here you will read about ideology in film; organisational communication; values in the new digital world; and how identity, privacy, deception and 'truth' have been redefined.

The third and final part, **Part 3: Communication and Control**, looks at communication today, exploring what it might be like to live in an increasingly digital world. Here you will read about how a 'friend' is no longer necessarily a 'traditional, geographically close friend'; how gamers can live, talk and act in a whole other world; and why it is that we 'pirate' things that we don't own. This final part also introduces the idea that we now (happily?) live in a surveillance society, a society that is increasingly populated by citizens who can, if they wish, assume different forms of identity.

A distinctive feature of this book is its diverse authorship. It was written by a number of communication experts, each with a special interest in the topics on which they write. As a result, the chapters have slightly different 'voices' and writing style; nonetheless, the diversity of views should be viewed as a strength. In an effort to reduce the impact of the 'different tones' throughout this book, the authors have employed a number of narrative devices to 'sew' the book together. These are described below.

As you work through each part and chapter, you will read a number of stories about 'Family X'. This fictionalised family is a really useful tool to help bring to life the often complex concepts and theories to be discussed. You may find that you identify with one family member; perhaps the life of the son has some resonance, and you too might be bored at university and a little lost. Perhaps it's the mother or father, feeling like society is telling them that their work life is drawing to a close and yet they feel young? Perhaps it's no one and everyone all at once? Here's a little about the family.

Introducing Family X

The X family is a family of four (two adults, two children) who live in a small, older house on the fringe of an inner-city suburb undergoing slow but constant gentrification. They decided to live near a reasonably large city because this provided ready access to jobs, public transport, schools and a range of social and sporting activities. Family X itself is not a large family. The two adults are well into middle age and their children are older and mostly independent; the daughter is in her first year of studying anthropology and space science at university, and the son who is older, has deferred his final year at university in order to work for a year to 'sort out' his priorities. Both children went to select-entry government schools and did fairly well in their final year of high school.

Life is busy in the X household (and has been since their son's first day at childcare some 20 years ago). Sport is a declining event because, when they turned 15, both children got a casual job at the local supermarket; cooking is organised on a (mostly) effective roster;

and boyfriends and girlfriends have come and gone over the years. Ms X is recovering from the stress of trying to prosecute an ex-boyfriend who turned into a nasty online stalker, cyber-bully and nuisance txter.

The X family would probably not identify themselves as tech mad or 'tech heads', but they all have laptops, their home has wireless internet and cable TV, they all possess mobile phones (the children, iPhones), and Mrs X loves small gadgets like PalmPilots, GPS, iPads and any other new toy she can afford. The children have always had a TV in their bedroom, and, as they have saved up, they replaced their PS3 and Xboxes as new models arrived. Occasionally, the dog is left to watch the TV alone, as the rest of the family sits around the lounge room, typing on their individual laptops. The X family is actually pretty mundane, relatively ordinary and an excellent vehicle to represent the ideas in this book.

You will find **vignettes** or short stories about Family X throughout the book. These focus your attention on a particular event, or character(s), to highlight the real world of a particular theory or idea, or to examine in detail a specific setting or object. Vignettes are useful because these short dramatic descriptions are used to typify a range of experiences, creating a composite of all the people or events studied. In short, they get your attention by bringing to life the theories and concepts in this book.

Other pedagogical tools used in this book are:

Case studies: This text also makes use of real life situations, using newspapers, the internet and many other interesting examples from everyday life. We encourage you to further explore how the ideas, concepts and theories contained in these pages might translate into the actions of your daily life. Turn your friends, family and workplace into a communications laboratory!

Side bars: These contain definitions of key concepts that are used in the main body of the text. The terms in these side bars are often cultural or local idioms, complex terms or words that are crucial to understanding the rest of the chapter. Feel free to pencil in your own definitions as well. What have you got to lose? You have already defaced the cover! (Here I should insert ;-) or LOL. More on that later.) Side bars also contain short reflections and activities.

Weblinks: One of the challenges of new media is the redundancy that comes from the speed of change and weblinks are no exception. At the end of each chapter (and in some cases, in the main body of the text) are lists of interesting websites for you to follow. We assume that as most of these links are from large, well-established organisations, they will be stable and enduring. But this is not always the case. As we started writing this book, LimeWire was enormously popular but, by the end of writing, it was gone! If you have trouble finding a particular website, make Google your friend!

Study questions: These are provided to sharpen your focus and direct your thoughts back to the central concepts in each chapter. As you answer, it is useful to also ask yourself why you hold a particular position and what informs your thinking. In other words 'What is it I think, and why?' These questions can be found at: www.oup.com.au/orc/chalkley.

Further reading and Bibliography: At the end of each chapter you will also find a list of references used to inform the writer and develop the structure of the chapter. In the final pages of the book, the bibliography is a list of sources and a useful place to find other information, quotes and greater detail about what has been discussed in the chapters.

Glossary: In the final pages of this text (immediately before the bibliography) you will find a glossary of terms. The glossary is a device that decodes and explains the language of communications studies. It might be useful to read through this glossary after you have finished this introduction and you might even photocopy it and refer back to it as you work through the chapters.

Facebook: Firstly, go online and review the many Facebook groups that have 'communication studies' as their focus. (Some might have titles such as 'organisational communication' or 'professional communication' but using the word 'communication' to initiate your search will uncover many options.) Even though most people perceive Facebook to be a social forum (for most, a lovely way to connect with others while wasting time!), it is also a really useful place to hear what others have to say about the study of communication.

The most important thing is to enjoy reading this book. Some theories you will disagree with, some concepts might be difficult to digest, and some of the stories you read might be quite personal and confronting. As you work through the book, revisit the earlier chapters to deepen your understandings, reframe your opinions, examine your values and ideologies and, most of all, use this new knowledge to develop and improve your own communication.

Further reading

Tolbert, P & Zucker, L 1997, 'The institutionalization of institutional theory', in S Clegg & C Hardy (eds), *Studying Organization: Theory and Method*, 2nd edn, Sage Publications, London.

Weblinks

Facebook: www.facebook.com

Google: www.google.com

For revision questions, please visit www.oup.com.au/orc/chalkley.

What Exactly Is Media and What Is 'New' in New Media?

chapter

Toija Cinque

Another night in the life of Family X

'How do you get to play as Mario?', calls out Ms X to her brother.

'You have to get to the final level', replies a confident Master X.

The Family X children are happily 'playing' *Super Mario* online together on their respective laptops at the dining room table. The television late news drones on in the background with no one paying much attention to the latest celebrity footballer to be before a tribunal. Miss X gets a call over Skype and catches up with her best friend from kindergarten, Saba, who now lives in Dubai. Saba has just renovated her apartment and 'shows' Ms X around. Via Facebook, Miss X has maintained contact with her friends from primary and secondary school, many of whom live either interstate or overseas. In minutes she can find out what they have done over the weekend and with whom. Even though they don't see each other in the 'real world', they have remained close.

She turns her attention to completing her uni homework on outer space. She is studying Astronomy and Space Science at university. Rather than using an encyclopaedia, she logs onto the Hubble telescope site (http://hubblesite.org) to view high resolution images taken in our galaxy. She realises that she has missed some key classes that would help her complete her work so she puts up the information she has on Google Docs with some pictures and invites some of her classmates to let her know if she has missed any important facts. One person points out that she has incorrectly noted the distance from the earth to the sun in one of her digital models, so Ms X googles the correct answer and amends her mistake. As she does this she responds to txt messages coming in on her iPhone.

Master X leaves her to her tasks and heads out to a club in the city. He is part-way down the main street when he gets the tweet 'crap go GC', by which he understands his destination to be a bust so he turns on his heels for a club around the corner where he meets up with friends who got the same message.

Meanwhile, Mr X sets the alarm clock on his BlackBerry for 5am. Not to check that Master X is home but to check his emails that have come in from overseas before going into the office. Mrs X plays a game of Mahjong online and reads another chapter from *Mortal Remains* on her iPad before turning out the light.

What you will learn from this chapter

This chapter provides a simple definition of the media. It outlines some of the various ways you might come to understand the term. It distinguishes between old and new media and what processes have brought about the change. It considers the impact on society that the widespread use of old and new media has. In the chapter you will learn:

- What constitutes 'the media'
- How we went from 'old' media to 'new' media
- What we mean by 'new' media
- Some of the issues that have arisen in the new media age.

Introduction

The twentieth century has seen rapid technological developments that have resulted in the media becoming prevalent in almost all aspects of daily life. The launch of social network sites such as Twitter and Facebook has revolutionised the way we communicate, both in our professional and personal lives. The introduction of Skype has also advanced the way we communicate through both voice and video contact. It has been used to reunite families and given opportunities to elderly people in nursing homes to speak with family interstate or overseas. Wireless devices such as the iPad allow us the convenience to work and communicate on the go, any time, anywhere. We can watch television and YouTube clips, upload our own pictures or stories, stay in touch with family and friends and network with colleagues around the globe. We are no longer tethered to a desk, working more efficiently and flexibly. More than that, we can contribute to the range of content being created where this was not the case under an old broadcast model for the delivery of media content. Indeed, most chapters on the new media will start with an explanatory statement defining the old in comparison to the new. This chapter is no different and includes an overview of what constitutes traditional (old) mass media in order to establish what is 'new' about emerging technologies and services.

Until fairly recently, the media (and what we do with it) was clearly defined and consisted of four key media industries including: (1) print (encompassing books, newspapers, magazines; (2) broadcasting (initially by radio and then television); (3) music (recordings on tape or vinyl); and (4) the cinema. It is now quite clear in countries with highly developed media systems that all these industries—print, radio, television broadcasting, music and film—have undergone profound change, primarily in terms of delivery (from analogue to digital means), method (from hard copy to virtual copy in the case of print; and the radio frequency spectrum, satellites and cables for broadcasting), content and program schedules, with resulting economic, social and political implications. These events have led to technical, regulatory and conceptual transformations.

The wider use of broadband services including the internet (via the personal computer/television as one unit), together with video services via mobile telephony, has regulators such as the Australian Communications and Media Authority (ACMA) reconsidering the definition of media markets due to these evolving technologies. The new media services, providing a diverse array of media forms and content choices, place demands on traditional media, requiring it to be more informative and competitive. According to Nielsen Online, Australian internet use has taken over television viewing for the first time (Nielsen Online, 2008: 1). A Cisco commissioned study found similar results reporting that where an average of 14 hours was spent viewing television, 22 hours were spent on the internet (Hendry, 2008). Many theorists are predicting that traditional broadcasting is on the way down (Levinson, 2009; Tapscott, 2009). We should, however, be cautious in anticipating the 'death of broadcasting' (to use Given's 1998 turn of phrase) because the introduction of radio did not see the complete demise of print, nor television the demise of radio. How traditional media industries respond to the new media environment will be an ongoing process as technology and audience expectations continue to change. An interesting point is that much of what is considered 'new media' is no longer new, so it is reasonable to question what happens to the old new media, a point taken up later in this chapter.

Have you watched 3DTV? Does it revolutionise the televisual experience or is it just bad for your optical health (note that it does come with health warnings)?

What exactly is 'media' and what does it mean to us?

The traditional media forms of the press and, later, broadcasting were originally meant to be independent institutions that could empower the people of liberal democracies (see Alexander, 1981). There is a well-established political imperative to the function of the media in its role as the 'fourth estate' (discussed further in Chapter 3). This is an accountability function—that is, the media acts as a 'watchdog' and is used to keep the public informed about what politicians are doing on their behalf or important events or issues that should be raised publicly, for example. This important role dates back to the eighteenth and nineteenth centuries in liberal democracies (for print because broadcasting as we know it was not yet invented) and was performed by journalists in the public interest (the first estate being God, the second the Crown, and the third the government) (Schultz, 1998: 48). For more than two centuries the traditional media forms have been largely defined by geography and limited by political and cultural boundaries. New digital technologies and the increasing array and distribution of ideas, choice and opportunities facilitate innovative methods of communication through the spheres of finance, economy, government, work, health, entertainment and leisure. All this has meant massive change for the traditional media.

While print media forms such as newspapers, magazines and books have existed for centuries, the term **mass media** gained widespread use in the 1920s with the creation of nationwide radio networks such as the ABC in Australia. It was then used with reference to the later introduction of television. Essentially, it is media for a large group of individuals engaging in similar activities. The various **media industries** are involved in developing, producing and disseminating content through a wide variety of formats including the press, electronic publishing, telecommunications, radio, music, cinema and television.

Using a different term, McQuail (2005: 81) describes the media as an institution (or institutions) that have the central aim to produce and distribute *knowledge* in the widest sense of the word. And that such knowledge 'enables us to make some sense of our experience of the social world, even if

Mass media: media for a large group of individuals engaging in similar activities, such as watching a particular television show during prime time (7pm to 9pm) or reading the Saturday edition of a newspaper.

Media industries: Media industries are involved in developing, producing and disseminating content through a wide variesty of formats including the press, electronic publishing, telecommunications, radio, music, cinema and television.

the 'taking of meaning' occurs in relatively autonomous and very diversified ways'. To this definition of the media's role in society is added a further clarification by Cunningham and Turner (2010: 5) that, in an ever more commercial environment, 'the media are increasingly providing entertainment rather than information—and thus attempting to second-guess people's taste preferences before information needs'. As a result, it is important when studying the media and its functions to be able to deconstruct the messages delivered by the media we consume—be it a television or radio program, a newspaper article or film.

The word 'media' means middle and is a term purposely used to describe its location between the media industry/institution creating the content (the sender) on the one hand and the audience member (or receiver) on the other. Many years ago, Harold Lasswell (1948), a leading American political scientist and communications theorist, made the important statement about the media as 'mediating' (being the conduit) between the sender and receiver:

Who (says) What (to) Whom (in) What Channel (with) What Effect

Here, Lasswell's theory of the media communication process can be modelled for clarity as:

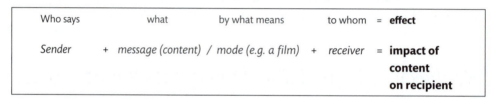

Figure 2.1 Modelling Lasswell's theory of media communication

Mediation: Mediation is a process whereby the sender relays versions of issues or events to the receiver that he or she cannot directly observe for him/herself by way of the media.

By definition, **mediation** is a process whereby the sender relays versions of issues or events (the world or reality) to the receiver that the receiver cannot directly observe for him/herself by way of the media (O'Shaughnessy & Stadler, 2008). However, the notion of mediation in the sense of the media intervening between ourselves and 'reality' is no more than a metaphor according to Denis McQuail (2005). This is because, according to O'Shaughnessy and Stadler (2008), the world impacts on the media (as the media might impact on the world/reality) and audiences are active in making meanings based on their own very individual learning experiences, cultural differences and psychological make-up. Importantly, audiences are not passive recipients of content. As a result, we might better understand our relationship to the world and the media via O'Shaughnessy and Stadler's (2008: 79) model of the world/media/audience relationship in Figure 2.2 below. The double arrows stress that the world/reality and audiences have mutual impact on the media:

Figure 2.2 The reciprocal nature of media communication

The media and the languages, sounds and images used in creating content (be it a television show or movie) are cues that audiences draw on (along with education, family, friends and the like) to make sense of the world and construct 'reality' as a result. We could say that the media is a system of representation (a concept that will be revisited in Chapter 3 but meaning here to look like, resemble or represent). However, because all representations come from humans (via the media organisations they work for) they come from a particular position and are, therefore, not completely unbiased, but relative. Further to this, the media can only represent issues/events/people and other things of the real world, giving a very realistic impression but never actuality. That is, realistic media is constructed either through selected camera angles and lighting, omission (editing) and increasingly digital photographic enhancements and other selection techniques. While offering a re-creation of the world, the media plays an important role in society.

McQuail (1987) has argued that the traditional media serve four main types of needs, namely: (1) *diversion* whereby there is an emotional release (for example, from day-to-day stressors); (2) *personal relationship* where the media provides both company for the individual when alone and serves as a point of conversation with others; (3) *surveillance* wherein the media delivers information about (or a version of) issues and events; and (4) *personal identity* as the individual comes to interactively locate (conceptualise, compare and contrast) themselves against the social practices, or other 'agencies of socialisation', to use Giddens' (1993: 76–80) term. The term includes family, peers and mass media. This final need of identity formation has been highlighted by audience reception studies underlining the theory that 'the presentation of social reality influences perceptions of collective and individual identity and the socialization process' (Hall, 1994: 189). That is, 'language' (comprising the visual language of television, film and other media industries) and culture provide representations that produce meanings (Hall, 1997a, 1997b). These meanings regulate social practices, affect people's conduct and, as a consequence, have real practical influence. There are, however, a number of widely divergent perspectives on the role of the media in society, which offer complexity to the study of media as more than simply industries and technologies on one hand, and audiences and what they 'do' with the media on the other. Remember that radio, television, cinema and the internet are all just inventions. It is what we do with them and for what reason that is significant to making sense of the media-rich world around us.

Understanding the media's role in society

A broad approach to making sense of the media's role in society, its process and effects, is through **structuralism** and **semiology**. As predominantly sociological methods of enquiry, their focus is on media systems and organisations and their relationship to the wider society (McQuail, 2005). The concern is with how meanings are produced or structured through codes or rules and discourses. Each of the media industries produces **texts** which are a collection of still or moving images and/or sounds put together, and functioning as a group to create meaning. Radio and television, for example, produce programming content; the press produces newspapers, books and magazines; advertisers create advertisements. Anything that generates meaning through signifying practices such as dress, television programs, images, sporting events, and vodcasts can be called a text. Indeed, a media text can take the form of a conversation, a book or article, a photograph containing a number of visual elements, a piece of music, a television show, a speech or a public demonstration, among other examples. The problem with the structuralist/semiotic approach is that understanding and meaning are largely subjective to particular individuals and cultures. For example, what we wear differs around the globe, as does the meaning conveyed about our clothing. Clothes can reflect cultural heritage (a Muslim woman might wear an abaya, an Indian woman a sari, an Ethiopian a gabi) or subcultural or subgroup identity (police, nurses, fire-fighters); colours have different cultural meanings (the West, for example, favours a white wedding and black for mourning, but in East India the bride traditionally wears red because white signifies death). But these categories are broad generalisations. Due to interpretation being largely subjective, any research findings (conclusions) using this approach are more difficult to replicate.

Another means of analysing the media is via **behaviouralism** or **empiricism**. These are psychological methods that focus on human behaviours, actions or acts rather than the characteristics

Do you think it is true that Rupert Murdoch is the last 'tycoon' or media player of real significance in the new media age?

Structuralism and semiology: This is the study of signs whereby the focus is on media systems and organisations and their relationship to the wider society (McQuail, 2005).

Texts: All media industries produce texts that are a collection of still or moving images and/or sounds functioning as a group to create meaning. Anything that generates meaning through signifying practices can be called a text.

Behaviouralism or empiricism: These are psychological methods that focus on human behaviours, actions or acts rather than the characteristics of industries.

of industries. This experimental method of research treats media use as a form of rational, motivated action where users choose, process and respond to communication messages (McQuail, 2005: 20). Content analysis was devised as a quantifiable and systematic method for description and analysis of the meaning of media messages (Sinclair, 2010b: 22), while the effects of mass media content were understood to have direct, immediate behavioural reactions on audiences like a 'magic bullet'. This 'magic bullet' theory has not gained wide acceptance, however, largely because it is not based on empirical analysis but rather on commonly held beliefs about human behaviour that assume people to be similarly controlled by their biologically based nature and that they react more or less homogeneously to whatever 'stimuli' they are exposed to (Lowery & DeFleur, 1995: 400). The empirical tradition continues to be used today but obstacles include the fact that technology and society continually change and, as a result, valid and reliable generalisations about the effects of the media can quickly become outdated. For example, Professor Howard Cantril's famous 1940 study of people's fearful reactions as a direct result of a 1938 radio play by Orson Welles, in which over 1 million Americans believed they were being invaded by Martians, would probably not find the same panicked reaction today due to the immediacy of technology and the fact-finding inclination of users (see Cantril, Gaudet & Herzog, 1940).

Political economy:
This is an empirical approach to understanding the economic structures and dynamics of media industries and the ideological content of media.

Yet another approach to understanding media texts and audiences is known as the **political economy** tradition. This is an empirical approach to understanding the economic structures and dynamics of media industries and the ideological content of media. Consideration of who has ownership and control of the media is fundamental, along with how media market forces are run; that is, media activity is an economic process resulting in a commodity—either media content/product or audiences for advertisers (McQuail, 2005: 99–100). Important questions from this approach would focus around mergers and acquisitions of media organisations such as Time/Warner/AOL, Bertelsmann AG or Vivendi/Universal (see: www.cjr.org/resources/index.php for a current and comprehensive list of what these and other major media companies own worldwide) and specifically the implications of such control over vast amounts of content for global consumption. For example, Disney controls film (through the companies Walt Disney Pictures, Touchstone Pictures, Hollywood Pictures, Miramax Films and Pixar); multiple national and cable television networks; music (Walt Disney Records, Hollywood Records and Lyric Street Records); and numerous titles via book and magazine publishing; as well as toys (including The Baby Einstein Company), theme parks and the Walt Disney Internet Group. Such power raises the issue of media organisations influencing government and policy to retain a dominant position in the market. More than this, the vast amount of content created, controlled and filtered to the wider public causes concern over the extent to which these top media companies influence the minds and behaviours of those who consume their media products.

In conceptualising 'the media', theorists have used the term 'consciousness industry' to argue that the media plays a substantial role in forming our consciousness; that is, what we think, how we think, and what we think about (Cunningham & Turner, 1997: 6; see also Enzensberger, 1974). If this is so, then *the media is extremely influential in our lives*. What is important here, though, is to acknowledge the capacity for audiences to negotiate and produce meaning from media texts that might be different from the intended meaning or preferred reading of the producer (the media). It is also probably inaccurate to use the word 'industry' to denote media organisations and what they offer us (consciousness) as we settle into the 'information age'. The problem with such a label, as Hartley points out, is that:

> Firms produce goods or services, while 'industries' are abstract aggregations of firms, actions, prices and the rest. 'Industry' is often used more loosely, interchangeably with business, trade, market, or even community … This does not mean that the term is useless or a lie; it means

that it must be used with care, carrying with it a full trail of analytical explanation. But instead, media studies imported it as self-evident and as real, with connotations that endowed vertically integrated industrial corporations not only with moral qualities (chiefly evil), but also with exorbitant or 'fabulous powers'.

According to Hartley (2009: 232), the term 'industry' brings connotations of power, control, hidden agendas and the objectification of audiences/consumers, which in turn provoke moralistic or ideological misgivings about wealth creation per se. A reasonable question has now arisen about whether or not it is possible to reconfigure the relationship between producer and consumer on more equal terms. Over 40 years ago, Alvin Toffler (1970) used the term 'prosumer' when he predicted that the role of producers and consumers would begin to blur and merge. Don Tapscott used the term 'prosumption' (production + consumption) in his 1995 book *The Digital Economy: Promise and Peril in the Age of Networked Intelligence*. More recently, Axel Bruns (2007: 6) has employed the term 'produsers' to describe partici-

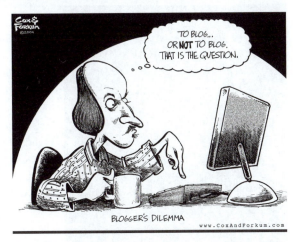

Figure 2.3 To blog or not to blog: 'If you're not online, you don't exist'

Source: www.coxandforkum.com

To blog or not to blog'? Is this a real question for you? It might be less a question of *whether* to blog as which type of blog you choose.

pants in interactive spaces who engage with content interchangeably in consumptive and productive modes and often at the same time. What is undeniable is that the top-down flow of information from a few companies to a mass audience has given way to user-created information distribution and sharing. This leads us to explore how new media is defined and understood.

What is new media?

Social network sites such as Facebook, Twitter, MySpace, WAYNE, hi5, Xanga, Bebo and many others are what we would call **new media**. The term 'new media' comprises content that is created, stored or retrieved in digital form ranging from text, still pictures, audio and video. New media forms are instantaneous, globally accessible, fast and efficient ways of passing on news and information. The new media has also created an almost virtual world. Games such as Second Life, where people have an avatar, live in a virtual world and become someone else, offer an escape from reality. Then there is Google, the search tool giant helping us make sense of the vast amounts of information online. While our searches are free, Google turns our clicks into money paid through advertising when we visit their sites. The advantage of this behavioural marketing for users is that the advertisements we see are based on our own search terms or tailor-made for people likely to buy the product or service.

The media, as part of all cultural activities, is being reconceived on many levels due to the processes of digitisation, convergence and globalisation (or marketisation). The media and what it does is now less a distinct sphere of life, offering, for example, print, television or radio services

New media: includes content that is created, stored or retrieved in digital form. New media includes digital forms of text, still pictures, audio and video.

alone, becoming an entity permeating everything from the design of cars, phones, software, furniture and clothing to new options for shopping and banking. Indeed, traditional (usually analogue) media including print, radio, film and television is a one-to-many broadcast system (to use Barr's 2000 term), which can be contrasted with the many-to-many interactive paradigm of today's new digital media.

A useful way of thinking about the new media is through the concept of **convergence**. The term can be used to describe how the previously separate businesses of (1) media, (2) telecommunications and (3) computing/information technology have come together, or converged, to offer interdependent services via digital networks.

Convergence: The term can be used to describe how the previously separate businesses of (1) media, (2) telecommunications and (3) computing/ information technology have come together, or converged, to offer interdependent services via digital networks.

For example, a television show (content) can be delivered to hand-held portable devices (computing/information technology) over the wireless communications network (once purely telecommunications). The term 'the convergence of modes' has been used by communications scholar Ithiel de Sola Pool (1983) and as early as 1979 by Nicholas Negroponte of the Massachusetts Institute of Technology (MIT). Negroponte was using three overlapping circles he characterised as (1) Broadcast and Motion Picture Industry, (2) Computer Industry and (3) Print and Publishing Industry, predicting that the overlap between the three circles would become almost total by 2000 (Gordon, 2003).

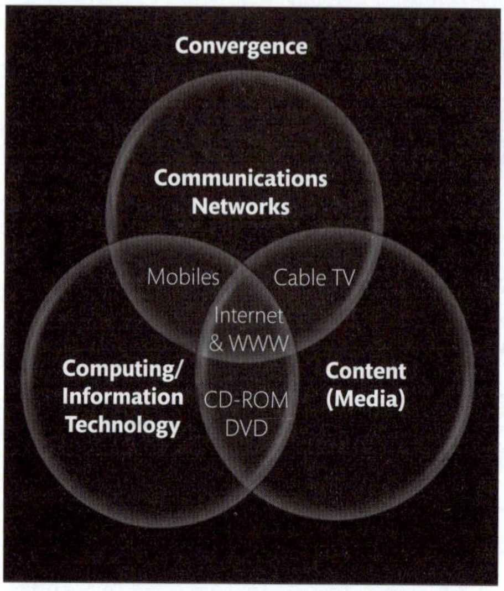

Figure 2.4 The process of convergence

Source: Trevor Barr, *newmedia.com.au*, Allen & Unwin, Sydney, 2000, www.allenandunwin.com

More recently the conceptual tool has been used by Australian scholars Trevor Barr (2000: 22–25) and Terry Flew (2008: 3). At its most basic level, Barr described the functional convergence between information technology (process), telecommunications (carriage) and media (content). For his part, Flew talks about the three Cs—(1) computing and information technology, (2) communications networks and (3) content (media). The authors consider the complex interaction between traditional media businesses with users' expectation that programs/content will be available at their convenience and coupled with greater interactivity where choice is important. As a consequence of convergence, program producers and content deliverers have to consider what audiences do with new media in order to engage them.

Fundamental to convergence is the digitisation of data and globalisation. **Digitisation** is the process of converting information (usually analogue) into a digital format or a series of zero and one digits (called binary code). What this means is that all information (whether from radio, television, newspapers, movies or blogs) is encoded in exactly the same format, eliminating distinctions between their forms and thus the need for multiple devices. Or as McQuail (2005: 39) puts it, 'information of all kinds and in all formats [is] carried with the same efficiency and also intermingled'. That is, there is no reason why we should not use the PC and a wireless connection for socialising, entertainment, communication, work, gaming, research, shopping—and indeed many users do. The Cisco study statistics noted above and current research indicate that internet use will rise as television use (via the set) declines. Tapscott (2009) found that internet users (significantly those born between January 1977 to December 1997) are:

Digitisation: Digitisation is the process of converting information (usually analogue) into a digital format or a series of zero and one digits (called binary code).

> more likely to turn on the computer and simultaneously interact in several different windows, talk on the telephone, listen to music, do homework, read a magazine, and watch television. TV has become like background MUZAK for them.

Clearly, the ability to access the television via the internet might appeal to many consumers rather than running a computer and a television at the same time. What the author points to is the trend for television to be just one of many simultaneous tasks that new (new) media users are engaged in at any given time. Again, it is too early to call the death of traditional media because there is a body of evidence demonstrating continuity in the mass audience (see, for example, von Hasebrink, 1997; Krotz & von Hasebrink, 1998; and Cinque, 2009, in relation to Australia's public broadcasters). McQuail (2005: 450) has argued that '[a]t the present time … it is too early to conclude that the mass audience will fade away. It still exists, albeit in somewhat new forms, and the mass media industries have shown a remarkable capacity to survive in familiar forms'. But will this trend continue as those born January 1998 to the present 'turn their backs on TV and other traditional media forms' (Tapscott, 2009: 42)?

Program producers and content deliverers have to consider what audiences do with new media in order to engage them. But this comes as users themselves are creating and disseminating content of interest to them and their peers. This will be an ongoing and dynamic process as technology and audience expectations develop, vary and adjust.

As noted above, an additional driver of the 'digital age' is **globalisation**. In his formative 1996 work *The Rise of the Network Society*, Manuel Castells stated that a global economy provides a marketplace that is vastly different from what consumers have had access to. A global marketplace operates in an electronic economy where information is currency and has the capacity to operate as a unit in real time on a universal scale, and capital is managed on a 24-hour basis in globally integrated financial markets. Moreover, despite protectionism and restrictions to free trade markets, goods, services and creative output are ever increasingly becoming global. According to Chang (2003), the widespread use of broadcast satellites and continuing policies of deregulation and privatisation facilitated the evolution of the media industries from a state of internationalisation (1960s–70s) to multinationalisation (1980s) and globalisation (1990s onward). By definition, globalisation is a process that sees nations integrating to form an interdependent global society, featuring its own economy, military, police, judicial system, parliament *and media*. Indeed, it is not possible to simply consider the global new (new) media from one's own local perspective because the medium is global. When it is asserted that the internet is global, our frame of reference is that the medium is not restricted by physical distance for distribution.

My four-year-old plays at checking email, 'working' on the computer and engaging with digital books, games and Skype. He, like his generation, will look to a single media device for applications anywhere, any time.

Globalisation: a process whereby industries are operating increasingly on an international basis as a result of the deregulation of communications industries and improved communications technologies.

What is 'new' in new media?

In establishing what is 'new' in new media it is important not to simply create a list of current technologies and uses and declare them new, because they won't be for long, as technologies and industries change and adapt to user demands. Media that might be termed 'old' now was once 'new' (see Flew, 2008; Pingree & Gitelman, 2003). Levinson (2009) distinguishes between the new media of websites, email and blogs, and the new new media of social network sites like Digg.com, social bookmarking sites like Delicious that allow users to locate and save websites that match their own interests and share them with others, and the virtual games like Foursquare played over a mobile application. Here, some theorists make a distinction between social network sites (SNS) and 'social networking sites' because being part of a social network, they argue, often means engaging with existing relationships online rather than forging new ones and net*working* as such (see Huijser, 2008; Boyd & Ellison, 2007; Ellison, Steinfield & Lampe, 2007). Research by Ellison et al. (2007: 1155) found that 'students view the primary audience for their profile to be people with whom they share an offline connection' and that 'students use Facebook primarily to maintain existing offline relationships or to solidify what

Figure 2.5 Information sharing via Delicious

Source: www.delicious.com. Reproduced with permission of Yahoo! Inc. © 2010
Yahoo! Inc. DELICIOUS and the DELICIOUS logo are registered trademarks of
Yahoo! Inc.

would otherwise be ephemeral, temporary acquaintanceships'. Problematically for such conclusions, however, is that the way social network/ing sites are used rapidly changes in a new media environment and users/uses are not globally uniform (more on this in Chapter 12).

Thus, we could question for how long new media technologies stay new; that is, what is the timeframe for 'newness'? I am not sure there is a clear answer to this question because technologies, applications and user needs change continuously, as noted above. A further point for consideration is what society does with the media and for what reasons it is new rather than just taking account of what the new media is (see Livingstone, 1999). Certainly examples are useful and currently include (at the time of writing) mobile hand-held devices such as the iPhone, iPad or BlackBerry; the internet; and Web 2.0. Web 2.0 as a communication platform is second-generation internet, which offers a more participatory understanding of the internet centred on virtual communities. The design of Web 2.0 is interactive and arguably improves the more people use and contribute to it. The best example might be Wikipedia, which offers a vast array of amateur scholarship on almost any topic.

New media issues

Current discourses of new media include recounting the forces for change of digitisation, convergence and globalisation. There are, however, a number of issues for concern in the new media environment such as the accuracy of information found online and, related to this, information overload. Here, Levinson (2009) argues that information overload is a misnomer because users experience no more anxiety online than they do walking into a large bookstore. Users, he contends, are capable at seeking out and accessing information that they are interested in and rejecting the rest. This view might, however, be too simplistic.

Tumber (2001) contends that the role of the media as the 'fourth estate' to act as the 'watchdog' of democracy and be an independent examiner of power might well be over, as traditional filters that enable verification no longer exist. Against this background, he argues that journalism via new electronic technologies might incorporate both *orientating journalism*, where background commentary and explanation are provided to the general public, and *instrumental journalism*, which makes available functional and specialised information (Tumber, 2001: 107–108). Without doubt, there is much data available from the internet and other media devices, but a question we must ask ourselves is whether data is the same thing as information and the answer is probably not. Further to this is the quantity of misinformation that is also accessible.

While the internet and online services provide information and services, without access to the tools of technology—including a computer, modem, phone line, connection to an Internet Service Provider (ISP)—the ability for some individuals to access and use information is diminished. Therefore, some groups in society will be advantaged over others in not only the tools that some have access to, but in education, skills base and knowledge. This is known as the **digital divide** and occurs not only between nations but *within* nations as well.

Other issues arise over the possibility for the internet and other computer-mediated communication devices to be a force for freedom and democracy. Internet 'freedom' is a term used by O'Loughlin (2001) in the negative—such as freedom *from* (for example, freedom from unwanted 'SPAM' emails or from state intervention); or as positive—such as freedom *to* (for example, having the enabled freedom to pursue one's goals). Democracy is a term that is contested and many versions exist; for example, representative versus direct democracy.[1] Dahlberg (2001) notes that much emphasis to date within internet democracy rhetoric and practice derives from three leading 'camps': (1) *communitarian,* which stresses the possibility of the internet enhancing communal spirit and values; (2) *liberal individualist,* which conceives of the internet as assisting the expression of individual interests: and (3) *deliberative,* which promotes the internet as the means for expanding the public sphere of rational-critical citizen discourse—discourse which should be autonomous from political and corporate influence. This latter aspect of democracy would be supported through wide-ranging and autonomous information flow which is independent from corporate or other vested interests.

Theorists taking a 'deliberative democratic' perspective view computer-mediated communications as capable of extending power to citizens (at both local and global levels) to participate in new democratic forums, not only between government and the people, but also among citizens themselves, effectively broadening the public sphere.[2] Dahlberg (2001: 616) sees the deliberative perspective as offering a more robust political model than the communitarian or the liberal individualist perspectives. He argues that both the communitarian and liberal individualist political models tend to present a unitary subject, whether the isolated ego or the undifferentiated communal subject, and therefore neglect the multiple differences between subjects within pluralist societies.

However, Poster (1997) has questioned the term 'democracy' in relation to computer-mediated communications. He argues that theorists need to be careful not to adopt a framework that limits the discussion from the outset to modern patterns of interpretation. Poster argues that the internet cannot be conceptualised simply as an extension of existing institutions and that we need to focus on the ways in which it establishes new social functions (Poster, 1997: 213). Ultimately, though, he concedes the best we can do is 'to examine phenomena such as the internet in relation to new forms of the old democracy, while holding open the possibility that what might emerge might be something other than democracy in any shape that we may conceive it given our embeddedness in the present' (Poster, 1997: 214).

Tumber (2001) has disputed the notion of a single public sphere as becoming obsolete where various groups uphold their own deliberative democratic forums. Gitlin (1998), on the other hand, is concerned that the increase in separate public 'sphericules' might impair the formation of a unitary public sphere. He states that the argument proposing that the sole public sphere becomes redundant where deliberative gatherings occur presumes that a rough equivalence of resources exists for securing overall justice. It also presumes that society is without divisions that could be made worse in the absence of repeated negotiation between members of different groups.

Digital divide: the situation in which some groups in society are advantaged over others in not only the tools that some have access to, but in education, skills base and knowledge. It occurs not only between nations but *within* nations as well.

Further confounding the issues raised above is that determining what acceptable 'speech' is in an online forum proves difficult, because ideology differs around the globe (for example, a terrorist in one country is considered a freedom fighter in another). Therefore, how the 'rules' are decided will vary. While there are content filtering software options for children—such as 'NetNanny' or using 'family-friendly' service providers such as the ABC and SBS—only two solutions are available for adults (O'Loughlin, 2001: 604). The first is a single authority or moderator (albeit the idea connotes George Orwell's all-seeing 'Big Brother' and arguably works against the general notion of free speech and expression), and the second is self-regulation or 'netiquette', which encourages users not to become irrational or overly emotional, or to use the forum for commercially oriented goals. O'Loughlin (2001: 604) argues that both options are a voluntary loss of negative freedom (to read or say anything) and an increase in positive freedom (freedom from unwanted information or influence).

Overall, in terms of equality, O'Loughlin (2001) regards netiquette as being the preferable means for limitation, because it removes the hierarchical (probably political) influence of the moderator. Additionally, warning codes for content could be offered on sites, much the same as those offered on free-to-air television (or cigarette packets).[3] Furthermore, netiquette and warning codes could be combined with self-regulation and supervision of children by parents/teachers. While an additional cost, another means is software at the user-end that filters content. Despite the various problems in determining the 'control' for the internet, the future that many will experience is still being shaped and there is much to be optimistic about.

Or is it just hype? In his investigation of the promotion of computer-mediated communication, using Ellul's work on the role of myth in **propaganda,** Karim (2001: 130) concludes that:

Propaganda: This term describes the situation of print or broadcasting being used strategically to influence the hearts and minds of citizens.

> The implications of information society's propaganda [be it political—selling peace, justice, freedom; or commercial—selling happiness and perfection] are enormous. Its ultimate aim seems to be complete absorption of everyone into a perfectly working system of production and consumption that benefits only a few. It conflates data and information with knowledge and wisdom, promising a paradisical state of happiness for all who plug into the internet.

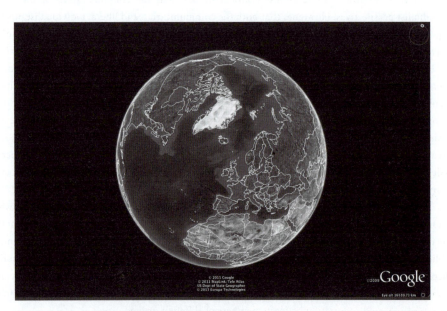

Figure 2.6 Google Earth: Where do you want to go today?

'Plugging into the internet' will never bring absolute freedom of expression, ubiquitous content dissemination or unfettered access to information for everyone due to issues of cost, access, skill level and individual inclination to use the technology—on this point the author is correct. Indeed, the gap between 'the haves' and 'the have-nots', surveillance of our private lives, cultural commodification, the effects of increased human–machine relationships with the isolation of individuals at computer terminals and the possible resulting effects of anonymity and reduced self-and-other awareness are all good reasons for evaluating how society is progressing. On the topic of privacy and security, individuals, corporations and governments must address how much information is held about subscribers and whether or not this data is cross-matched across services (for example, from one government department or private corporation to other government departments and corporations). In a similar vein, one wonders where our personal data is stored and, importantly, who has access to it.

Certainly **interactivity** is a key aspect of new media. Unlike traditional media, which selectively excludes as well as includes information for public consumption, a great deal of content available via the internet gives power to the user to choose what information they will consume or disregard and when they will do so. That is, fewer time restrictions mean that users have greater control over access to content as well as the production of content. Overall, it would seem that the internet is the medium of the consumer—quick, efficient, varying, anonymous and non-committing.

Rheingold (1993: 118) was one of the first to argue that the internet is an 'anarchic, unkillable, censorship resistant, aggressively non-commercial, voraciously growing conversation among millions of people in dozens of countries'. However, Brown questions these assumptions, stating '[N]oncommercial? Anarchic? No way! For one thing, the launch of the internet, and its remarkable rise into the high-flying reaches of business development, was initially triggered by public funding. Now it is managed by a group of telecom companies. Its continued operation depends not only upon their physical infrastructure but upon a distinct software protocol as well' (Brown, 1997: 180). Other critics also see the ideals of cyberspace as illusory. Robins (1999: 166) established a number of years ago that interaction in cyberspace represents a withdrawal from reality to be among like-minded people in an artificial space, avoiding the wider problems of the 'real' world. However, Chenault (1998) is of the view that it is inconceivable that people leave their foibles at the 'cyberdoor'; rather, they are more likely to take their real-life problems and personalities to their virtual lives. All this might lead us to question how one arrives at a perception of rational citizen participation in a globalising, liberalising, decentralising, converging world of media sound bites, manufactured personalities, commercial/political propaganda and artificial lifestyles.

Summary

This chapter has outlined some of the key methods for conceptualising media functions in the West and the resulting implications for audiences/users. Current discourse of new (new) media includes recounting the forces for change of digitisation, convergence and globalisation. The social changes brought about by new (new) media, technological convergence and globalisation as outlined above are giving users an increased choice of media in different formats and on different platforms.

- As content—be it text, sound or vision—is made available from multiple sources, it becomes apparent that audiences will continue to fragment.
- Changes to employment patterns and lifestyles will dramatically affect when and what audiences choose to watch and listen to.

- Issues of concern are information overload, accuracy of information found online, cyberbullying/cyberstalking, privacy of information and security, among others.
- As media and communication students, we must keep in mind that the media does not simply reflect what or who we are. Rather, it plays an active role in shaping social relations.

Further reading

Barr, T 2000, *Newmedia.com.au: The Changing Face of Australia's Media and Communications*, Allen & Unwin, Sydney.

Castells, M 1996, *The Rise of the Network Society: The Information Age—Economy, Society and Culture*, vol. 1, Blackwell, Massachusetts.

Flew, T 2008, *New Media: An Introduction*, 3rd edn, Oxford University Press, South Melbourne.

Levinson, P 2009, *New, New Media*, Pearson, Sydney.

Tapscott, D 2009, *Grown Up Digital*, McGraw-Hill, New York.

Weblinks

Delicious: www.delicious.com (a social bookmarking site).

Wired magazine: www.wired.com (information on new media in society and future trends).

www.theory.org.uk (a website about the mass media and its relationship to popular culture).

For revision questions, please visit www.oup.com.au/orc/chalkley.

Endnotes

1   See, for example, John Nieuwenhuizen, 'Computers in politics', *Australian Rationalist*, no. 47, Spring 1998, 27–30.

2   See, for example, Pavlik, J 1994, 'Citizen access, involvement, and freedom of expression in an electronic environment', in F Williams & J Pavlik (eds), *The People's Right to Know: Media, Democracy, and the Information Superhighway*, Hillsdale, New Jersey, 139–62; the work of The Berkman Center for Internet and Society at http://cyber.law.harvard.edu/projects/deliberation; and The Civic Exchange Strong Democracy in Cyberspace undertaking at: http://webserver.law.yale.edu/infosociety/civicexchange.html.

3   At the moment there is no global requirement that websites be labelled by their owners, nor agreement about labelling criteria (see www.caslon.com.au/censorshipguide8.htm).

3

chapter

Subtext: Are We Really Just Mass Media Sponges?

Toija Cinque

Family X engage with mass media

It is 7 October 2001 and the federal election campaign has just begun in Australia. An issue has arisen on the political scene. Everyone is talking about it. Everyone has an opinion.

'They threw their children into the ocean—I can't believe it! Those poor babies!' screams Mrs X as she watches the evening news on television (the information is delivered as fact by a handsome and well-spoken television news anchor).

The accusation of refugees throwing their children over the side of a sinking vessel, the *Olong*, was made by Prime Minister John Howard, Immigration Minister Philip Ruddock and Defence Minister Peter Reith. The incredible 'news' of these callous asylum seekers putting their children at risk caused an immediate media frenzy and for two days the media is awash with 'information' that illegal asylum seekers threw their children into the ocean in a bid to be rescued and allowed entry into Australia. The incumbent government seeking re-election is known to stand strong on matters of unauthorised arrivals to Australia. The pictures in the press and on television of children floundering in the sea send chills through the Australian community and the act is seen as desperate and even psychotic by the wider public (a sure vote-winning issue!).

In the consequent Australian Senate *Select Committee for an inquiry into a certain maritime incident*, it was found that *no* children had in fact been thrown overboard and that the government had known this prior to the election. Subsequent criticism was levelled at the government for misleading the Australian public and playing on voters' fears of a wave of illegal and cruel immigrants (see, for further detail, Marr, 2006; Arlington, 2004).

What you will learn from this chapter

This chapter introduces you to the reasons why we have the mass media models we do.
- How the mass media models for the press and broadcasting differ around the world
- Why they differ
- Whose interests they serve.

Introduction

The mass media circulates information and ideas in the form of print, radio or television. Are we, the audience, mass media sponges as a result? Most would answer 'certainly not!' We all know that visual images are extraordinarily common in everyday life. We are aware of the media, from the radio news that wakes us up in the morning to the many advertisements we see or just block out on the way to work or study. What we might not be conscious of, however, when we watch television, listen to the radio or read the news is that the media is standing between us and the world of reality, helping to shape our sense of self and what we believe. **Representation** is the way we use images and language to create meaning from what we see and hear in the media. Images from the media help us make sense of the world around us and are active in the ideologies (beliefs or world views) we have as a result. A central point to take from this chapter is that 'the players' that create the content we consume have different reasons for making it available to us. Chapter 8 explains how symbols and signs depicted in the media are used to convey meaning and can have effects on our behaviour as a result. This chapter will look at the reasons behind the introduction of mass media to society (not including new media forms), its impact, and whose interests are really being served.

Representation: the ways in which images and language are used to create meaning, e.g. from what we see and hear in the media.

Think about the television shows you watched, radio programs you listened to or magazines you read when you were growing up. Do you think they have helped to shape the beliefs you have now?

Figure 3.1 *The Father of Television*
Source: *The Father of Television* by John Parker Dilworth

Ideology and the media: Is what we see and hear on TV real?

Ideologies are the cultural frames around which we organise our actions (see also Chapter 10). It is important to note that different countries have different ideologies, including beliefs about how to create the 'best' society for its citizens, and this thinking has shaped the way audiences receive the mass media as a result. The notions of **the public sphere** and **the fourth estate** (briefly explained in Chapter 2) are ways that audiences of democratic nations are meant to get accountability and the truth from their media reportage.

The public sphere: Providing circumstances for 'ideal speech' and the free flow of ideas

Emphasising the importance of free-flowing information for unimpeded communication is not new. Indeed, the democratic philosophers of the seventeenth and eighteenth centuries—often writing at great personal risk—firmly established the notion that sovereignty (the condition of political independence and self-government) belongs in the hands of the citizen.

> One of the central tenets of their sense of democratic order was the idea that government should never be allowed to condition public perception by exercising a stranglehold over the exchange of ideas. Democratic thinkers of the eighteenth century like Edmund Burke, David Hume, and Thomas Jefferson understood that political liberty depended crucially on an informed citizenry (even if citizens were often, at that time, defined as white male property owners), and that this was best cultivated by guaranteeing a free press operating within a shared civic space.
>
> (Brown, 1997: 168)

A shared civic space or public sphere has been examined in relation to 'ideal speech' by German philosopher Jürgen Habermas. Ideal speech, according to Habermas (1989), is the opportunity to hold and voice an opinion or to engage in 'discourse' whereby all in the public sphere have the ability to raise matters according to the ideal, that what they say is true and honest and that they can confirm their claims. Similarly all have the duty to listen. This, he argued, would set the public standard for social discourse. In examination of the word 'public', Habermas (1989: 1) notes that the word has a 'multiplicity of concurrent meanings'. Of relevance to this chapter is the meaning of 'public' most commonly associated with 'public opinion' or 'informed public':

> The subject of this publicity is the public as carrier of public opinion; its function as a critical judge is precisely what makes the public character of proceedings … meaningful. In the realm of the mass media, of course, publicity has changed meaning. Originally a function of public opinion, it has become an attribute of whatever attracts public opinion … The public sphere itself appears as a specific domain—the public domain versus the private. Sometimes the public appears simply as that sector of public opinion that happens to be opposed to the authorities. Depending on the circumstances, either the organs of the state or the media, like the press, which provide communication among members of the public, may be counted as 'public organs'.
>
> (Habermas, 1989: 2)

Habermas' view that publicity has simply become an attribute of whatever attracts public opinion is too simplistic in that, while the sole aim of some media is to seek public acceptance in line with economic imperatives, this is not uniformly the goal of all media, as will be discussed subsequently. Habermas argues that, in certain circumstances, the media can be counted as a public medium.

By definition, because the state took up the role of looking after particular groups in private business, the public sphere (once the exclusive domain of private people who were most often involved

Public sphere:
Habermas' theory of the public sphere encapsulates a central belief for liberal democracy: that of rationalising public authority under the established practice of informed discussion and reasoned—open, free and equal—agreement.

Fourth estate:
This is the ideal by which audiences of democratic nations are meant to get accountability and the truth from their media reportage.

in commercial activities and had the capacity to engage in educated, rational debate and discussion) became a wider concept and not just a sphere of a 'private elite' (Habermas, 1989).[1]

This public sphere was common to democratic nations characterised by commodity exchange and social labour governed by its own regulations. Habermas (1989) located this public sphere between *civil society,* which was made up of commodity owners with private autonomy, and *the state,* which is the part of a liberal, mercantile economy that comprises state-owned institutions, including nationalised industries and services provided by local governmental (public) authorities. Habermas claimed that the state or public authority has the important role of promoting the public or common welfare of its rightful members and thus providing a *public service,* and certainly the media is useful for this purpose.

In consideration of the media addressing the needs of 'public welfare', there are important public goods which we might consider fulfil specific human values (common to us all) in the general benefit of particular societies and should, therefore, be taken account of. While Bonney and Wilson (1983: 77) argue that there is no single, overarching concept of 'public interest'—instead, 'there are class interests, individual interests, fluctuating group interests [and] to suppose that there is such a thing as the public interest is to suppose that there is a single "public" with a unified set of interests which somehow override conflicting and varying individual, class and fractional interests'—we can still argue that some values are common to us all and not sectional. Some broad aspects to be promoted as the public good are educational (the desire to self-actualise or better one's lot), cultural and democratic, together with notions of equality and identity, and having universal access to these.

At a more specific level, the essential public good provided by media and communications industries might include: (1) a commitment to editorial freedom, diversity of view, consumer access and choice, and the absence of state political or editorial control; (2) commitment to fairness in general political debate and news coverage; (3) protection of audiences, particularly children, from broadcasting certain things such as violence and pornography; and (4) protection of national and regional cultural identities, and the stimulation of innovative, artistic, creative, educational and productive activity (Hollick, 1995). The promotion of the public good can be accomplished when public sector organisations (and those that fund them) see that they are crucial in advancing an educated and informed citizenry with the ability to judge public affairs, which is deemed necessary for the proper functioning of a democracy.

The fourth estate

One of the public interest roles undertaken specifically by the media is traditionally associated with being the 'watchdog' of democracy and an independent scrutiniser of power, or the 'fourth estate' (Schultz, 1998). Originally the press emerged as a fourth estate by the practical application of the principles of freedom of expression that were actively sought during the eighteenth and nineteenth centuries (Schultz, 1998: 48). The fourth estate ideal primarily holds that the role of the news media is to act as a channel for information, ideas and opinions, with the aim of assisting good governance in society; to act as *a check on the powerful* (especially executive government) by reporting, analysing and criticising their actions on behalf of the people who were traditionally without direct access to information or power (Schultz, 1998: 51–52). Arguably, the fourth estate fulfils a political role that transcends any commercial commitments (Schultz, 1998: 1). A central purpose of the contemporary notion of the fourth estate is to stimulate the existence of an educated and informed electorate that can make decisions about public affairs (Dennis & Merrill, 2002: 5).

The press informally gained standing as the fourth estate in Australia and Britain during the nineteenth century. Acceptance of the ideal of accountability to the public was established in custom and practice rather than under official constitutional protection (Schultz, 1998: 233). This is unlike the United States, which has freedom of expression and freedom of the press guaranteed by law in the free press clause of the First Amendment to the US Constitution, which states that:

> Congress shall make no law respecting an establishment of religion, or prohibiting the free exercise thereof; or abridging the freedom of speech, or the press; or the right of the people peaceably to assemble, and to petition the government for redress of grievances.

Essentially, the fourth estate is assumed to secure the fulfilment of a democratic society's need for a maximum flow of information and opinion (Dennis & Merrill, 2002: 6). Social theorists such as Herman and Chomsky (1994) would, however, criticise this notion of the fourth estate, claiming that no media altruistically works for the good of the people but necessarily controls and marginalises democratic society through **agenda setting** on behalf of dominant elite groups in society. The media does this by selecting, shaping and restricting the types of information that we are exposed to. In essence, mass media controls the opinions that appear.

In a critical examination of whether we are indeed 'mass media sponges', then, it might be useful to now examine the differences between the *media models, each of which has its own purpose for the dissemination of ideas*. Three main models emerged in the context of the political and cultural traditions of the societies that created them. These were the state model, the commercial model and the public model, and each has its own purpose for how information should be presented and what the desired effects should be.

Agenda setting: is arguably undertaken on behalf of dominant groups in society by the media via selecting, shaping and restricting the information that we are exposed to, thus controlling the range of opinions that appear.

The state model

This mass media system is a model in which a single, central print or broadcasting organisation is operated by the state for its own purpose. The state model is usually associated with totalitarian and authoritarian regimes and characterised by direct government propaganda whereby *print or broadcasting is used to influence the hearts and minds of citizens*. A form of state broadcasting, for example, has existed in the past in some Western nations such as Spain, France and Italy. It was recognised that in different ways in different societies and cultures certain forms of *public expression should be 'controlled'*. This was to avoid possible harm from certain forms of public expression that are outside the society's moral norms (Garnham, 1998: 212). This avoidance is presumed to protect the state and its people from outside corrupting or divisive influences. More specifically, however, print and broadcasting could be used to encourage respect for the legitimate authority of public institutions such as the Crown, parliament and government (Lopez-Escobar, 1992: 166).

State-controlled media was adopted in Soviet zones of occupation such as Berlin, areas normally characterised as totalitarian. The state model here was a means for bringing the socialist order to fruition, and therefore of exercising political control over citizens (Gerber, 1990, cited in Hoffmann-Reim, 1992: 43). In Italy, the early years of radio broadcasting (like print) were strongly connected to Benito Mussolini's fascist dictatorship (1922–1943). The privately owned Union Radiofonica Italiana (URI) was granted a broadcasting licence in 1924, but was subject to strict, direct government censorship. Realising the power and popularity of broadcasting, the fascist government transformed URI into Ente Italiano Audiozioni Radiofoniche (EIAR) in 1929. This was a semi-governmental company, whose supervision was shared closely by the fascist *Vigilanza* organisation (Noam, 1991: 149). During the Second World War, government control was tightened further with RAI (Radio Audironi Italiane and later Radiotelevisione Italiane) being established to operate alongside EIAR, which the Mussolini government controlled (Noam, 1991: 149). Italian television broadcasts were introduced in 1952, which saw the popularity of the state broadcasting services increase. The then ruling Christian Democratic Party used RAI extensively as a propaganda machine, as Noam (1991: 150) argues:

> As a result of that Church-allied party's domination of Italian politics through the past decades of the post-war period, RAI's programs tended to be relatively straight-laced.

Direct control of radio, and later television broadcasting, by the state also existed under the Falangist (fascist) Franco regime in Spain. This led to a public monopoly with only two state television channels. These two national public channels commanded the attention of all available viewers until the 1980s, when competition from commercial operators was introduced (Lopez-Escobar, 1992: 161). Because of its partisan composition, Lopez-Escobar (1992: 169) argues that Spanish public broadcasting currently operates according to political considerations, rather than to programming standards:

> Spain has not yet developed an effective framework of broadcasting regulation for enforcing values … Many of the values concerned have been expressed in the form of general principles without elaboration into more definite obligations. The regulatory machinery is either non-existent or politicized.

In France, broadcasting was explicitly organised as a state institution after the Second World War. Radio-Télévision Française was placed directly under ministerial control in November 1945, and remained there until 1964. During this period broadcasting was considered a legitimate agency of government information, as Raboy (1990: 10) explains:

> Even after creation of the formerly autonomous Office de la radio-télévision française (ORTF) in 1964, the French Cabinet took an active daily role in programming television news. The government could use the air as it wished, while opposition politicians were not entitled to access at all, even during a presidential election campaign.

But state control has been used in Australia and America as well, usually during wartime. Remember the targeting of the 'axis of evil' by the United States—this is a term initially used by the former US President, George W. Bush, to describe the governments of Iran, Iraq and North Korea, which he thought were responsible for terrorism.

In summary, under a state model for the dissemination of information, the government strictly controls what audiences view, listen to or read.

The public (service) broadcasting model

Public broadcasting:
a government-funded form of broadcasting (at arm's length) charged with the responsibility of contributing to a sense of national identity as well as informing and entertaining audiences.

The Canadian broadcasting system adopted a combination of privately owned, commercial broadcasters (in line with the US) and **public broadcasting** elements (based on the BBC model discussed below). The dual system of broadcasting was also chosen in Australia. While Australia would initially align itself closely with the United Kingdom and aim to create a national identity imitating the 'homeland', this was not the case for the Canadian Radio Broadcasting Commission (CRBC). Established in 1932, it became the Canadian Broadcasting Corporation (CBC) in 1936. In Canada the 'national' purpose of Canadian broadcasting was, on the one hand, the main cultural component of the federal strategy for maintaining a political identity distinct from the US. On the other hand, broadcasting was to serve as a strategic tool against the internal threat to Canada's national integrity posed by cultural resistance among French Canadians in Quebec (Raboy, 1990: 8).

The American form of market-driven cultural democracy (giving the people what they want) was resisted in the United Kingdom. The establishment of the BBC also reflected public concern over the potentially damaging cultural, security and moral effects of European content in radio programming in the United Kingdom after the First World War. Early arguments in favour of broadcasting, demonstrating the influence of the government in 1922, were outlined in an official document of the British General Post Office (GPO). As cited in Briggs (1961: 137), these include:

a   Country.

   1   England at present behind in the development of radio art, which is of great future importance, c.f. U.S.A. where large Engineering firms are directly interested.

   2   Possibility of **propaganda** (indirectly).

   3   Let amateurs hear English music rather than Dutch only, or French.

   4   **Unifying effect**.

b   People.

   1   Broadcasting forms a most important social activity and should not be prevented, though it may be necessary to impose some limits.

   2   Educational.

As outlined above, the GPO saw that broadcasting was something to capitalise on in the face of international competition for the technology and content. Moreover, it suggests that broadcasting *had a significant effect on the individual and the collective orientations of citizens*. The GPO understood that broadcasting could be significant to all aspects of life. In Western democratic countries considerable value was being placed on an independent broadcasting system allowing access to the free flow of information whereby the public could draw their own conclusions from material presented to them. In response, the government granted a monopoly to the BBC to go to air (Burns, 1977). The BBC was initially created from mergers between principal interests pursuing radio licences (as was the ABC). The BBC became a Corporation by Royal Charter in 1927 (Inglis, 1983). John Charles Walsham Reith was the BBC's first general manager.

Reith insisted that no rival to BBC radio services be endorsed in the United Kingdom. His reasoning was that each would be under pressure to maximise its audience. This would arguably be at the expense of minority and quality programming, in favour of that which was preferred by the greatest number—or, as Crisell (1998: 117) has summarised Reith's view, '*if listeners were allowed a choice they would be likely to avoid the challenge of new experiences inherent in mixed programming and opt for less demanding fare* that a competitor of the BBC would almost certainly provide'.

In Australia, the ABC and SBS are governed by their own charters and founding Acts where neither one is a branch of government. Moreover, neither organisation's employees work directly for the government, as public servants, but have autonomy. The level of independence is debatable, however, given that members of the board are appointed by government. Nevertheless, the ABC and SBS are not strictly part of the 'public service' but are part of the public sector.

In essence, section 6(1)(a) of the ABC's Charter (a key section of the *Australian Broadcasting Corporation Act 1983* that outlines how the ABC is legislated to operate) states that the public broadcaster must: 'provide within Australia innovative and comprehensive broadcasting and television services of high standard as part of the Australian broadcasting and television system' and provide 'broadcasting programs and television *programs that contribute to a sense of national identity and inform and entertain,* and reflect the cultural diversity of, the Australian community'. Moreover, section 6(2)(iii) of the Act states that it is the responsibility of the ABC as a source of independent national broadcasting and television services to 'provide balance between broadcasting programs and television programs of wide appeal and specialized broadcasting programs and television programs'.

SBS's Charter is set out in a similar manner to that of the ABC. The functions and duties of SBS as a public broadcaster are outlined in section 6 of the *Special Broadcasting Service Act 1991.* As stated in its Charter, the principal function of SBS is to 'provide multilingual and multicultural radio and television services that *inform, educate and entertain all Australians,* and, in doing so, reflect Australia's multicultural society'. As well as this mandate, SBS's Codes of Practice explain the principles and policies used to direct its programming; for example:

> SBS believes that its audiences are best served by exposure to a wide range of cultures, values and perspectives. As a result, SBS's programming can be controversial and provocative and may at times be distasteful or offensive to some. SBS will present diversity carefully and responsibly, ensuring a balance of views over time.

Conflict over the perceived need for public service broadcasting is ongoing, as Barr (2000: 62) argues:

> Commercial broadcasters have to deliver the largest possible audiences to their advertisers, as measured each quarter of an hour by the ratings. However, the role of the public broadcaster is that they must relate to audiences as a public, rather than a market ... Hence their charter is to be comprehensive in programming, unlike commercial broadcasters, yet critics of public broadcasting have long labeled their programming as being 'elite' or 'minority' or 'alternative' or patronising 'niche' offerings.

In summary, public broadcasting is a service to the public rather than being 'public service' broadcasting. Public broadcasting is not fully controlled by government, having a level of independence in the programs made and put to air. The amount of influence exercised by the government is debated, however, given that the government provides funding for public broadcasting, appoints the chair and people to the ABC's board and might, therefore, indirectly influence editorial practices.

The commercial model

The adoption of a commercial model for its press reflected the United States' broader cultural and political traditions. In this light, when television broadcasts began in 1939 they were according to the same ideal of free market operation. The Federal Communications Commission (FCC) established the current regulations for the United States' television in 1941 (Straubhaar & LaRose, 2004: 189). According to the Centre d'Etudes sur les Medias (Centre for Media Studies) in Quebec (2002: 9), after numerous debates about the capacity for broadcasting to serve the public interest, it was decided that the United States would be better served if broadcasting was left to private entrepreneurs who would provide listeners, it was claimed, with what they wanted to hear:

> Supply and demand were expected to serve the interests of both the audience and private broadcasters. Advertising as a means of financing broadcasting, it was believed, ensured that

private broadcasters would seek to meet public demand at all times—after all, the rate paid by advertisers for commercials was linked to the broadcasters' ability to reach the widest possible audience. And if the audience tuned in, it was assumed that the public was satisfied overall with the programs offered.

In the context of a liberal, capitalist market-driven society, proponents of the commercial model spoke as vigorous advocates of private enterprise involvement and initiative as the best means of developing such a service (Walter, 1998: 108–9). Supporters of a fully commercial model took it for granted that the community would get what it wanted and that fears of adverse effects were unwarranted, while advocates of private enterprise spoke of market-driven choice or 'democracy and freedom' (Walter, 1998: 109). Essentially, an unconstrained, commercial, advertising-supported broadcaster would provide programs based upon maximising advertising revenue (Noam, 1991: 47–8). Simply, this would lead to a maximisation of audience. In the phenomenon described as **radical pessimism** (see Curran, 1998: 83), print and radio/television programs are provided under a commercial model according to what audiences want rather than what might afford a 'public benefit' such as information or opinions which might add to or challenge an audience member's personal beliefs. To be more specific, the commercial model offers the press and broadcasters the ability to attract greater audience numbers by offering the public what they want in terms of what suits their existing knowledge base and personal beliefs. This 'dumbed-down' content is considered preferable to audiences because it arguably produces less anxiety than material invoking questioning, analysis and challenge.

An alternative to the 'radically pessimistic' view described above is the concept developed by Noam (1991: 48) in which advertising revenues are not simply related to growing the size of an audience but to an audience being weighed by its consumption power. As Noam (1991: 48) clarifies:

> We assume that consumption power equals income, and that income and preference for upper culture are, on average, positively and linearly correlated because of the higher educational levels commonly associated with higher incomes.

In other words, when audience income is factored into the types of programs offered by a commercial broadcaster in order to maximise its profit, then the quality of programs is raised to reflect the interests of those with higher education levels.

Radical pessimism: the theory that print and radio/television programs are provided according to what audiences want rather than what might afford a 'public benefit'.

From broadcast to multicast: Now anyone anywhere can have a say

It must be pointed out here that content via the internet is not technically broadcast because one person can communicate with one other person or hundreds, even millions, of others. Further, many people can communicate with many others simultaneously when online. This is not the case with the broadcast model, which is about a few select players being able to control the airways to communicate (one-way) with the mass audience. And you will note here that there is really no such thing as a 'mass audience'. Indeed, users can now create and disseminate their own content, bypassing the traditional mass media corporations and put their views online for all to read and comment upon, thus encouraging active participation.

Today the accountability function of the fourth estate faces challenges in the new media age. O'Shaughnessy and Stadler (2009: 468) note here that the global reach of information has an impact on transparency and accountability with regard to journalistic practices in a competitive, global, financially driven new media environment. Competition for audiences from multiple sources (such as talk shows, interest groups, various websites) sees the public's reception of news and current affairs further fragmented from points of context. Howard Tumber (2001) argues that journalism in the information age is becoming less a product than a process being witnessed in real time and in public, and such pressure allows journalists (print and broadcast) less time to ascertain what is true and significant. As a result, the public gets the raw details with little context. For this reason, *audiences need to be active in decoding the media* they are exposed to. But how easy is that when we are not always sure of a content creator/reporter's agenda—how or why a story has been framed in a particular way or for what purposes?

Summary

This chapter has presented a brief history of the thinking behind demands for a 'free press' in democratic nations and independent media more widely. It explained that information needs to be able to circulate widely to allow the general public the opportunity to hold and debate a range of ideas. It considered the notion of the public sphere as a 'stage' whereby this democratic function takes place and highlighted the key role of the media as a carrier of public opinion and a forum for social change. Habermas' theory of the public sphere holds the tenet for liberal democracy ('liberal' in this sense denotes social and political views favouring progress and reform): that of rationalising public authority under the established practice of informed discussion and reasoned—open, free and equal—agreement. That is, power relationships can be neutralised as political authority is transformed into rational authority when dealing with the needs of civil society. The public is the crux for liberal democracies as all authorised decisions, as well as repercussive private decisions, are justified as being in the public's welfare. The role of public defender is taken up by journalists and the like under the principle of journalistic integrity and fourth estate ideals whereby the media is the public's voice. As outlined in this chapter, while governments did initially aim to control the content of programs put to air by public broadcasters, this practice became unacceptable to the public in the United Kingdom and in Australia. Public broadcasters in Australia ultimately gained protection for the independence of their programs and programming schedules through legislation. Advocates of the public broadcasting model addressed issues of citizenship, including educating citizens to employ reasonable choice, ethics and the duty of 'responsible citizens to be informed and have opinions about current affairs' (Livingstone & Lunt, 1994: 8).

- Presently, the commercial model of print and broadcasting prevails in Western countries.
- The state model, where it still exists, is losing its influence in a global media environment where publics can access international content via new media.
- The public broadcasters remain relevant where there is concern about the limits of content available via commercial media.

Further reading

Briggs, A 1961, *The History of Broadcasting in the United Kingdom, Vol. 1: The Birth of Broadcasting*, Oxford University Press, London.

Burns, T 1977, *The BBC: Public Institution and Private World*, Macmillan, London.

Centre d'études sur les medias (Centre for Media Studies) 2002, *Public Broadcasting: Why? How?* A report compiled in cooperation with the Canadian Broadcasting Corporation at the behest of the World Radio Television Council, retrieved 7 February 2010, <www.cmrtv.org/documents/radio-publique-en.htm>.

Habermas, J 1989, *The Structural Transformation of the Public Sphere: An Inquiry into a Category of Bourgeois Society*, trans. T Burger with F Lawrence, MIT, Cambridge.

Herman, E S & Chomsky, N 1994, *Manufacturing Consent: The Political Economy of the Mass Media*, Vintage, London.

Inglis, K S 1983, *This is the ABC: The Australian Broadcasting Commission 1932–1983*, Melbourne University Press, Melbourne.

Weblinks

Australian Broadcasting Corporation: www.abc.net.au

Jerry Mander, 'The Homogenisation of Global Consciousness: Media, Telecommunication and Culture': www.lapismagazine.org/the-homogenization-of-global-consciousness-media-telecommunications-and-culture-by-jerry-mander

The Noam Chomsky website: www.chomsky.info

Special Broadcasting Service: www.sbs.com.au

For revision questions, please visit www.oup.com.au/orc/chalkley.

Endnotes

1   The traditional definition of 'public' offered by Habermas has been criticised for not encompassing all people, in that civil and political rights extended to only about ten per cent of the population to which he referred. Women, young people, non-citizens and slaves were not represented in this public sphere. Indeed, it took many centuries for democracy to become the form experienced in relative democracies such as the United Kingdom, the European Union, Canada, the United States and Australia.

4 Narrative, Communication Tools and Making Meaning: 'Tell Me a Story!'

Adam Brown

Master X's blog

Today has been a rollercoaster of a day! A real bummer. And 4 that reason, itz probably a strange time to start keeping a blog, but here we go …

At 10 in the morning, I woz all set to stay indoors until 10 that night, curled up on the couch in front of the TV, reading a book while The Big Bang Theory played in the background. When I moped down to the kitchen, my sister was grinning at me, showing the large gap between her front teeth.

'Don't know whether I should smile back or kick a field goal,' I told her. She threw a set of keys @ my head. I really h8 her sometimes.

'Oooh, my poor luv-sick brother.' It was my turn with the keys.

She was kind of right, though. I'd been waiting for my girlfriend 2 call, or email, or send a message in a bottle, or something! for days!! I had the feeling she was avoiding me, and couldn't stand all this waiting around! Finally, I got a txt msg that evening:
I DUN THINK ITZ WORKIN OUT
At least she sent a message. My sister didn't annoy me after that.
That's my story.

What you will learn from this chapter

This chapter introduces you to the concept of narrative and the various ways in which we make meaning through stories and their conventions. You will be able to:

- Reflect on the role of narrative in everyday life
- Understand how narratives are constructed according to genres and conventions
- Identify the role of noise as an obstacle to meaning-making
- Consider the importance of intertextuality for narrative and communication
- Analyse the effects of new media on language, and vice versa.

Introduction

How many times have you communicated today? How many processes of meaning-making have you engaged in? Whether we take a vow of silence or aim to become a politician during parliament's question time, we are always 'saying' something—intentionally or unintentionally, clearly or unclearly. Master X's story reveals that almost every moment of every day, whether we are using words, facial expressions or an act of physical violence, we are communicating to others, to no one in particular, or perhaps even to ourselves. Another key, though obvious, point is that *all* communication has meaning. Even when we wake up in the morning and wonder what the dream about drop-bears taking over the world was all about, we are grasping for meaning. But, as in dreams, sending and receiving messages in everyday life is not always a simple, clear-cut process.

Communication often revolves around the construction of a **narrative**, or story, using a series of **conventions** that will (possibly) be understood by the reader. While it might confidently be claimed that, most of the time, we 'get' the message, the delivery of information between a sender and receiver might at times be impeded by what is called **noise**. For example, if a reader of Master X's blog did not understand the use of the words 'moped' or 'bummer', there would be, to some degree, a breakdown in communication. Of course, these might be translated into other words, and other languages, but the requirement of shared understandings would still remain. Likewise, the use of 'text-speak' abbreviations such as '2' and 'h8' might also prove an obstacle to meaning-making if a reader did not know of or frequently use similar language. The shared cultural understandings that communication so often relies on is also known as **intertextuality**, which reveals how all communication—both in terms of sending and receiving messages—relies on pre-existing knowledge of language, conventions and texts. This chapter therefore focuses on several key aspects of communication in everyday life: narratives, the conventions that make up these narratives, and how noise and intertextuality influence the way meaning is (or is not) made.

The stories of our lives: 'All the world's a stage'

The widely known (and, when it comes to high school students around the world, widely disliked) English dramatist William Shakespeare once wrote: 'All the world's a stage, / And all the men and

Narrative: a story that is constructed using various **genres** and other **conventions** in order for people to make sense of the world.

Convention: an established practice or constructed device that is understood by a wide audience through its repeated use over time.

Noise: a disturbance in a communications system that interferes with or prevents reception of a signal or of information.

Intertextuality: the inherently interrelated or interconnected nature of all **texts** and **conventions**.

women merely players: / They have their exits and their entrances' (1999: 622). Love him or loathe him, it is clear that Shakespeare had a point. Without very often thinking about it, we live our lives according to stories. The ways in which we make sense of the world and our experiences within it are constructed through narratives. From our earliest years as toddlers, when our parents place picture books in front of us; to our time as teenagers, when we laze on the couch and watch an episode of *MasterChef*; to our adult years, when we are asked the worst of all interview questions—'So, tell me about yourself … '—we engage with our own or others' narratives. Narrative is a very broad topic and can only be addressed briefly here, but there is a massive literature on narrative theory, which will help broaden your understanding of communication tools and meaning-making (see, for example, Phelan & Rabinowitz, 2005; Bal, 2004; Culler, 2000; Richter, 1996).

Narratives are made up of conventions, which are practices or devices that are established and reinforced by their recurring use over time, and are thus widely understood by audiences. Conventions might relate to the style, structure or content of a story. If you've studied literature or linguistics before, you will have already been introduced to various narrative conventions, some of which we'll follow up on here. To examine narrative at its most basic level, it is the case that (most) narratives consist of a beginning, a middle and an end. Master X's blog constructs a narrative of his experiences by starting with the morning's events and finishing with the evening's revelation.

Generally speaking, all texts have some kind of 'start' and 'finish'. When reading, watching or listening to a story, we don't usually think about this—it just seems natural that that's the way things are. A particularly powerful convention that all narratives rely on is **closure**—or, sometimes, a lack of closure. In literary terms, closure, to use Chris Baldick's words, involves 'the sense of completion or resolution at the end of a literary work or part of a work' (1990: 38). Nonetheless, closure is not specific to novels and plays alone. Looking at narrative broadly, the vast majority of stories in everyday life are constructed to provide at least some sense of closure. For instance, 'open' endings, in contrast to the 'closed' endings seen in most Hollywood films, are much less common.

We simply can't understand the world without narratives. Many of the 'rules' that govern narrative are the 'rules' that govern our lives and help us construct our identities. As Shakespeare pointed out, our lives *are* narratives that we constantly perform for ourselves and those around us. In relation to a human being's life, different narratives exist about when this begins and when it ends. The issue of abortion has led to debate over when a human life 'starts', whereas recent scientific advances have transformed the definition of death—the 'end' of a life—from when the heart stops to incorporate other medical factors. This also shows that conventions can and do change over time. On the other hand, when you are asked to write essays, these are expected to be structured according to similar conventions, with a body of analysis framed between a beginning and an end: an introduction that outlines the argument you will make and a conclusion that sums up the points that precede it.

The conventions that a narrative employs often rely on what kind of **genre** the narrative falls into. *Genre* is the French term for 'type', and consists of a set of conventions that has been established over time. From browsing the local video store, you will already be familiar with many different genres. An audience's expectations about a certain narrative will depend on the genre it belongs to. A person who wants to set a romantic mood in the early days of a relationship would usually be better served by a different choice of movie than *Wolf Creek* or *Rambo: First Blood*. The power that genres exercise over our imaginations is clear when considering the recent films *Shaun of the Dead* (2004), which was marketed as 'a romantic comedy with zombies', and *Hot Fuzz* (2007), which also plays with many of the generic conventions that we as viewers are used to seeing utilised in a more clear-cut manner. Such films confront us with the fact that narratives are entirely constructed—although this doesn't detract from the power that stories have over our lives.

Closure: the degree to which a **narrative** offers a resolution to the tensions within it.

Reflection on narrative: Are there any texts you have read or seen recently that did not 'finish neatly'? What is your impression of narratives that do not have a sense of closure? Do you find it frustrating? Why?

Genre: a 'type' of **narrative** consisting of a set of **conventions** that has been established over time.

Figure 4.1 Poster for the film *Shaun of the Dead* (2004)

Source: The Kobal Collection/WT2/Big Talk

Another crucial aspect of the construction of stories is **narrative perspective**, or what is often called point of view. All narratives are constructed from a certain vantage-point, where the events and characters described are narrated from a certain perspective. The narrative that Master X constructs in his blog draws on what is termed first person narration, which is signalled by the use of words like 'I', 'my' and 'we'. One of the main effects of this convention is to position readers to identify and sympathise with Master X, therefore accepting his version of events and the views he expresses within it. We will return to this process of audience identification in Chapter 10.

On the other hand, stories are often written using a third person point of view, which can generally be identified by the use of 'she', 'he' and 'they'. In this case, the constructed narrator gives the impression that she or he is more 'objective', narrating the events from a distance. This, again, is a convention. Newspaper reports are most often written using a third person mode of narration in order to make an implicit claim to authorial credibility: *this is true*. On the other hand, some narratives have multiple narrators, allowing a more complex interaction between narrative perspectives.

Narrative perspective: the point(s) of view from which a **narrative** is told.

Of course, there are many other conventions that are used to construct meaning through narratives. While Master X uses a first person point of view in his blog, he employs many other narrative strategies to position the reader to sympathise with his situation. An author's use of tone, diction and humour—just to name a few—are often crucial aspects of the message(s) a reader receives. Master X's characterisation of his sister, for example, relies on comical observations (or inventions) regarding her physical appearance, facial expression and behaviour. The use of short, fragmented sentences, colloquial diction and abbreviated words develops an informal tone, encouraging the reader to identify with the story's main character. But the ways in which a narrative is constructed through language do not stop here: the (often unconscious) use of very complex **rhetorical devices** also informs how language operates in our everyday lives.

Broadly defined, rhetorical, or figurative, devices consist of conventions or techniques that are used with the intention of persuading an audience to adopt a certain idea. Figurative speech involves the use of words that departs from their 'literal' meaning(s), gesturing to some kind of associative meaning, which can be understood through shared cultural experiences. People use numerous rhetorical devices, including similes, metonyms, irony, allusions, personification, clichés, analogies, oxymorons, allegories and alliteration, among many others. While it would be useful to research and keep a glossary of these concepts, we will focus here on just one rhetorical device, which is arguably the most significant and widely used figure of speech: **metaphor**. A metaphor is constructed when an object, concept or action is referred to through words or language generally used to mean something else (i.e. a different object, concept or action).

To take a brief example, Master X begins his blog with the sentence, 'Today has been a rollercoaster of a day!' Obviously, Master X is not intending the reader of his narrative to think that

Rhetorical device: a **convention** or technique that is used with the intention of persuading an audience to adopt a certain idea.

Metaphor: a common figure of speech where an object, concept or action is used through language to refer to another object, concept or action generally used to mean something else.

he spent his daylight hours at a theme park. The metaphor of the rollercoaster is being used for the **connotations** attached to it—the fluctuation between moments of calm and tension, and feelings of happiness and anxiety, which one might associate with riding a rollercoaster, can be connected to Master X's representation of his experiences. This is not to suggest that the intended meaning(s) behind this metaphor will automatically be understood by all readers of his blog. The understanding of what a rollercoaster is and what a ride on one entails is required for the metaphor to be fully grasped. This suggests that there are potential obstacles to communication to be negotiated in the construction of narratives in texts and in our everyday lives.

Connotation: a secondary latent meaning of a sign, which operates at the 'second order of signification', building upon the denotative features of a text to convey a **mythic** message.

The meaning of noise ('Huh?')

Imagine this: an international student from Sri Lanka arrives at Tullamarine airport in Melbourne to undertake a university degree in Media and Communication Studies. The young woman, let's call her Nisita, thanks the flight attendant, who gives her a smile as long as Friday. Retrieving her suitcase from the baggage claim, Nisita follows the signs to the public transport area. Typing a text message on her phone, Nisita halts just before walking into a bus driver. 'How are you going?', the man asks in a thick Australian accent. Boarding the vehicle, Nisita replies: 'By bus'. One week later, after hearing numerous other Australians in conversation, Nisita realises that she misunderstood the man's question.

This story points to an integral aspect of human communication: *mis*communication. No matter how well constructed narratives are, or how knowledgeable a writer or film-maker is of the genre and conventions they are using, there is always the possibility that the process of meaning-making will break down. Likewise, miscommunication is a constant presence in our everyday lives. When talking to another person who has had very similar social, educational and cultural experiences, even when you are staring them in the face and speaking very clearly, there is no absolute guarantee that the intended message will 'get through'. The problem of miscommunication is clearly revealed in the game commonly known (rather problematically) as 'Chinese whispers', which involves a circle of people whispering a message to the person next to them until the—often *very different*—message reaches the last person in the circle. There is always the chance, if not likelihood, that a message or intended meaning will be altered by what is termed 'noise'.

Sky Marsen explains that a 'noise source' exists outside the intended message and can interfere with the communication process, resulting in the message 'reach[ing] the recipient in a distorted form and [causing] failures of communication' (2006: 14–15). Noise is not something that should necessarily be frowned upon, but by understanding the potential obstacles to communication we are much more likely to become more effective communicators. Nisita's misunderstanding of the bus driver's question points to the fact that shared or different cultural understandings influence the way meaning is made. In this case, the comprehension—or lack thereof—of an Australian colloquialism is a source of 'noise'. Of course, cultural (mis)understandings are not the only form of noise.

Marsen highlights several main categories of noise, including contextual factors, technical factors, perceptual factors and cognitive factors (2006: 18–19). Contextual factors relate to aspects of the environment in which communication takes place. For example, a marriage proposal in a sports stadium during the last five minutes of a football grand final could probably have been thought through more carefully. Technical factors cause a message to be distorted due to problems with the mode of transmission used. With the widespread use of digital technologies in everyday life, there is always the possibility that the medium will 'fail us'. When compiling a resume for a job application, it's important to make sure that you don't accidentally change the font type of the entire document to Wingdings at the last moment.

On the other hand, the noise that occurs in situations where someone's physical and/or psychological condition impacts on the communication process can be classified as a perceptual factor. When a student has stayed awake all night to finish a written assignment, the 9am lecture the following morning might not make as much sense as it usually would (probably the lecturer's fault, of course!). The example from Nisita's story above highlights the importance of cognitive factors, which come into play when 'the sender and receiver do not speak the same language or have vastly different systems of reference for the knowledge communicated' (Marsen, 2006: 19). This category of noise reveals how important cultural understandings are in human communication, which leads us to the concept of intertextuality.

Brainstorm:
Under the headings 'contextual', 'technical', 'perceptual' and 'cognitive', make a list of examples of noise sources. What do you think are most influential? Does this depend on the circumstances? Can noise be avoided? How?

Intertextuality and meaning-making: Connected through texts

A true story: ever since the film *Pirates of the Caribbean* (2003) was released, followed by its sequels, Luke has developed a great liking for the phrase 'Ello, Poppet!', which is used every now and again by one of the film's characters. Luke, who has the good fortune to possess a mobile phone paid for by his work, frequently rings his sister Abbie without anything particularly important to communicate and the conversation goes like this: Abbie answers her phone with 'Hello?' Luke simply says, 'Ello Poppet!' Abbie laughs, responding 'Ello Poppet!' Luke laughs, they both laugh, and then they hang up. For those people who have seen the films, this scenario is (for some reason) funny, or a bit sad—but probably still funny. Why do Luke and Abbie do this? The answer is that they share an intertextual understanding of the film and it has 'meaning' for them.

John Stephens defines intertextuality as involving 'the production of meaning from the interrelationships between audience, text, other texts, and the socio-cultural determinations of significance' (1992: 84). This is a rather complex way of suggesting that *everything* is interconnected—people, texts and cultural meanings. Our personal views and values, everyday experiences, educational backgrounds and the historical context in which we live constantly influence how we interpret texts and understand other people. In addition, all texts share intertextual meanings. The point of the example above is to demonstrate that much of the meaning we make in our everyday lives is intrinsically related to texts. Indeed, any reader of this chapter who has seen the Australian film *The Castle* (1997) at least a few times might have associated the last line of Master X's blog—'That's my story'—with the last line of dialogue by the film's narrator, Dale Kerrigan.

A bit of theory:
In 1959, Swiss psychoanalyst Carl Jung coined the term 'collective unconscious', arguing that everyone shares common understandings of the images of the unconscious (expressed in dreams and texts) and therefore make meaning in similar ways.

Figure 4.2 'Ello, Poppet!' The characters Ragetti and Pintel in *Pirates of the Caribbean: Dead Man's Chest* (2006)

Source: The Kobal Collection/Walt Disney

To further highlight the power of intertextuality, many films explicitly make reference to other films (think of the *Scary Movie* franchise, for instance), thereby constructing meaning through the texts they draw on. Nonetheless, intertexts do not necessarily consist of specific earlier texts (or pre-texts), but can also include subsequent texts (sequels and adaptations), well-known stories, socio-historical narratives (stories from history), and other discourses or media, such as songs, advertisements and photographs (Stephens, 1992: 84–85). If a *Harry Potter* fan reads or views a version of the *King Arthur* narrative, they may find *many* similarities. Likewise, many connections can be made between the recent blockbuster film *Avatar* (2009) and earlier films such as *Pocahontas* (1995) and *Fern Gully: The Last Rainforest* (1992). The plot elements, genres and conventions used in these texts reveal the heavily intertextual nature of films, which will be discussed further in Chapter 10.

It should be clear at this point that the intersection of everyday life and narratives is immensely important and immensely complex. This is reflected in Michael O'Shaughnessy and Jane Stadler's statement that 'as we consume fictions, we leave behind the mundane practicalities of everyday life to travel deep into the heart of ourselves, discovering our core beliefs, feelings, and desires' (2008: 352). What is being suggested here is that narrative, and representation in general, affects our lives and the way(s) in which we view the world around us. By extension, the ways in which we construct the world through language change over time, hence changing our perceptions of the world. This transformation of language in contemporary culture is increasingly affected by the ever expanding use of new media.

New media and the place of language in cultural transformation: 'LOL b4 ☹?'

While it is essential to understand the major aspects of human communication, such as narratives, the various tools that are used to construct these, and the many ways in which we make or mistake meaning, it must be noted that language is constantly changing. Much of this book is concerned with the implications of new media for everyday life. The impact of new media on language is impossible to estimate. Every day, new forms of mediated communication become available to consumers and users of the internet. But one thing always remains the same: they are all used to communicate, often by telling stories. A much discussed subject in recent years is how new media is affecting everyday language. The frequent use of abbreviated English words on the internet is continually commented upon, positively and negatively. The following article briefly surveys the issue of whether or not traditional spelling is being replaced by 'netspeak', and whether or not this is cause for concern:

Internet words form the language of 2moro

BY MARTIN BECKFORD

THE AGE

January 3, 2010

So traditional spellings could be killed off by the internet within a few decades, a language expert has claimed.

The advent of blogs and chat rooms meant that for the first time in centuries printed words were widely distributed without having been edited or proofread, said Professor David Crystal, of the University of Wales.

As a result, writers could spell words differently and their versions could enter common usage and become accepted by children.

Within a few decades, the spellings favoured by many internet users could replace the current, more complex versions, he said. Current spellings were standardised in the 18th century with the advent of dictionaries.

It could mean that internet slang—such as '2moro' instead of 'tomorrow' or 'thx' for 'thanks'—may enter into mainstream publications. Professor Crystal, a pioneer of language theory, said many spellings bore no relation to meaning or pronunciation.

'The vast majority of spelling rules in English are irrelevant', he said. 'They don't stop you understanding the word in question.

'If I spell the word rhubarb without an 'h', you have no trouble understanding it. Why do we spell it with an 'h'? Because some guy in the 16th century said it was good to put an 'h' in to remind us of the history of the word'.

Professor Crystal said that before the internet, nobody could write something in print without an editor or a proofreader checking it.

But now simplified and phonetically spelt words were likely to enter the vocabulary. 'There's been a huge movement over hundreds of years to simplify English spelling, because it is complex for historical reasons'.

'What you consider to be atrocious now may be standard in 50 years', he said.

'There are people around who would treat what I said to be the voice of the devil, but one has to remember that spelling was only standardised in the 18th century. In Shakespeare's time you could spell more or less as you liked'.

Professor Crystal told the 20th anniversary conference of the International English Language Testing System that the internet would not lead to a complete breakdown in spelling rules. 'All that will happen is that one set of conventions will replace another set of conventions', he said.

He said schools should not abandon the teaching of traditional spelling.

'Kids have got to realise that in this day and age, standard English spelling is an absolute criterion of an educated background', he said.

'You're not going to get certain types of jobs if you don't spell well. The point is that they haven't been taught well.

'Teachers don't know how to teach spelling because they haven't done the appropriate linguistics … The blame is being put on the kids, but most of the kids I know who have got poor spelling regret the fact'.

As the author of this article notes, the idea of 'correct spelling' is relatively new; however, it continues to be held up as a very important part of education and knowledge. At times, gaining employment might rest on an applicant's ability to spell the company's name properly. If a person hands in a cover letter to express interest in working at 'Darrels Wea' rather than 'Darrel Lea', they might have diminished their chances. And many teachers have by now seen the number '2' instead of the letters 'to' while marking exam papers. Is this a bad thing? It is a complex issue, and only one of many issues that we confront in society when it comes to the effects of new media on language.

Many people are sceptical of the ever increasing ability of people to communicate through social networking technology, with emails, text messages, Facebook updates and 'tweets' replacing—to some degree—our need to meet with someone face-to-face. It's true, housemates can just 'Skype you' from the other end of the hallway now. But on the whole, we still interact physically with each other *a lot*! And communication is not only verbal. As Master X and Nisita's narratives revealed, communicating with other people involves many non-verbal processes as well, to which we now turn.

Summary

This chapter has demonstrated that:

- Language, and particularly narrative, is fundamentally important to our understandings of the world and our place within it.
- Through various genres and conventions, our construction of stories has considerable implications for the meanings we make in our everyday lives.
- Shared cultural understandings between human beings constantly see meaning evoked and maintained through intertextuality.
- Processes of meaning-making are often limited by the existence of noise.
- The role of new media in contemporary developments in language and narrative will continue to be a contested issue as we move further into the twenty-first century.

Further reading

Bal, M (ed.) 2004, *Narrative Theory: Critical Concepts in Literary and Cultural Studies*, Routledge, London & New York.

Baldick, C 1990, *The Concise Oxford Dictionary of Literary Terms*, Oxford University Press, New York & Oxford.

Culler, J 2000, *Literary Theory: A Very Short Introduction*, Oxford University Press, Oxford.

Marsen, S 2006, *Communication Studies*, Palgrave Macmillan, Houndmills.

Moon, B 2001, *Literary Terms: A Practical Glossary*, 2nd edn, Chalkface, Cottesloe.

O'Shaughnessy, M and Stadler, J 2008, *Media and Society: An Introduction*, 4th edn, Oxford University Press, Melbourne.

Phelan, J & Rabinowitz, P J (eds) 2005, *A Companion to Narrative Theory*, Blackwell, Oxford.

Richter, D H 1996, *Narrative/Theory*, Longman, White Plains.

Stephens, J 1992, *Language and Ideology in Children's Fiction*, Longman, London.

Weblinks

For revision questions, please visit www.oup.com.au/orc/chalkley.

5

Non-verbal Communication: Why Are You So Defensive?

Tony Chalkley

Accidental admission: We don't like your friend

The Family X is planning a weekend away to celebrate a significant birthday: their aunt (and great aunt) is turning 90! As they plan the trip, Master X asks if he can bring an old friend from school (one his parents have never really approved of) and drive his own car so they can stay on a couple of extra days. Even before his parents have spoken a word in reply to his question, their son knows that they don't want this to happen and, even more importantly, he realises that they don't actually like his friend. He is offended.

What you will learn from this chapter

- Non-verbal communication asks (and answers) the question: 'Why do we (want to) belong to a group?'
- This chapter describes how we use our appearance to establish a sense of belonging and communicate about ourselves. You will also learn how 'neo-tribes' are the result of this process.
- Here you will read how we use clothing as a symbolic presentation. A doctor in board shorts and a Mambo 'poo-shooter' T-shirt made Mrs X worry about his ability as a medical practitioner. Why?
- This chapter will also explore the physical elements of non-verbal communication: eye contact, posture, sound and how we use 'affect displays' to say 'stuff' without using words.
- This discussion will introduce you to 'gestures and emblems' and will describe how these gestures and emblems are culturally informed and used in different ways to communicate a range of messages.
- This chapter also looks at how we use emoticons in text language as a form of non-verbal message. This can sometimes go wrong, as it did for Mrs X and the death of the family dog (see p 50).
- You will also discover how the media uses non-verbal communication to send a message, even when we think 'nothing' is being communicated.
- The chapter concludes with a telling comment about robotics, where the biggest challenge is making them 'real' and 'human-like'; the manufacturers of robots have found non-verbal communication very hard to replicate, even for humans, but especially for robots.

Introduction

For most of us, 'non-verbal communication' conjures up images of the rude (say, 'flipping the bird') or the silly, like Borat's double thumbs up (*Is good, I like*). This understanding is, to some degree, accurate. But non-verbal communication is much more than this, and in this chapter you will learn about the many elements of communication that don't involve words and yet can produce a potent message. You will learn that non-verbal communication is simultaneously very simple and yet terribly complex. The stories from Family X illustrate how a girlfriend can hate her birthday present, even though she says, 'Thanks, it's just what I want'. The story at the start of this chapter illustrates how non-verbal communication can sometimes 'accidentally' give away our inner, private feelings. In this chapter, you will also learn how Mrs X inadvertently used a cheery text message to forward some very sad news and you will discover how their father is sometimes (quite inaccurately) thought to be 'distant and rude'.

Object communication: We want to belong to a group

Some readers will disagree with this statement and perhaps feel a little like the member in the crowd who, in the Monty Python film *The Life of Brian*, shouts out that they are 'not an individual'. In the film, Brian attempts to lose his gourd-carrying followers by telling them that they 'don't need to follow anyone, you are all different'. True. We are all different, but the majority of people will actively seek out and enjoy the sense that we are also 'the same'. This chapter is concerned with how we communicate our 'sameness' without using words.

Most people, especially when very young, expend quite some energy on a process called object communication. Object communication is part of the process of creating a sense of belonging to a group in order to 'feel like an insider'. The simplest way to understand object communication is to examine the clothing we wear. The style, branding, colour and fashionability of our clothing is often used by outsiders to assess (accurately or inaccurately) our personality traits. Social groups will often use a common form of clothing to set themselves apart from 'others', using object communication to create a sense of 'insider' and 'outsider'. Skaters do this, as do 'goths', 'emos' and sports 'jocks'. Object communication includes our clothing, but it also extends to other body adornments, such as hair colouring and styles, tattoos, piercing and branding. Object communication also includes things that might be considered as a status symbol. Consider Figure 5.1. The concept of 'bling-bling' is an excellent (albeit extreme) example of object communication. Rappers use their 'bling' to display success, power, wealth and status. For those who are not famous rappers, object communication still plays an important role in our communication. At different stages in our lives the importance of object communication changes: you must have the 'right' type of pencil case in primary school, the 'cool' sneakers at high school and the 'best' phone and computer for university. I re-member a group at my university who wanted to be different and as a result they all dressed in clothing purchased from charity op shops. They all looked different and yet somehow the same! Through their consumer choice, they used object communication to create group identity and, in turn, a sense of belonging.

Figure 5.1 Rapper Rick Ross shows us his 'bling-bling'

Source: Getty Images/FilmMagic/Shareif Ziyadat

Using objects to communi-cate is not simple. Like most communication practices, using non-verbal communication can

Figure 5.2 Not cool. Stupid.

Photographer: Donna Edwards

be ambiguous, primarily because the character of the sender of the message plays an important role in the process of 'making meaning' from the object.

What do I mean? Well, a good example is aviator sunglasses. When my 16-year-old son wears them, he looks 'cool'. When his 45-year-old father puts them on, he looks 'stupid'. This is a good example of how the context of the message influences the meaning produced by the message—in this case, the message transited by the object ('the aviators') is influenced by the status of the person (me) transmitting it.

Problems with object communication: 'If you are a doctor, why aren't you dressed like one?'

> On a recent beach holiday, the X family had to visit a medical centre in order to clean and suture a cut on the foot of their 'wannabe' surfer son. As they sat in the waiting room, Mrs X noticed something about the doctor that disturbed her.
>
> He was young, which is not really a problem. But he was wearing a pair of oversized shorts with huge flowers on them, his shoes were Crocs and his T-shirt had an enormous screen print of a dog with 'poo' shooting out its anus. This was an issue because their usual doctor back home wore a tie, or if the weather was hot, just a collared shirt, slacks, simple leather shoes and a white jacket for examinations.

Generally, we have expectations for the appearance of professions and those individuals we call professionals. The doctor in the Mambo 'poo-shooter' T-shirt disrupted the expectations of Mrs X (this is a form of 'noise',—see Chapter 4) because, to her, this is not the way a 'doctor' should appear. These specific and 'agreed' expectations of the 'correct' appearance provide us with a type of non-verbal communication 'short cut'. When I buy a burger, I know what the staff should look like; at the hospital I can easily identify a doctor, and ditto for the nurses and cleaning staff. When I was at an AC/DC concert, I could easily use clothing and appearance to identify the security guards, the police, the first aid staff and the outlaw bikers too.

The skilled suturing and confident manner told Mrs X that the doctor was indeed a competent medical practitioner, but his clothing did not.

Finally, there is another way we use objects to communicate about our **identity**, status and self. As new media devices are increasingly entrenched and naturalised into everyday life, we have begun to use them (and their functions) to tell people about ourselves: our ring-tones, the design of our Facebook page and the wallpaper background on our laptop are all relatively new and emerging forms of object communication.

Identity: A much-debated term, though scholars generally agree that the (ongoing) construction of one's sense of self is not concrete or static, but fluid, multiple and constantly changing.

Non-verbal communication: Eye contact, posture and sound

Take a look at Lawrence Yang's artwork *Emo Boy* (Figure 5.3). Even if Yang removed the title 'Emo Boy', most viewers would look at this image and ascertain that it's not necessarily a happy or cheerful one. Some viewers would take the decoding process even further, observing the long, feathered fringe, the down-turned eyes, the lowered head and the use of soft sepia tones to create a sombre feeling. This is an 'emo' boy. What exactly 'emo' is, and what ideology and beliefs are communicated by members of the 'emo community', are open to debate and discussion. But for the purpose of this chapter, I will simply define 'emo' as what Bennett calls a 'neo-tribe', a group of people who identify with each other in order to share 'style, musical taste and collective association' (Bennett, 1999)

Neo-tribes are a common part of our social lives and, even if you don't belong to one, chances are you will encounter them as part of your everyday life (most of us can decode and understand Yang's *Emo Boy*, even though we are not necessarily 'emo' ourselves). A really simple and easy way to explore the concept of neo-tribes is to watch a 'college' or 'high school' movie. Take the 1988 Film *Heathers*, for example (www.imdb. com/title/tt0097493). *Heathers* is a movie that uses neo-tribes in a crude, blunt and yet highly effective way. The viewer can immediately and very easily identify the sports jocks (shorts, white socks), the nerds (thick-rimmed glasses), the unpopular kids (large, shapeless sweaters), the cheerleaders (short skirts, letters on shirt), the science geeks (multiple pens in pocket), the beautiful, popular girls (grooming, grooming, grooming)

Figure 5.3 Lawrence Yang's *Emo Boy*

(Reproduced with permission of the Artist: www.suckatlife.com/digital.html)

and the dark, unhappy outsider (trench coat, smoking). The producers of *Heathers* use non-verbal communication to ensure that viewers are aware of the status, identity and role of each character, even before they speak a single word.

The use of objects to 'send a message' is only one of the many ways we communicate non-verbally. Another way is the use of kinetic transmission: that is, posture, eye contact and the arrangement of our body. In his book *Communication Theory*, Mortensen provides a simple typography of the sorts of kinetic messages we encounter every day:

> *Batons*: movements which emphasise particular word or phrase (*such as describing a catch; 'the fish was this big'*)
>
> *Ideographs*: movements which sketch the path or directions of thought (*'first, write a small plan, then next a draft and {click fingers} you are finished'*)
>
> *Deictic-movements*: pointing to an object, place or event (*'there he is, over there!'*)
>
> *Spatial movements*: movements which depict spatial relationships (*it's the one, two … third house on the left'*)
>
> *Rhythmic movements*: movements which depict the speed and rhythm of an event (*'time just flew' {make spinning motion at watch}*)
>
> *Kinetographs*: movements which depict bodily action or some non human physical action (*the car screamed past like this …)*
>
> *Pictographs*: movements which draw a picture in the air of the shape of the referent (*'the burn mark was like this, donut shaped'*)
>
> *Emblematic movements*: emblems used to illustrate a verbal statement, either repeating or substituting for a word or phrase. (*sssssshhh!! The recital has started*).

(Mortensen, 2007: 279)

These **kinetic** messages play a really important role in message-making: they provide an opportunity to tell someone what we 'really' think, often contradicting the words we speak.

Kinetics: the study of body movements, gesture and posture.

In the case of the Family X, this happened when their son gave his girlfriend of three years an eighteenth birthday present. As she had her own car, he spent many hundreds of dollars on an auto sound system, subwoofers, MP3 player, pre-amp, LED display and speakers. It was a 'fully sick' system. When she opened the boxes she said, *'Thanks, it's great and just what I need'*. Yet he knew, almost immediately, that she hated it and was disappointed. How? By ignoring her verbal response and decoding her kinetic message, he recognised that she had turned away from him and was not smiling; nor was she making eye contact with him, but instead looking at his sister. His girlfriend was also touching her hands to her face, her tone of voice was flat and monotonous and she seemed to open the last box in a slow and resigned manner. When his sister hissed 'jewellery, idiot, jewellery', his interpretation of her non-verbal messages were confirmed. He had stuffed up.

To varying degrees, we are all attuned to the messages in our friends' and family's unconscious and unintentional behaviours and take these non-verbal cues (such as those listed above) into account when communicating (Adler & Rodman, 2009). If you were to make a list of kinetic messages (that is, common posture and eye contact messages), chances are you might come up with messages and meanings such as these:

Down-turned eyes when talking	*means*	Shy, rude or disinterested.
Sparkling, wide open, direct view	*means*	Flirting? Interested, connected.
Crossed arms	*means*	Hostile, guarded, closed.
Hands behind head, legs sprawled	*means*	Arrogant, domineering.
Looking around while chatting	*means*	Bored with conversation.
Smiling all the time	*means*	Happy, content.

These forms of non-verbal communication are called 'affect displays'. Affect displays are body movements which are thought to reveal our affective, or emotional, state. Facial cues are the primary way we reveal our feelings non-verbally. Affect displays are most often used in an attempt to influence others, and their success relies on the experience and knowledge of the receiver to accurately decode these kinetic devices.

My list of affect displays and their possible meanings is simultaneously accurate and yet inaccurate. In the film *Little Miss Sunshine* (www.imdb.com/title/tt0449059), the young competitors walk the stage with radiant smiles and yet we know (from the happenings backstage) that they are far from happy children. So, smiling all the time does not necessarily mean happiness. Likewise, some of the non-verbal messages on this list have a cultural context. In some Aboriginal communities in Australia, it is considered rude to stare at the person speaking to you, so to assume that down-turned eyes means disinterest can sometimes be wrong.

Mr X has never been all that comfortable around people and at times his non-verbal cues have created offence. People think he is bored with them. Here's how his daughter sees it:

> I think that when dad was little, his teachers probably wrote 'doesn't play well with others' in his school report [laughs]. But really, he looks at the ground when he is concentrating on what you are saying. He doesn't smile much, but he would say that he is happy. He's actually pretty shy and when he's nervous he crosses his arms, which looks kinda hostile.

Mr X is sending all the 'wrong' messages. His down-turned eyes suggest rudeness, his crossed arms imply hostility and his infrequent smiling suggests that he is miserable. Yet his daughter, who knows him well, believes that these are false conclusions to draw from his body language. How can that be? Adler and Rodman argue that 'it's virtually impossible to not communicate nonverbally' (Adler & Rodman, 2009: 135) and, in Mr X's case, this seems particularly true. Unfortunately for Mr X, the messages he is sending are being decoded by the receiver in a manner that produces unintended and sometimes inaccurate meanings. Some readers may have experienced this when a friend or family member looks at you and asks 'What's wrong? What's up?' They read your body language and decide that you are unhappy. Allan and Barbara Pease have been writing, researching and talking about body language for more than thirty years. Here's what they have to say about this:

> Every person's body language very often reveals that what they say is different from what they think or feel. It is a scientific fact that people's gestures give away their true intentions.

(Pease, 1985)

Gender, culture, expectations and relationships also have a role to play in the process of sending and receiving non-verbal messages. For the most part, every day we send and receive many non-verbal messages, without issue. But misreading these messages can sometimes have dire consequences, and the disappearance of Azaria Chamberlain is one such case.

On 17 August 1982, a family lost a child. The Chamberlains' baby, Azaria, was snatched and killed by a dingo at an Uluru (then known as Ayers Rock) camping ground. I remember this story because it dominated the media, my family, my friends and most conversations. My school friends speculated that the mother (Lindy) was guilty because she didn't look 'sad enough', the local talkback radio hosted endless callers who, as self-appointed experts, pointed out how the Chamberlains 'should have behaved and looked'.

The point of including this story is not to criticise the legal or forensic process that resulted in the wrongful imprisonment and eventual release of Lindy Chamberlain, but to show how easy it is to misread non-verbal cues, produce false meanings and jump to conclusions. In 1982, many people felt that the Chamberlains had killed their baby simply because they looked guilty but some thirty years later we know for certain that 'a dingo took her baby'.

Figure 5.4 The Chamberlains entering the courthouse

Source: Newspix/News Ltd Archive

Gender: While still contested by theorists, gender is defined here as a socially constructed performance determined by cultural assumptions and expectations. Importantly, gender is different from biological sex ('male' or 'female') and sexual preference.

Gestures and 'emblems': How do we use emblems to communicate?

'Emblems' are movements which have a direct verbal translation, generally a word or phrase. These are often culturally specific and what might be acceptable in one country is considered offensive in others (see Figure 5.5's 'Flipping the bird' and 'Up yours').

One of the really useful functions of the emblem is to act as a physical substitute for words that have a similar meaning. The young Ms X is constantly being told not to shrug her shoulders when

Figure 5.5 Gestures and emblems

Photographer: Donna Edwards

people ask her a question. This gesture normally implies *'I don't know the answer'*, but in this case, her mother reads the shrug as *'I don't care'* and this irritates her. But not all emblems are ambiguous; some emblems are very precise. A nod of the head means 'yes' and shaking the head means 'no'. The vigour of the nod or shake adds emphasis to your answer (anyone who has tried to feed a baby understands that we 'get' the concept of 'no' as a head-shake very early in life! This is a very effective way to experience an emblem at work because babies can be quite good at 'NO!'). When Ms X's mother 'tells her off' for shrugging her shoulders, Ms X responds (behind her back) with a single finger gesture that has a very clear meaning!

Some sports make very effective use of emblems to communicate play strategies (for example, baseball), noisy workplaces employ emblematic movements to communicate (to signify a lunch break in a loud workshop) and I have used emblems to get the attention of noisy students at the back of a very large lecture hall. Some emblems are specific to a particular age group and stage in life; for example, making a 'W' with your thumbs and fingers, then rotating them to become an 'E', signifying 'What ever' (Figure 5.6) seems to be more popular for people (especially girls) in their early to mid teens.

Like most forms of non-verbal communication, emblems and gestures can have differing meaning across different cultures. My 'OK' gesture in Figure 5.6 is a good example. This emblem is a

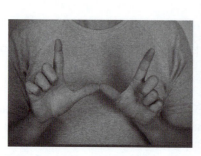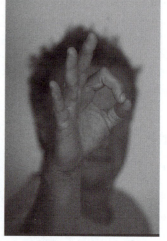

Figure 5.6 'Whatever!' and 'OK'

Photographer: Donna Edwards

positive one, an affirmation to most people in Australia. But in parts of France (and other places in Europe) it is used to signify the fact that someone or something is 'worthless' and without value. In some parts of Greece and Turkey this emblem is a rude invite for sex, mostly used in an insulting manner (Adler & Rodman, 2009). So, it's not always OK to use 'OK'!

A note about gender and non-verbal communication

It's very difficult to generalise about the way men and women use non-verbal communication, and the work of socio-linguist Dr Deborah Tannen (see Chapter 6 on gendered communication for more on this) suggests it is risky and potentially inaccurate to do so. Tannen's work proposes that social factors have the most significant influence on our ability to communicate, to send and read the many non-verbal messages we encounter as part of our everyday lives (Tannen, 1993). A really interesting exercise in non-verbal gendered communication is to watch a production (television or film) with 'gender swap' as the main theme. For an example of a woman pretending to be male, watch the film *She's the Man* (www.imdb.com/title/tt0454945), with Amanda Bynes attempting to substitute for her brother in his soccer team. For an example of a man attempting to be female, see David Walliams' extreme portrayal of Emily Howard in the BBC comedy *Little Britain* (www.bbc.co.uk/comedy/littlebritain/characters/emily.shtml). As you watch these (and other) 'gendered' stories, look for the way the actors over-enunciate non-verbal cues and exaggerate typically 'male' and 'female' gestures. Is it really like this? Adler and Rodman argue that to some degree, yes, men and women do use non-verbal communication in different ways:

> For example, women are more likely to face conversational partners head-on, where as men are more typically set at an angle. Women express more emotions via facial expressions then men. Most noticeably, women smile considerably more than men. Women gesture more, but men use more expansive gestures.
>
> (Adler & Rodman, 2009: 142)

The simplest explanation for the differences in the way men and women communicate might be found not in our physiology, but in the way we are socialised by our family, peers and community more generally. The comedians in *Little Britain* and *She's the Man* take easily identified, gendered behaviours/gestures and inflate them until they become humorous clichés of non-verbal communication from our everyday lives. Gendered communication will be discussed in greater detail in Chapter 6.

Emoticons r gr8t :-D

Like the Facebook page and mobile phone ringtones discussed earlier, emoticons are a relatively new form of non-verbal communication. The Concise Oxford Dictionary defines an emoticon as *'a representation of a facial expression such as a smile, formed with keyboard characters and used in electronic communications to convey the writer's feelings'* (Oxford University Press, 2008). Emoticons are now so common that the software used to type this chapter automatically converts the combination of my individual keyboard characters into stylish icons. When I type ':' followed by '-'and then ')' I get ☺.

Most people will be familiar with emoticons such as these (you might understand their meaning to be slightly different):

:D	means	large grin/smile
:)	means	happy/smiling
:-(	means	unhappy/sad
;-)	means	wink
:-P	means	sticking tongue out
>X3	means	naughty, playful, flirty
:O	means	shocked, surprised, outraged
:I	means	bored, unimpressed
:S	means	confused

Emoticons are primarily used when we employ our mobile phones or internet to communicate (MSN, Twitter, Skype, etc.). The key function of the emoticon is to demonstrate to the receiver the emotion accompanying our message, to display the feelings and intentions that might not be readily apparent in the written message. In my official role as a university academic, I receive and send many 'formal' email messages, using 'proper' English and impersonal language, very dry salutations and certainly no emoticons. When 'talking' to students who are my 'friends' on Facebook, this changes and the rigidity is removed. On Facebook, I LOL, ;-) and even use $#@!! words; the language is relaxed, the spelling often wrong; and it's in places like Facebook that you discover another, related non-verbal device, 'initialisms'.

Initialisms are also a form of emotional representation. Initialisms are a word formed by abbreviation of the first letter or letters of words in a phrase (for example, 'WAGs' for Wives and Girlfriends—especially in football), syllables or components of a word ('ISP' for Internet Service Provider), or a combination of words and syllables ('ESP' for extrasensory perception) and pronounced by spelling out the letters one by one rather than as a solid word. Initialisms can also be abbreviations that are formed using the initial components in a phrase or name. These components may be individual letters such as in 'rofl' (roll on floor laughing) or even the more enthusiastic, capitalised 'ROFL'. Some initialisms are parts of words, such as 'staph' to represent 'staphylococcus'.

Like emoticons, one function of initialisms is to act as emotional representations in our message-making. Another task they perform is to act as short cuts, and to reduce the volume of text we use in our messages. Instead of writing 'Asymmetric Digital Subscriber Line', we can use 'ADSL' as an abbreviation (here I will confess that, until now, I had no idea what the letters ADSL stood for!); most people who use MSN Messenger probably call it 'MSN'; and when medical staff call for an 'IV' they need an 'intravenous peripheral cannula'. These short cuts usually start out as a communication device that is specific to a certain industry, social group or interest. The expression 'laugh out loud' or 'LOL' was, at first, used in text form on mobile phones and computers. Last week, while on the train, the Family X were amazed to find a group of high school students who, instead of laughing at a joke, called out 'LOL'! This migration from technology to everyday life is a result of convergence. One way of thinking about convergence is to look at the way previously separate technologies such as phones, data (software and applications) and video now share resources and interact with each other, creating new language and symbols. So, shouting out 'LOL!' seems strange, but when you understand how convergent our lives have become, it makes some sense.

The Wikipedia entry for Technological Convergence (at the time of writing) includes the following statement: 'Today, we are surrounded by a multi-level convergent media world where all modes of communication and information are continually reforming to adapt to the enduring demands of technologies, changing the way we create, consume, learn and interact with each other' (Unknown, 2010b). I agree.

Similar to all the other non-verbal devices discussed in this chapter, the use of emoticons and initialisms is not entirely straightforward. Last year, after the family's 14-year-old dog (Toby) died, Mrs X sent the entire family this text message: *'arrvd hm & found toby passd away LOL Mum xx'*. What? Laugh out loud, the much loved family dog has died? The issue here is that Mrs X thought that 'LOL' was an abbreviation for 'lots of love' and that she had used 'LOL' appropriately. What is interesting in this story is the fact that her family was able to use the context of the message, and previous experience of their mother's use of text language, to easily work out that she actually meant 'lots of love'.

Emoticons and initialisms have yet another use. We employ these devices to soften the impact of a negative message, to moderate unpleasant news or to balance out the rejection embedded in our text. In most cases we use emoticons and initialisms to stand in for a tone of voice, gesture or emotion. For example, some readers might be familiar with messages such as the ones I found on my Facebook page:

> Sorry can't make it 2nite ☺
> Ouch! Stapled own finger LOL
> Drinks any one??? Lonely here ;-)
> Idiot drivers, stupid bikes, footpath not safe *ROTFL*
> Boys!!! ☺

In spite of the brevity of these messages, we decode them in a manner that produces complex meaning. Take, for example, *'boys !!! ☺'*. Combining this person's gender, age, their profile and the message, it seemed likely that the sender had some issues with her relationship. Similarly, *'Ouch! Stapled own finger LOL'* is not simply about physical pain. It also hints to the reader that this person was probably a little embarrassed at such a silly injury.

The simplicity of emoticons and initialisms enables the sender to turn simple and literal messages into ones that produce complex and multifaceted meaning.

How does the media use non-verbal communication to send messages?

An extraordinary thing happened during the red carpet arrival of the stars at the 2008 Academy Awards. Seventy-five of the world's most famous and fabulous actors arrived in 'green' (fuel efficient, hydrogen or hybrid) cars. I was amazed, and wondered what the message here was. Cameron Diaz, Ed Norton, Will Ferrell and Jay Leno all arrived in BMW Hydrogen 7 vehicles, and many others arrived in cars like Tahoes, provided by General Motors. Teamed with this 'green' arrival, a number of stars seemed to be wearing 'awareness' wristbands, folded ribbons and even black arm bands. One interviewee told the camera that she was wearing faux fur, but feared that even fake fur was 'sending the wrong message'.

What is remarkable about this case is the overwhelming number of non-verbal messages that came from the simple act of arriving and then walking up a strip of carpet. Imagine the number of non-verbal messages we must be exposed to over the many hours spent watching television, going to the movies and surfing video websites.

Figure 5.7 The Trunchbull and Miss Honey

Source: Kobal Collection/Tri Star

Some non-verbal messages in the media are easy to spot. 'Gender' as message is one example and 'villainy' is another.

Most programs portray the criminal/villain as a male, sometimes tattooed, always a little unkempt and mostly sinister-looking. In dramas involving a school, the teacher will almost always be female and the principal male. In the case of the film *Matilda* (1996), this is still true, because the character 'The Trunchbull' is heavily masculinised, large, strong and stereotyped! Miss Honey (as her name suggests) is the teacher, caring, feminine and fragile. These non-verbal messages are embedded and enduring and they perform an important role in the process of meaning-making: they too are short cuts. Non-verbal media messages about gender don't need to be as brutally obvious as those in *Matilda*. Producers very effectively make meaning through the use of things such as the type of jobs the male and female characters perform, the layout of their house/apartment, their pets and even their cars. All these things tell us something about the character. In Paramount Television's 1960s program *The Brady Bunch*, gendered non-verbal messages are very easy to spot. The mother is most often in the kitchen (looking in the refrigerator and talking to the maid), the girls in their bedrooms with a hairbrush, the boys in their rooms with guitars, and their father, after arriving home from his job, retires to his architect drawing board in 'the den'. All of these actions and objects tell us something about the roles and status of the characters and hint at how we might use these understandings to produce meaning.

Finally, there is another form of non-verbal communication commonly used by the media, and it's called product placement. Product placement is the process of 'discreetly' inserting a product, service or company into the narrative/scene of a program or movie. Here are some examples:

- In *American Idol*, Coca-Cola cups are always seen on the judges' table.
- *Biggest Loser* (Australia): Adidas tops, Coles deli meats and Bürgen bread all appear.
- *Mission: Impossible* uses only Apple computers.
- *Happy Gilmore* wears a Subway T-shirt.
- In *Back to the Future*, Marty drinks Pepsi.
- *Austin Powers* checks his email using AOL software.
- In *I, Robot*, look to see who's NOT wearing Converse footwear.

The function of product placement is very simple. It provides a non-verbal prompt that encourages us to consume the product on display. For a humorous take on product placement, watch the film *The Truman Show* (1998). As you watch, look for the way Truman is pushed to stand in front of the fried chicken sign, the food his faux wife prepares, the utensils she purchases, Truman's favourite drink 'Mococoa' and the beer his friends bring over. For an almost exhausting array of real products, watch *Transformers*. This movie has many product placements, from music players to cars. Finally, examine the media you consume: How many non-verbal product placement messages do you devour every day?

To conclude: How hard is it to make a realistic humanoid robot?

This last section will use the concept of the 'humanoid robot' to illustrate how all the elements of non-verbal communication discussed in the chapter are incredibly complex and yet painfully straightforward. In this chapter you have learnt about object communication, kinetic transmission, affect displays, emblems, gestures, emoticons, initialisms and many other non-verbal communication devices that perform an important and often subconscious role in our everyday life. A list such as this is a programming nightmare for those charged with making a robot seem human.

Wikipedia defines a 'humanoid robot' as:

> a robot with its overall appearance, based on that of the human body, allowing interaction with made-for-human tools or environments. In general, humanoid robots have a torso with a head, two arms and two legs, although some forms of humanoid robots may model only part of the body; for example, from the waist up. Some humanoid robots may also have a 'face', with 'eyes' and 'mouth'. Androids are humanoid robots built to aesthetically resemble a human.

> (Unknown, 2010a)

What is missing from this description is an important function of the humanoid robot. The ultimate humanoid robot will need to communicate in a manner which exactly replicates human interaction. The simple act of producing a smile is an enormously complex process: we have sad smiles, fake smiles, seductive smiles and even Mona Lisa smiles!

One thing we learn from trying to produce the perfect humanoid robot is that human non-verbal communication is a highly complex process which transmits many thousands signals, cues and messages that (most of us) simply decode and understand. The complexity of non-verbal communications means that the arrival of a convincing humanoid robot seems some way off.

Summary

One thing that we can conclude from all the material in this chapter is that non-verbal communication is complex. We often communicate things we thought were private, we all rely on non-verbal cues to serve as communication short cuts and some use non-verbal communication to transmit messages that make us feel uncomfortable. The parents of Family X did it when their son asked if his friend could come away for the weekend. If you slam this book closed, sigh loudly and drop it ostentatiously in your bag, those around you will ask 'What's wrong?'

Try it now.

Further reading

Adler, R B & Rodman, G 2009, *Understanding Human Communication*, Oxford University Press, New York.

Bennett, A 1999, 'Subcultures or Neo-Tribes? Rethinking the Relationship between Youth, Style and Musical Taste', *Sociology*, vol. 33, no. 3, 599–617.

Mortensen, E 2007, *Communication Theory*, Transaction, New Brunswick.

Oxford University Press 2008, *Compact Oxford English Dictionary of Current English*, Oxford University Press, Melbourne.

Pease, A 1985, *Body Language: How To Read Others' Thoughts By Their Gestures*, Camel, North Sydney.

Tannen, D 1993, *Gender and Conversational Interaction*, Oxford University Press, New York.

Unknown 2010, 'Humanoid Robot', retrieved 9 March 2010, <http://en.wikipedia.org/wiki/Humanoid_robot>.

Unknown 2010, 'Technological Convergence', retrieved 9 March 2010, <http://en.wikipedia.org/wiki/Technological_convergence>.

Weblinks

BBC Television: www.bbc.co.uk

The Internet Movie Database (IMDB): www.imdb.com

The Star Pulse Internet News: www.starpulse.com

Suck at Life (the blog of Lawrence Yang): www.suckatlife.com

Wikipedia: www.wikipedia.com

For revision questions, please visit www.oup.com.au/orc/chalkley.

6

Gender and Communication: Why and How Men and Women Communicate

Tony Chalkley

Are you wearing that?

In the middle week of her university holidays and close to her own birthday, Ms X was invited to the eighteenth birthday of one of her friends. This created much excitement; it was a nice interruption to holidays that seemed to be filled with uni homework, and the venue, the Arts Centre, was a spectacular place to party. She spent hours in the bathroom and changed at least a dozen times before the party and, finally, raced downstairs, leaving just enough time for her father to drive her to the venue. After asking 'What do you think?' and a quick 'cat walk' through the lounge room, she turned to her parents:

'You look nice, but will you be cold once it gets dark?', was the comment from her father.

'You're not wearing that, are you? I thought this was a classy venue', said her mother. Tears ensued.

What you will learn from this chapter

- How men and women use different (and similar) communication devices to get their message across. You will read how we negotiate meaning and work to establish a rough consensus between the sender and receiver of messages.
- How non-verbal communication described in earlier chapters also plays an important role in gendered communication.
- That, in the late 1990s, bookstores seemed to carry a number of surprisingly popular bestsellers about communication between men and women. In this chapter you will learn what these books had to say and why they were so prolific and popular.
- About meta-messages and how Deborah Tannen's research into professional communication exposed differences in how men and women communicate in the workplace.
- How 'saving face' is a cultural practice that spans both geography and gender.
- About the issues and challenges posed by virtual classrooms and online dating. This chapter will also include a discussion on the role played by new media in gendered communication.
- And finally, as you navigate through this chapter, you are encouraged to reflect on your own communication—in particular, how you produce and interpret meta-messages.

Introduction

This chapter introduces you to the thorny and complex world of 'gendered' communication and I would like to qualify the contents of this chapter with a rider: making any definitive statement about how men and women communicate is a risky business. The reason for this is very simple. There is no 'correct' way for men and women to communicate and, as a result, not everyone employs a gender-stereotypical approach to communication. In other words, not all females talk in a 'female' way and, equally, not all males talk in a 'male' way, because there is no such thing. Hopefully, you will find yourself dis/agreeing with some of the theories outlined here and you may discover that even though some assertions seem to be rational and logical, they just don't apply to you.

To start the chapter, let's return to the Family X 'leaving for a party' story and find out why an 18 year old is crying, ruining her make-up and now running late.

Meta-messages: 'You're not wearing that, are you?'

In her book *You're wearing that?* (2006), Deborah Tannen (sociologist and linguist) provides an insight into what might have occurred in the X house, just before the party. The father's response was fairly non-committal and was mostly concerned with the mechanics of the night—would she be adequately warm once the thermal protection of the sun was removed? Some might argue that this is a fairly typical male response to a query about appearance, clothing and attractiveness. It's bland, safe and provides a relatively useless appraisal that Ms X politely smiled at, but largely dismissed. But, when she asked her mother *'How do I look?'* her mother responded with the question *'You're not wearing that, are you?'* And this created some friction and tears (some readers may even have first-hand experience of this). Why?

When her mother asked *'You're not wearing that, are you?'*, her daughter heard *'I don't approve of your clothing and/or appearance'* and while it's entirely possible that her mother did not intend to insult or offend and was genuinely interested in her daughter's choice of clothing, it seems unlikely. Why? In her book, Tannen explains an almost identical experience of a 'dressing up to go out' event in the life of 'Loraine', a participant in her research. (Like in the Family X, Loraine's question 'How do I look?' was answered with 'You're not going to wear that, are you?'). Here's how Tannen explains the interaction:

> A way to understand the difference between what Loraine hears and what her mother said she meant is the distinction between message and meta-message ... Everything we say has meaning on these two levels. The message is the meaning that resides in the dictionary definitions of words. Everyone agrees on this. But people frequently differ on how to interpret the words, because interpretations depend on meta-messages—the meaning gleaned from how something is said, or from the fact that it is said at all.

> (Tannen, 2006: 13)

In the case of Ms X, the issue is not the literal meaning of her mother's statement *'You're not wearing that, are you? I thought this was a classy venue'*, it's the **meta-message** that the daughter heard. What she heard was *'Your appearance is not suitable for a classy venue'* and, possibly, *'You are not classy'*. Tannen believes that everything we say has meta-messages to indicate how our utterance should be interpreted: Mrs X expressed her disapproval through a meta-message and her daughter heard this loud and clear.

The reason for including a story such as this in a chapter that is primarily concerned with inter-gender communication is that, through her research, Tannen has established that the early experiences with our parents (of both genders) shapes and influences conversation and communication for the rest of our lives. These meta-message-rich conversations teach us how to identify the not so well hidden messages in communication and educate us about what sorts of comments we can expect and how to interpret them: 'The long history of conversations that family members share contributes not only to how listeners interpret words, but also to how speakers choose them' (Tannen, 2006: 14).

Meta-messages: the 'hidden' meanings behind (and among) the words we hear.

Bestsellers about gender: Are men and women really from different planets?

Figure 6.1 was included with some trepidation. It is biased, heterosexual and, to some, offensive. But, at the same time, we view it and might find that we agree with at least some of the connotations and embedded meanings. John Gray, in his aptly titled bestseller *Men are from Mars, Women are from Venus* (1993), uses this planetary metaphor to explain how he believes part of the problem with gender communication is the very fact that men and women even attempt to communicate directly with each other!

Gray's theory that men and women 'seldom mean the same things even when they use the same words' (Gray, 1993: 61) also reflects some of Tannen's research findings: that the sexes communicate differently because 'boys and girls grow up in different worlds, even if they grow up in the same house' (Tannen, 1992: 125). Gray believes that this difference in upbringing results in a phenomenon he calls 'the cave and the wave'.

The 'cave and the wave' metaphor relates to the way different genders react under stress. Gray believes that many men 'retreat into their cave' until they find a solution to a problem. Gray uses the second term, the 'wave', to describe a natural propensity for women to give/share with other people.

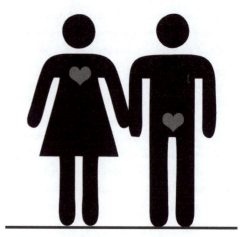

Figure 6.1 Surely we are more sophisticated than this?
Source: Shutterstock/Korinyuliya

This 'cave and wave' approach has its problems, flaws and challenges: overall, the use of such a simple metaphor works quite well, as does his use of intense and emotional language, but do the theories and concepts embedded in the 'cave and the wave' hold up to close scrutiny? Deborah Tannen does not have a 'cave' or a 'wave', but some of her research uncovered similar issues with gender communication. In her book *You Just Don't Understand*, she describes how men and women differ:

> For males, conversation is the way you negotiate your status in the group and keep people from pushing you around; you use talk to preserve your independence. Females, on the other hand, use conversation to negotiate closeness and intimacy; talk is the essence of intimacy, so being best friends means sitting and talking. For boys, activities, doing things together, are central. Just sitting and talking is not an essential part of friendship. They're friends with the boys they do things with.

> (Tannen, 1991: 78)

Tannen believes that one of the biggest challenges for men and women in conversation is caused by something very simple: 'Male–female conversation is cross-cultural communication. Culture is simply a network of habits and patterns gleaned from past experience, and women and men have different past experiences' (Tannen, 1992: 125). She also described how 'complementary schismogenesis' can undermine the success of our communication and, eventually, the health of our relationships. Complementary schismogenesis is how two different people, often in a close relationship, react to each other's actions. For example, the interaction between them is such that a particular behaviour (e.g. leaving the milk out of the fridge) from one side elicits a particular behaviour (e.g. confront and complain) from the other side. After a while, this action/reaction becomes an unnoticed and unhelpful form of **patterned behaviour**. Complementary schismogenesis can be found in most relationships, irrespective of gender.

These two behaviours complement one another, and often exemplify the dominant–submissive roles we play in particular parts of our relationships. Furthermore, these behaviours may exaggerate one another, leading to a severe rift and possible conflict. Tannen describes this as the 'mutually

Complementary schismogenesis:
'Complementary' means 'forming a satisfactory or balanced whole'; 'schismogenesis' means the 'creation of division'. When combined, they describe a situation where two people work with and against each other to act and then respond, in a predictable, often destructive manner.

Patterned behaviour
is any action(s) repeated over and over. Typically, it: 1) feels like it's beyond our control; 2) is cyclical and very had to change; 3) is a response to a familiar, long-standing problem.

aggravating cycle' that undermines long-term relationships (Tannen, 1992: 125). Perhaps it is a little like the notions expressed in the 'cave' and the 'wave' analogy? In their humorously titled book *Why Men Can Only Do One Thing at a Time and Women Never Stop Talking* (2003), Allen and Barbara Pease use humour to argue that women talk in order to build relationships, connect with people and demonstrate that they are keen to develop a friendship. Pease and Pease believe that this 'talking to build relationships' explains why women can spend all day together and then, later the same day, telephone each other in order to catch up. For men, it's different. Men talk in order to pass on facts and information. The telephone is a device for the transmission of these facts and information.

Of course, both these statements are a little outrageous and deliberately provocative—but the extreme nature of statements such as these highlights the possibility that men and women do communication in different ways (Pease & Pease, 2003: 35).

So, perhaps the concept of the 'cave' and 'wave' is actually too complex? Is it possible that these problems stem from something much more basic—the seemingly simple process of talking? Tannen found that some of the communication problems we experience are the result of issues that seem incredibly straightforward. For example, she found that words and their many meanings are the biggest challenge for men and women in conversation, pronouns in particular. Tannen's research found that little things like the way men use 'I' and 'me' was often the cause of unintended hostility. This happens often in the Family X household: when Mr X loudly announces *'I'm having a coffee'*, his wife gets upset, because what he actually means is *'I'm making coffee, would anyone else like one?'* Similarly, when the weather is fine and a walk seems like a pleasant idea, he simply announces *'I'm going to walk the dog'*. When his family protests that they would like to be invited, his reply is *'You don't need an invitation! Just say "I'm coming too"'*.

Pronouns: Can Ms X expect a few reassuring words from the cave?

The use of pronouns is an issue in the Family X house, but there are other equally challenging communication issues, one of which is the type of words employed to illustrate how upset one member becomes about a particular issue.

And it's very often a simple issue, such as replacing the empty toilet paper roll: as the two teenagers share a common bathroom, this is a long-standing issue and it seems to bother Ms X more than her brother. *'You NEVER, EVER replace the roll when you finish it, I ALWAYS do it'* is a fairly common argument from the second-storey bathroom. Of course, it's not factually correct because, very occasionally, he does replace the toilet roll. But that's not the point: Ms X has used the very definitive 'always' and 'never' in order to express her annoyance, fury and frustration after discovering no toilet paper, again. Gray (1993) theorises that this happens because women tend to use superlatives, metaphor and exaggeration to more fully express emotion, mood and sentiment. As a result, the very literal men (the 'Martians') miss the 'true' message because they don't understand that women (the 'Venusians') use dramatic language to reinforce how important the subject of the conversation is. Ms X actually wants her brother to acknowledge that she replaces the toilet paper much more often than he and she would like this to change, even if it's just a little change.

The book *Men are from Mars, Women are from Venus* contains a similar example of how a woman might tell her partner that *'we never go out'* instead of stating more directly what she means: *'I'm bored and restless and would like to go out'*. In her work, Tannen describes a similar situation: how a powerful female CEO might say *'How certain are you of that?'* rather than *'No, that is incorrect, you are wrong'*. This approach, 'sneaking up' on a difficult topic, is called 'indirectness' and is a major theme in most gender communication literature. In the following section, I will discuss and explore some of the issues associated with 'indirect' communication.

Indirectness: 'Why don't you say what you mean?'

Then you should say what you mean, the March Hare went on. 'I do,' Alice hastily replied; 'at least—at least I mean what I say—that's the same thing, you know.' 'Not the same thing a bit!' said the Hatter. 'You might just as well say that "I see what I eat" is the same thing as "I eat what I see"!

(Lewis Carroll)

Sometimes, like Alice, we mean what we say, even when we don't say what we mean. This is the complex process of 'indirect' communication. What exactly is the difference between 'direct' and 'indirect' communication? The Oxford Dictionary provides a very simple definition of these two terms:

Direct: (of a person or their behaviour) going straight to the point; frank: he is very direct and honest.

Indirect: avoiding direct mention or exposition of a subject: an indirect attack on the Archbishop.

(http://oxforddictionaries.com)

Communication theorists believe that the decision to use direct or indirect communication depends on the nature of the message, the relationship between sender and receiver and the motivation of the person making the utterance. What do I mean? Here's an example. When Mrs X went into the lounge room, it was cold. Instead of saying *'Oh, it's freezing in here, shut the window, I'm cold!'*, she asked *'Would you like me to close that window a little?'* The first is a direct message, blunt and unambiguous. The second, the indirect message, is presented as a slightly vague, impersonal enquiry. Even though she used a form of indirect enquiry, we still understand that she is cold and wants the window closed. So, why do we (sometimes) decide to be deliberately indirect? The male stars of *Sex and the City* were often subject to indirect communication that they frequently (and comically) failed to understand:

Mr Big: Nice dress.

Carrie: Meaning?

Mr Big: Nice dress.

(*Sex and the City*, Season 4, Episode 18, June 3, 2001. First screened February 10, 2002
(Star, 2002))

Tannen (1984) explains how and why we use direct and indirect conversational styles by taking Lakoff's 'theory of politeness' as a model. According to Tannen, Lakoff's 'Rules of Politeness' follow three principles:

1   Don't impose on people (keep a distance).

2   Give people options (develop deference).

3   Be friendly and open (a sense of 'camaraderie').

Lakoff argues that when we make a choice to employ a particular principle ('distance', 'deference' or 'camaraderie'), this naturally results in a specific communication style, and with each style comes either directness or indirectness. When using the first principle, 'don't impose', we tend to use formal expressions, technical language and routine expressions in order to exclude personal emotions. To see this principle in action, watch a televised meeting between two important heads of state!

The second principle, 'give people options', is characterised by saying things hesitantly, by not stating directly what you mean and, often, using euphemisms to articulate difficult and unpalatable ideas or contentious proposals. Giving people options involves the status difference of the sender and the receiver, and usually the sender acquiesces to the receiver by leaving them the option of making the decision. Tannen points out that women often behave in this way to show consideration to others, or to leave some of the decision-making to others. This is a classic example of how indirect communication allows people to 'save face'.

The third principle, 'be friendly and open', is slightly different because this approach accentuates the sense of equality between the sender and receiver, and enhances closeness between them. In this principle, indirectness can be also employed when the sender and the receiver have a high level of interpersonal understanding and there is little need to talk. In this case, indirectness is employed to produce empathy.

Tannen's research found that women in positions of power more often used the second principle ('give people options') when working with staff employed in subordinate positions. This happens for a number of reasons: first, because 'it seems that the women were keenly aware of the power inherent in their authority and expended effort to avoid wielding it carelessly' (Tannen, 2005: 180). The second reason this happens is more complex. Here is how Tannen explains it: 'it might seem that saving face is primarily something one does for oneself, saving face works especially well if two people do it for each other, as often occurs in ritual exchanges characteristic of women's conversations'. Why? In order to preserve your 'face', 'you speak in ways that present a certain face to the world, but the world must do its part in supporting that face. If others refuse to treat you as deserving of authority, you can't "hold up" your face on your own' (Tannen, 2005: 180–181). Successful 'face saving' is a two-way process.

One of the most potent uses of 'indirect' language is to use it to save face. Mrs X is a good example: she is a senior manager in a firm that is, on the whole, male dominated. When working with the younger managers, she finds herself taking care to avoid offending them, even when criticism is needed and justified. *'I've just read your report and, I'm sorry, there are a couple of mistakes. Let's fix them together'* and *'I really appreciate the time you have put into this project and it's brilliant. With your permission, I would like to make a couple of small improvements'* are the kind of indirect messages she uses to negotiate with staff, critique their work and allow them to save face. Tannen found that men do this as well, but women are more likely to do so. Later in this chapter, you will read what happens when this process is removed as organisations increasingly depend on electronic communication for decision-making, consultation and to stand in for other traditional face-to-face interaction.

The use of direct and indirect communication is not just a gender issue; there is also a cultural element to this communication approach. The majority of communication literature cited in this book includes lengthy discussions about the fact that different cultures use indirect language to save face. Face saving is a complex process that depends on a very simple principle: it's the desire to restore balance to a conversation and take into account the effect of one's words on the other person (Tannen, 2005).

New media and gender: What happens in the virtual world?

Describing how men and women communicate online is a much more difficult process. This is a relatively new and under-researched area, and the nature of communication depends on the nature of the forum (e.g. online gaming, learning and dating would all result in very different communication styles) and communication changes as technology evolves. One of the most interesting elements of this topic is the fact that the concepts of 'identity' and 'reality' have been completely dismantled in online worlds; just because someone claims to be a 32-year-old male from a distant country does not necessarily mean that is who they are: they may well be a 14-year-old girl from three streets away!

In an effort to gain a glimpse into this sometimes murky world of virtual communication, the following section explores three (relatively) well-established phenomena—online learning, computer-mediated communication and virtual dating.

Online/**virtual learning** is very popular: most universities offer a number of subjects online, using chat rooms, bulletin boards and **i Lectures** to stand in for traditional lectures and tutorials.

Ms X is in her first year at university and studies two units this way. She doesn't like it at all. Her older brother has also studied online and thinks that it 'rocks': no class, no one knows who you are and you can study (or not) in your pyjamas. What might explain their very different experiences of online learning? The first and simplest explanation is personality—some people really like the idea of time-shifting (studying whenever you like), they enjoy being anonymous and would much rather type than speak up in a classroom. Some people hate it and would much prefer 'traditional' face-to-face learning.

There is another, more contentious, explanation. Men and women experience online learning differently. In her 1999 study, Kimberly Blum found that inequity between male and female students is often caused by gender differences in communication styles, resulting in a tolerance of male domination in online communication patterns, effectively silencing female students (Blum, 1999). Blum's research discovered that male students responded to more questions and, overall, posted 58 per cent more than their female classmates. More importantly, Blum found that the nature of these postings was also very different.

She observed that the messages produced by male students had a 'tone of certainty', often using polite language, but producing messages that were overly decisive, sometimes 'pushy' and mostly resolute in their conviction (Blum, 1999: 6).

But, when she examined female students' responses, she found that their messages tended to be more moderate, considerate and much less 'arrogant' in tone. It appeared that female

Virtual learning: a mode of computer-based education whereby the teacher interacts with students either via video conferencing internet broadcast or email (or combination of the above).

i Lecture: a digitally recorded lecture that is available as media file, live steam or podcast.

students valued messages that worked to produce a relationship, allowing both the sender and receiver an opportunity to disagree and simultaneously reaffirm. Words such as 'thanks', 'great' and 'sorry' were more common in messages produced by female participants (Blum, 1999: 7).

Perhaps this 10-year-old finding is not so contentious after all, because, to some degree, this also happens in face-to-face tutorials: loud and confident (often male) students can dominate with definitive statements, the quiet go unnoticed and some students (often female) meet afterwards for a coffee and a de facto tutorial. Blum's findings also confirm some of the theories discussed earlier in this chapter, especially Deborah Tannen's research into how men and women communicate in the workplace.

In August 1999, a group of researchers in the United States undertook a small but significant research project with 70 students enrolled in a university business degree (Dennis et al., 1999). The experiment was quite simple: the students were divided into three work groups (all male, all female and mixed) and required to problem solve in order to achieve a number of office-type tasks, first using face-to-face communication and, for the second task, only computer-mediated communication (CMC). What they discovered was quite startling. The first thing they noticed was that all the groups took longer to make decisions using CMC (this makes sense: typing is slow; it is much quicker to talk). The second finding was that the all-female groups took significantly longer to make their decisions when using only CMC. The reason why this might be the case is linked to the ideas and concepts covered in the previous chapter:

> Computer mediated communication interferes with women's use of nonverbal communication and consensus seeking behaviour by eliminating nonverbal communication— a channel more important for women than men. Therefore, use of CMC will have a greater impact on women performing the more equivocal task compared to their face-to-face performance.
>
> (Dennis et al: 1999)

A group study as small as this, which is now quite old, is by no means conclusive, but the findings are intriguing. What does this mean to organisations (businesses, government and schools, for example) that are increasingly dependent on CMC for discussion, decision-making and the production of action?

Online dating: 'Tall, fit, good sense of humour, seeks same'

Online dating is an entirely different, unpredictable and exciting new world, and it seems fair to say that in the past five years, online dating has become progressively more popular and increasingly socially acceptable. Some five years ago, university students made shocked and horrified faces when this topic was mentioned, but now the response is a little different. A quick scan of the most popular Australian dating websites reveals services such as 'intelligent matching based on compatibility and partner preferences'; some aim to 'connect, engage and entertain singles: making single life an exhilarating and complete experience'; and a new site promises to assist people who are 'looking for extra thrills and romance through discreet relationships, casual encounters and extra-marital affairs. Meet for romantic adventures with local married women or attached men'.

Facebook offers many dating groups, as does MySpace, and even eBay has a tab for 'dating'! Why might online dating be popular? Back in 1995, when online dating was relatively new, Bradford Scharlott and William Christ found that online dating was becoming popular because:

> the ability to communicate with others without revealing details about oneself enables the shy user to interact without fear of rejection. Moreover, as the questions about their personalities and fantasies reveal, (online) 'Matchmaker' enables these users to communicate in ways that in other contexts they might feel too socially inhibited to do.
>
> (Scharlott & Christ, 1995: 201)

The personal motivation for why people participate in online dating is interesting, but this not the most important issue here. As this chapter is concerned with how men and women communicate, it's important to see if anything changes online. Do we behave differently in the online dating world? As far back as 1995, researchers were discovering that:

> The pattern of sending and receiving messages on [Matchmaker] suggests that, generally speaking, men and women on the system employ different communication strategies. Most men seem inclined to maximize the number of users they contact, presumably to increase their chances of finding someone interested in a physically intimate relationship; most women, by contrast, seem inclined to contact fewer men and then try to establish more sustained communications.
>
> (Scharlott & Christ, 1995: 202)

This observation seems to be a little like a high school biology lesson in mammal reproduction: 'a successful male should have many matings'. Surely it's not that basic? This early research found that the way men and women communicate on dating websites was actually very complex. Women had different motivations and expectations to start with, women were more successful at meeting a partner (and sustaining a relationship), and men disclosed less in their profiles and wrote less in their messages. Women log in and reply more frequently, men tended to infrequently log in and would tend to bulk post their replies. Men tended to not initiate (or would abandon) conversations that didn't assist them in their 'quest', but women would occasionally contact other female members (the 'competition') to share their online experiences.

These new worlds of virtual classrooms and online dating are not places where the existing norms and rules of communication no longer apply. It would seem that most of the problems and challenges we experience in the 'real' world exist in the virtual world as well: we use direct and indirect language, meta-messages (especially in the way we construct our online identity) and continue to experience misunderstanding and misinterpretation when we 'talk' to each other.

Conclusion

Communication is never simple and rarely straightforward. Gendered communication is no exception to this rule: men and women are fundamentally different and, as a result, adopt different approaches when communicating with each other. Some commentators use metaphors to explain complex theories in simple ways, some break our messages down into small parts and attempt to explain the function of each component, and some use 'scientific' measurement tools to assess how we 'talk'.

One limitation shared by all these research approaches is the fact that it is impossible to develop a comprehensive, permanent and definitive understanding of how and why men and women communicate in different ways. Some theorists (including the author) argue that nowadays in the online world this distinction is being dismantled.

It seems a reasonable conjecture that significant developments in gendered communication might be on the way. Our increasing dependence on mediated communication, the acceptance of virtual friends and the popularity of digital lovers will reconstruct (or has already reconstructed) our identities and, once again, the way men and women communicate will be transformed.

Summary

In this chapter you have learnt:

- How men and women use different (and similar) communication devices to get their message across, how we often struggle to negotiate meaning and how establishing a 'rough consensus' is actually quite difficult
- How contentious 'truisms' (self-evident and obvious truths) are embedded into our daily lives and can, sometimes without us realising, affect the way we communicate
- How Deborah Tannen's research around issues in professional communication provides a useful insight into how men and women communicate; in particular, what she has discovered about how men and women 'talk' differently in the workplace
- That 'saving face' is cultural practice that spans both geography and gender; we moderate our communication in order to manage issues of power, status and 'face'
- The final part of this chapter briefly introduced you to three emerging forms of communication: the virtual classroom, CMC and the increasingly popular world of online dating. The primary aim of this chapter was to encourage you to develop a better understanding of your own communication, to develop an appreciation of how the sexes use different narrative devices to make meaning and to provide you with some insight into how we negotiate our way in the world.

Further reading

Blum, K 1999, 'Gender Differences in Asynchronous Learning in Higher Education: Learning Styles, Participation Barriers and Communication Patterns', *Asynchronous Learning Networks,* vol. 3, no. 1, 46–66.

Dennis, A R, Kinney S T & Hung, Y C 1999, 'Gender Differences in the Effects of Media Richness', *Small Group Research,* vol. 30, no. 4, 405–37.

Gray, J 1993, *Men Are from Mars, Women Are from Venus! A Practical Guide for Improving Communication and Getting What You Want in Your Relationships,* HarperCollins, Hammersmith.

Pease, A & Pease, B 2003, *Why Men Can Only Do One Thing at a Time and Women Never Stop Talking,* Camel, Boston.

Scharlott, B & Christ, W 1995, 'Overcoming Relationship-initiation Barriers: The Impact of a Computer-dating System on Sex Role, Shyness, and Appearance Inhibitions', *Computers in Human Behavior,* vol. 11, no. 2, 191–204.

Sex in the City 2002, television program, Home Box Office, New York. Star, D (prod.).

Tannen, D 1991, *You Just Don't Understand: Women and Men in Conversation*, Random House, Milson's Point.

Tannen, D 1992, *That's Not What I Meant! How Conversation Style Makes or Breaks Relationships*, Ballantine, New York.

Tannen, D 2005, *Talking From 9 to 5: How Women's and Men's Conversation Styles Affect Who Gets Heard, Who Gets Credit, and What Gets Done at Work*, Virago, London.

Tannen, D 2006, *You're Wearing That? Understanding Mothers and Daughters in Conversation*, Random House, Westminster.

Weblinks

For revision questions, please visit www.oup.com.au/orc/chalkley.

7

Designing Desire:
Advertising, Consumption and Identity

Mitchell Hobbs

Ms X needs retail therapy

Ms X felt bored. Lying on her bed and ignoring her overdue anthropology essay, she distractedly flicked through the pages of her favourite magazine, wondering what it would be like to be famous. 'Surely Paris Hilton is never bored?', she thought, pausing to read a story about the hotel heiress's latest party exploits. Blonde socialites simply don't get bored; they're too busy creating their own brand of perfume or underwear. Or they are at some wild party, in a little black dress, making out with Justin Timberlake in a toilet cubicle. Or perhaps they're out walking a red carpet for some film première. Or simply being chased by the paparazzi up a Hollywood boulevard, while trying not to trip in their designer high heels or drop their little, handbag-sized dog. Either way, thought Ms X, Paris would not be lying in a boring suburban bedroom, wasting her Saturday morning. And with that revelation, she knew how to fill the present emptiness: it was time for some retail therapy.

Calling her closest friends and arranging to meet them at her favourite shopping centre, Ms X grabbed her headphones, left her suburban bedroom and began to make her way to the local train station. While en route, she tuned her mobile phone to her favourite commercial radio station. Connecting her headphones and ignoring the ad breaks, she sang softly to herself, happily cocooned in her own private media bubble. Arriving ten minutes prior to the scheduled departure of the next train, she had sufficient time to browse the station's newsagency for the latest fashion and celebrity magazines, before standing with bored anticipation of the arrival of the next train. Intermittently sipping from a bottle of water she had purchased while in the newsagency, she updated her Facebook status on her phone, before standing staring at the large billboards advertising underwear. Well, it was hard not to stare: the models were practically naked!

Finally arriving at her intended destination, Ms X collected her friends and made her way through the shopping centre towards the section most devoted to her style. Ignoring freebies and shopping centre touts pushing everything from make-up to the alleviation of global poverty, she entered the familiar sanctuary of her favourite clothing shop. This was her space. Everything here—the jeans, the shoes, the dresses, and even the staff—matched how she felt about herself and the world. The only problem was choice: at times she felt slightly anxious about choosing the right outfit, about identifying the jeans or tops that were the best possible reflection of her personality and sense of fashion. Thankfully her friends also understood her predicament, and together they happily helped each other choose new dresses, complimenting each other as they charged their selected clothes to their well-used credit cards. It was only after Ms X had purchased her new clothes and returned to her bedroom, some four hours later, that she felt slightly uneasy about the money that she had just spent. This sensation was compounded by another source of anxiety—as she was now finding it increasingly difficult to ignore her overdue anthropology essay. 'What on earth', she thought, 'could possibly be learnt from studying the symbolic and ritualistic meaning of cultural artefacts'?

What you will learn from this chapter

This chapter explores how advertising and consumption shape our identities and daily experiences. In particular, it focuses on the social roles and meanings of commodities (such as clothing, cars and other material products) as they are defined by the advertising industry. After reading this chapter, students will better understand:

- The history and structure of the Australian advertising industry
- How advertising influences how we see ourselves, each other and our 'stuff'
- The cultural mechanisms used by the advertising industry to sell us all manner of goods
- The formation and presentation of social and self-identity in the age of the consumer society.

Introduction: 'I shop, therefore I am'

The above vignette is fiction, yet it illustrates experiences, behaviours and feelings that are common to many young adults living in the developed world. Indeed, for many individuals living in Australia today, shopping is not merely about meeting one's material needs (such as those for food or clothing), but is rather a form of leisure, where 'shopaholics' engage in 'retail therapy', seeking to distract themselves from boredom or anxiety with the satisfaction of commodity consumption. Even for those with relatively small levels of 'disposable' income, shopping, or simply hanging out at the 'mall', can be a form of entertainment and recreation, where we can find hours of pleasure in window shopping and bargain hunting, happily losing track of time in the glittering labyrinths of our consumer society.

While shopping can be fun and is necessary for the purchase of essential material goods and services in modern societies, it can also be seen as a self-destructive form of behaviour, with potential negative psychological consequences. For example, in recent years clinical psychologists and behavioural therapists have begun to treat a growing number of patients suffering from shopping disorders, with the American Psychological Association having estimated that 'oniomania', or 'compulsive buying', is afflicting somewhere between 1 and 6 per cent of people living in the United States (Benson, 2000: xxi). Although for some individuals compulsive buying is thought to be a reflection of 'deep-seated psychological problems', such as feelings of low self-esteem or anxiety, the compulsive behaviour is also attributed to social circumstances, such as stemming from a desire to avoid boredom, loneliness and sources of stress (DeSarbo & Edwards, 1996: 252–253). In contrast to what one might expect from the expression 'retail therapy', for some shopaholics mass consumption can become its own psychopathology, straining financial independence and damaging personal relationships as consumers spend more than they can afford (Benson, 2000; Dittmar, 2004).

Thankfully, the majority of us are not addicted to shopping, in that we do not possess a chronic and overpowering repetitive urge to buy consumer goods. Yet, while the majority of us may not be suffering from a behavioural shopping disorder, we might in fact be affected by a less acute socio-pathology: 'affluenza'. According to the popular Australian academic Clive Hamilton, 'affluenza' can be defined as:

1   The bloated, sluggish and unfulfilled feeling that results from efforts to keep up with the Joneses.

2   An epidemic of stress, overwork, waste and indebtedness caused by the dogged pursuit of the Australian dream.

3   An unsustainable addiction to economic growth.

(Hamilton & Denniss, 2005: 3)

Hamilton, along with co-author Richard Denniss (2005), views affluenza as a fairly recent cultural phenomenon that reflects a growing adoption of the values of materialism and mass consumerism. The core of their argument is this: Australians, in chasing a materialistic vision of ideal lifestyles, now ignore the social relationships and community participation that makes for a truly enriching and ennobling society. Their evidence: despite earning incomes three times higher than they were in 1950, two-thirds of Australians today feel they cannot afford to buy all they 'need' and report to be less happy than previous generations, with close to a third of the adult population currently dependent on anti-depressant drugs or other substances 'to [help] get them through the day' (Hamilton & Denniss, 2005: 188). Their conclusion: the emptiness of material culture is making Australians sick and creating a shallow and self-centred society.

While we can debate the extent to which mass consumption is adversely affecting our mental health and relationships with each other (an idea explored later in this chapter), what is less contentious is the proposition that developed societies are becoming more concerned with consumerism, with advertising identified as the ideological force helping to drive this cultural transformation. Indeed, since the end of the Second World War and the rise of mass consumption, advertising has emerged as a conspicuous cultural phenomenon, selling us material goods and other commodities by promoting lifestyles and ideal versions of the 'self' (or who we would like to be). The power of advertisements lies in their ability to build an ideological relationship between a consumer good—be it a personal computer, dress or car—and the individual, so that shopping becomes, in part, a symbolic project of identity construction and wish fulfilment, with consumer items selected and purchased according to what the shopper feels such things will say about their personality, character and taste. In other words, we identify and purchase products that **advertising agencies** have successfully marketed as matching our desired identity or lifestyle. We then use these goods, heavy with their ideological meanings, to say something, at a symbolic level, about who we are to those we encounter in our daily lives.

This chapter is dedicated to exploring this interconnected relationship between advertising, consumerism and identity. It seeks to review not only the history and methods of the advertising industry, but also the key role that commodities and industrial production have played in creating our modern consumer societies. Through exploring the social roots of the consumer society, we will better understand how advertising agencies use our desires to sell us 'stuff'. More importantly, such an exploration will allow us to better consider the extent to which we are manipulated by advertising messages and consumer culture more broadly, so that our relationships with each other, and indeed our impact on the environment, might be adversely affected. This discussion begins with a closer look at the history and structure of the advertising industry.

Advertising agencies: connect their 'clients' (the regional and national advertisers) and the media, purchasing advertising space and creating content. While some advertisers produce their own ads, the agencies produce the majority of Australia's national advertising.

Advertising: A short introduction

While most textbooks discuss the importance of advertising in relation to sustaining and shaping the content of the commercial media, few focus on the manner in which advertising has impacted on the economy and society in which we live. This is an unfortunate oversight, for the stuff we buy to decorate our homes and use to construct a sense of style—in what has been labelled the 'aestheticization of everyday life' (Featherstone, 1991)—are products of an industrial system of mass production that was shaped by advertising. In other words, we cannot understand the social effects of advertising unless we discuss the interconnected development of the mass media, mass (industrial) production and the growth of the advertising industry.

For most of the nineteenth century, the sale of commodities was characterised by the movement of unbranded merchandise. Small factories or individual artisans created goods, which were purchased by middlemen and other merchants, who then sold them on to small retailers and marketplaces, before they were finally bought by the consumer (Windschuttle, 1985: 11). The problem with this early system of commodity exchange, commonly known as classical capitalism, is that it was exceedingly vulnerable to the vagaries of the market, with the forces of supply and demand creating an inherently unstable economic system, prone to boom/bust cycles. The heart of the problem related to market saturation and the efficiencies of industrial production (which was gathering global momentum since its emergence in seventeenth-century Britain). When too many manufacturers flooded a market with the same (or similar) consumer goods, prices were forced down, sometimes dramatically, as industries were forced into a dog-eat-dog period of price reduction (Windschuttle, 1985: 11). In some cases, this collapse in prices resulted in factory closures as primary producers and manufacturers struggled to stay financially viable. Such closures generated considerable social hardship, particularly during the severe depressions of the 1840s and 1890s, and often killed off smaller corporations.

This boom/bust cycle began to change with the advent of larger, more economically robust corporations and product branding, both of which began to emerge in the latter half of the nineteenth century. Larger corporations—particularly those that had implemented vertical and horizontal integration—had greater financial stability, and were therefore better able to survive a downturn in market prices. Yet it was product branding, more so than a company's size, that gave producers the ability to control the output and demand for their goods. By distinguishing their products from those created by a competitor, manufacturers could use product branding to influence the market so that the forces of supply and demand no longer dictated the price of consumer goods. By gaining a degree of control over the demand for their products, manufacturers could generate more profit, which in turn was often re-invested in the expansion of the company's assets and market share. This process saw the creation of what some economic historians have called 'monopoly capitalism', where the unfettered forces of marketplace competition are suppressed as fewer corporations, and their brands, come to dominate the national, and indeed the international, distribution of goods and services (see Windschuttle, 1985).

With branded consumer goods—including Australian household brands such as Foster's and Rosella—becoming commonplace in industrialised countries towards the end of the nineteenth century, **advertising** began to play an important role in both the distribution of goods and the operations of the media (see Sinclair, 2010a: 191). In particular, advertising played an important role in the development of financially and politically independent media sources, such as the mass circulation newspapers and magazines that began to emerge towards the end of the nineteenth century. Whereas columns of classified advertisements were common in most of the world's newspapers during the 1800s, much of a newspaper's total income came from sales (Windschuttle, 1985: 10–13). This meant that the early newspapers in the Australian colonies, such as the *Sydney Gazette* and the *Australian* (the latter of which should not be confused with the modern day newspaper of the same name), were fairly expensive when compared to the average worker's wage, and, therefore, many of them had comparatively small circulation figures. This was also broadly the case for newspapers in Britain and the United States during this period (Windschuttle, 1985).

This situation changed, however, with the implementation of two interrelated innovations in newspaper content: the creation of 'display' advertisements and an increase in the type of news which had already proven popular with working-class readers—scandal, tragedies and sport (Windschuttle, 1985: 13). Newspaper owners such as Lord Northcliffe in Britain and William Randolph Hearst in the United States were market leaders in relation to identifying the financial advantages of display advertising and tabloid journalism. In Australia, Keith Murdoch (father of the famous international media proprietor, Rupert Murdoch) also saw the lucrative benefits of such techniques (which he learnt from his mentor, Lord Northcliffe), and in 1920 brought such content innovations to Australia with great success (see Shawcross, 1993: 31–44). Moreover, the 1920s saw a further advertising innovation, with advances in printing technology making the widespread use of visual images possible (an illustrative technique that had been inspired by the official propaganda cartoons during the First World War, and that was further strengthened with the use of photographic images from the early 1930s—see Crawford, 2006). Collectively, these content changes allowed media proprietors to increase their market share by making their publications more affordable and attractive to working class readers.

Importantly, the increases in newspaper circulation figures that accompanied such content changes created truly mass media, which could deliver large audiences to prospective advertisers (such as the emerging corporate giants eager to sell their branded goods to as many buyers as possible). Thus the early decades of the twentieth century, both in Australia and abroad, saw the emergence of the interconnected relationship between expanding manufacturers and the mass media. Importantly, this relationship between big business and mass media saw the inception of the world's first advertising agencies, giving rise to what has been labelled modern society's 'manufacturing-**marketing**-media complex' (Caro, 1981: 5, cited in Sinclair, 2010a: 189).

Advertisers: regional, national or transnational corporations and businesses that seek to market their goods and services through national and/or regional media.

Marketing: is used by companies to create and communicate a branded message to a desired consumer group. Advertising should be thought of as a central technique within a broader marketing strategy.

The next major development in the history of advertising occurred with the arrival of commercial radio, which in Australia began with the launch of 2SB Sydney in November 1923. While radio broadcasting began in the early 1920s, it was not until the late 1930s that it started to challenge the visual display advertisements of the press as a mass medium for commercial messages (Crawford, 2006; Sinclair, 2010a: 192). It is also during the 1930s that 'market research', or the study of the social demographics of the audience (from age and gender to income and cultural tastes), became a key part of the business of advertising, as agencies sought to reach those consumer groups most likely to purchase their product. At the outset, radio advertisements took the form of program sponsorship, with a commercial message played before the airplay of the regularly scheduled content. Yet some advertising agencies even produced entire programs for transmission—typically in the form of quiz shows and plays (see Sinclair, 2010a: 192). This system of 'program sponsorship' was slowly replaced with 'spot advertising' (in the form of 'ad breaks') following the arrival of commercial television in September 1956.

Initially, television programming in Australia was heavily dominated by content imported from the United States and the United Kingdom, despite the requirements specified in section 114(1) of the now superseded *Broadcasting and Television Act 1942* (as amended 1956): 'licensees shall, as far as possible, use the services of Australians in the production and presentation of radio and television programs'. While the federal government was largely unsuccessful in its attempts to encourage the new television stations to carry Australian-produced programming (at least until the implementation of content quotas from the mid-1960s), it was nonetheless successful in regulating the nation's changing advertising industry, with the commercial stations regulated so that they could only carry Australian-made advertisements (Sinclair, 2010a: 192). This policy was enacted in order to create local production houses, and thus further the development of jobs and skills within the Australian television industry. Moreover, it is a policy that continues today, with the **Australian Communications and Media Authority (ACMA)**—the government agency now responsible for the regulation of the nation's broadcast media—requiring that 80 per cent of television commercials broadcast between 6am and midnight are produced in Australia (for further details, see ACMA, 2010).

From the 1950s onwards, Australian industries and markets became increasingly interconnected with those in other nations as US corporations, in particular, began to invest overseas to further their process of corporate conglomeration and market expansion (part of a process now called 'globalisation'). This process of transnational expansion was not restricted to the manufacturers of consumer goods, but was also undertaken by the U.S. advertising agencies of Madison Avenue. Indeed, following the arrival of commercial television, US advertising agencies began a rapid colonisation of the Australian advertising market (from 1959 onwards), taking over many local advertising agencies in a process of 'common accounts management' and 'global alignment' (a method of market expansion where a transnational advertising agency seeks to service the same clients in several different countries—Sinclair, 2006). So rapid was this US corporate takeover of the Australian advertising industry that by 1972 'at least three-quarters of the Australian advertising business had been brought under US ownership' (Sinclair, 2006: 113).

However, as the processes of globalisation gathered momentum in the early 1980s, new transnational corporations from Britain, France and Japan challenged the market dominance of the US agencies. In particular, the 1980s saw the emergence of 'global advertising groups', such as the British 'mega groups' Saatchi & Saatchi and Wire and Paper Products (WPP) (the former of which became the world's largest agency group in 1986, only to be surpassed in size by WPP in

Australian Communications and Media Authority (ACMA): is responsible for the regulation of the broadcast media, the internet and telecommunications. ACMA promotes 'industry self-regulation', while ensuring that media businesses comply with relevant licence conditions, codes and standards.

1990—Sinclair, 2006). As John Sinclair (2006) notes, the global advertising group acts as a holding company or parent corporation for a collection of subsidiary global advertising agencies. The strength of this business model lies in its ability to allow a mega group to rise above potential conflicts of interest—which arise when a single agency manages the marketing campaigns of two competing clients—by having different agencies within the parent corporation manage the accounts of competing advertisers.

As the commercial strength and market share of the global mega groups grew throughout the late 1980s and early 1990s, the Australian advertising industry became increasingly integrated into the 'globally aligned' system of advertising. This process of globalisation and market colonisation placed solely Australian-owned agencies at a commercial disadvantage, in that they could not access many of the global brands being marketed in Australia unless they were part of an international mega group. Such commercial pressures have resulted in a high level of foreign ownership of the Australian advertising industry as local firms have sought multiple global connections. Indeed, global corporations own (or partially own) approximately 80 per cent of the advertising agencies operating in the Australian market (Sinclair, 2006: 119).

Following the transnational rise of the global mega-agencies, two final historical developments have helped to shape the current structure and practices of the Australian advertising industry. The first occurred in 1997, when the system of self-accreditation used by the advertising agencies and commercial media was abolished. Prior to this period, the advertising agencies and the commercial media cooperated in the implementation of self-accreditation programs, which required advertising agencies to prove that they had the requisite technical and professional expertise, as well as the financial assets, to act as effective 'agents' between the commercial media and advertisers. While this system created a stable industry, it militated against new entrants and favoured the larger, established agencies (Sinclair, 2006). Moreover, many national advertisers (as represented by their industry body: the Australian Association of National Advertisers, or AANA) felt the relationship between the advertising agencies and the commercial media was too close, and open to inflated pricing practices (Sinclair, 2006: 217–18). A governmental inquiry into the system found that the practice of self-accreditation was indeed anti-competitive, and thereafter abolished the practice entirely (see Sinclair 2010a: 217–18). The AANA was subsequently given the task of creating a new system of self-regulation for the industry. The end result of this restructuring was the creation of Australia's current system of advertising self-regulation, and its three primary parts: (1) The AANA Advertiser Code of Ethics; (2) the Advertising Standards Board; and (3) the Advertising Claims Board.

Self-regulation: Adopted by many industries seeking to avoid direct government regulation, which they consider to be interference in the workings of the marketplace.

Advertising Standards Board: Responsible for investigating and ruling on complaints made by members of the community regarding advertisements that might be misleading or offensive.

Advertising Claims Board: Responsible for investigating and ruling on complaints made by advertisers about each other, so as to ensure competitive, fair and truthful conduct.

Advertising Regulation in Australia

Self-regulation is adopted by many industries seeking to avoid direct government regulation, which they consider to be interference in the workings of the marketplace. In Australia, the **Advertising Standards Bureau** is responsible for coordinating the system of self-regulation governing the practices of the domestic advertising industry, and receives its operational funding from a levy placed on the purchase of advertising space (this levy is set at 0.035 per cent of gross media expenditure). In essence the role of the Advertising Standards Bureau is to provide administrative support for its two boards, the **Advertising Standards Board (ASB)** and the **Advertising Claims Board (ACB)**. Rather than the overarching secretariat, it is the two boards (the ASB and the ACB) that seek to ensure that advertisements comply with the **AANA Advertiser Code of Ethics**, which in turn aims to prevent the circulation of advertisements that are offensive, false, misleading or socially irresponsible.

The two boards perform very different functions. The role of the Advertising Claims Board is to provide a forum where 'competitor complaints' regarding the truth or accuracy of a particular advertisement can be heard (by relevant lawyers), so that both parties can avoid costly legal battles. In contrast, the Advertising Standards Board—or rather its 20 independent board members, chosen to represent the broader community—considers complaints made by the general public. As such, many of the complaints considered by the ASB concern the appropriateness of advertising content, particularly in regards to sexualised images.

However, while an advertisement might provoke considerable outrage amongst certain sections of the community, the ASB often dismisses complaints regarding sexualised content, after closely considering an ad in relation to the AANA Advertiser Code of Ethics. For instance, the GASP Jeans billboard advertisement below was the most complained about advertisement in 2009, and resulted in around 250 letters of complaint to the ASB (many of which came from cities where the billboard could not have been seen—Jolly, 2009). In contrast to the complaints which argued that the billboard was offensive and exploitative, the ASB found that the 'advertisement was not demeaning or degrading to women and that the woman depicted in the advertisement appeared to be a strong, healthy looking female … and did not … engender a sense of what might constitute a "problematic" body image'. Subsequently, the complaint was dismissed (see Advertising Standards Bureau, 2009).

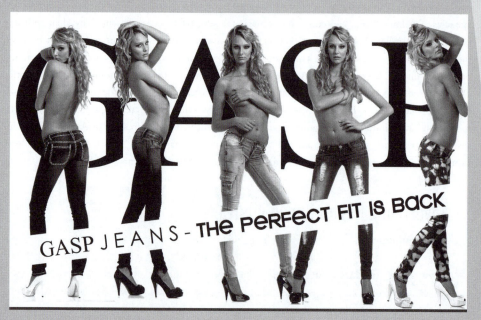

Figure 7.1 GASP Jeans billboard

Source: GASP Jeans 2009. This advertisement is used with the kind permission of the copyright holder.

After the creation of Australia's current system of advertising self-regulation, the final major historical development that has shaped the current industry is the advent of online advertising. While many advertisements on the internet's webpages are similar to the display ads found in newspapers and magazines, new forms of marketing have been made possible through the interactive nature of new media. In particular, 'keyword search ads', which appear when you use a search engine such as Google, are an effective way for advertisers to connect their products directly with a desired market, with marketing messages filtered to match the search terms provided by the user. Likewise, advertisements on **social networking** sites—such as MySpace and Facebook—can be matched with the lifestyle information provided by their users. In others words, online advertisements are increasingly being matched to our interests, tastes and desires, thereby blurring the distinction between commercial messages and sought-after or useful information.

Social networking: the building of online communities through the movement of non-virtual human relationships into the virtual world via the use of various technological devices.

As a medium for advertising, the web has had a significant impact on the profits of the 'old media' (that of print and broadcasting), which have long relied on 'selling' large audiences to advertisers in order to remain financially viable (Smythe, 1977). In particular, significant amounts of the classified advertising that once supported the expensive investigative journalism of the press have dried up, as consumers increasingly turn to the internet for online dating (e.g. RSVP or eHarmony), online auctions (e.g. eBay) and the purchase of new and used goods (e.g. Amazon or iTunes). Likewise, the faster download speed made possible by broadband technology has seen many young people turn to cyberspace for their desired media content, such as the latest episodes of their favourite television programs, leaving fewer people watching the channels of the commercial broadcasters—a trend that has only recently become apparent and yet will likely see the further restructuring of the media landscape in the coming decades.

However, while the rise of online advertising is forcing many media proprietors to rethink their business models, it is far too soon to say we are moving to a post-mass media era. As is made clear in Figure 7.2, advertisers and their agents continue to choose newspapers and free-to-air television as their preferred destination for their marketing, as these mass media continue to maintain large audiences. Indeed, the advertising industry in Australia continues to invest significant amounts in the old

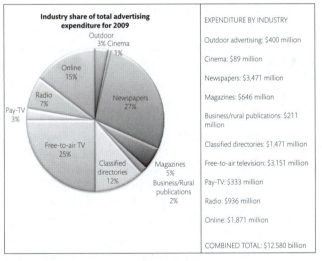

Figure 7.2 Advertising expenditure in Australia for 2009

Source: Commercial Economic Advisory Service of Australia.

media, ensuring that many of the core elements of the manufacturing-marketing-media complex will continue to remain significant features of modern societies. Exploring how and why this complex works is the subject of the following discussion.

Marketing techniques

While advertising agencies seemingly possess an endless repertoire of creative techniques for capturing our attention and conveying information, they must consider the various features of the social world when crafting a marketing strategy. In particular, marketing strategies must target consumers across four dimensions of the social and physical world, using market research data on the 'demographic', 'geographic', 'temporal' and 'cultural' factors that may affect the sale of certain consumer goods (see MacRury, 2009: 70–1). For instance, demographic information is used to understand the 'purchasing power' and 'wants' of a group of consumers, and refers to data regarding age, gender and socio-economic status. Geographical and temporal information is used to understand a group's daily routines and lifestyles, in order to target advertisements when and where they are most likely to be effective. Cultural information is used to understand the complex cultural identifications, values and practices of a consumer group, so that the creative department of an advertising agency can produce evocative and relevant marketing strategies.

In chasing their desired consumer groups, advertisers employ what has traditionally been known as 'above the line' and 'below the line' marketing. However, as media studies academic Iain MacRury (2009: 106) argues, the changes brought to the business of advertising by new media technologies necessitate that we add a third category to our typology of marketing: 'through the line' marketing. Above the line marketing is the most common form of advertising and is concerned with the use of traditional media outlets—television, the press (both newspapers and magazines), outdoor media (such as billboards), radio and cinema—for the display of spot advertisements. Thus, the pervasiveness of above the line marketing makes it the most obvious form of product/brand promotion, with advertisements clearly discernible from unbranded content. In contrast, 'through the line' marketing can be both overt and covert. It refers to: the sponsorship of television programs, the use of product placement in films and other video clips, the use of mobile phones for SMS advertisements and participatory marketing, and online marketing techniques (such as connecting advertisements to keyword search queries and/or the location of an ISP address).

Much like through the line marketing, below the line marketing utilises both overt and covert methods to engage consumers. Common marketing techniques here include direct mail; telemarketing; retail marketing (sale posters, in-store features or events); and point-of-purchase displays (which are placed near the checkout aisles of a supermarket). More recently, however, below the line marketing is seeing the proliferation of covert promotional strategies that often rely on 'buzz marketing' and 'word-of-mouth marketing'. These covert forms of marketing rely on publicity stunts or 'viral media' (such as the publication of a humorous or controversial video clip on YouTube) to generate word-of-mouth interest in an advertiser's message. Moreover, word-of-mouth marketing is often used in conjunction with 'influencer marketing', the latter of which seeks to identify the influential individuals of a particular social network in order to convince them to use or promote a branded good to their peers (a service for which they may or may not be paid). While below the line marketing can be both intelligent and effective, a number of its methods are intrusive (such as telemarketing) or manipulative (such as influencer marketing), and thus these techniques risk provoking a hostile or negative reaction from savvy consumers weary of 'brash and insistent commercialism' (see MacRury, 2009: 107).

Advertising and the meaning of 'stuff'

In order to understand how the advertising industry sells us consumer goods, it is necessary to explore the role and meaning of commodities within our society. Advertising does not, of course, take place in a historical vacuum, removed from the wider sociocultural systems that shape our understanding of the world. Indeed, while advertising is quite effective in getting us to see an object in a different light, the resources used by advertising agencies to ascribe meaning to things are drawn from the cultural values and discourses of a given society. Accordingly, if we are to appreciate how advertising can persuade us to buy things that we may or may not need, then we must examine the place of material goods in society, as our attraction to stuff existed long before the invention of either marketing or the mass media (as anthropologists are quick to point out). Such an investigation necessitates a chronological review of some the core ideas of those social scientists that have helped to explain the meaning of commodities and consumption in the modern age.

Perhaps the single most influential thinker to write on this topic was Karl Marx (1818–83). Born in Germany in the early nineteenth century, Marx wrote many influential publications on the early system of capitalism that had come to characterise the industrial societies in Europe and North America (as well as parts of Australia) (see Marx, 1959, 1973, 1990). For Marx, capitalism was an exploitative system of commodity production, which de-humanised workers by alienating them from the fruits of their labour. He argued that, whereas workers in the pre-capitalist/pre-industrial societies were intimately connected with commodities that were skilfully crafted by hand, in capitalist economies, workers are forced into factories and other methods of mass production, where a segmented 'division of labour' (epitomised in the repetitive tasks performed by individuals on a production line) often robs them of the skills of a craftsperson, and alters their relationship to the goods produced by their collective labour (Marx, 1990). Marx argued that this capitalist system of mass production ensured that the ruling classes (who own and run the factories) profit from the labour of their workers (who have no choice but to sell their labour). Marx (2002) considered this system to be both exploitative and inherently unstable, and argued that it would eventually be replaced by a more equal system of socio-economic relations known as 'communism'.

While Marx's writings on capitalism and politics were extensive (and had a violent revolutionary impact in several countries), it is his work on commodities that concerns us here. At the heart of his critique of mass production is an explanation of the meaning of material goods, which he defines according to their 'use-value' and their 'exchange-value' (see Marx, 1990). The use-value of a commodity is calculated by determining the total material and labour costs that have been used in its production. In contrast, the exchange-value of a commodity refers to the price someone is willing to pay for the good in the market-place. The difference between these values is what Marx labels 'surplus-value'—i.e. the profit made on a good by the cost-efficient system of mass production. As commodities in a capitalist society are defined by their 'exchange-value', Marx argues that they obtain almost 'magical' properties that mask the different manufacturing processes (as well as the human and environmental costs) that go into industrial methods of production. Drawing on anthropological research on the 'fetishes' of pre-modern societies (i.e. inanimate objects that are seen to have godly powers), Marx labelled the magical properties of modern consumer goods 'commodity fetishism'. Marx's terminology might be complex, but his point is relatively simple: consumers see only the socio-economic meaning of a 'thing' (be it an iPhone or a car), and do not see the minerals, nor the labour hours and working conditions, which have all gone into the commodity's creation.

This idea, that goods have meanings beyond their use, was picked up by the American sociologist Thorstein Veblen (1857–1929) in his research on 'social emulation'. In his influential book *The Theory of the Leisure Class* (originally published in 1899), Veblen examined the leisure and shopping practices of the newly wealthy class in New England (USA)—those who had recently become rich due to the rise of various manufacturing industries. Veblen (1994) noted how the 'newly rich' of New England emulated the consumption and leisure practices of upper-class life in Europe, seeking to demonstrate their social status by engaging in a display of the 'conspicuous consumption' of expensive and fashionable commodities. Importantly, Veblen's research highlights the modern heart of consumer culture, applicable to all classes in a capitalist society: namely, that individuals positioned lower in society's socio-economic hierarchy seek to emulate the lifestyles and fashions of those with the wealth and time to become the arbiters of 'style'. This is, of course, a social phenomenon often utilised by the manufacturing-marketing-media complex, which uses celebrities and flawless models as key ingredients in a standard advertising recipe used to sell us everything from pimple cream to perfume.

Writing around the same time as Veblen, the German sociologist Georg Simmel (1858–1918) also sought to understand the meanings of commodities and the processes of top-down social emulation. In particular, Simmel's work *The Metropolis and Mental Life* (first published in 1903) focused on the experiences of living in a large urban environment, where individuals become merely faces in a crowd. In such urban landscapes, Simmel (1997) believed that we use fashion (or the consumption of different clothes) to re-assert our individuality and sense of identity. Thus, in cities, the conspicuous display of wealth and fashionable consumption leads to an increased awareness of style, which will later spread to regional towns and country areas. Yet, where for Veblen social emulation was a trickle-down process from the upper to the lower classes, Simmel (1997) argued that the practice of fashionable consumption by modern consumers often involves both 'generalisation' (or imitation) and 'specialisation' (or differentiation) (Paterson, 2006: 22). In other words, Simmel saw that fashion operates according to a continual cycle of establishing a consumption pattern (or fashion norms), challenging it, and thereby driving new forms of style (see Paterson, 2006: 23). This dynamic and antagonistic process that we see within fashion—which allows personal values to be expressed through the modifications and re-interpretations of the dominant style—is found in the consumption of other commodities (from cars to cuisine). Indeed, it is a dialectical social phenomenon that manufacturers and advertisers from a range of industries have sought to understand and map, so as they might become the company to sell the latest fashionable commodities—thereby establishing their role as the 'merchants of cool' (see, for example, the Frontline weblink at the end of the chapter).

Simmel, Veblen and Marx do, then, offer complementary insights into our attraction to stuff. For Marx, such products are fetishes, where their use-value has been replaced by an abstract exchange-value (which in contemporary society can be defined more by the marketing of a brand, rather than by the quality or functionality of a consumer good). For Veblen and Simmel, consumer goods are used by the wealthy middle classes (or the new 'bourgeois') to distinguish themselves from the masses, while simultaneously demonstrating and legitimising their higher socio-economic status. While these ideas are still relevant for understanding how advertising uses our tastes and desires (including those for social status, power and prestige) to sell us products that represent particular lifestyles, they do not tell us how consumer goods communicate their particular meanings. For this we need to turn to the work of the French cultural critic and semiotician, Roland Barthes (1915–80).

In his influential book *Mythologies* (first published in 1957), Barthes examined the meanings of mass culture (or culture which is widely disseminated by the mass media), in order to expose the **myths** that shape our interpretations of the physical and social world. In particular, he analysed how

Myths: the common ways of thinking of a particular culture. Myths define our perception of certain events, objects or ideas. Thus myth has an ideological quality that shapes how we perceive and value its referents.

myths signify particular ideas and values, by drawing on our deeply held social and cultural ideas (Barthes, 1973). For example, when we encounter an object, be it a media text or pair of skinny black jeans, we 'decode' its meaning according to our cultural repertoire. Thus, we understand that a BMW is more than merely an average car—it is also a sign that connotes wealth, success and social status. Likewise, we understand that skinny black jeans are, at least for the moment, fashionable, and connote youthfulness, sophistication and style. This process of 'signification', where we read the signs that texture our daily experiences, refers to the communicative properties of all commodities (or 'texts'), which cannot be understood outside the 'sign systems' of our cultural context. Importantly, myths often seem both timeless and natural, and thereby militate against alternative understandings of a text (see Chapter 8 for a more detailed discussion on semiotics and the meaning of signs).

The significance of the work of Roland Barthes lies in its instructive lessons for understanding the semiotic properties of advertisements. For the vast majority of advertisements rely on connotative messages—ideological ways of seeing a particular thing—to convince you that this is a product that you must buy if you hope to consume (and thus be part of) a particular lifestyle (see MacRury, 2009). As such, Barthes provides us with a method for analysing and understanding the hundreds of advertisements we encounter in our daily lives. Moreover, he demonstrates how consumption can be a symbolic activity, where the messages of the commodity (which are often defined by marketing and advertising campaigns) are used to say something about the individual—'I buy this product because I am that type of person'.

Commodities and culture

Writing in the 1950s, Roland Barthes was analysing a very different form of consumer society to that studied by Veblen, Simmel and other social scientists of the late nineteenth and early twentieth century. Indeed, following the Second World War, a new period of 'mass consumption' came first to North America, Britain and Australia, before then spreading to Western Europe. This period of mass consumption, or consumerism (as it is more often known today), was made possible because of greater levels of mass production and corresponding increases in wages—thereby allowing formerly marginalised socio-economic groups to participate more fully in consumer capitalism. In this new age of relative economic prosperity, new consumer lifestyles were emerging, as identity and branding became more important in determining consumption patterns. In many nations, such as Australia, Britain and the United States, this economic prosperity, coupled with the proliferation of branded goods, led to the formation of 'sub-cultures'—such as the Teddy Boys of the 1950s, the famous mods and rockers of the 1960s, or, indeed, the emos or punks of contemporary society—the members of which defined themselves, if only partially, by their clothes, vehicles and haircuts, rather than by more fixed and traditional social bonds (such as those which stem from the world of work or the family) (see Hebdige, 1979).

For some scholars writing after the Second World War, the rise of consumerism and the aspirational classes merely magnifies the exploitative tensions first identified by Karl Marx. For instance, members of the Frankfurt School of scholars, such as Theodor Adorno and Max Horkheimer (1973 [1947]), and Herbert Marcuse (1968 [1964]), argue that consumer capitalism and mass culture rob the masses of their ability to collectively overcome the exploitative features of capitalism. Marcuse (1968), in particular, argues that the 'ideology of consumerism' instils 'false needs', so that individuals distract themselves from the drudgery of their daily existence by purchasing consumer goods (an idea that is echoed in the concept of affluenza). For Marcuse (1968), consumer society and mass culture leads to depoliticised conformity, where the consumer can be seen as merely the 'passive dupe' of the advertising industry.

The concept of consumer society as a type of cultural prison, or a gilded cage from which there is no escape, is also a core theme of the early work of Jean Baudrillard. Drawing on the ideas of both Marx and Barthes, Baudrillard (1998: 192–3) argues that commodity fetishism has been replaced entirely by the consumption of signs, where the symbolic exchange-value of commodities keeps people trapped in an exploitive relationship, in that we relate to each other through semiotic systems of communication distorted by the micro-politics of interaction (i.e. games played to determine social standing). Thus, for Baudrillard, consumption is a type of symbolic language, where one's vocabulary depends on their economic and cultural resources (see also Bourdieu, 1986). Moreover, the later, more postmodern work of Baudrillard argues that there has in fact been an 'implosion of the social', where we become merely empty carriers of signs, and have no inner depth below our manufactured symbolic identities.

However, while many social scientists have been intensely critical of the interconnected relationship between commodities, advertising and culture, for Daniel Miller (a British anthropologist specialising in understanding everyday activities like shopping and the meaning of 'stuff') consumerism should not be characterised as mindless exploitation (see Miller, 2010). Indeed, he argues that much of the literature on the meaning of consumption falls victim to the myth of the 'prelapsarian society' (where we romanticise about societies that existed prior to capitalism, assuming that their relationships between people and things were more natural). Rather than merely seeking to understand consumption as a symbolic project, Miller (2010: 4) contends that 'the best way to understand, convey and appreciate our humanity is through attention to our fundamental materiality'. He does, then, challenge the orthodox way of thinking on consumerism, arguing that our culture has a subtle ideological bias, a 'depth ontology', which suggests that the experiences of material culture (such as shopping and mass consumption) are 'shallow' and inauthentic social practices. For Miller (2010: 16–17), this 'depth ontology' is misleading, as it suggests that the clothes and other stuff we buy are merely commodities that hide our true 'inner selves' (which he argues is merely a metaphor that we use when thinking about our identity). Instead, we need to consider the meanings that we give to commodities, as such material goods become incorporated into our sense of identity. In other words, our 'true' self can be constructed and represented through clothing (an idea that has also emerged in the study of different subcultures—see Hebdige, 1979).

The importance of Miller's work lies in its reminder that we cannot rob people of their 'agency' (of their ability to think freely and act independently from the social influences in our society). We must consider their views on their activities, and not assume they are simply the victims of capitalism and the global advertising industry. For, while advertising saturates our everyday experiences, we are both 'suckers' for their commercial messages and 'knowing consumers' capable of rejecting their symbolic content (see Hall, 1980). Indeed, advertising is a type of cultural feedback loop, where certain social trends and desires are identified and articulated, and then sold back to us as we search for identity and meaning in our daily experiences. Within this system, we are neither passive dupes nor entirely free and knowledgeable consumers—rather we reside somewhere in between.

Conclusion: Advertising and consumption

Social groups do, then, seek to construct and maintain different identities, distinguishing themselves in part through acts of consumption (see Bourdieu, 1986). Moreover, we possess both 'social identities' (how we are seen by others) and 'self-identities' (how we see ourselves). As such, we purchase commodities that we feel reflect who we are, and that will communicate our values and tastes to others. As the most prominent features of consumer culture, advertising is a key part of this process of identity construction and definition, giving certain brands, logos and styles magical values beyond their utility.

Yet this does not necessarily mean that we become alienated from such commodities or that we are mindlessly exploited by capitalism, as Karl Marx would contend. Indeed, capitalism has both positive and negative features. On the one hand, the abundance of consumer goods in our society allows for new forms of identity expression and a greater level of material comfort. Yet our consumer culture comes at a price, and we should not ignore the conditions of commodity production (particularly as experienced by factory workers in the developing world, or the environmental costs of wasteful consumerism). As capitalism has both positive and negative features, so too does advertising. At its best, advertising provides truthful product information and promotes creative ways of seeing material objects. At its worst, it manipulates us into buying things we cannot afford, and influences how we view each other (where individuals who lack the money for a certain style might be seen as 'less than' the savvy fashionista or wealthy businessman). In short, as long as we look beyond the brands, logos and commercial messages of consumer society in our daily interactions with each other, then we resist becoming merely 'consumers' and remain citizens, brothers, sisters, mothers, teachers, nurses, neighbours, and so on.

Summary

- Advertising promotes lifestyles and ideal versions of the 'self' (or who we would like to be).
- Advertising has played an important role in the development of modern capitalism by manipulating the demand for consumer goods.
- Australia's advertising industry is governed by a system of self-regulation, which uses the AANA Code of Ethics to enforce content standards regarding truth, accuracy and decency.
- The power of advertisements lie in their ability to build an ideological relationship between a consumer good and the individual, so that shopping becomes, in part, a symbolic project of identity construction and wish fulfilment.
- Advertising draws on our innate desires, such as those for social status and sex, to capture our attention and persuade us to buy.
- While we can be manipulated and deceived by advertisements, at their best they provide useful and truthful product information in an imaginative manner.

Further reading

Baudrillard, J 1998, *The Consumer Society: Myths and Structures,* Sage, London.

Crawford, R 2006, 'Truth in Advertising: The Impossible Dream?', *Media International Australia: Incorporating Culture & Policy*, no. 119, 124–37.

Featherstone, M 1991, *Consumer Culture and Postmodernism,* Sage, London.

Hamilton, C & Denniss, R 2005, *Affluenza: When Too Much Is Never Enough,* Allen & Unwin, Sydney.

Hebdige, D 1979, *Subculture: The Meaning of Style,* Routledge, London.

MacRury, I 2009, *Advertising*, Routledge, London.

Miller, D 2010, *Stuff*, Polity Press, Cambridge.

Paterson, M 2006, *Consumption and Everyday Life*, Routledge, London.

Weblinks

The Australian Advertising Bureau: www.adstandards.com.au

The Australian Association of National Advertisers: www.aana.com.au/codes.html

The Australian Communication and Media Authority: www.acma.gov.au/WEB/HOMEPAGE/
PC=HOME

Frontline investigative report: 'The Merchants of Cool' (video): www.pbs.org/wgbh/pages/frontline/
shows/cool

The Story of Stuff (video): www.storyofstuff.org

For revision questions, please visit www.oup.com.au/orc/chalkley.

chapter

8

Semiotics: Making Meaning from Signs

Mitchell Hobbs

Master X reads the signs

Master X listened for the raw, distorted sounds that would signify that the music had begun. He was standing in line with a few thousand fellow festival-goers, waiting—with considerable patience—for his turn to be ID-checked, searched for drugs and waved through to the chaotic revelry that inevitably accompanied 'Splendour in the Mud'—Australia's greatest music festival. Not that it showed any sign of raining today, Master X thought. The clouds were soft and the half-hidden sun was warm: it was a good day for a little rock 'n' roll. Turning his attention back to his fellow music lovers, his eyes searched the faces behind for any sign of his friends. No luck. Yet he was not surprised. Glancing at his watch, he realised they must have made it here ahead of him. By now, they should be within the perimeter fence, and heading for the rendezvous location: in front of the sound stage, under the striped ceiling of the main tent. While shuffling forward a few more steps, he removed his festival map from his tight back pocket. This was not his first festival experience, so he instantly recognised the iconography that represented the different stages, the banks of toilets and the bars. There, he thought. That white-striped, umbrella-looking icon represents the main tent. If I can get inside within the next half-hour, I'll meet the others before the first act begins. 'You can move forward', said a polite female voice behind him. Taking three steps closer to the gate, Master X mumbled his apologies over his shoulder for holding up the queue. Suddenly he was aware of being alone in a crowd. Yet the crowd was friendly. The group of girls behind him were laughing and talking excitedly about the acts they wished to see. And they were clearly his type of people. That is, they too wore the right attire, the black Ray-Ban sunglasses, the music T-shirts and the skinny black jeans. All of which were signs that these were girls he should talk to—when he found a friend for support. 'That's a great shirt', said the same girl. 'My friend has that shirt, and they're an awesome band.' 'Err, thanks', Master X responded, mind racing for a witty remark that would be sure to convey a cool image of a fun-loving, free-spirited, intelligent muso. 'But do you think that it's kind of funny that we're all wearing the same uniform?'

What you will learn from this chapter

This chapter introduces you to 'semiotics', a research method useful for examining media representations and other forms of verbal and visual communication. In particular, this chapter covers:

- The history of semiotics
- The components of the 'sign' and their importance to communication
- The role of ideology and myth in shaping the meaning of everyday objects
- The methodological questions raised by different interpretations of a text
- How to apply semiotics in the study of media texts and the signs of everyday life.

Introduction: The 'study of signs'

Whereas the previous chapter explored the social roots, functions and consequences of advertising, this chapter provides students with a research tool capable of analysing media representations and their meanings. Yet semiotics—or 'semiology', as it is sometimes called—is more than merely a method of analytical enquiry. It is a research philosophy, dense with a specialist terminology, used for explaining and analysing the communication of meaning (Chandler, 2007). As such, this chapter offers a taxonomy of the semiotic method through exploring the ideas of three influential semioticians, developing a glossary of key analytical terms useful for both understanding the 'codes' of the media and those of the social world. For, whether we are at the pub, on the sports field or in the street, we cannot escape being saturated by the meanings of **signs**.

Signs: words, sounds, images or objects that serve as vehicles for the communication of meaning. As such, they represent concepts, objects, people and things.

As communication is made possible due to sociocultural phenomena in the form of sounds, gestures and images—all of which we call 'signs'—semiotics should primarily be thought of as the study of the 'nature of *representation*' (Gottdiener, 1995: 4). In other words, semiotics concerns the study of sign systems, such as the verbal and textual manifestation of languages. Yet semiotic analysis can go beyond the traditional focus of linguistics to analyse a wide array of media forms that communicate particular ideas, concepts, messages and ideologies. For signs are not only written or spoken words (in the form of symbols or sounds), but can be images, photographs or other '**texts**'— such as clothing, billboards, foods or cultural artefacts.

Texts: documents, objects or things that comprise one or more signs. We 'read' texts, such as newspapers and clothing, for their meaning.

Moreover, semiotics is not solely concerned with the apparent 'surface meaning' of a sign. As this chapter will make clear, signs can have multiple meanings and often communicate ideological messages that influence how we feel about an object or event (as the previous chapter's discussion on advertising made clear). Accordingly, semiotics is interested in the deeper (or latent) meanings that are potentially present within a media text, and seeks to describe the manner in which sign systems communicate cultural **codes** that conceptually structure how we understand the physical and social world (Gunter, 2000: 83). This is why an appreciation of semiotics is important, as it is through the study of signs that we become aware of ideological messages that may not have otherwise been apparent. Indeed, we see that signs common to the media often naturalise certain ideas or values, in that they construct a commonsensical view of 'how the world is'. Such a way of seeing influences how we relate to the natural world and to each other, and can serve to mask or 'justify' social inequality. As Daniel Chandler (2007: 11) argues, the research implication of semiotics is clear: 'to decline the study of signs is to leave to others the control of the world of meanings which we inhabit'!

A short history of semiotics

The term 'semiotic' is derived from the ancient Greek word '*Sēmeíon*' (Saussure, 1983: 15), which was used to describe the medical practices of Greek physicians who studied the symptoms, or rather the 'signs', of disease (Gottdiener, 1995: 4). Thus the 'study of signs', before it was later championed as a 'science of signs', has been an element within the work of many thinkers throughout history, from ancient Greek philosophers, such as Plato and Aristotle, to the political and social theorists of the Enlightenment, such as Thomas Hobbes and John Locke (see Eco, 1976: 166). Yet it is only with the arrival of the twentieth century that the study of signs was transformed from a reoccurring theme of Western philosophy to something approaching an analytic method of textual analysis, with modern semiotics emerging concurrently, and coincidentally, on two continents.

In Europe, teaching a course in general linguistics at the University of Geneva, the Swiss linguist Ferdinand de Saussure (1857–1913) called for the creation of a new science: **'semiology'**. Saussure contended that semiology, through the study of signs and the 'laws that govern them', would shed new light on the 'rites and customs' of human communities, thus helping to explain the social world and the significance of its cultural practices (Saussure, 1983: 15–17). Saussure viewed language as a social institution—and, therefore, a social construct—defined by the conventions and culture of its users. At the time, his approach to signs was revolutionary in that he moved away from the 'diachronic' (or historical) study of the evolution of a particular language, to a 'synchronic' perspective that sought to understand and explain the communicative properties common to *all* languages.

Independently of Saussure's work, in the United States the philosopher and logician Charles S. Peirce (1839–1914) developed 'semeiotics' (or what would later be called **'semiotics'**). Unlike Saussure, Peirce (pronounced 'Purse') was concerned less with language as a mode of communication, and more with how people think (Gottdiener, 1995: 9–10). He argued that semiotics could be used to explain the role of language in supporting the 'truth claims' made by the findings of the natural sciences. In other words, Peirce was concerned with how well the signs of a language system can represent actual phenomena and forces in the natural world (the reality beyond our cultural subjectivity). For Peirce, semiotics was a necessary research method for understanding the symbolic conditions underpinning the creation of both meaning and truth, as constructed and communicated by the signs of a particular language. Despite his different research focus to Saussure, Peirce's model for the study of signs has much in common with the approach of the Swiss linguist. Indeed, most versions of modern semiotics incorporate the ideas of both Peirce *and* Saussure within their analytical framework. In both cases their work was published posthumously by students and other followers, and has led to the proliferation of scholars concerned with the roles and the processes of '**semiosis**' (the act of making meaning from signs).

Codes: frameworks of meaning that define how we interpret a sign. For example, a language is a code that defines the meanings of its verbal and symbolic units for those fluent in its use.

'Semiology' or **'semiotics'?** 'Semiology' is the label most often used by European scholars, whereas academics from English-speaking countries tend to use the term 'semiotics'. Both terms refer to the study of signs.

Semiosis: the interpretative process that occurs as we decode the meaning of a sign. It is often used interchangeably with its synonym 'signification' (which originates from the Saussurean tradition of semiology).

As this chapter is concerned with introducing a research method, more so than exploring the entire historical development of semiotics, what follows is by no means an exhaustive account of all the different concepts used since its modern inception in the early twentieth century. Instead, through an exploration of the key ideas of Ferdinand de Saussure, Charles S. Peirce and the French cultural critic Roland Barthes, we lay the foundations for a common and practical method of textual analysis capable of studying both media representations and the signs of the social world.

The components of 'the sign'
The semiology of Ferdinand de Saussure

As a linguist, Saussure (1983) considered language to be the quintessential structure of social life. The importance of his work lies in his contention that language systems, and indeed communication in general, was only made possible through its structural relationships, with meaning created through the sequencing of culturally specific signs (Saussure, 1983). In other words, meaning is made from our choice and use of certain words, as opposed to others. Saussure asserted that, as there are no labels or words inherent within the human mind at birth, the system of language in to which we are born provides and defines the conceptual framework through which we perceive reality (Bignell, 1997: 6). The implication being, 'we cannot think or speak about something for which there are no words in our language' (Bignell, 1997: 6).

Signifier: the physical elements of the sign, such as a spoken word or the features of an image. It is, then, something that can be seen, heard or felt, and communicates meaning.

Saussure's arguments highlighted the importance of language systems in limiting and shaping an individual's understanding of the world. He was not, of course, arguing that a material or physical world, one outside of language, does not exist. Rather, his point was that the signs used in communication (the sounds or symbols used to represent an object or concept) are specific to that particular culture. Their meanings are not intrinsic, but arbitrary, and are established over time (by convention) within a particular community (see Saussure, 1983: 65–70). At the core of his argument, Saussure contended that all signs communicate meaning in a similar manner and can be broken down into two primary conceptual categories of the **signifier** and the **signified** (see Figure 8.1).

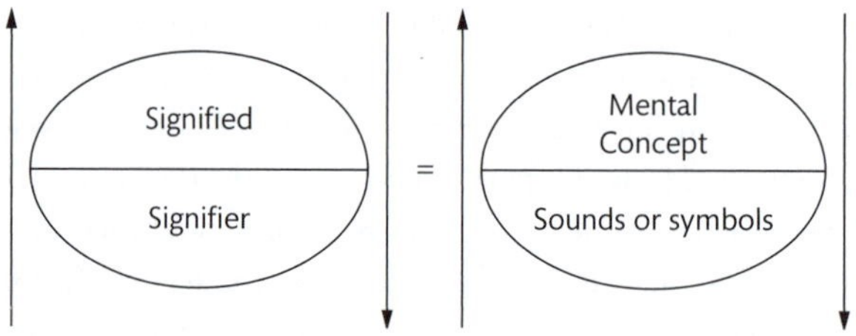

Signified: the mental concept that results from our encounter with the signifier.

Figure 8.1 The workings of the sign

Source: adapted from Saussure (1983: 67)

Referent: the object, concept or event represented by the sign (such as an actual living tree or the concept of God). Most, but not all, referents exist independently from our language or belief systems.

The signifier refers to the actual sign. For example, the signifier for the sign 'cat' are the sounds that the human mind decodes as 'c'-'a'-'t' or the symbols read as producing the sound 'cat'. Whereas the signified is the concept stimulated by the sign (in this case, the mental image of a small mammal commonly owned as a domestic pet). These categories, the two layers that together comprise a sign, denote a **referent** (in this case an actual living creature), and perform the communicative act of 'signification' (or 'semiosis'). For Saussure, both sound and thought (or the signifier and the signified) were 'intimately linked', with 'each triggering the other' upon being heard and decoded by the mind (Saussure cited in Chandler, 2007: 17). This relationship is illustrated in Figure 8.1, with the directional arrows denoting the rapid process of interpretation that occurs when our senses (whether vision, hearing or touch) are stimulated by a sign.

Moving from the micro-level of the composition of the sign to the more macro realm of language systems, Saussure found that, while languages may differ from one sociocultural context to another, the units of meaning within such languages—the signs—operate according to similar rules necessary to the facilitation of communication. For instance, Saussure (1983) argued that the linguistic sign must reside within a language system (what he labelled '*langue*'), which determines the rules for its use as a 'speech act' (or what he called '*parole*'). Furthermore, he argued that the meaning of a linguistic sign is defined by a series of surface-level relationships, with signs gaining meaning through their conceptual, or 'paradigmatic', differentiation: thus, 'cat' is defined by what it is not, such as a 'dog'.

This paradigmatic differentiation—or the selection and use of certain signs as opposed to others that would also fit the syntax of a sentence—can be thought of as two intersecting axes (see Figure 8.2). The vertical Y-axis represents our choice of signifiers, the words and their meanings that are the focus of a sentence. The horizontal X-axis represents the 'syntagmatic order of the act of communication', or the sentence's sequential articulation of meaning from the first word to the last (moving from left to right). Hence, the communicated meaning or message of a set of spoken or written words is defined by both the selection of certain signs, as opposed to others that would fit the sentence structure (such as 'cat' rather than 'dog'), and the linear procession of other signs, the meanings of which are dependent on the meanings of those signs which both proceed and follow them (thus, the mat cannot sit on the cat). In altering the 'paradigmatic' aspects of a sentence—analogous to the spinning columns of a poker machine—a different sequence of words is created, which changes the meaning of the sentence. For instance, in altering the sentence 'the cat sat on the mat', the word 'sat' can be paradigmatically replaced with a number of other signs that would significantly modify its meaning (as is illustrated in Figure 8.2).

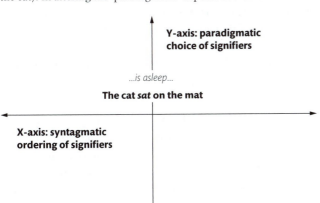

Figure 8.2 Syntagmatic and paradigmatic structure of a sentence

Source: adapted from the theories of Saussure (1983: 121)

Although this might seem like an unnecessarily complicated approach to understanding language and communication, it helps to highlight the interpretative and evaluative processes we engage in when we speak or write, whereby we choose different linguistic signs to represent the world around us. Moreover, this approach to the study of language and communication helps to highlight that the words we choose to describe an event often come loaded with a series of values designed to tell our audience how they *should feel* about the subject of the sentence. Consider the following example from O'Shaughnessy and Stadler (2006: 63) regarding a couple engaged in an intimate act:

- They are making love.
- They have gone to bed together.
- They are having sexual intercourse.
- They are fucking.
- They are fornicating.

All of these simple sentences can be used to describe the one event, and yet each sentence tells us something different about what is taking place due to the paradigmatic choice of certain signifiers. Whereas the tone of the first sentence is positive and suggests that the subject is something we should feel good about, the tone of the last sentence is aggressive and carriers a clear moral judgment within its structure. What this example highlights is that language constructs a version of reality (that we can either embrace or reject), based on the selection and sequencing of signifiers that are often heavy with ideological values.

From this brief exploration of Saussure's theories, it is relatively easy to see why he is considered the father of 'linguistic structuralism', with his concepts demonstrating the manner in which 'language divides up the world of thought, creating the concepts which shape our actual experiences' (Bignell, 1997: 12). Indeed, his work had repercussions far beyond the discipline of linguistics, influencing the development of Claude Lévi-Strauss's (1972) 'structural anthropology', Jacques Lacan's adaptation of psychoanalysis, and Roland Barthes's 'sociology of culture' (see Boyne, 2000: 176).

Yet our understanding of signs and languages has continued to develop since the publication of Saussure's ideas. Some scholars feel that Saussure's work places too much emphasis on the study of the structures of language, arguing that he neglects the contextual and historical dimensions to communication (Derrida, 1976). Moreover, Saussure's belief that the sign has only an 'arbitrary relationship' with a referent has generated some criticism, for it implies that language constructs reality (rather than reflecting it) according to the dominant social understandings and conventions of a culture. As such, many academics today feel the semiology of Saussure needs to be complemented by the ideas of other semioticians, who consider more completely both the context of communication and the different forms of a sign. Indeed, many of the more recent books on the practice of semiotics draw upon the ideas of Charles S. Peirce to provide additional concepts capable of analysing both linguistic and non-linguistic signs, be they photographs, images or symbols (Bignell, 1997: 14–16).

The semiotics of Charles S. Peirce

Developing his ideas independently of Saussure, Charles S. Peirce's approach to understanding the communicative properties of the sign shares several close similarities with the theories of his Swiss counterpart. Yet, where for Saussure signs are dyadic units composed of both signifier and signified (or word and concept), Peirce's (1960: 135) model of the sign is 'triadic' in that it consists of three parts: the 'representamen', an 'interpretant' and an 'object'. In the Peircean model of semiotics, the 'object' refers to a material form, and is conceptually similar to Saussure's 'referent'. The 'representamen', on the other hand, refers to the form that a sign takes, and is synonymous with the term 'signifier'.

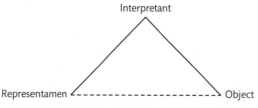

Figure 8.3 Peirce's model of the sign

Source: Daniel Chandler (2007:30)

Likewise the 'interpretant' has a similar meaning to the term 'signified'. This triadic relationship is represented in Figure 8.3—the broken line connecting the object and the representamen indicates that 'there is not necessarily any observable or direct relationship between sign vehicle and the referent' (Chandler, 2007: 30).

The first major difference between the Peircean and Saussurean semiotic models is the former's emphasis on the 'object' (or referent) in the composition of the sign—the referent was largely outside Saussure's (1983) focus on language as a structured system that is only arbitrarily connected to the world it represents. There is also an important distinction between Peirce's 'interpretant' and Saussure's 'signified'. Peirce, being concerned with how people think, believed that the interpretant becomes manifest as a 'psychological event', taking the form of an equivalent or a more developed sign within the mind (Gottdiener, 1995: 11). He argued that this new mental sign is the interpretant of the first sign and facilitates the meaning of the communicative act through a process of interpretative contrast. In other words, Peirce believed that our encounter with a sign immediately stimulates the mental creation of other, conceptually related, signs that help to define the meaning of the first.

Although Peirce's (1960: 135) idea regarding signs referring to other signs does not seem a particular revolutionary development within our understanding of semiotics, his idea contains a troubling implication embedded within its logic. As all signs, including those conceptual signs within our minds, are constructed from the interactions of signs referring to other signs, then the act of 'semiosis' can, at least in theory, regress *ad infinitum* (or continue forever). While Peirce believed that the reality of the 'absolute object' is inescapable in a person's daily experience—or that there is a real world of 'objects' generating the systems of signs, which prevents endless conceptual interpretations—some postmodern thinkers have seemingly disagreed. For example, the controversial postmodern philosopher Jean Baudrillard (1929–2007) has used this idea of '*regressum ad infinitum*' to argue that 'true meaning' (or reality) is infinitely deferred from our powers of perception. Baudrillard (1983) argues that we are all trapped in a 'hyperreal' world dominated by media representations and advertising slogans, and where signs are no longer connected to true referents (or Peircean 'objects'). Instead, we are said to live in a society dominated by the circulation of 'empty signifiers' (such as advertisements or biased media representations), where signs are defined in relation to other signs rather than by a truthful connection to a real world. According to Baudrillard, our modern media-saturated culture situates us in a hall of mirrors, where we are incapable of seeing the deeper truths that reside behind media representations and that influence how we live our lives (see Chapter 9 for a more detailed discussion of Baudrillard's critique of postmodern culture).

Yet, while Baudrillard is right to highlight the problematic relationship signs have with an objective reality, we need not push our philosophical logic to his hyperbolic conclusion that we can no longer see the forces which shape our experiences and that make up the world around us (which, if taken literally, suggests a theory similar to that of philosophical idealism). It is important to remember that signs are shaped by the common understandings of a particular community. As such, signs are units of a broader cultural code, the meanings of which are anchored by 'semantic fields' (or common assumptions regarding the use and meaning of certain signs as opposed to other signs), and are thus the product of the linguistic and communicative conventions of a group of language users (Eco, in Gottdiener, 1995: 24). If the meanings of linguistic and visual signs were not both defined and *contained* by cultural codes of language users, than the act of communication would be impossible. In other words, the cultural codes of Baudrillard's hyperreal world can be studied if we wish to assess the truthfulness of different media representations (this is an idea that will be explored in greater detail later in this chapter).

While Peirce's point regarding the psychological manifestation of signs is useful in that it highlights the interpretative processes of semiosis, his triadic model of the sign is used less by contemporary media and cultural researchers than that conceived by Saussure. As such, this chapter follows the convention of accepting Peirce's points regarding the interpretative nature of semiosis and the importance of studying the object (or the referent) when analysing signs, while retaining the conceptual terminology of the Swiss linguist.

Peirce's contribution to modern semiotics lies less in his model of the sign, and more in his typology of signs. His work here extends the semiotic critique beyond the linguistic sign to the world of natural signs, symbols and non-human languages. Daniel Chandler (2007: 36–7) offers a useful definition of the three most important (and widely used) categories of this typology:

1   *Symbol/symbolic*: a mode in which the signifier does not resemble the signified but which is fundamentally arbitrary or purely conventional—so that this relationship must be agreed upon and learned: e.g. language in general (plus specific languages, alphabetical letters, punctuation marks, words, phrases and sentences), numbers, morse code [sic], traffic lights, national flags.

2   *Icon/iconic*: a mode in which the signifier is perceived as resembling or imitating the signified (recognisably looking, sounding, feeling, tasting or smelling like it)—being similar in possessing some of its qualities: e.g. a portrait, a cartoon, a scale model, onomatopoeia, metaphors, realistic sounds in 'programme music', sound effects in radio drama, a dubbed film soundtrack, imitative gestures.

3   *Index/indexical*: a mode in which the signifier is *not arbitrary* but is *directly connected* in some way (physically or causally) to the signified (regardless of intention)—this link can be observed or inferred: e.g. 'natural signs' (smoke, thunder, footprints, echoes, non-synthetic odours and flavours), medical symptoms (pain, a rash, pulse-rate), measuring instruments (weathercock, thermometer, clock, spirit-level), 'signals' (a knock on a door, a phone ringing), pointers (a pointing 'index' finger, a directional signpost), recordings (a photograph, a film, video or television shot, audio-recorded voice), personal 'trademarks' (handwriting, catchphrases).

From these examples, we can appreciate the important contribution made by Peircean semiotic theories. For with a sign such as a photograph the signifier has a much closer relationship with the referent, and is not the 'arbitrary' product of a particular socio-linguistic context (Bignell, 1997: 14–15). Indeed, we can see that a photograph is an 'indexical sign', which merges the signifier, the signified and the referent together. It is because of this implosion of the three common elements of signification that Bignell (1997: 15) believes 'that the photographic media seem to be more realistic than the linguistic media'. Accordingly, any analysis that deals with both visual and linguistic signs should have these Peircean theories incorporated into the methodology.

Beyond the surface: Denotation, connotation and myth

Perhaps even more important than the contribution to semiotics made by Peirce is that made by French cultural sociologist Roland Barthes. Helping to pioneer the sociology of popular culture, Barthes produced two of the most important books of twentieth century structural semiotics, *Mythologies* (1973) (first published in 1957 and containing essays on different aspects of French culture, from the 'World of Wrestling' to the 'Striptease') and *Elements of Semiology* (1964) (a detailed treatise on Saussure's structural linguistics). In these texts Barthes extended Saussurean semiology, taking it from the basic structures of language to the 'metalanguage' level of objects situated within ideological codes. Barthes (1973) labelled these codes 'myths', arguing that such ideologies are an integral part of the communication of different meanings. As such, Barthes (1973: 117) believed that 'myth is a type of speech', one that operates on a second, higher order of signification (see Figure 8.4).

Looking at Saussure's model of the sign, Barthes argued that his predecessor's structural linguistic approach was useful for revealing only the 'denotative' function of the sign. That is, Saussure looked merely at the most obvious, first level meaning of the sign. We call this '**denotation**'—what the sign 'denotes' or points to. Yet Barthes believed that objects, and their textual/linguistic representation,

Denotation: the first-order meaning of a sign. It is the blatant, standard, primary meaning of the sign—its primary signification. For example, a photograph of a shoe denotes a clear referent (footwear).

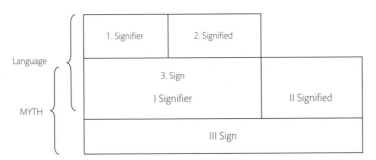

Figure 8.4 Roland Barthes's model of second-order signification

Source: Barthes (1973: 115)

communicate information beyond the level of denotation, arguing that they also 'connote' meanings peculiar to one's social milieu. For example, a 'cat' may only be a pet in contemporary Western societies, but in the historical context of ancient Egypt such creatures (as well as the signs used to denote them) communicated a very different set of sociocultural values (cats were sacred to the Egyptians—ownership of them was an indication of one's social standing and religiosity).

Operating at the second order of a sign, connotation signifies a second-order meaning of the original sign, built on top of its first order meaning (as represented in Figure 8.4). For Barthes, sign systems articulate with cultural values (or ideologies) as connotative codes, producing 'richer structures of meaning than was assumed by de Saussure' (Gottdiener, 1995: 15). Like Peirce's theories regarding the infinite regress of meaning, Barthes showed that, through connotation, certain signs are capable of building upon other signs (and so on) ultimately to connote cultural and political values. For such ideologically loaded signs, this higher order of signification feeds upon itself, with the connotation sometimes becoming its own referent, communicating at the level of myth. Thus, rather than seeing the truth behind a sign, we see only the myth connoted by the image. Such mythic signs, rich in connotative meaning, can condense an entire ideology into a single word or image. For example, an image of a Rolls-Royce will denote a car, yet at the connotative level it will draw upon the myths of an interpreter's social context to communicate ideologies of wealth, prestige, social status and power (Bignell, 1997: 16). Rather than seeing merely a car (or the industrial conditions involved in its manufacture), we read a social symbol for a person's social status and wealth.

Barthes believed that myths are an integral part of the ideologies that make certain aspects of society appear 'natural' or 'normal', effectively erasing the historic processes leading to the development of certain social structures and beliefs, and thereby validating the existence of the socio-political status quo. In his famous essay 'Myth Today', which concludes his seminal work *Mythologies*, Barthes (1973: 55) argues:

> What the world supplies to myth is an historical reality, defined, even if this goes back quite a while, by the way in which men [sic] have produced or used it; and what myth gives in return is a *natural* image of this reality ... [M]yth is constituted by the loss of the historical quality of things: in it, things lose the memory that they once were made ... The function of myth is to empty reality: it is, literally, a ceaseless flowing out, a haemorrhage, or perhaps an evaporation, in short a perceptible absence. It is now possible to complete the semiological definition of myth in a bourgeois society: *myth is depoliticized speech*. [Original emphasis]

Having opened the semiotic method to the study of ideologies as cultural forms, Barthes essentially reoriented semiotics to its distant roots in theories of social order. He argued that myths are powerful forces in social organisation in that they build (at the second order of signification) the ideological ways of seeing that permeate social practices and cultural beliefs (as can be seen quite clearly in advertisements—see Chapter 7 for a more detailed discussion on this point).

Barthes did, then, see the study of signs as a tool for the 'demystification' of reality, whereby commonsensical ideologies could be exposed to the light of critical reasoning. For example, Barthes (1973: 121–7) showed how the linguistic signs used to discuss clothing appropriate different cultural values in order to connote messages about one's status in a particular society (see Barthes, 1983).

Yet perhaps his most famous example of his semiotic method in action was his analysis of the French magazine *Paris Match* (Barthes, 1973: 121–7). Here Barthes (1973) demonstrated how a magazine cover depicting the image of an African soldier saluting an unseen French national flag, could connote complex myths of the 'naturalness' of French imperialist rule in Algeria—published during a time when many of France's colonies were struggling for political independence (see Figure 8.5).

Such a 'social semiotic' approach to understanding the uses and communicative properties of words and objects clearly influenced the work of many social and cultural theorists (including the less radical work of the 'early Baudrillard', particularly his writings on the consumer society). Moreover, it helped to pave the way for the 'epistemological correction' away from the Saussurean 'structural' semiology focused on units of language to the more flexible version of social semiotics commonly used today.

Figure 8.5 The June/July 1955 cover of *Paris Match*, which Barthes argued connoted the 'naturalness' of French colonialism

According to Barthes (1973), the dominant denotative meaning of this text is simply that of an African soldier, whereas the connotative meaning is that of the 'rightness' of French imperialism in Algeria. Unlike most signs, this image of the African/French soldier has two referents: the African soldier and the French Empire.

Reality and the sign: Content vs. perspective

Whereas in the late 1950s and early 1960s Barthes's theories had a significant impact on the development of semiotics and its underlying philosophies, by the early 1970s 'post-structural' arguments had emerged that seemingly challenged the validity of some of his earlier ideas. In particular, Jacques Derrida's (1976) critique of the work of Saussure was seen as particularly damaging for the structuralist semiotics on which Barthes built his ideas. Drawing upon Peirce's notion of infinite regress, Derrida (1976) argued that the Saussurean model of semiology tacitly assumed the existence of a 'transcendental signified' that could circumscribe the signifier. Or, in other words, that outside the system of language we use to categorise and label the world, there exists an unproblematic referent—a real thing or object—possessing both a stable and absolute meaning (Chandler, 2007: 263). For Derrida, the problem with structuralist semiology, such as that practiced by both Saussure and the early Barthes, is that it assumes that meaning is inherent within the sign, waiting to be exposed by the structural categories of the researcher. This ignores that *we think with signs and assign meaning to referents*, understanding texts through the subjective values and beliefs embedded in our particular language. As such, Derrida argued that signs, as units of meaning within a language, are defined by the ontological values of a particular community of language users and cannot be studied, or understood, in isolation from their broader cultural context. The implication of his thinking is that no object, event or thing has meaning beyond that given to it by language users (some of these ideas will be explored in more depth in the discussion of postmodernism in Chapter 9).

Derrida's post-structural theory forced researchers to reflect on their analytical categories and generalisations. In particular, semiotics from the late 1960s onwards came to consider more seriously the 'problem of perspective' in the creation of meaning, with signs increasingly seen as possessing 'polysemic' properties. **Polysemy** (where a sign can convey several different meanings to different readers) is a concept that acknowledges that both 'circumstance and context' play integral roles in a communicative act and, as such, it implies that the meaning of a text is always 'volatile' and dependent on the perspective of the viewer (Gottdiener, 1995: 20). In other words, polysemy is created by the 'epistemological crisis' resulting from one text producing multiple messages and meanings for different readers. It explains why issues such as media bias are often said to reside 'in the eye of the beholder', as people read a text through the prism of their own values and beliefs. It also highlights the significance of other texts in **intratextually** and intertextually shaping the meaning of a particular sign. This problem of interpretation is, of course, magnified according to the visual (or sensory) complexity of a text—with a greater number of signs increasing the likelihood of disparate interpretations amongst groups of individuals.

Although the epistemological issues let loose by the 'discovery' of polysemy were not easily dismissed, the rise of post-structural/postmodern theories of language and culture did not entirely discredit the more structural emphasis of the 'early Barthes' (such as is exemplified in *Mythologies*). Indeed, Barthes's idea that objects are encoded with social functions that, simultaneously, act as a 'sign function' (thus connoting mythic values), was to give rise to the theories of a number of postmodern thinkers, such as those of the late Jean Baudrillard. In particular, the early (more structuralist) semiology of Barthes—that concerned with ideology, myth and the fashion system—is manifest in the early (more empirical) and sociological work of Baudrillard, who in *The System of Objects* (Baudrillard, 1996 [first published in 1968]) argued that, as mass consumption has become tied to the cultural/mythical values inscribed into things by the ideologies of advanced capitalism, the signification processes of consumer products 'commodify everyday life'.

Likewise, Barthes's later theories are evident in Baudrillard's more controversial work on hyperreality. For instance, when Baudrillard argued that the system of signs—and hence the processes of signification, from referent to signified—had in fact been broken, his argument was running parallel to some of the conclusions of the 'later Barthes' (see Barthes, 1989 [1970]; 2006 [1968]). Indeed, Baudrillard (1983) was drawing upon Barthes's post-Saussurean/post-structuralist idea that signs have no fixed meaning, and that interpretation and polysemy (or multiple meanings) are, in fact, key features of signs, texts and the processes of signification.

While both Jacques Derrida and Jean Baudrillard are correct in highlighting the problems with signs and texts as purveyors of an absolute truth, their work goes too far when interpreted as denying the existence of a real world outside, and independent of, language systems. Texts may be open to interpretation (and thus can be read incorrectly), but they are still capable of conveying factual information regarding the world and our society. Likewise, although signs might have only an arbitrary relationship with the 'reality' they represent, they can effectively stand in for real referents (such as the example of the sign 'cat' discussed above, or that of a photograph, or that of a mathematical formula). Indeed, while we can quickly identify texts that clearly distort different 'truths' (such as in the case with deliberate news media bias), the technologies and sciences of the modern world would not be possible without a degree of knowledge being accurately conveyed by a text (such as a

Polysemy: refers to the capacity of a sign to be interpreted differently by different readers. As such, signs can signify 'multiple meanings', as defined by the social and cultural context and values of the audience.

Intratextuality: the process whereby the different features of a text help to shape the semiotic interpretation of the whole. For example, a newspaper headline helps to frame the meaning of a story.

medical science textbook instructing university students on the symptoms of disease). Likewise, the polysemic meanings of the sign are anchored and contained by the rules and conventions governing the use of language, and thus by the conceptual schema employed by the individual in the process of interpretation (or by what Stuart Hall (1980: 134) has labelled one's 'maps of meaning').

Post-structuralism has not, then, buried semiotics as a research method concerned with analysing the meanings of signs. Rather, it merely serves as a reminder not to be too rigid when analysing the units of a language, and that we must understand texts in reference to the cultural codes of their social context. As Stuart Hall's (1980) seminal work on ideological codes showed, texts communicate **dominant readings** (where the reader accepts the 'truthfulness' of a particular text), **negotiated readings** (where the reader accepts some aspects of the author's interpretation but rejects others) or **oppositional readings** (where the reader rejects or dismisses a text as entirely untruthful). Yet, despite this potential for conflicting interpretations by different readers, polysemy is not the same as unlimited plurality of meaning, as the author of a text intentionally (and, sometimes, unintentionally) inscribes, or rather 'encodes', preferred meanings and messages (Hall, 1980: 134). In other words, regardless of how a text might be read by its audience, it is the goal of the semiotic critique to expose the dominant ideological assumptions and messages that have gone into its creation (i.e. what was the preferred reading intended by the author, and what does it not say about the referent).

Post-structuralism: social theory that reminds researchers to avoid making generalisations about the universal meanings of signs or the structures of languages. Instead, researchers must consider the contextual basis of meaning.

Dominant, negotiated and oppositional readings: Dominant readings of texts are those generally intended by their creators. However, Hall argues that individual 'readers' have the capacity to resist, to produce negotiated or oppositional interpretations.

What is the message? Sex, porn, art or clothing?

The image immediately below is part of a controversial advertisement campaign run in Australia by Lee Jeans during 2006. Intended for publication in magazines such as *Yen*, *Oyster* and *Russh*, this advertising campaign was labelled pornographic and criticised for its 'Lolita' imagery (referring to the novel by Vladimir Nabokov, infamous for its depiction of a sexual relationship between a middle-aged man and a 12-year-old girl). At the heart of this controversy was the concern that young people might be influenced by the morals represented by such media texts, incorporating such values into their everyday actions. While the images were clearly drawing on the familiar marketing technique of attaching sexual desires and images to cultural commodities, Lee mounted a defence of their risqué advertisements, stating that they were neither offensive nor derogatory, but rather that they showcased 'sexuality in its most beautiful light' (see Wilson, 2006). This view was upheld by the Advertising Standards Board, which dismissed complaints regarding the ad's sexualised imagery (see Jolly, 2006). There are, then, at least two conflicting interpretations of the text (see Figure 8.6). What does this advertisement say to you? What are the communicative elements of this sign, and what are the messages?

Semiotics can allow us to dispassionately analyse and understand such texts by focusing on their communicative properties. For example, the referent of this advertisement is a young woman, aged somewhere in her early twenties. Her photographic representation is the primary signifier, and signifies the concepts of youth, beauty and desire. At the denotative level, the text shows merely a young woman, enjoying a lollipop, while being photographed by an unknown (and almost unseen) photographer. Yet it is at the connotative level that this text becomes a controversial image, drawing on different ideological codes to suggest forms of sexuality and cultural practices. Here, different features of the sign become important.

Intratextually, it is the lollipop, the woman's tongue, the photographer's flash, the half-exposed breast, the positioning of the legs and the location of the word/brand 'Lee' that give this image its sexual connotations. Both the lollipop and the brand stand in for the phallus, while it is the photographer's flash that suggests this is a desirable behaviour, worthy of photographic capture. The lollipop and the photographer's flash are of further connotative significance in that they intertextually draw on wider cultural codes to suggest fame and youth. It is here that we can identify the source of the controversy that accompanied this image, for it seemingly weds symbols of childhood innocence with the bright hot lust of the porn industry, offering a Lolita-like myth of the sexually precocious teenage girl. And it is this very connotative message that lends this image its raw artistic authenticity—cultural values that the indented reader is meant to attach to Lee Jeans products. The photographer, Terry Richardson, becomes part of this story of the commodification of sexual desire, in that he is a self-styled cultural provocateur using sexual desire and our society's veneration of fame and youth to fashion an image that most young people would decode as authentically 'cool'.

Figure 8.6: Lee Jeans advertisement

Source: Art Partner/Terry Richardson

Conclusion: Semiotics for life

This chapter offers what can be considered a 'post-postmodern' method of semiotic analysis (which should always be referred to simply as 'semiotics'). It does so on the epistemological basis that semiotics (when used with caution) can be an appropriate (although imperfect) method for researchers seeking to understand cultural texts as products of a social world modulated and shaped by human agency and power (following the insights of Gottdiener, 1995: 25). The discussion above is intended to highlight not only the strengths and weaknesses of the research method, but to provide the definitions of the key terms used in the application of semiotics. In essence, the user of semiotics should:

1 search for how meaning is constructed and framed through the use of words, images, ideologies and narratives

2 identify the different layers of meaning within a sign, from the denotative to the connotative

3 analyse the ideological codes present within a text in order to expose the myths used to communicate and reinforce particular ontological perspectives of 'how the world is'.

The semiotic enterprise is far from over. Rather, it has evolved as new ideas have emerged to help refine the critique. Indeed, a semiotic method that situates the text within the contextual parameters of culture and society remains of fundamental importance to both media studies and the broader social sciences, helping us understand the signs that help to texture and shape our daily experiences.

Summary

- Semiotics involves the study of visual and linguistic 'signs'.
- Signs are the units of meaning within a language and make communication possible.
- Signs 'stand in' for events and things in the real word. However, different signs can be used to represent the one event and thus can present different or competing versions of 'reality'.
- Semiotic research allows us to analyse how different texts create meaning, and thus we can critically assess their 'truth claims' (or the accuracy of their representations).

Further reading

Barthes, R 1973, *Mythologies*, Paladin, London.

Bignell, J 1997, *Media Semiotics: An Introduction*, Manchester University Press, Manchester.

Chandler, D 2007, *Semiotics: The Basics*, 2nd edn, Routledge, New York.

Gottdiener, M 1995, *Postmodern Semiotics*, Blackwell Publishers, Massachusetts.

Hall, S 1980, 'Encoding/Decoding', in S Hall, D Hobson, A Lowe & P Willis (eds), *Culture, Media, Language: Working Papers in Cultural Studies, 1972–79*, Hutchinson, London, 128–39.

Weblinks

Daniel Chandler's Semiotics for Beginners: www.aber.ac.uk/media/Documents/S4B

The Gruen Transfer, Episode 4: Head & Shoulders and Semiotics (YouTube clip): www.youtube.com/watch?v=fLPKmA18Rzc&feature=fvwrel

The Gruen Transfer: The panel discuss Dove advertisements and the *reality* of body image (YouTube clip): www.youtube.com/watch?v=BaSRWnv_KLo&feature=fvsr

For revision questions, please visit www.oup.com.au/orc/chalkley.

chapter

9

Postmodernism:
Why Should I Care?

Brad Warren

Ferris Bueller's Day Off

> 'Isms, in my opinion, are not good. A person should not believe in an ism, he should believe in himself.' (Ferris Bueller, 1986)

The X children are settling down to watch *Ferris Bueller's Day Off*, a cult teen-movie from the mid-1980s. The lead character is prone to voicing opinion on a range of topics, in ways that are often amusing, and nearly always misinformed. Ferris also has a knack for stating concerns frequently held by people his age. In the case of the passage above, he is talking about how many young people feel that theoretical paradigms—or 'isms'—have little or no relevance to everyday life.

Introduction

Is Ferris correct? This is an easy one: the answer is no. Theoretical paradigms, or 'isms', such as postmodernism, feminism and structuralism, can be defined in general terms as 'ways of looking at things'. Consider for a minute that our vision is rarely, if ever, crystal clear. The things we see, or more accurately the ways we *interpret* the things we see, are affected by the perspectives and attitudes that we bring to them. These perspectives and attitudes, in turn, are the products of our history, prior experiences and beliefs.

A simple example illustrates this point: imagine opening your window one morning, seeing a clear blue sky and feeling a warm breeze caress your face. Surely this is a straightforward scene of a pleasant spring or summer morning, with no room for differing or misinterpretations? Isn't it?

Again, the answer is no. Consider the following:

If you worked a night shift somewhere, this 'pleasant' scene would likely evoke dismay or anger, because it means the alarm didn't go off and you're six hours late for work.

If you're a farmer, it's likely your reaction would again be dismay, although probably not surprise. At the time of writing, drought is affecting many rural areas in Australia, and the 'pleasant' scene would mean 'just another day without rain'.

Or maybe you'd been desperately hoping to go snowboarding on this particular day. Again, the reaction to the blue sky and the warm breeze would be negative, but in this case the extreme difference between your expectations and the reality of the morning probably just means you're a bit thick.

The only difference between these differing interpretations of a sunny morning and Ferris's 'isms' is that 'isms' are a bit more complicated. Nonetheless, they are basically the same: they are simply different perspectives, different *ways of looking at everyday life*. So, 'isms' are indeed relevant to everyday life—they are different ways of interpreting and understanding it. And looking at things in different ways sometimes sheds light on different aspects of everyday life that we perhaps hadn't considered or noticed, and extending knowledge and understanding is always good.[1]

The modern-to-postmodern shift (or perhaps it's more like a plummet)

What characterises twenty-first century university life, for students undertaking Media and Communication/Arts/other related degrees (i.e. the kinds of students likely to be reading this book)? Limited contact hours? Juggling study and work, and struggling to find a balance? Cheap beer on Wednesdays? Lots of coffee? And a ton of big words? All of these things, probably.

Many of those big words are addressed in these pages (semiotics; panopticon; paradigm, with a silent 'g' and a hard 'i'; cappuccino …), but one of the most perplexing is undoubtedly postmodernism, because it has so many different elements, and can mean different things in a variety of contexts. It's one of those words that, when it comes up in conversation (say, over some of that coffee just mentioned), eyes tend to glaze over slightly, there are lots of polite smiles and half-nods to sort-of indicate understanding … and that's about it. Further conversation on the subject frequently goes along the lines of 'Maybe you should ask your lecturer …'.

And that's fine, but pick a friendly one, and ask them when there's time to spare, otherwise you'll likely invoke a brush-off non-answer along the lines of 'It's very complicated …'.

Such non-communicative lecturers are correct: postmodernism *is* complicated, but only to a point. You *can* get a handle on it, if it's approached in a logical manner. Despite what Ferris Bueller says, we should care about isms, as they can show us a new way of looking at life. There are some postmodernist theories that are useful in understanding new media: hyperreality, simulacra and pastiche/bricolage. Notwithstanding the negativity of some theorists (Baudrillard in particular—more on this shortly), postmodernism's idea of shifting/transient meaning is useful. The trick is to not let an ism—such as postmodernism—become an ideology that we cannot see beyond, but rather to use it as a theory/paradigm for understanding reality.

A logical approach to postmodernism: The first things you need to know

When did **postmodernism** begin? The more you research to find an answer to this question, the more confused you are likely to become. The reason it's hard to pin down a straight answer is because *there isn't one!* As suggested above, 'postmodernism' is a term that covers a vast range of phenomena and ideas, across a great many disciplines. For example, it relates to various things in the fields of literature, architecture, critical theory, music and drama (among others), not to mention *culture in general*. It was first used in the 1920s by British artist John Watkins Chapman, with reference to the 1870s, another half-century earlier (no kidding!) (Jencks, cited in Appignanesi et al., 2004: 3).

If we were to leave the question of origin here, it would appear we have a clear answer, but unfortunately things aren't that simple. One of the greatest problems with this starting date for *post*-modernism is that the height of the **modernist** period is usually held to be between 1890 and 1930 (Bradbury & McFarlane, 1976: 3). How is it possible that the heyday of modernism occurs so long *after* the emergence of *post*-modernism, when the literal meaning of 'post-' is 'that which comes later'?

To complicate things still further, Dada, one of the cultural movements associated with modernism, began in Zurich during the First World War (Young, 1981: 22). One of the characteristics of Dadaist art was to 'cut words out of a newspaper, shake in a bag, paste at random on

Postmodernism should be understood as a *lack of faith in the modernist project*. Postmodernists claim that modernism's search for answers through progress is fundamentally flawed, because there are no final answers, just multiple and transient meanings.

The period of high **modernism** is generally agreed to have fallen between 1890 and 1930. It was characterised by a belief in reason, and in (primarily Western-capitalist) notions of progress. Through progress, it was felt that perfection was possible.

a page' (Marcus, 1989: 199) (much the way you might have done with pictures from magazines when you were in kindergarten ☺). Problematically, though, this kind of artistic practice bears a remarkable resemblance to the postmodern practice of 'pastiche', as described by Fredric Jameson in his seminal article 'Postmodernism, or The Cultural Logic of Late Capitalism' (1984: 64). This is more than just the later, postmodern form growing out of its modernist predecessor—the practices are essentially identical. And, just in case you're not confused enough, 'late capitalism' is a period Jameson sees as beginning after the Second World War, which would put the emergence of postmodernism after 1945.

Enough of this. To restate, elements considered to be 'postmodern' have arisen at different times across a great many disciplines. With apologies to those who like neat, tidy answers, there really aren't any in this instance. The best that can be done is to accept that inconsistencies exist and put them aside, or at least try to work around them.

Figure 9.1 Dadaist 'pastiche' art, years before its time

Source: Kurt Schwitters, Theo van Doesburg, Kleine DADA Soirée, 1923, colour lithograph, 29.8 × 29.8 cm. Purchased 1984. Collection: Art Gallery of New South Wales. Photograph: AGNSW.

Some things to cling to: A couple of ports in the storm

The concept of 'post-' ('that which comes later') is very important. Despite the contradictions outlined above, one of the basic truths often neglected in attempts to get a handle on postmodernism is that you can't understand 'post-' anything unless you have a basic understanding of 'that which came before'. And so, with regard to studies of the media, and of modernism (that which comes before postmodernism), there are a few things to say.

Like postmodernism, modernism also takes—or should that be took—a great many forms. In general, however, modernism is characterised by a belief in progress, and by the pursuit of perfection. Birch et al. (2001: 29) provide a good working summary, describing modernism as:

- the partial replacement of religion by 'human' values (liberty, equality, fraternity, individualism)
- the rise of science and scientific methods
- a belief in reason, rationality and the civilising effects of culture and technology, and
- a belief in 'progress'.

Expanding further on these ideas, consider the following, an extract from www.artcollecting. co.uk/Modernism.html:

Modernism is a period characterised by … industrialisation … it is a period defined chiefly by a deep held belief in the idea of progress towards some kind of better world. This belief in Utopia led to huge advances and sacrifices being made, in order to distance humanity from a cruel and barbaric past, and lead them forward to a state of harmony and plenitude …

Modernism is characterised by a never ending pursuit of the 'new' over the 'old'—this impulse is one that arguably does not belong to any one period of history, but one that is particularly prevalent in the Modernist period. This coincides directly with the Modernist striving toward Utopia. … This is a position that … undeniably led to progress … Problematically, this meant that no sooner was something new, than it soon became old, thus necessitating ever faster artistic developments.

To paraphrase, then, modernism was the belief in, and pursuit of *bigger, better, faster, more*. Modernists sought an ideal world through progress, and believed that it was possible.

And now *post*-modernism. First, and most importantly …

Postmodernism, put as simply as possible, can be described as a lack of faith in the modernist project. The belief in progress, and in ultimate answers to big questions—another element contained in the notion of utopia—were superseded in many cases by a sense of futility and pessimism. Not only do many postmodernists fail to believe in ultimate answers, they claim to not even know what the big questions *are* (so much for the meaning of life ☹).

Although there are several contenders for the title of 'Most Negative Postmodern Pessimist', the award should probably go to **Jean Baudrillard** (not that he'll appreciate it, on account of his being dead). A few select passages serve to illustrate this point:

'… the extermination of meaning' (1988: 10)

'… the end of history' (1988: 13)

'… the death of culture' (1988: 97)

'… what is hanging over us now is … more or less long term … melancholia' (1990: 11).

Nonetheless, while a focal point of much postmodern writing, this characteristic negativity does not really concern us here. What does concern us, however, is where that negativity comes from. Rather than the pursuit of progress and the 'ever new', postmodernism is characterised by shifting and transient meanings, and multiple possible interpretations of cultural forms. However, theorists such as Baudrillard take this element a step further, and argue that *because meanings are not fixed, then nothing means anything at all!* This actually seems a bit illogical, the more you think about it, but it's essentially what they're being so negative and upset about.

It must be stated plainly that while this book agrees with (in fact, embraces) the idea of shifting and multiple meanings of cultural forms, it does not take the additional leap into postmodern depression and melancholia. This author has argued elsewhere (Warren, 2000: 90) that the meanings attributed to cultural phenomena *can* shift and change, and that they remain valid, provided they are considered within the grounded cultural contexts in which they occur. For example, to revisit the simple example of a sunny day cited at the beginning of this chapter, just because the meaning

Jean Baudrillard (1929–2007):
One of the major theorists associated with postmodernism, Baudrillard was a French intellectual/sociologist. He is credited with developing the concepts of hyperreality and simulacra.

changed depending on the perspective of the person viewing it, this does not mean that any of the meanings were diminished or irrelevant, especially not to the person experiencing them.

So, shifting and multiple meanings = valid and good, and this is a large part of the relevance of postmodernism to new media and everyday life—consider the multiple uses/meanings attributed to iPods, Facebook and so on (for a further exploration of Facebook, see Chapter 13).

The possibility of multiple valid meanings for cultural forms, under postmodernism, also needs to be considered in light of semiotics (see Chapter 8). In a sense, a postmodern paradigm can be seen as actively disrupting the semiotic chain (Signifier + Signified = Sign), recasting the equation along the lines of 'Signifier + Signified may or may not = a particular Sign, under certain conditions and in specific cultural circumstances'. Or something like that. Put another way, while a postmodern paradigm doesn't necessarily do away with the semiotic chain, it does suggest strongly that the chain is made of rubber bands!

To delve a little deeper, the remainder of this chapter examines a number of other relevant postmodern ideas:

- hyperreality (Baudrillard)
- simulacra (also Baudrillard)
- pastiche (Jameson) / bricolage (Lévi-Strauss).

This is by no means a comprehensive list of postmodern concepts, or of postmodern theorists. Lyotard (*The Postmodern Condition*, 1979) and Foucault (see discussion of his concept of the panopticon in Chapter 17) are also worthy of mention, as are many others.

Reality imitating media imitating reality. **Hyperreality** is more than just exaggerated media images. It's a process, whereby emphasised or accentuated media is accepted as a true reflection of reality, and behaviours are affected as a result.

Baudrillard's hyperreality, as explained by Master X

Master X wanted to be a suicide bomber. But he didn't know how to begin. He had a vague idea what was involved, and sort of understood that it was about standing up for something you thought was really important, but he didn't have anything like that. Master X just thought it all sounded really exciting, and that it would look great on his resumé. So he researched making explosives from common household ingredients, and googled everything he could think of with regard to local terrorist cells, until he thought he was up to speed.[2]

But he still wasn't sure about how to actually get out there and make it happen. You know, niggling details like how to identify a target, make contact, put yourself in the right time and place, stuff like that …

But then something wonderful happened: a plane was hijacked, and a string of improbable coincidences taught him everything he needed to know:

Improbable coincidence no. 1: There was a passenger on the plane with a video recorder on his phone. The phone had enough battery and storage to film all three hours and 27 minutes of the hijack.

Improbable coincidence no. 2: The passenger managed to film everything that happened in great detail, without any of the hijackers pausing casually to kill him, just for getting in the way.

Improbable coincidence no. 3: The phone and its video footage not only survived the destruction of the airplane, but somehow found their way, complete and intact, into the hands of a reporter from Master X's local television station.

At this point, however, things got a little strange. (This is not where hyperreality comes into play—please keep reading, we're not quite there yet.) The reporter who obtained the camera-phone was relatively new to his position and, perhaps as a result of this, was extremely enthusiastic about playing the entire recording from beginning to end as a documentary special, shown on prime-time television.

However, his superior, a producer from the network, had been in the media game a lot longer. He explained to the young reporter, as gently as possible, that the footage could not be shown in its entirety, because it contained too many boring bits, like extended scenes where people were just sitting around looking scared. Instead, the producer proposed that, instead of a lengthy special, the footage could be given a 90-second slot on the evening news.

The young reporter was understandably disheartened—he'd already imagined himself winning all sorts of journalism awards—but he did as his producer instructed. He went away and made a 90-second edited version of all the most exciting and dramatic bits of his 3+ hours of footage, with the result being an action extravaganza that was far more exciting, more-real-than-real, than the original footage would ever have been. (But this is still not hyperreality as such. It's just clever video-editing. Hyperreality comes next; please keep going just a little bit further.)

The 90-second segment aired as the leading story on the 6 o'clock news that night, and Master X sat there riveted. This was exactly what he'd been waiting for! He now had a detailed 'how-to' guide that would walk him through every stage of his own intended hijacking. (This is the beginning of hyperreality: *it's all about how media influences and directs (elements of) society—in this case the intentions and behaviour of Master X.*)

So, Master X strapped on his homemade C4, clamped his 10-inch safari knife firmly in his teeth (this last bit was old-school, but he'd always been a fan of the Rambo movies), and off he went to stage his own hijacking.

In his mind (intended outcome): Master X stages his hijacking, but does so in a way that is bigger, better, faster and more exciting than the original one had ever been, *because Master X DID NOT learn from the original hijack, but from the media's excitement-laden, more-real-than-real version of it.* (This, precisely, is hyperreality: it's not just the way the media exaggerates reality (that's only half of it), it's the way such media feeds back into society as it is received and used (as Master X did), creating a bigger, faster, more-real-than-real[3] version of actual reality the next time around.)

In reality (factual outcome): Master X was apprehended by representatives of a government agency (so secret they don't have a name) while checking his letterbox at the top of his driveway. He spent the next three weeks in solitary confinement and under interrogation, until the secret agents realised that his homemade explosive was almost as dangerous as cookie-dough, and that Master X was too dumb to be any real threat to anyone.

Further consequences of hyperreality, and a more believable example

In addition to the adventures of Master X just described, it also needs to be recognised that hyperreality can become a cycle, with no visible end in sight. To retain Master X's hijacking example a moment longer, imagine that someone on Master X's plane also had a video camera, that the entire event was again recorded (only 1 hour and 10 minutes this time, so not as much battery life was needed—hyperreality in action), that the recording made it to the media, was edited down and then viewed by *another* wannabe suicide bomber, who then staged his own hijack that was even faster and more exciting than Master X's had been …

… and so on. Round and round we go.

Implausible, I know. So let's abandon Master X at this point, and look at the phenomenon of hyperreality in a more general sense: things (any things, it doesn't really matter) are shown by the media in an accelerated or exaggerated manner, and people watching the programs mistake what they see for actual, exact reflections of the real world, and incorporate them into their everyday lives, seeking to emulate them in their day-to-day practices. Now that we've left Master X to his own devices, suddenly the process of hyperreality doesn't sound quite so far-fetched.

One more example, this one based firmly in reality: According to ninemsn (and this was news printed on the internet, so it must be true)—see http://news.ninemsn.com.au/entertainment/1003397/demi-moore-in-new-photoshop-storm,24/01/2010—Demi Moore is again facing criticism for the extensive photoshopping of her image for a new perfume commercial. Please copy the link into your net browser and consider the pictures before reading on …

Had a look? Good. But what's this got to do with hyperreality? A great deal, actually. Although not at an entirely conscious level (most of the time, anyway), the message received by many consumers will be that buying and using the perfume will enable them to look more like digital-Demi. And this is, of course, exactly what the perfume manufacturers want you to think, so that you will buy their product. That is to say, the perfume makers are seeking to instil in the consumer public *hyperreal* expectations of what the perfume can achieve. This then feeds back into the actual actions of the public, not in terms of hyper-enhanced appearances (bad luck on that score), but in terms of perfume sales. Ironic, really, since clear ethanol-based products don't change your appearance a single bit (unless you swallow rather a lot of them).

To illustrate the extent to which fashion magazines, advertisements and so forth seek to encourage hyperreal reactions from their audiences, we might ask how much of what we see in these places is modified, enhanced—in short, photoshopped? Answers to this question aren't easy to find, since excessive photoshopping isn't something magazine producers readily admit to, because of the negative stigma attached. Just the same, if we view the question from a different angle, then maybe we can intuit the answer.

In February 2010, popular Australian model/television presenter Jennifer Hawkins appeared makeup- and photoshop- (and also clothing-) free on the cover of *Marie Claire*, supposedly in an effort to promote positive body images for women. The results can be viewed at: http://sweettater.files.word-press.com/2010/01/jennifer_hawkins_marie_claire-large.jpg. Considerable debate has arisen as a result of this well-known image, not least around whether a former Miss Universe represents a normal (read: attainable) image that women can aspire to—regardless of whether she's been photoshopped or not. More interesting in the current context, however, is the sheer weight of the publicity that the 'Photoshop-free' magazine-feature generated (try googling for yourself to see the immense range of hits that show up, but use search terms like 'Jennifer Hawkins' and 'Marie Claire', rather than 'naked photoshoot').

The volume of publicity begs a question: 'What percentage of magazine articles with similar content are *not* photoshopped?'

The answer seems fairly self-evident: None of them![4] This says a great deal about the potential for hyperreal effects developing in contemporary society. We could even go so far as to ask: 'How could they *not* develop, when the media is so saturated with exaggerated, more-real-than-real images?'

To see the extent to which images can be 'touched up' using software programs such as Photoshop, check out the following link: www.youtube.com/watch?v=mUYwC4HkIV0.

Baudrillard's simulacra

Like hyperreality, the idea of **simulacra** is also directly concerned with the media, and with the ways in which meanings can become distorted as events are reported. However, it is with simulacra that Baudrillard goes a step further (some would say a step too far) and suggests that the constant repro-duction of images, events and so forth through media leads to *the collapse of meaning altogether*. The argument goes something like this:

1 Events are reported by the media.

2 They are received as images, not as reality (i.e. they are consumed as banal entertainment at best).

3 This process gets worse as the original events are (re-)reported over and over again, to the extent that the original meaning is lost (no matter how serious or horrific the originally reported event may have been).

4 Somehow, meaning collapses altogether, and nothing means anything anymore.

Writing about Baudrillard's simulacra, Lash and Urry (1987: 289) describe the process as follows:

> Everyday life and reality itself … become 'imploded' into the hyperreality of the spectacle. Baudrillard's world of spectacle is a world of 'simulacra', that is, where there is no original and everything is a copy. The masses simulate the media which in turn hypersimulate the masses.

This passage makes it clear that, for Baudrillard, hyperreality and simulacra are closely intertwined. Further, to expand on simulacra in Baudrillard's (1990: 227) own words:

> Simulacra are today accepted everywhere in their realist version: simulacra exist, simulation exists. It is the intellectual and fashionable version of this vulgarization which is the worst: all is sign, signs have abolished reality.

As the tone of this sub-section has probably made clear, Baudrillard's simulacra is not a concept that this author is willing to accept, at least not in its complete, full-blown form. It's a fascinating idea, pushed to an illogical extreme. It *does* make sense that tragedy seen on the nightly news loses some of its original meaning when it's reported—obviously, we don't feel the terror of an earthquake shown on the news as much as if we actually lived through it—but most of us still feel *something*. Furthermore, meaning is not lost altogether, no matter how many times the story is repeated (it's even plausible that meaning *diminishes* with repeated re-telling—it's the irrational leap to the *end of everything* that's hard to swallow).

Jameson's pastiche/Lévi-Strauss's bricolage

This section cuts some corners, as it were, albeit only a little bit: technically speaking, **pastiche** and **bricolage** are not the same, but for our purposes they're close enough to warrant discussing them under a single heading. Pastiche, which has already been mentioned a little earlier in this chapter, is a practice of combining elements of past style (art, culture, fashion, whatever) in an apparently random manner to make something new.

Jameson coined the term 'pastiche' as a postmodern concept in the mid-1980s, describing it as a kind of 'irrational eclecticism' (1984: 64). The Dadaist artwork reproduced earlier still stands as a good example of the pastiche idea, despite its troubling location within the modern (rather than postmodern) movement.

Simulacra are closely related to Baudrillard's hyperreality. He argued that the media re-reports events / re-broadcasts images covered by other media, in a never-ending cycle. In the process, *meaning is held to have become lost.*

Fredric Jameson (1934–): Another important postmodern theorist, Jameson is an American Marxist critic. His engagement with postmodernism covers a range of areas including, famously, architecture, through his discussion of the Los Angeles Bonaventure Hotel.

Also, consider the example in Figure 9.2, which is more firmly grounded in the postmodern epoch.

However, there's a problem with all this: in fairly typical postmodern style, pastiche has also been described as 'speech in a dead language ... a neutral practice ... without ... motive ... [and] blank' (Jameson, 1988: 16). That is, pastiche is apparently without purpose, without meaning, and it is here that the concept becomes very troubling.

So, here we are again. Can you hear the echoes of Baudrillard's stubborn insistence on the end of everything? Like Dada before it, pastiche is apparently committed to 'the utter rejection ... of reason and all rational systems—the most acceptable system is on principle to have none' (Tristan Tzara, one of Dada's main protagonists, from his *1918 Manifesto*, cited in Young, 1981: 22).

But it can't be done ...

Everything means *something*!

It doesn't have to be very important, but *everything means something*!

In fact, even to seek to mean nothing has a meaning—a political agenda, if you like: to reject meaning (how's that for confusing?).

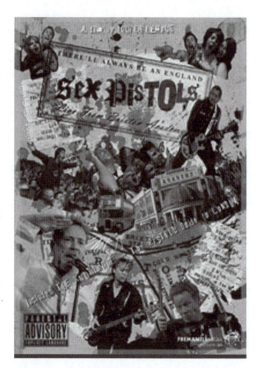

Figure 9.2 DVD sleeve for The Sex Pistols' *There'll Always Be An England* (2008)

Source: DVD packaging design © 2008 Freemantlemedia Enterprises. Artwork: Jonny Halifax & John 'Rambo' Stevens. Photography: Paul Bargess & David Wainwright.

Likewise, the Sex Pistols DVD cover above clearly has a meaning: it's packaging that advertises one of the band's products ... or, with regard to the work at hand (this book), its meaning is to help demonstrate a theoretical concept.

To reiterate a point, the secret to escaping postmodernism's recurrent pessimism is to ground things in context—to ask what things mean in particular places, times and to particular people, whatever those contexts might be.

And so we come to bricolage. The reason for grouping this term together with pastiche is that, at least on the surface, the process of engaging with these concepts is frequently much the same. That is, both pastiche and bricolage are concerned with making new things out of other things already in existence.

Bricolage, as a concept, belongs to Claude Lévi-Strauss, and first appeared in *The Savage Mind* (1966: 16–17). In a nutshell, bricolage can be described as a kind of improvisation, of making something to suit your needs out of whatever materials you might happen to have on hand at the time. Clearly, then, bricolage makes no claim to the lack of meaning associated with pastiche—everything made using bricolage has a purpose (to suit your needs)—but then, as just demonstrated, the supposed lack of meaning in pastiche is highly questionable, so perhaps the two practices are not so far apart.

Lévi-Strauss's work and reputation are not so readily associated with postmodernism as the other theorists considered in this chapter, but his name does appear in such contexts from time to time.

Jameson's concept of **pastiche** is not too dissimilar from Lévi-Strauss's **bricolage,** or even the more common notion of collage: bring together a more-or-less random collection of stuff, and stick them together to make something new.

Bricolage: is all about making the best out of whatever you've got on hand, combining and re-combining elements (of whatever) to best suit your needs. The practice of bricolage carries within it connotations of a do-it-yourself ethos.

Claude Lévi-Strauss (1908–2009): Lévi-Strauss is more firmly associated with anthropology than postmodernism, and his work has also been instrumental in the fields of sociology, philosophy, social theory and, particularly, structuralism.

A conclusion (of sorts)

The key point of this chapter is that Ferris Bueller was wrong: 'isms' are extremely useful in making sense of everyday life—they arise out of people's observations of life, and they become the 'lens' through which we see it. Sometimes we may not even be aware of this—the dominant ideology or 'ism' of the day is frequently passed off in everyday life as 'just the way things are'. (Such insidious prevalence of the dominant ideology has a name, by the way. It's another one of those big words—'hegemony'—which is discussed in more detail in Chapter 18.) To get beyond 'just the way things are' and actively examine things from a different perspective(s) takes an act of will. It's not always easy, but it can be very rewarding.

Where did we come in? Oh yes, multiple interpretations of a sunny day. Well, it's still a sunny day, so forget postmodern negativity (while at the same time embracing its capacity for multiple meanings and interpretations)—I'm going for a swim.

Summary

In this chapter we found that:

- It *is* possible to make sense of postmodernism, so long as you hold on tight and ground yourself in what the movement was/is all about—largely a reaction to modernism—and accept that it is many things across many disciplines all at the same time.
- The postmodern concepts explored in this chapter—hyperreality, simulacra, pastiche/bricolage—are all useful tools for understanding everyday life (or, indeed, taking part in it), and you are encouraged to take them up or put them down as need be. You should focus on the elements of postmodernism that make the most sense to you, or are most relevant to whatever it is you're doing.

Further reading

Appignanesi, R & Garrett, C with Sardar, Z & Curry, P 1995, *Postmodernism for Beginners*, Icon, Cambridge.

Baudrillard, J 1988, *America*, trans. C Turner, Verso, London and New York.

Baudrillard, J 1990, *Cool Memories*, trans. C Turner, Verso, London and New York.

Birch, D, Schirato, T & Srivastava, S 2001, 'Modernity, Postmodernity and Postcoloniality', in D Birch, T Schirato & S Srivastava (eds), *Asia: Cultural Politics in the Global Age*, Allen and Unwin, Crows Nest, 25–53.

Bradbury, M & Mcfarlane, J (eds) 1976, *Modernism 1890–1930*, Penguin, London.

Jameson, F 1984, 'Postmodernism, or the Cultural Logic of Late Capitalism', *New Left Review*, no. 146, 53–92.

Jameson, F 1988 'Postmodernism and Consumer Society', in E Kaplan (ed.), *Postmodernism and its Discontents: Theories, Practices*, Verso, London, 13–29.

Lash, S & Urry, J 1987, 'The Semiotics of Everyday Life', in S Lash & J Urry (eds), *The End of Organised Capitalism*, Polity Press, Cambridge, 288–376.

Marcus, G 1989, *Lipstick Traces: A Secret History of the Twentieth Century*, Harvard University Press, Cambridge.

Young, A 1981, *Dada and After: Extremist Modernism and English Literature*, Manchester University Press, Manchester.

Weblinks

Marie Claire (cover). 'The Naked Truth—Jennifer Bares All for Charity': http://sweettater.files. wordpress.com/2010/01/jennifer_hawkins_marie_claire-large.jpg

ninemsn. 'Demi Moore in New Photoshop Storm': http://news.ninemsn.com.au/ entertainment/1003397/demi-moore-in-new-photoshop-storm.

For revision questions, please visit www.oup.com.au/orc/chalkley.

Endnotes

1   The author of this chapter acknowledges that this last statement is, itself, a product of his own particular perspective/view of the world. It is, of course, up to you whether you agree or not.

2   And, valued reader, before you even *think* about using the internet to emulate either of these activities, even if only to 'see what's out there', please read Chapter 17 of this book, 'Surveillance'. As a result of Master X's online searches, his activities were flagged by several government agencies across the globe, to the extent that he couldn't type a shopping list without a range of law-enforcement bodies knowing all about it—so, *this is not a joke: do not try this at home!*

3   Note the similarity here between (postmodern) hyperreality and the summary of *modernism* provided earlier in the chapter. This is partially the effect of postmodernism growing out of modernism (i.e. it's not out of the question that they should have some things in common)—and, as discussed, it's also due to the modern/postmodern distinction or break being hazy at best.

4   Or as close to 'none of them' as makes little difference.

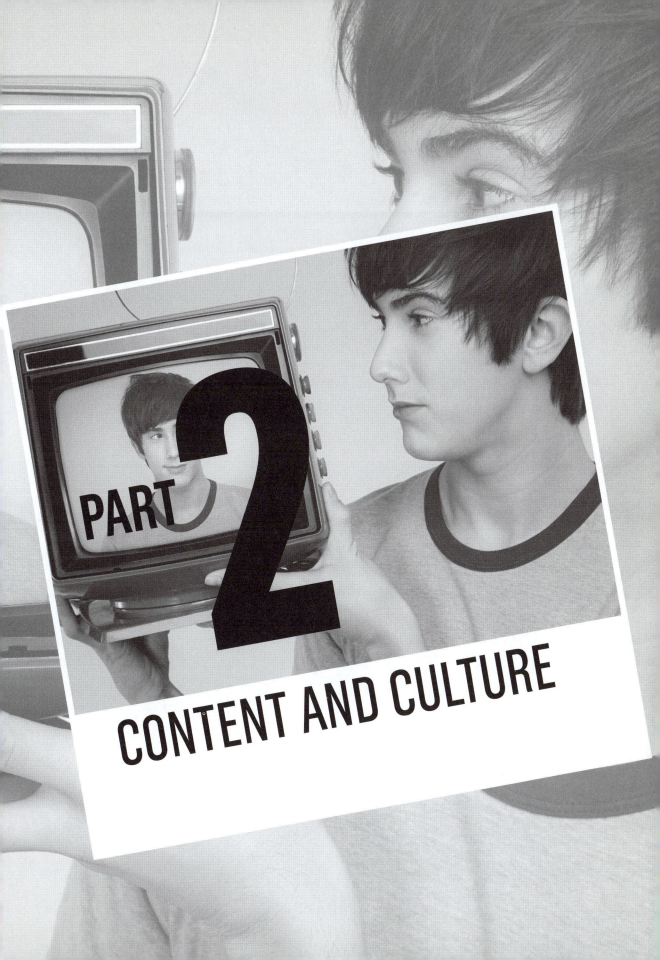

PART **2**

CONTENT AND CULTURE

10 Ideology and Meaning in Film: Life in Surround Sound

Adam Brown

How to hire the right (or wrong?) movie

Several years ago, when the X family decided to make up the spare room and organise for an African-American exchange student named Celia to visit them, there was a lot of chaotic discussion about how to make the young woman feel 'at home'.

'Imagine how you would feel flying over to the other side of the world and having to stay with strangers!' Mr X exclaimed. Celia was a bit shy, but very polite and would have been very embarrassed had she known of all the trouble they were going to.

The first night that Celia arrived, Mrs X instructed her children to hire a film that everyone would enjoy. Within seconds, the brother and sister had decided on *The Lion King*, reasoning that: 1) it was an American film; 2) it was well-liked by everyone they knew who'd seen it; and 3) it was, of course, their own personal favourite. They thought they couldn't go wrong.

They were wrong.

While watching the film, the children noticed that Celia wasn't laughing at many of the scenes. They couldn't help asking Celia later why she didn't seem to enjoy the film. Celia hesitated, but then told them.

'I can't stand how these films always portray minority groups. I mean, I know the characters are animals and everything, but they're always given human features. The three hyenas are obviously supposed to be African-American, Latino and what appears to be someone with a mental disability—just listen to their accents and see how they behave! And they live in some scummy ghetto-like place as outcasts, have to beg for food, and are always just stupid or evil, or both! It's like that in heaps of films, and people say that society's moved beyond discriminating against people ... '

The X children weren't sure what to say. They'd never thought of the film (in fact, any film!) in that way before—they thought it was just a story. They could see Celia might have a point, but they weren't sure. Did it really matter what films 'meant'?

What you will learn from this chapter

This chapter introduces you to the ways in which meaning(s) are communicated through films. You will be able to:

- Understand the role of ideology in films, and how and why filmmakers engage audience emotions
- Identify the potential effects that ideologies in films have on viewers
- Explain how film techniques are used to communicate ideological messages
- Undertake a critical film analysis.

Introduction: Simply a story or something beneath the surface?

We go to the movies to be entertained. We rent or buy DVDs to relax, to reward ourselves for doing all the chores or to 'escape reality'. Films tell us great stories—and sometimes, not-so-great stories. Some theorists claim that the 'principal function [of films] has always been to take their viewers away from the pressing issues and mundane details of everyday life, rather than to focus their attention on them' (Dennis & DeFleur, 2010: 127). But is it all just a matter of having 'fun'? Is a trip to a cinema or stocking up your collection of the latest blockbusters all about seeking entertainment? Or is there something else going on? This chapter will examine this question and provide a means by which you can discover what meaning(s) are being communicated behind the obvious storyline—what ideas are being put forward 'beneath the surface'.

Narrative: a story that is constructed using various **genres** and other **conventions** in order for people to make sense of the world.

Chapter 4 revealed how stories—**narratives**—are used to help us understand everyday life. Of course, these stories are always constructions that hold certain meanings for us, and the narratives in films are an important example of this. While watching a film, an audience is being told lots of different things that they 'should' believe, whether they realise they are being told these things or not. This is where the key concept of this chapter—**ideology**—becomes important. We'll think about ideology in more detail later in the chapter, but it suffices to say here that, in the story about Family X, Celia identified a certain, very problematic, ideology being communicated in *The Lion King*, which, arguably, most viewers of the film will not have spotted.

Ideology: a collection or system of views and values shared by a certain group of people.

There are many different ways to study film, and books that engage with the subject take a number of different approaches. This chapter deals only with the ideological aspects of films and how these are communicated. While important and interesting, we are not concerned here with the history of film in relation to how the technology has developed, or film's commercial and industrial aspects, such as how studios produce and market their films, and how these are censored with ratings. We are also focusing on fictional feature films, rather than documentaries, short films or amateur movies made for YouTube. While these are all films in their own right and worthy of discussion, feature films often reach a worldwide audience and attract millions of viewers, and therefore the effects of these films' ideologies have the potential to be widespread. We will first consider what ideological messages are present in films, then how these are communicated through **audience identification** and film techniques, before finally combining these elements to conduct **film analysis**.

Audience identification: the process by which viewers are positioned or encouraged to sympathise with a character or group of characters within a film's narrative.

But first, an important note: one of the most common reactions of a student who is just starting to analyse films is annoyance, if not anger. Every teacher who has ever discussed a film in class has been confronted with the accusation: 'But you're ruining the movie! Movies are supposed to be fun!' This is particularly the case when teachers offer a critical analysis of films like *Shrek* (2001) or *Harry Potter and the Philosopher's Stone* (2001) and their students are fans of these. This reaction is perfectly understandable. We don't want our favourite characters to be dragged away from their heroic feats and detained in a classroom discussion. In 1994, *The Lion King* was criticised for reinforcing sexism and racism. In response to the critics, Disney spokesperson Terry Press declared: 'These people need to get a life. It's a story. It's fiction' (Foster, 1994). After reading this chapter's opening vignette, you might have had a similar feeling towards the criticism of such a beloved film as *The Lion King*. Read this chapter, then return to this section and ask yourself the question: Does it matter?

It takes some effort and an open mind to explore what film analysis has to offer. But there is much useful knowledge—and enjoyment—to be found here. By gaining an understanding of the ideologies being communicated through films, you can feel empowered and satisfied that you are getting much more out of the movies than overpriced popcorn. And you can still be entertained by what you watch—there's nothing wrong with that. So, keep an open mind and enjoy studying films!

Film analysis: the critical engagement with film **narratives** that investigates the ideological messages within films and how these are constructed through **film techniques**.

The construction of meaning in film: Defining ideology

As media texts, films have transformed from being a few minutes' worth of black-and-white visual images accompanied by little or no sound, to immensely complex audio-visual representations of the past, the present and the future.

Throughout its long history, film has always been used—consciously or otherwise—to present messages of one kind or another to the public. As part of culture, films serve many purposes. Stanley Baran writes that culture 'helps us categorize and classify our experiences; it helps define us, our world, and our place in it' (2010: 9). Films play an important role in this. All texts—all narratives—have specific messages or meanings embedded within them, and the popularity of films guarantee that these messages are communicated to, if not accepted by, a very wide audience. In short, all films contain ideologies and these can influence the way people think.

'Ideology' is a term that is used in different ways in many different fields of study. Here, the concept of ideology is broadly defined as a collection or system of views and values shared by a certain group of people. Of course, all forms of media—not only films, but also magazines, newspapers, songs and so on—contain ideologies. When an advertisement is 'telling' us to buy something, it is putting forward an ideological message that supports consumerism—i.e. that it is good to buy things, even things that are not necessities. What is more, we ourselves have ideologies embedded within us.

We all hold ideas and beliefs about who we are, how we relate to people, what groups we are part of and where we belong in the world. All of these ideas make up our own personal ideologies, and these will vary from one individual to the next. When we read or view a text, our own ideologies interact—usually without us being conscious of this—with the ideologies contained in the text. This process is highly complex and important to grasp if we are to see how cultural products, not least of all films, benefit or disadvantage us. Michael O'Shaughnessy and Jane Stadler point out that 'ideology is capable of reinforcing existing power relations and social structures in a manner that inevitably works to the advantage of one group (the dominant group in that context), and disadvantages others by

It can be useful to think about film in relation to the concept of **new media** (see Chapter 2). Recent developments in the '3D' movie experience suggest that changes in film are ongoing.

making them seem abnormal, different, or deviant' (2008: 179). To fully understand the potentially damaging effects of ideology, there are several key distinctions that must be made when considering the ideologies being put forward in a text:

- positive or negative
- dominant or subversive
- surface or passive.

First, while the term 'ideology' is often thought of as referring to a 'bad' thing due to its use by Karl Marx to critique the imbalance of power in capitalist societies, under our definition, ideologies can be positive or negative. In Andrew Milner's words, ideology is 'any set of shared assumptions and beliefs seen as in some sense "governing" how people think and act' (1996: 41). This not only suggests that ideology is essential, since we all (especially when we're young) need to be taught positive messages about how to live and understand the world, but also potentially dangerous, because the 'wrong' messages can be communicated through a text. Racism, sexism and homophobia are clear examples of what might be called negative ideologies, whereas environmentalism and feminism can be viewed as positive messages.

On an even more fundamental level, ideologies generally tell us what is 'right' and 'wrong', who is 'important' and 'unimportant', or who is 'good' and 'bad'. Think about the endless stream of action movies that are released from Hollywood. Which group of people are usually the 'good guys'? Who are the 'bad guys'? Is it significant that these questions highlight 'guys'? Does anyone seem to be considered 'unimportant'? Of course, it is not always easy to distinguish positive and negative ideologies, as all people hold different personal beliefs and will interact with ideas presented to them in different ways. The reference to consumerism above is one such example, as people will differ in their attitudes towards certain ways of living. Judgments often depend on what is being said about such things—i.e. if a wealthier group is considered more important than a 'lower class', or vice versa, this would be a negative ideology.

Dominant ideology: a construction of ideas about people and the world that privileges more powerful social groups while marginalising other groups.

As suggested in the above quotation from O'Shaughnessy and Stadler, constructions of ideas about people and the world involves certain power relations, with many ideologies benefiting a dominant group. These are termed **dominant ideologies**. For instance, the most 'powerful' group in society has previously been, and arguably remains, middle-class, white, heterosexual males. Let's consider the last of these categories in relation to the genre (see Chapter 4) of action movies. The main characters of the action movie, which has been described as 'an intensively male category of film' (Hayward, 2007: 11), continue to be predominantly men. This trend partially reinforces the common idea in society that men are more 'courageous' or 'heroic'. This is therefore a dominant ideology, and is part of what we understand as sexism. In addition to this, it might be argued that the considerably larger number of male leads in the 'hero' role is still considered 'normal'.

Process of naturalisation: the ways in which certain messages are portrayed over time and in numerous texts as 'normal' or 'common sense'. Similar to the process where something becomes **normalised**.

Ideologies that are most common or dominant in society undergo what is called a **process of naturalisation**, which means that certain messages are portrayed over time and in countless texts as 'normal', beyond question—just 'common sense'. We will return to this process in the discussion of surveillance in Chapter 17. When you read the above questions about who usually plays the 'good guys' and 'bad guys' in movies, did it seem 'normal' or 'natural' that the questions were phrased in this way? While sexism in society has decreased considerably over the past half century, it can still be argued that discrimination against women is widespread. Sexism can therefore be considered a dominant ideology that has been naturalised. Of course, there can be exceptions to the dominant ideology. Men are not always the heroes of action movies and women are not always merely the 'love interests' or 'damsels in distress'. A film that portrays women as independent and capable of what men are usually considered *naturally* capable of could be classified as a film with a **subversive ideology**—one that challenges, contradicts or undermines a dominant ideology.

The third key distinction regarding ideology is that films have both **surface ideologies** and **passive ideologies**. A surface ideology is an explicit message that seems to be consciously communicated through a film's narrative. To take a recent example, James Cameron's well-known film *Avatar* (2009) communicates the positive message that respecting the environment is important. The film's plot revolves around the suffering of the indigenous 'people', the Na'vi, of Pandora at the hands of the invading humans. Along with the themes of 'race', 'disability' and war, the destructive effects on the environment by the powerful corporation and military force make up a significant part of the film, and are continually depicted and commented on by the characters. Environmentalism, therefore, is a positive surface ideology in the film.

Even more importantly, film texts also have ideologies that are implicit, or passive: those that can only be found 'beneath the surface'. This reflects the fact that many ideologies 'inform our everyday lives in often subtle and barely noticeable forms' (Sturken & Cartwright, 2001: 21). The reason passive ideological messages are so crucial is that they are always more difficult to identify. This is because they are naturalised and even communicated without the film-makers' knowledge. While a film might seem to have a positive message on the surface, a critical analysis could locate a negative message that contradicts this. For example, the film *Tomb Raider* (2001) might at first glance be viewed as promoting the belief that women are equal to men. However, an analysis of the ideologies beneath the surface could find this apparently positive message is contradicted by the ways in which the action hero(ine) Lara Croft is portrayed as a sexual object for male viewers. We will look at a detailed example of the ways in which a film's passive ideology puts forward ideas about **gender** in the analysis of *The Castle* (1997) at the end of this chapter, but for now we need to consider *why* it is so important to be aware of what ideological meanings are being communicated through film. Do we as viewers actually 'take in' the messages contained in the films we watch?

Subversive ideology:
a set of ideas that challenge, contradict or undermine a **dominant ideology**.

Surface ideologies:
explicit messages that seem to be consciously communicated through a **narrative**.

Passive ideologies:
implicit messages that are present 'underneath' the **surface ideology** of a **narrative**.

Framing our emotions and affecting our ideas: 'But I love them, they can't die!'

There is something very powerful about films. The volcanic rise of television half a century ago led to a widespread feeling that the cinema would not survive (Gorman & McLean, 2009: 177); yet, while ticket sales have remained stable, the cinema still thrives on the whole.

The cinema's ability to resist the 'threat' of television would seem to indicate that it possesses a considerable amount of power—social, political and economic. To further emphasise this, films—especially the kind we go to see at the cinema—are, above all, about money. Lots of money. When filmmakers design, produce and market their movies, they give top priority to box office receipts (followed by DVD sales and often movie-related merchandise). The commercial success of American 'Hollywood blockbusters' in particular reveals how important their messages can be, since they are viewed—and obviously enjoyed—by so many people around the world. However, in order to get us to invest our money in a film, filmmakers know that they must also get us to invest our emotions in it.

A major objective of a filmmaker is to establish audience identification with a character or group of characters. These characters are almost always those that we are supposed to 'like'—or, in the case of Harry Potter, love. Think about this: have you ever identified with a character in a

There is currently much discussion of the new 'threat' to the cinema in the form of home theatre systems and video-on-demand digital technologies. What do you think?

movie and then they die in a hail of gunfire or some freak yachting accident? Were you sad? Even angry at the director for letting this happen? When we as viewers 'identify' with a character, we sympathise or empathise with them, putting ourselves in their shoes. As we will see shortly, there are many strategies and devices that filmmakers use to position us to identify with specific characters. When this happens, it might be assumed that we are much more likely to (unconsciously) accept the views and values these characters stand for. At the same time, we might reject the beliefs and values represented by characters we are encouraged to keep our (emotional and intellectual) distance from. We are not likely to agree with those characters we *want* to die. But do we really take on board a film's ideologies?

The issue of whether or not—or more precisely, to what extent—films influence our thoughts and actions is far from clear-cut. It is undeniable that our personal ideologies influence how we behave in our everyday lives. Watching movies may help to reinforce the way we think about the world, but there are various other factors to take into account, such as our personal experiences; how we were raised; what education we have obtained; which political, religious and social groups we belong to; and what cultural products we have encountered. The last of these factors might not only include the movies we watch, but also the music we listen to, the books we read and even the clothes we wear. Yet the fact that there are a multitude of influences on our lives does not mean that the potential impact of films is too small to be worth considering.

There has been a lot of debate in relation to just what ideological effects films have on viewers. Many theories of film spectatorship have been developed for over half a century regarding whether audiences adopt (or refuse to adopt) the ideologies that are communicated to them (Pramaggiore & Wallis, 2008: 335–6). While well-known theorists such as Theodor Adorno, Jean-Louis Baudry, Christian Metz and Laura Mulvey differ widely in their approaches, the one similarity they all share is that films *have the potential* to affect viewers. For this reason alone, it can be argued that ideology in film is an important topic of discussion.

A bit of theory

The early 'transmission' model of understanding the audience as passive receptacles of whatever messages they are given by filmmakers has long been considered redundant. Reception theory, for example, which was inspired by reader-response criticism in literary theory, has stressed the role of the audience in constructing meaning(s) from the films they watch. Roland Barthes conceived of the idea of the 'death of the author', arguing that a text only 'exists' in the act of reading (or viewing) it, and that the audience is the primary source of meaning (Phillips, 2007: 160). Other scholars contend that this idea goes too far, suggesting that a balanced approach is needed between considering the impact of a filmmaker's intentions and a viewer's response.

In one sense, no ideas are set in stone. The ideologies that define us and how we see our own and others' place in the world can, and invariably do, alter over time. We always encounter ideas that conflict with our own. In such cases, we have a choice: to change the way we think and accept the message being suggested to us, or to reject the contradictory ideology and maintain our own beliefs. Our engagement with films works in the same way. We might subconsciously accept or (perhaps more consciously) reject the ideological meanings a film is communicating to us. The second option here is termed a **resistant reading** (or viewing), where we refuse to grant legitimacy to the views and values being promoted by a film.

In order to offer a resistant reading, we obviously have to be able to identify what passive ideologies are constructed within films. Film analysis, therefore, involves being able to understand the relationship between: 1) what films are saying (ideologies); and 2) how they are saying it (through audience identification and **film techniques**). Being able to spot the points at which ideology and techniques intersect is therefore the crucial skill required for analysing films. But first, we need to understand what film techniques are and how they position us to identify with (or distance ourselves from) certain characters.

Resistant reading: a process by which a reader or viewer rejects the ideological messages a text encourages its audience to accept.

A 'visual grammar': Film and the tools of meaning-making

Just like the stories told in books, the narratives constructed in films are made up of a series of **conventions**, or codes, of which we all have a shared **intertextual** understanding (see Chapter 4). The techniques or conventions used by film-makers, such as music, camera movements and editing, are extremely powerful. Think of digitally animated films such as *Up* (2009) and *WALL-E* (2008). These films do not actually use camera technology in the way that traditional movies do, where actors stand in front of a film crew and perform—the images are created with the use of computers only. However, when you watch these films closely, you might notice that their narratives are still separated into scenes and the 'camera' cuts between these using familiar devices, such as a dissolve from one picture to the next. The filmmakers of *Finding Nemo* (2003) did not have to use these techniques, but the expectations of film audiences are so deeply ingrained that such techniques seem to be essential for a movie to be made comprehensible to its viewers, not to mention commercially successful.

It would seem that film conventions exercise considerable power over our imaginations. Due to the shared cultural experiences of any given group of people—in this case, people who watch films—we know what a certain technique 'means' even without thinking. This is, in other words, part of our intertextual understanding of the film medium. The technique itself can therefore tell us certain things: what we should think, how we should feel. When we hear a dripping tap or creaking floorboards on a movie's soundtrack, the convention creates suspense and we 'know' we are supposed to be anxious or fearful (whether or not we actually feel these emotions).

Film techniques: the various devices utilised by film-makers to construct meaning through moving images and sound.

Film techniques

	Shot size
Setting	• Establishing shot
Lighting/shadow	• Long shot
Colour	• Medium shot
Costume	• Close-up shot
Décor and props	• Extreme close-up
Acting/characterisation	• Shot-reverse shot
Dialogue	• Point of view shot

Camera movement	Editing (fast/slow)
• Tracking	• Cut
• Panning	• Wipe
• Tilting	• Dissolve
• Zooming	Soundtrack (music/sound effects)
• Hand-held	Special effects
Camera angles (high/low/eye-level)	Narration/focalisation/voiceover
Focus (deep/shallow)	Captions/titles

A key concept in film studies is **mise-en-scène**, which originated with the theatre term for 'staging'. Mise-en-scène is essentially the overall shot composition, the combination of devices used to construct what is represented within a **frame** or shot (what you see when you pause a film). This raises a crucial point in discussing film: techniques never work in isolation; their effect is a combined one. Let's return now to the notion of audience identification. How does a filmmaker position her or his audience to identify with or against certain characters of the film-maker's choosing? You may already be familiar with a number of the techniques listed in the table provided, which is far from comprehensive. There is insufficient room here to discuss all of these; however, introductory film studies texts will provide further details and examples.

Above all, it is important to remember that nothing you see or hear in a film is a simple recording of 'reality': every single detail is artificially constructed by a large number of people, from directors, to costume designers, to the actors themselves. Watch the credits rolling at the end of a movie to get a sense of this (though perhaps don't do this with a *Lord of the Rings* film). The complexity of film-making is such that even analysing a single frame frozen from a motion picture can provide a wealth of information about the interaction between film and viewer. Look at the two images provided from the recent Hollywood blockbuster *Twilight* (2008). The appeals that these images are making to our emotions and intellect may seem obvious, but the ways in which these effects are created needs to be examined closely.

Mise-en-scène: the overall shot composition of what is visually depicted on film.

Frame: the visual contents of a particular camera shot.

Figure 10.1 Edward gets to know Bella in *Twilight* (2008)

Source: Aquarius/Summit

The first image (Figure 10.1) depicts *Twilight*'s two main characters and love interests, Bella and Edward, in a romantic encounter. Perhaps most prominently, the construction of space in the scene, with both characters physically positioned very close together, enhances the focus on their developing relationship. The body gesture of Edward's character, leaning in towards Bella's face from a slightly higher angle, suggests that he is attracted to Bella and is flirting openly with her. The description so far could also be used for an image that suggested sexual harassment. So what other elements of the frame position the audience to view the tension between Bella and Edward as something else? First, the casual body language and clearly happy facial expressions suggest that the characters are relaxed in one another's company and the attraction is mutual. Additionally, the external setting of the shot allows a great deal of natural lighting to accentuate the colour (or lack thereof) of the characters' skin and clothing. The use of a light blue shirt and a green jumper that resembles the shading of the tree helps establish a calm, non-threatening mood

Figure 10.2 Edward gets to know James in *Twilight* (2008)

Source: Aquarius/Summit

for the scene, positioning the audience to identify with these characters and sympathise with their hopes of being together.

In stark contrast to the first image, the second frame (Figure 10.2) portrays a confrontation of an entirely different kind between Edward and the main villain of the film, James. Lighting is used in this shot to create a considerably more pessimistic atmosphere, namely through the shadows being cast over Edward's face. This is further emphasised in the colours of the costumes worn by the characters, which are only dark brown, black or grey. The viewer is positioned to view the situation in two different ways here. First, the focus on Edward's worried facial expression as he grasps at a dirty hand wrapped menacingly around his neck encourages the audience to sympathise with him and be concerned for his welfare (even if he is immortal).

On the other hand, viewers are clearly positioned to identify against James and reject his apparently violent character. The strategic placement of a mirror in the background allows the audience to see the contempt in his expression as he threatens to strangle Edward. The contrast in the cleanliness and dirtiness of each figure's hand, which might usually be considered an unimportant feature of one's personality, plays an integral role in the moral judgments the audience is being asked to make about the characters, therefore influencing who they will most likely identify with and against.

It is important when analysing a film not simply to describe what is happening, as this will merely result in a plot summary or synopsis. The terms highlighted in the above discussion of the *Twilight* images demonstrates the value of explicitly identifying and interpreting film conventions and their effects. If you draw on the appropriate terminology when discussing a film, such as the various techniques used, it is literally impossible to just 'describe' rather than analyse a movie.

Now, let's put all of this together in a film analysis by considering how ideologies and techniques intersect. What follows is a critical discussion of the 1997 Australian film *The Castle*, which received much national popularity and was watched widely overseas. In order to stress the kind of detailed observations that can be made in closely analysing a film, the discussion will focus primarily on the passive ideology of gender and how this is communicated in the opening ten minutes of the film. *The Castle* is readily available and it would be a good idea to watch at least the first few scenes before reading the following analysis.

Gendered power relations in *The Castle:* 'A man's house is his castle'

The Castle depicts the story of the Kerrigans, a close-knit, working-class, Australian family that finds itself in a fight with the authorities over the right to remain in their home, which has been slated for demolition. One might characterise the film's surface ideology as the value of family bonds and, following the Australian catchphrases, the right to a 'fair go' for the 'little Aussie battler' or 'underdog'. While not an explicit theme of the film, *The Castle* also reveals strongly conservative or dominant ideas about the place of men and women in the family and society, a passive ideology that is consistent throughout the narrative. The following analysis will focus on this aspect of the film. Chapter 6 revealed that gender, or the social constructions of how women and men are expected to think and behave, is often communicated through language. The **binary oppositions** of 'masculine' and 'feminine' attributes, which are seen to distinguish men and women respectively, continue to play a large part in many people's attitudes and behaviour, and, as you will see, in this film.

> **Binary oppositions:** the construction of a clear-cut distinction between two concepts that are perceived to be opposites, with one concept dominant over the other.

The pervasiveness of gendered ideologies

Essentially all films, even those without human characters, contain (usually passive and usually dominant) ideological messages about gender. Ideologies of gender are so powerful that movies portraying animals, robots or alien creatures, such as children's animations, still have characters that are obviously intended to be viewed as male or female. Think about how they are generally portrayed in these films. Do they communicate dominant or subversive ideas? Of course, gendered ideologies are only one form of passive ideology that we should be aware of, as films also frequently communicate ideas about socio-economic class, ethnicity and 'race', age, disability and sexuality, among countless other issues relevant to the contemporary world.

'My name is Dale Kerrigan. And this is my story.' *The Castle* begins with this apparently simplistic line of dialogue, yet a lot of information can be taken from this alone. Most obviously, the character Dale is identified as the narrator of the story the film will tell. The initial close-up, eye-level shot of Dale in front of a black background suggests that Dale-as-narrator exists outside the constructed narrative; however, this is an artificial device that serves an important function. Dale's personal reflections on all members and aspects of the Kerrigan family throughout the first scene reveal that he is positioned as the **focaliser** of the story.

Focalisation is essentially 'the anchoring of narrative discourse to a specific subject position [or character] in the story' (Fulton et al., 2005: 89), similar to the narrative point of view in novels we read. As the narrator and focaliser of the story, Dale is granted authority by the film-makers, positioning the audience to view what he says as important. At the same time, Dale's simple, even naïve, dialogue encourages viewers to see him as innocent, childlike and, above all, trustworthy. Therefore, the overwhelming attention Dale—and therefore the film's narrative—gives to his father, Darryl Kerrigan, is naturalised.

> **Focaliser:** the subject position or character through which a viewer is positioned to understand a **narrative**.

Early in *The Castle*, Dale's narrative voiceover comments that his father 'reckons power lines are a reminder of man's ability to generate electricity. He's always saying great things like that. That's why we love him so much'. The language used regarding 'man's ability' can be seen to passively communicate a gendered idea about who is responsible for 'human progress'. This is one of many examples in which Darryl's character is idolised by Dale, whose dialogue characterises Darryl as the 'head of the family'—or, in other words, its most important member. The male character's central place of leadership in/of the family is further emphasised through Dale's selection of Father's Day to describe the family's love of giving and receiving presents. A medium shot portrays the family sitting around a couch, with Darryl situated in the centre of the frame. The focus on Darryl by both the camera and the family positions the audience to view his opinions and activities as the most worthy of attention, to sympathise with his views, and to regard the lives of the women in the family as less important.

It is significant that Dale's descriptions of all other family members rely on their relationship to Darryl and his evaluation of them. This is particularly the case in the brief portrayal of Sal, the family's maternal figure, who is marginalised throughout the scene. Despite the fact she has a part-time job, her ability to cook for the family is the main quality that is focused on in the short depiction of her role. As Dale states, 'Dad reckons Mum is the greatest cook on Earth'. The uneven power relations in the marriage are also shown when Darryl decides to build a patio. Standing prominently next to his much shorter wife in the middle of the frame, Darryl ignores her worried facial expression and suggestion that 'we finish the back room first'. Upon his dismissal of her idea, the camera cuts immediately to the next scene, allowing no opportunity for her to make her case further.

The daughter of the family, Tracy, is given more screen time than Sal, although the viewer is positioned to see her only as, in Dale's words, his father's 'favourite' child, who 'constantly gave Dad proud moments'. The sentimental musical score, which is heard while Darryl stares lovingly at Tracy's framed TAFE graduation certificate, encourages the viewer to adopt the father's perspective, focusing attention once again on Darryl's role in the family. Furthermore, when Dale recounts Tracy's decision to take up kickboxing, which would seem to have the potential to subvert gender norms, it is revealed that she only did so because she was following her husband's lead.

There are many other elements of this scene alone, and of course the rest of the film, that promote unequal power relations between men and women. The editing of the many shots or sequences of shots in this scene enables all aspects of the family to be immediately related back to Darryl. Interestingly, the cuts between Darryl's towtruck, his speedboat, his pet greyhounds and his 'pool room' seem to suggest that he is practically the only family member who has any substantial possessions. Indeed, the title of the film itself, which is connected to the well-known saying that 'a man's house is his castle', also reinforces the film's gendered ideology. Dale's voiceover suggests as much at the end of the film's introductory scene, declaring that 'all in all, 3 Highview Crescent was a happy home. Dad called it his castle'.

One potential counterargument to the above analysis is that the makers of *The Castle* are 'just making fun' of people like this. The genre of the film—a comedy—should also be taken into account, as the use of humour always has ideological consequences. Whether we are asked to 'laugh at' or 'laugh with' certain characters, we should always think about what effects this has. It is true that the filmmakers of *The Castle* are constantly playing with **stereotypes**—simplistic, generalised versions or representations of a particular group of people. However, the many comedic moments in the film serve only to make the family—and Darryl in particular—likeable to the audience, and never question the gendered ideological messages beneath the film's surface.

Stereotypes: simplistic, generalised versions or representations of a particular group of people.

One last piece of advice: the most effective way to analyse a film is to watch it, or at least the relevant scenes, a number of times. Particularly when starting out, this is the only way to spot the use of specific film devices and think about their effects. Pausing and rewinding the film while taking notes is a good method. Your remote control is your best friend! Enjoy!

Summary

This chapter has demonstrated that:
- In positioning us to identify with or against certain characters, film-makers undertake a complex process of meaning-making.
- It is important to critically engage with films in order to understand what ideologies are being constructed within their narratives.
- Ideologies of various kinds are (often unconsciously and implicitly) communicated to audiences through the use of film techniques.
- There is potential for films to subvert dominant ideologies by offering positive representations of marginalised groups.
- There remains the danger of stereotyping and discrimination in films against those with less social and political power.

Further reading

Baran, S J 2010, *Introduction to Mass Communication: Media Literacy and Culture*, 6th edn, McGraw-Hill, New York.

Fulton, H, Huisman, R, Murphet, J & Dunn, A (eds) 2005, *Narrative and Media*, Cambridge University Press, Port Melbourne.

Hayward, S 2007, *Cinema Studies: The Key Concepts*, 3rd edn, Routledge, London & New York.

Phillips, P 2007, 'Spectator, Audience and Response', in J Nelmes (ed.), *Introduction to Film Studies*, 4th edn, Routledge, London & New York, 143–71.

Pramaggiore, M & Wallis, T 2008, *Film: A Critical Introduction*, 2nd edn, Laurence King, London.

Sturken, M & Cartwright, L 2001, *Practices of Looking: An Introduction to Visual Culture*, Oxford University Press, Oxford & New York.

Weblinks

For revision questions, please visit www.oup.com.au/orc/chalkley.

chapter 11

Organisational/ Professional Communication: Modelling the World of Work

Tony Chalkley

Uniforms, work photos and a hug from the boss

On Sunday evening, as the family sits and watches the television, they take turns to press one item each from their overflowing ironing basket. As they work, both Mr and Mrs X receive messages on their phones. Mostly, they email back their replies, but one message is so serious, Mr X steps outside to phone the person, in order to speak directly to them. At around 9pm, Ms X's work roster for the next week is finally emailed to her. As the son has been off work, unwell, he checks his work Facebook group to find that the office soccer team has won the semi-final. The photos of his boss intoxicated, with his shirt off and his arm around an uncomfortable looking young colleague is not such good news. He decides not to post a comment on the photo, as fellow workers have been unkind enough already.

The family all take turns with the iron, and by the end of the evening the room is filled with freshly pressed garments. The result: a significant pile of business shirts, three logo-embroidered jackets, four uniforms, one netball skirt, three ties and a scout uniform that has been in the very bottom of the basket for years.

What you will learn from this chapter

- What the phrase 'organisational communication' means
- How a new form of organisational communication called 'digital/mediated' communication is transforming the workplace
- How email and other forms of electronic communication have changed the way we communicate at work and, consequently, the 'world of work' in general
- How a number of new problems are really a case of 'same old problem, different communication media'
- That organisational communication is not new: Egyptian builders, factory managers, blacksmiths and members of the clergy (and many others) have long relied on 'good' organisational communication to get their message across
- 'Organisational' communication is not a distinct entity: it is constructed from and by the talk of individuals. When we criticise an organisational communication system, do we criticise ourselves?

Introduction

Organisational communication is incredibly complex and interconnected and most of us do it every day. As a result of this interconnection, this complexity, you will revisit and revise topics such as non-verbal communication, surveillance and social construction. There are a number of ways to understand organisational communication.

Some theorists argue that it should be viewed as a 'science' and the proponents of 'scientific' organisational communication argue that, after studying, dissecting and cataloguing the rudiments of organisational communication, it is possible to better understand, manage, manipulate and control how effectively organisations work.

Some communication theorists (such as Nobel Laureate Herbert Simon) argue that it's not that simple and that communication is not best studied through the application of 'pure science'. These theorists believe that organisations are best examined through a rubric of social construction. This approach is favoured because organisations are made up of individuals, some of which may behave in a predictable and rational manner, but most do not. Social constructionists argue that some individuals share the organisational goals promoted by their workplace and some do not. The nature of communication is influenced by the experience, values, attitudes, behaviour and actions of the individual staff members.

Finally, some communication theorists argue that 'Communication is primarily a mechanical process, in which a message is constructed and encoded by a sender, transmitted through some channel, then received and decoded by a receiver. Distortion, represented as any differences between the original and the received messages, can and ought to be identified and reduced or eliminated'. (This is a quote from one of many 'organisational communication' groups on Facebook, but by the time this book went to press, it had become inactive! Many more have sprung up in its place.)

In this chapter, you will discover that all of these very different approaches to understanding organisational communication are helpful because they assist us to better appreciate the complexity of organisation(s), the challenge of communicating with/in a diverse workforce and the difficulty of interaction when stakeholders have different (sometimes conflicting) values and priorities.

(Note: the primary focus of this chapter is the workplace, but all of the concepts covered here apply also to other organisations: tennis clubs, churches, social groups, retirement villages, student clubs and book groups are all organisations!)

First, what exactly is organisational communication?

In this text, 'organisational communication' is defined as 'the sending and receiving of messages among interconnected individuals in a particular environment, workplace or organisation in an effort to work towards individual and shared goals'. Organisational communication is a complex practice that is culturally dependent, and is not easily isolated from the many other practices of our daily message-making (for example, talking to your family and friends about your work is a form of organisational communication, as is using the vernacular of your work in everyday life). One of the most significant challenges for organisational theorists is the fact that the nature (and definition) of organisational communication is ever-changing: individuals have traditionally sent messages through face-to-face interaction and written correspondence, but in the second section of this chapter, you will read how, increasingly, members of organisations now communicate in a technologically mediated way (for example, email) (Gorman & McLean, 2009).

Irrespective of the medium used, the majority of organisational communication aims to build relationships, or establish an ongoing pattern of successful interpersonal interaction between the individuals connected to the organisation. 'Good' organisational communicators do this both with internal organisational members (for example, workmates) and interested external publics (for example, customers and outside stakeholders). As you read through this chapter, you will notice that there are a number of common characteristics in all the definitions of organisational communication. A search of the internet will uncover many thousands of documents about communication in organisations, some very scientific, some very theoretical, some very **new age** and some a mixture of all of these.

Rather than attempt to comprehend the content of these many thousands of documents, here is a really simple description of what organisational communication is and how it works:

* It occurs within a complex open system which is influenced by, and influences, its internal and external surroundings.
* It involves messages and their flow, purpose, direction and media.
* It involves people and their attitudes, feelings, relationships and skills.
  Organisational communication is important because it helps us to:
* Accomplish important day-to-day tasks in order to 'succeed' (for example, meeting targets in industry, working together as a community and participating at school)
* Understand and cope with organisational change
* Successfully complete mundane (but important) tasks through the application of organisational policy, procedure and regulation
* Develop relationships where 'human messages are directed at people within the organisation—their attitudes, morale, satisfaction, and fulfilment' (Goldhaber, 1990: 20)
* Coordinate, plan and control the operations of organisations through what is commonly referred to as 'management'.

New age: a philosophy, originating in the late 1980s, characterised by a belief in alternative medicine, astrology, spiritualism, etc.

Organisational communication is how workplaces, clubs and other organised groups constitute, represent and share the climate and culture of the group, telling 'outsiders' about the attitudes, values and goals that characterise the organisation and its members.

For any organisation to be successful, it must have competent and skilled communicators. Research has found that prospective employers (that is, representatives from organisations) seek people who can follow and give instructions, listen precisely, provide useful feedback, relate to both workmates and customers, 'network', provide practical assistance, work well in teams (even poorly structured, dysfunctional teams), and creatively and critically solve problems and present ideas in an understandable manner. In other words, in order to develop 'good' communicators, organisations need to realise that:

> Developing organisational communication awareness and effectiveness is more than just having know-how or knowledge. Efficient organizational communication involves knowing how to create and exchange information, work with diverse groups or individuals, communicate in complicated and changing circumstances, as well as having the aptitude or motivation to communicate in appropriate manners.

For more on organisational communication, see the source of this definition: http://en.wikibooks.org/wiki/Survey_of_Communication_Study/Chapter_11_-_Organizational_Communication.

Digital/mediated communication: The modern world of organisational communication

Most of us will be familiar with digital/mediated communication and use it each and every day. Businesses depend on mediated communication to connect with customers and we, the customers, are annoyed and inconvenienced when it fails. Digital/mediated communication is best understood as any form of communication that uses a 'third party' to transmit a message (mostly, this third party will be some form of technology). The majority of readers will probably have had extensive experience with mediated communication: using a telephone, a fax machine, online messaging, Facebook or perhaps, many years ago, a horse-riding messenger! Mediated communication has resulted in a number of significant transformations to the way we work—some good, some bad. This problem is not a new one, nor is it exclusively a 'new media' problem. The introduction of telephones and pagers into homes also changed the concept of privacy and 'down-time', and introduced the possibility that workers might now be 'on call', available to their boss and co-workers at the press of a few buttons. The arrival of the smartphone introduced an added dimension: your 'office desk' was now a device that could fit in your pocket! The smartphone changed the way we work by introducing the possibility that we might always be at work. For some, this had dire consequences. In 2009, Reuters reported that for France Telecom staff, this constant connectedness meant that work had gradually and negatively encroached on workers' personal lives (Carew, 2009). Sadly, since 2008, 22 workers had committed suicide and another 13 had attempted to kill themselves. Some managers believe that, to some degree, a lack of rest, relaxation and personal space has contributed to this phenomenon.

What does this mean? When staff feel that they are never off duty and rarely off guard, it seems logical that they will feel a great deal of pressure to always be at their [digital] desk. These exciting new technologies have blurred the long-standing boundary between 'work' and 'play' by refining the construction of personal and public life (and vice versa).

The Carew article was not so much about mediated communication itself—it's more about the impact of mediated communication on our daily life, the popularity of mobile technology, increasing pressure for workers to be available 24/7, affordable phone and data charging and the popularity of mobile new media devices (for example, the laptop as a portable office). Mediated communication is not to blame for the increasing number of stressed out workers but it has contributed to the problem because mediation is now cheap, popular and fast. Most of us will know or have encountered someone who is always on their mobile, always 'at work' and increasingly unable to 'turn off'.

Mediated communication is not all bad! The very accessibility that has workers stressed out also makes it possible to work from home, it allows people with disabilities to contribute in ways that were not available ten years ago and it has enabled small business to compete, expand and grow. Most of us enjoy the connections created through Facebook, appreciate the simplicity of digital photos shared in a 'cloud' and feel more connected and informed as a result of email.

For organisations, mediated communication reduces the isolation created by offices separated by geography; it also allows staff to communicate in ways that are fast and efficient; and reduces the environmental impact of print, post and copying. It does have its risks, though. In my local area, a copy of a rude and abusive (and real as it turns out!) email was spread via **viral distribution**.

Viral distribution: spread by distribution, from person to person.

I received a copy and while it was amusing to read, it also had some diabolical consequences for the sender. Here is how the local paper represented the story:

Abusive message sent by mistake spreads over internet

Kerri-Ann Hobbs

The Geelong Advertiser

1 August 2009

A Geelong account manager's internet brain fade has cost her her job because she mistakenly sent a foul tirade to a client.

The email, in which she called the client a 'd--k' and said he was 'f----d in the head', has become an overnight internet hit, with its 'viral' spread seeing it pop up in inboxes all over the globe.

The woman appears to have accidentally sent her abusive email back to her client instead of to a colleague, causing her sacking and the client to cancel his account with her company.

But her victim, a prominent Geelong businessman, didn't resort to name calling; he merely replied that he would terminate all agreements with the woman's company and would then send the explosive email to other company heads in the region.

Email is an excellent organisational communication tool which works best when those communicating are skilled, considered and understand the nature of the device that is mediating their message-making. The 'reply' button commands respect; once sent, an email is around forever, and with the signs and symbols of non-verbal communication removed, an email message is very easily misread and misinterpreted. In the case of the story above, simply by clicking the 'reply all' tab and writing down her frustration, the sender lost her job.

But how did we get here? How did we arrive in a world with instant and potentially 'deadly' email, Facebook postings that can cost you your job and an environment where a negative online campaign can cost organisations many hundreds of thousands of dollars?

A brief history of organisations and communication

If there is any great secret of success in life, it lies in the ability to put yourself in the other person's place and to see things from his point of view—as well as your own.

(Henry Ford, 1926)

Organisational communication is not new. Ancient Egyptian society had communication rules and sophisticated records for technical information, many thousands of slaves were observed and managed by a matrix of interpersonal communication, and the production of complex plans and drawings allowed Egyptian builders to construct structures that were both incredibly intricate and vast (Kemp, 2006). As early as the fourth century, scholars in China examined the 'problems of communicating within the vast government bureaucracy as well as between the government and the people' (Murphy et al., 1997: 7). These ancient Eastern scholars focused on information flow, message fidelity and quality of information within their governmental bureaucracy (Krone et al., 1992). These are still, even today, the key elements of successful organisational communication! Later still, the industrial revolution bought about significant, irreversible changes to the way people lived and worked, but the revolution also ushered in new ways of communicating, managing staff and ensuring that a large and disconnected workforce worked to the same rules, plans and goals. In more recent times, communication is conducted by telephone, video conference, email and many other digitally mediated forms.

Later in this chapter you will learn how 'models' are a useful way to understand the complex theories, concepts and practices that make up the matrix of organisational communication. There are numerous models in existence and probably many more being written as you read this, but two communication theorists really stand out in history of communication: Frederick Taylor (1947) and Max Weber (1947). Taylor is famous not so much for his work in communication, but more for the result his ideas had on communication. The key to his work was what he called 'the four Principles of Scientific Management'. These principles are:

1   Change longstanding and informal work processes with methods based on a scientific study of staff responsibilities

2   Scientifically choose, teach, and develop the individual worker rather than allowing them (and their peers) to train themselves

3   Collaborate with the workers to ensure that the 'scientifically' developed methods are being followed

4   Divide work nearly equally between managers and workers; the managers then apply scientific management principles to planning the work and the workers undertake the tasks.

These principles were implemented by many industries, immediately increasing productivity, speeding up production and increasing profits. But these principles had a downside: 'Taylorised' work was dull, repetitive and boring. Staff became isolated, rarely were they challenged to problem-solve or work collaboratively, and the camaraderie of the factory floor was diminished and in some cases disappeared entirely. Taylor's model had a powerful effect on the practice of organisational communication (especially at the front line) and these principles seem to be deeply entrenched in the practices of some modern-day factories and workplaces.

Maximilian Carl Emil ('Max') Weber was a little different. While Taylor's interest in organisations was its practical elements, Weber's interest was more theoretical; in particular, the idea of 'bureaucracy' in organisations. Weber devised what he called an 'ideal type' of bureaucracy: these were organisations with elaborate hierarchical structures that served to divide up the labour of the workplace by rigid enforcement of explicit rules (that were formally and consistently applied). Weber's 'ideal bureaucracy' would be staffed by full-time, life-long professionals, who do not 'own' the 'means of administration', or control the priorities of their work or the sources of their funds (in other words, the means of production). Instead, staff would receive a predetermined annual salary, which would not come from the income/profit derived directly from the performance of their job. Does this description sound familiar? It should, because the above characteristics include many features found in the modern public service and large private industries that are staffed by salaried professionals.

Weber's ideas struggled to work in the 'real world'. The reason is simple: when you attempt to implement Weber's ideas with 'real people' in 'real organisations', things go wrong. Weber's first and most significant issue was that even though bureaucracies are (in theory) highly rational, people aren't! Managers in 'Weber-ised' organisations would need to expend significant energy making certain that staff were gathered in what Weber called 'the iron cage of rationality' (Weber, 1968). Because people are irrational, ambitious, curious, social beings, Weber's theories work well to frame the structure of an organisation, but struggle to control and direct the communication of individuals. Most social constructionists would simply shake their heads in disbelief at Weber's attempts to implement an 'ideal bureaucracy'.

It's important to note that the modern organisation now relies on digital/mediated communication to transmit what Weber called 'rational messages' in order to ensure 'rigid enforcement of explicit rules'. What Foucault tells us is that individual agents (the staff) then use narrative to resist, conform to and de-construct these messages! Organisational communication is sometimes a never-ending tug of war!

Models help us understand the complexity of communication

> Dwight Schrute: Studies show that more information is passed through water cooler gossip than through official memos, which puts me at a disadvantage because [picks up water bottle] I bring my own water to work.
>
> (*The Office*, US version, Winter Season, 2005)

The work of Taylor and Weber is useful to develop a basic understanding of what exactly constitutes 'an organisation', how it is structured and how members communicate, but the models in the following section take a different approach to understanding organisational communication. The following models examine the role of the individual, the culture of the organisation and the production of messages. They are directly focused on the 'producers of messages' and the 'makers of meaning'.

The first model (Robbins & Barnwell, 2006) examines the culture of organisations and evaluates the 'health' of the workplace by posing a number of questions. The second model (Belbin, 2010) is focused on the role of individual team players. As you read the descriptions and discussions, you might like to evaluate your our team work and see where you fit on the Belbin inventory. The final model (Gibb) attempts to define what makes for a 'positive climate' in which to send and receive messages. Gibb attempts to identify what 'exactly' makes a good message and how managers might better develop the skills needed to be a producer of positive meaning.

First, Robbins and Barnwell identified the following key elements that work to make a positive workplace and, as a result, influence the success (or otherwise) of business communication:

Individual initiative—how much freedom and independence do members have?

Risk Tolerance—are employees encouraged to 'go out on a limb'?

Direction—is it clear what the organisation does and stands for?

Integration—are groups in the organisation coordinated?

Management contact—how accessible are the leaders and senior staff?

Control—to what degree do rules and regulations govern the behaviour of staff?

Identity—are staff encouraged to identify with the company image?

Performance—is individual performance rewarded, or group, or both?

Conflict tolerance—is there a mechanism to positively use conflict?

Communication patterns—are they hierarchical or diverse?

(Paraphrased from Robbins & Barnwell, 2006)

A quick glance at this list should allow you to identify what type of organisation you work in. Are you allowed a good deal of independence to take control of and work on risky projects, with open access to your senior managers, confident in the knowledge that you will be rewarded for your efforts? Or is your work very prescriptive, tightly controlled, undertaken in an environment where isolated teams work to task, with little or no reward beyond a pay packet? Robbins and Barnwell theorised that the nature of the organisation (as described in the characteristics above) will directly affect the nature of its communication. This makes sense: a company such as Google, for example, with relatively flat structures and the 'ten things we know to be true' philosophy (see the end of this chapter for what those things are) promotes the idea of open, fluid and flexible communication between members of all levels of the organisation.

Conversely, members of an old, well-established 'traditional' law firm might experience a very different form of organisational communication. This type of organisation is traditionally arranged in a very hierarchical manner, with the most senior staff (often called 'partners') having very clear power and authority that requires little or no contact with the more junior staff. This type of organisation has very rigid lines of communication, clear rules around 'who says and does what' in the workplace and well-established and historically significant formal patterns of communication. Both these types of organisations would provide very different (even polarised) answers to Robbins and Barnwell's ten questions about communication.

The next communication theorist, Meredith Belbin, suggested that the best way to understand organisation communication is to first understand the type of people that make up these organisations. To do this, he came up with the following 'team roles':

Plant

Plants are creative, unorthodox and a generator of ideas. If an innovative solution to a problem is needed, a Plant is a good person to request help from.

Resource Investigator

The Resource Investigator gives a team a rush of enthusiasm at the start of the project by vigorously pursuing contacts and opportunities.

Coordinator

A Coordinator is a likely candidate for the leader of a team, since they have a talent for stepping back to see the big picture. Coordinators are confident, stable and mature and, because they recognise abilities in others, they are very good at delegating tasks to the right person for the job.

Shaper

The Shaper is a task-focused individual who pursues objectives with vigour and who is driven by nervous energy and the need to achieve—for the Shaper, winning is the name of the game.

Monitor Evaluator

Monitor Evaluators are fair and logical observers and judges of what is going on in the team. Since they are good at detaching themselves from bias, they are often the ones to see all available options with the greatest clarity and impartiality.

Teamworker

A Teamworker is the oil between the cogs that keeps the machine (the team) running smoothly. They are good listeners and diplomats, talented at smoothing over conflicts and helping parties under-stand one another without becoming confrontational.

Implementer

The Implementer takes their colleagues' suggestions and ideas and turns them into positive action. They are efficient and self-disciplined, and can always be relied on to deliver on time.

Completer Finisher

The Completer Finisher is a perfectionist and will often go the extra mile to make sure everything is 'just right,' and the things he or she delivers can be trusted to have been double-checked and then checked again.

Specialist

Specialists are passionate about learning in their own particular field. As a result, they are likely to be a fount of knowledge and will enjoy imparting this knowledge to others. They also strive to improve and build upon their expertise.

(For more detail, visit: www.belbin.com)

As you read through this list of team roles, it's possible to identify with a number of the charac-teristics and even disagree with some of the descriptors. Belbin believes that this is often the case; we perform different roles in different situations and alter our communication as we deem appropriate. Belbin's inventory is interesting and thought provoking, but how does it impact on organisational communication? These roles are important because they allow us to deconstruct the complex process of organisational message-making and to then examine the role of each individual element (that is, 'people') in the process. Belbin argued that in order for teams (and therefore, organisations) to communicate effectively, work together and be productive, they needed to have a mix of his nine types of team roles.

The final model, Gibb's model of a 'positive climate', introduces the idea that there are catego-ries of 'defensive' and 'supportive' communication that stem from our behaviour. Gibb proposed a number of behaviour types than can 'boil' or 'freeze' the communication climate.

These types are:

Defensive and Supportive Message Behaviour	
A *supportive* communication climate encourages open, constructive, honest and effective interaction. A *defensive* climate, on the other hand, leads to competitive and destructive conflict. The skilled organisational communicator endeavours to maintain a supportive communication climate.	
Defensive Behaviour	**Supportive Behaviour**
Evaluative: The evaluative message is engulfed in judgment. The message can be blatantly evaluative or can carry non-verbal overtones of judgment. 'When are you going to start coming to meetings prepared?'	*Descriptive*: Descriptive messages are clear and specific assertions. The creator of descriptive messages strives to avoid loaded words and is aware of non-verbal cues.
Control: Control messages are not honest attempts to persuade, but rather, attempts to impose one's will on others by coercion or manipulation.	*Problem Orientation*: This message poses an invitation to the group to work together on finding a solution to a mutual problem. This approach focuses on the issues.
Strategy: Strategic messages convey an air of deceiving, or misleading. Although the receiver's perception plays a central role, speakers should attempt to avoid producing strategic messages.	*Spontaneity*: Spontaneous messages are characterised by openness and honesty. This forthright message indicates that the speaker's contribution is unplanned and free of ulterior motives.
Neutrality: The neutral message demonstrates a lack of empathy or interest: 'I don't care what my team members do.'	*Empathy*: The empathetic message is responsive to others' feelings and thoughts. It conveys understanding and interest.
Superiority: These messages not only attempt to portray the speaker as superior but also imply the inferiority or inadequacy of the listener. These messages also discourage interaction since the speaker is indicating a lack of desire for input or feedback.	*Equality*: These messages indicate worth in the other and in others' contributions. An equality message asks for others' input and follows up with confirmation or clarification of others' comments.
Certainty: Certainty messages portray something as an absolute. The creator of these messages sees the world in black and white, and believes to have a corner on the reality market.	*Provisionalism*: The provisional message poses a point of view, but with an open attitude. This is an invitation to investigate or explore alternatives.

(Gibb, 1961: 141–8)

The above typology is by no means comprehensive and, similar to your experience with the previous models, you may find that you disagree with the generalised nature of the categories. In some organisations we move between supportive and defensive behaviour, some staff seem able to only use controlling and evaluative messages and yet some take a prescriptive, problem oriented approach. The best time to critique which of these message types dominates your workplace is to observe what happens when things go wrong. As workers and managers react to a problem, you should observe how senior staff respond, which Belbin characteristics workers exhibit and monitor whether the solution to the problem is communicated in a supportive or defensive manner.

'What we have here is a failure to communicate.'

(Cleveland Brown in *Family Guy*, quoting the film *Cool Hand Luke*)

It is important to note that the nature of meaning-making is determined by many factors: the content of the utterance (is it good or bad news?), the context of the message, interference (often referred to as 'noise'), non-verbal contributions and many other factors influence whether the message is perceived in a positive or negative manner. A really useful exercise is to combine the work of Taylor, Weber, Barnwell, Robbins, Belbin and Gibb to produce a 'matrix of models'. Doing this will provide an insight into the complex process of messages, meaning and organisational communication.

So far, this chapter has focused on verbal and written communication, but there is another powerful form of organisational communication (particularly to 'outsiders') and this is the non-verbal communication of uniforms.

Uniforms: What do they 'say'?

First, read this newspaper article about the proposal to change the uniform issued to the Victorian Police:

New Victoria Police uniform 'to give cops harder edge'

- First uniform overhaul since 1979
- New look to toughen up officers
- Plans for cargo pants and dark colours

Police in Victoria are to get new uniforms so officers can command more respect on the streets.

The outfit is likely to be dark blue, similar to the uniform worn by New York Police, the *Herald Sun* reports.

Cargo pants could be part of the new look, which will cost taxpayers millions of dollars.

It is the first overhaul of the uniform since 1979 and is backed by the state's top cop, Simon Overland.

The Chief Commissioner and other senior officers believe the sky blue shirts worn by police for the past 30 years are seen by the public as 'soft'.

Mr Overland has written to police about the possibility of a new uniform and 'the impact it has on community perception and behaviour'.

Police want Victorians to provide feedback on the change. A committee led by Deputy Commissioner Ken Lay has been established to oversee the new uniform, with first designs just weeks away.

Victoria Police believes its current uniform is 'too soft' and wants to harden it up with darker colours

Source: Newspix/Craig Burrow

The uniform worn by officers from 1925 to 1959, when it was relatively easy to command respect on the streets

Source: Victoria Police Image Library

Victoria Police is looking at uniforms worn by New York cops for inspiration

Source: Getty Images for IMG/Katy Winn

Cargo pants and breathable fabrics are being considered to fit in with the force's new protective vests, which are now being rolled out.

The committee has been looking at uniforms worn in the UK and New York.

Young officers want a hard-edge look. 'There's a lot of research to say darker colours are professional. These are the things we're looking at,' committee member Acting Supt Debra Abbott said.

Women officers have complained that standard-issue pants do not flatter their hips.

Ceremonial uniforms—used for graduations, funerals and court appearances—could be phased out for most rank-and-file police.

The blue and white chequered band, a world-wide police symbol, will remain.

Research by the committee has also revealed police want innovative or 'smart' fabrics, shirts to be breathable and odour-resistant, pants to be less restrictive, longer female shirts with pockets, and lightweight boots.

Supt Abbott said officers wanted uniforms that met the demands of modern-day policing. 'This is not about fluffing around with the uniform when there are much more pressing issues we have to address,' she said.

'We've got new equipment, such as our new vests and semi-automatic pistols, and they have to work with the uniform. We want to have more of an impact.'

Police Association secretary Greg Davies said changes should be practical and police should be immediately identifiable.

But he said more police on the beat, rather than a change of colour, would earn respect on the streets.

(*Herald Sun*, 2010)

This is an interesting article because it articulates a commonly held belief that uniforms 'say' a great deal about the organisation they represent (in this case, the police). The various commentators quoted in this newspaper article use phrases such as 'impact', 'respect' 'professional', 'soft' and 'harden up' to describe how the police service (formerly known as the police 'force', a name change which is, in itself, interesting) needs a uniform that communicates power, authority, strength and, perhaps, just a little bit of fear. Is it possible to use clothing to change people's perception? You may recall the story about the X family visiting the doctor (see Chapter 5).

> On a recent beach holiday, Family X had to visit a medical centre in order to clean and suture a cut on the foot of their 'wannabe' surfer son. As they sat in the waiting room, Mrs X noticed something that disturbed her about the doctor.
> He was young, which is not really a problem. But he was wearing a pair of oversized shorts with huge flowers on them, his shoes were Crocs and his T-shirt had an enormous screen print of a dog with 'poo' shooting out its anus. This was an issue because their usual doctor back home wore a tie, or if the weather was hot, just a collared shirt, slacks, simple leather shoes and a white jacket for examinations.
> Generally, we have expectations for the appearance of professions and those individuals we call professionals. The doctor in the Mambo 'poo-shooter' shirt disrupted the expectations of Mrs X because, to her, this is not the way a 'doctor' should appear.

Uniforms are a form of symbolic representation (that is, a **semiotic device**) and we rely on them to quickly and efficiently tell us about the nature of the organisation and its members. Nurses wear them, construction workers have them, supermarket staff wear them and you need only glance around you to see many other examples. Even organisations that do not have a formal uniform often have a type of 'uniform'. Most teachers do not have a uniform, yet are required to meet dress standards; you expect your university professor to 'dress like one'; and Mrs X clearly has expectations of what a doctor 'should look like'.

Uniforms provide a form of communication 'short-cut'. A quick glance at the grey uniform, utility belt, gun and sunglasses tells me that the man with the trolley is from a secure cash delivery service; and the white shirt, tie, black trousers and pushbike allowed me to identify the representatives of the Church of Latter Day Saints ('Mormons') even before they knocked on my door. Uniforms can also be deceptive. For example, the security guards at my local shopping centre wear uniforms that, at first glance, look very similar to that of the police. Also, a group of people have been 'conning' local residents into paying a deposit on a driveway treatment that never appears. The newspaper described these people as wearing a 'standard road workers uniform'. Uniforms are a very effective and powerful form of organisational communication. They work to guide us to assistance, they signal 'professionalism' and communicate (without words) the role, status and function of the people around us (Taylor & Cooren, 1997).

Semiotic device: an action of or pertaining to signs.

Conclusion

Like so many of the topics covered in this book, organisational communication is complex. In this chapter you have read how a number of communication theorists have attempted to describe this complexity and understand the nature of organisation communication. They have employed models, measurements, experiments and many other devices to deconstruct and explain how organisations work and how the members of these organisations communicate.

The biggest challenge for those attempting to understand organisations is the fact that the people who make up organisations are not easily studied; people are irrational and 'unscientific', and rarely do they communicate in the same way every time!

Summary

The work of these communication theorists tells us that:

- In order for an organisation to be successful, its members rely on 'healthy' communication.
- There are many and varied models of organisational communication, each with strengths and weaknesses.
- As individual team members we employ a number of constructive and destructive strategies to get our message across.
- Technology is/has reformed the way organisations communicate, in good and bad ways.
- Organisational communication is not just printed and spoken word. Non-verbal cues such as uniforms play an important role here too.

Further reading

Belbin, M 2010, 'Home to Belbin Team Roles', retrieved 1 September 2010, <http://www.belbin.com>.

Gibb, J 1961, 'Defensive Communication', *Journal of Communication*, vol. 11, 141–8.

Gorman, L & McLean, D 2009, *Media and Society into the 21st Century: A Historical Introduction*, 2nd edn, Wiley-Blackwell, Malden & Oxford.

Kemp, B 2006, *Ancient Egypt: Anatomy of a Civilisation*, Routledge, Oxford.

Krone, K, Garrett, M & Chen, L 1992, 'Managerial Communication Practices in Chinese Factories: A Preliminary Investigation', *Journal of Business Communication*, vol. 29, no. 3, 229–52.

Murphy, H, Hildebrandt, H & Thomas, P 1997, *Effective Business Communications*, 7th edn, McGraw-Hill, New York.

Robbins, S & Barnwell, N 2006, *Organisation Theory: Concepts and Cases*, Prentice Hall, Frenchs Forest.

Taylor, F 1947, *The Principles of Scientific Management*, Harper & Brothers, New York.

Taylor, J & Cooren, F 1997, 'What Makes Communication "Organizational"? How the Many Voices of a Collectivity Become the One Voice of an Organization', *Journal of Pragmatics*, vol. 27, 409–38.

Weber, M 1947, *Max Weber: The Theory of Social and Economic Organization*, Free Press, New York.

Weber, M 1968, *Economy and Society*, Bedminister Press, New York.

Weblinks

Belbin Team Roles: www.belbin.com

The Age newspaper: www.theage.com.au

The Geelong Advertiser newspaper: www.geelongadvertiser.com.au

For revision questions, please visit www.oup.com.au/orc/chalkley.

12

Values, Ideals and Power in the Brave New Digital World

Toija Cinque

Ms X states the implications for keeping a digital low profile

With the hope that the old mobile phone number still works, Ms X sends a text to her friend from high school:

'Hey J, I just tried to find you on Facebook ... you don't exist!'

What you will learn from this chapter

This chapter introduces you to the innovation of the internet. Specifically, you will learn:

- How the internet differs as a new media form
- About how it works (packet switching, TCP/IP, the WWW)
- How our values differ in terms of ethics and regulation
- What is possible in terms of regulation of the internet.

Introduction

You can hardly ignore the internet. Even though it has only achieved major public acceptance since the early 1990s, it seems to be everywhere in developed nations. The way the internet operates as a decentralised communication system was premised on the open/freedom-loving values of the hippy counter-culture movement on the west coast of the United States during the 1960s. The development of a data transmission mode called **HTML** (Hyper Text Mark-up Language) by English researcher Tim Berners Lee, working at the European Particle Physics Research Centre, meant that information could be easily shared between users in the research sector. Use of the internet became more prevalent in the public sector when a ruling that it not be used for commercial purposes was lifted in the 1990s. John Perry Barlow has long been an advocate for libertarian ideals continuing online (i.e. no state control, no laws and the freedom of the individual) but increasingly these values are at odds with the recent marketisation of the internet with the likes of Bill Gates' Microsoft, the rich and influential Google search engine and the corporatisation of big media companies which continue to make vast quantities of content for distribution via electronic means. Moreover, in order that citizens of nation states are protected no matter where they live and no matter where a digital crime is perpetrated, international laws must be enacted. This might seem unrealistic in an online world when agreement across real borders on what is 'right' and 'fair' differ quite considerably. Further, attempts to constrain the flow of information around the internet through the processes of filtering and censoring might slow it to such an extent that it becomes unproductive. With these important issues in mind, this chapter examines what we might expect of the new digital world and what we have come to value.

Internet innovation and libertarian values to swift marketisation

The internet began as a result of military intercontinental ballistic missiles (ICBM) research after the Russian launch of Sputnik in 1957. The Russian spaceship was widely considered to be a spying technique during the Cold War. Thus, the United States military began counter-spying research and developed the Advanced Research Projects Associated Network (ARPANet, later DARPANet for 'Defence'). After these early beginnings, the internet was adopted by the university sector when the desktop publishing revolution of the 1970s and 1980s required networked computing for printing. A series of applications was developed for the purposes of communication, file transferral and information exchange. The internet is based on sending and receiving messages. It operates on a system of transmitting and sending data through **packet switching**. The basic languages used in packet switching are a combination of Transmission Control Protocol (a language for sending data) and Internet Protocol (a language for addressing data). **TCP/IP** forms the basis of the internet communications applications.

The internet is actually a collective term for a series of applications that take place using packet switching technology. These applications include email, **File Transfer Protocol** (**FTP**) and the ubiquitous **World Wide Web** (**WWW**). The basis for the WWW's data sharing success was invented in 1989 by Tim Berners Lee (Freiberger & Swaine, 2000). The internet is based on addresses that primarily use numbers and these numbers are not an easy means of identifying the content of a website; for example, it might not be as easy to find Google if you had to remember the IP (Internet Protocol) address http://216.239.51.99. As a result, domain names were introduced as a means of

HTML: Hyper Text Mark-up Language

Packet switching: The basic languages used in packet switching are a combination of Transmission Control Protocol (a language for sending data) and Internet Protocol (a language for addressing data).

TCP/IP: Transmission Control Protocol and Internet Protocol. TCP/IP forms the basis of the internet communications applications.

FTP: File Transfer Protocol

WWW: World Wide Web

easily identifying internet content. This task was initially undertaken by a single computer scientist, Jon Postel, at the Stanford Research Institute (SRI) as part of the US Defence Department contract to 'build' the internet (Goldsmith & Wu, 2008: 33). Postel devised the top-level domains such as dot. com, dot.edu and dot.net. and for many years was known as 'the' naming and numbering authority (Goldsmith & Wu, 2008: 34). As the internet grew, domain names came to be administered on an international basis. Since 1998 the role has been undertaken by the Internet Corporation for Names and Numbering (ICANN), a non-profit private sector body based in the US. ICANN is a coalition of the internet's technical, business, non-commercial and academic communities (see: www.icann.org).

When studying the internet as a new media form, it is important to consider how the internet differs from traditional media including film, print and television, not just in terms of content and control, but in terms of regulation and policy. With every other medium such as print, radio or television, a strong infrastructure of accountability and control has preceded the introduction of the medium into a localised market. We must consider that, first, *the medium is global*. So, unlike traditional media, the internet is not limited by geographical distribution mechanisms or cultural expectations. Secondly, *the medium has grown from research*. While it began as a military experiment, the internet as we know it now was developed primarily by the university and research sector. Third, *the medium is interactive*. In contrast to traditional media, which might be described as few-to-many communications, the internet requires user intervention to progress through content. Finally, *the medium is immediate*. That is, content available on the internet is often available on demand and interactive responses can occur immediately. Content can change quite literally before the eyes of the audience.

The libertarian ideals of early internet advocates such as Barlow have become more interesting in recent times. Once it was thought that the nation state was dead and that the rule of law might no longer apply in the virtual world, allowing an ideal and 'free' existence online. If anything, however, the role of national governments and legislation has become more relevant. As Goldsmith and Wu (2008: vii) argue, many internet users are coming to demand that their local government act to protect the internet from perceived threats such as the circulation of spyware and spam emails, invasions of privacy and security, unsavoury content like child pornography and defamatory comments, and fraud. But legislating for the internet is complex.

From a legal point of view, a high-profile attempt to define the internet was undertaken through the US *Communications Decency Act 1995*. According to Mawhood and Tysver (2000: 119), the most widely publicised portions of the Act attempted to limit the transmission of indecent material such as pornography over the internet. These sections were later found to be unconstitutional in 1997 for reasons of limiting free speech and expression in the United States, specifically because it is difficult to define what is pornography in one example and fine art or basic anatomy in another. Sections of the Act do, however, remain in force and serve in part to protect service providers and web users from being charged as the speaker or publisher of information provided by another party (Mawhood & Tysver, 2000: 119). In Australia, the senate passed an Act to control offensive online material in 1999 by giving the then Australian Broadcasting Authority the power to order the removal or blocking of illegal and highly offensive material. Internet content is currently regulated under amendments to the *Broadcasting Services Act 1992* (Cth) since January 2000.

In *American Civil Liberties Union v Reno*, a US legal case dealing with the nature of the internet, several important points about the technology were described and are noted below:

1   The Internet is not a physical or tangible entity, but rather a giant network which interconnects innumerable smaller groups of linked computer networks. It is thus a network of networks.

Have you worked collaboratively on a document using Google Docs (http://docs.google.com) or contributed to a wiki? You would have noted that changes can be made online in real time.

2   Some networks are 'closed' networks, not linked to other computers or networks. Many networks, however, are connected to other networks, which are in turn connected to other networks in a manner which permits each computer in any network to communicate with computers on any other network in the system. This global Web of linked networks and computers is referred to as the Internet.

3   The nature of the Internet is such that it is very difficult, if not impossible, to determine its size at a given moment. It is indisputable, however, that the Internet has experienced extraordinary growth in recent years. In 1981, fewer than 300 computers were linked to the Internet, and by 1989, the number stood at fewer than 90,000 computers. By 1993, over 1,000,000 computers were linked. Today, over 9,400,000 host computers worldwide, of which approximately 60 percent are located within the United States, are estimated to be linked to the Internet. This count does not include the personal computers people use to access the Internet using modems. In all, reasonable estimates are that as many as 40 million people around the world can and do access the enormously flexible communication Internet medium. That figure is expected to grow to 200 million Internet users by the year 1999 [World Bank data had the figure at 1,586,272,555.0 for 2008]

...

11 No single entity—academic, corporate, governmental, or non-profit—administers the Internet. It exists and functions as a result of the fact that hundreds of thousands of separate operators of computers and computer networks independently decided to use common data transfer protocols to exchange communications and information with other computers (which in turn exchange communications and information with still other computers). There is no centralized storage location, control point, or communications channel for the Internet, and it would not be technically feasible for a single entity to control all of the information conveyed on the Internet.

The final point above demonstrates the 'levelling' aspect of the global internet in that there is no central point of control, storage location or communications path. From a legislative and regulatory point of view this final statement outlines the problem of applying rules to online activities when 'it would not be technically feasible for a single entity to control all of the information conveyed on the Internet'. As a result, local law and custom remains useful in certain circumstances such as libel and defamation cases, for example. Where American libel law places a higher burden of proof on the alleged victim of defamatory speech, the Australian legal custom is, by contrast, for the burden of proof to lie with the publisher and requires the publisher to reasonably believe that its statement against an alleged victim is true, and to provide the alleged victim with the opportunity to reply (*Lange v Australian Broadcasting Corporation*, 1997). This is a problem for the US because they see Australian laws 'chilling' free speech on the internet as a result of its 'restrictive' laws (Goldsmith & Wu, 2008: 148; see also http://libertus.net/censor/netcensor.html for a wider overview of Australian internet legislation since 1999).

Indeed, we must be mindful that the internet does not herald the demise of the nation state as was once predicted—the case of China is another good example here. While a wealth of information is now freely available in the nation, dissenting comments about the Chinese Government are still not permissible and are strictly controlled. Goldsmith and Wu (2008: 94) maintain that Chinese censorship and control over information is efficient and subtle:

No screen appears saying 'Blocked by the Chinese State.' Instead, the blocking takes on the appearance of a technical error. A user who tries to reach, say, freechina.net, will get a 'site not found' screen, a network timeout screen, or any number of HTTP error codes. And it can be difficult to know whether the problem is in fact censorship or technical difficulties. The mandated list of blocked sites changes as political events develop. For example, sometimes the *New York Times* website is available on computers in China and sometimes it isn't. This uncertainty, coupled with the general unreliability of the internet, helps mask efforts at censorship.

While the examples above might appear restrictive to certain groups using the internet, Goldsmith and Wu (2008: 152–3) make a strong case for the continuation of national sovereignty, 'the rule of law and government coercion' (139):

> Consider what would happen when three nations with equal populations of 100 people—A, B, and C—tried to decide whether web gambling should be allowed in their country. Assume that 75 percent of the people in A, 65 percent of the people in B, and 35 percent of the people in C want to ban web gambling, with the remainder of the population in all three countries opposed to the ban. If the countries decided on a 'global' rule reflecting majority preferences among the 300 people in the three territories, the result would be a global ban on web gambling with 175 people pleased and 125 displeased. But if each country can decide whether to ban web gambling for itself, A and B will ban web gambling and C will not, and the aggregate 205 people will be pleased and 95 displeased. In this way, decentralized government can respond in a more fine-grained way to what people want and can best enhance overall welfare.

As the authors suggest here, the future of the internet might be shaped to a lesser degree by the visions and desires of web-users/creators and increasingly by domestic politics and international relations between countries and businesses. It is the consideration of users' welfare online that is the focus of the following section, which evaluates the rise of social networks.

The true cost of free: Behavioural marketing, social networking and privacy

As outlined earlier in this chapter, the internet was a tool of the university sector to share information and advance research and collaboration. It is this idea of collaboration and networking which provided the platform for today's commercial use of the technology. And commercial use here includes the actions we perform online 'for free' such as Google searches, book quests via Amazon.com, holiday bookings through lastminute.com or free email accounts from Google mail (gmail.com). These services are, of course, not gratis but paid for by us when our online activities are monitored by the providers and collated into meaningful information to be sold to marketers who then tailor their advertisements in such a way as to increase the probability of our buying their product or service. So every time we use Google, for example, we make them money. Problematically, in the last example of Gmail, Google scans the contents of our emails in order to tailor ads that we see on the webpage alongside our messages. For example, if you mention travel you will get ads for beach holidays and the like. Many of us don't mind because the service is fun or convenient. Cookies, which are the devices that track our online actions, are the trade-off.

Location-based social networking service and game, Foursquare, is another way to do this. It is used via a mobile hand-held device like an iPhone and requires users to 'check in' to venues that they visit, such as cafes, bars, restaurants and workplaces in order that friends and potential acquaintances can meet up with them. Conjuring notions of 'Big Brother', it allows the user to 'track the history of where they've been and who they've been there with' (Foursquare, 2010). Here arises the 'slight' problem that someone might upload your photo and mention hanging out with you at a bar when you told your boyfriend you would be studying at the library! There are yet other uses to which the service might be put and 'players' might consider the following stalking scenario outlined by Hickman (2010):

> Louise has straight, auburn hair and, judging by the only photograph I have of her, she's in her 30s. She works in recruitment. I also know which train station she uses regularly, what supermarket she shopped at last night and where she met her friends for a meal in her home town last week. At this moment, she is somewhere inside the pub in front of me meeting colleagues after work
>
> Louise is a complete stranger. Until 10 minutes ago when I discovered she was located within a mile of me, I didn't even know of her existence. But equipped only with a smartphone and an increasingly popular social networking application called Foursquare, I have located her to within just a few square meters, accessed her Twitter account and conducted multiple cross-referenced Google searches using the personal details I have already managed to accrue about her online presence. In the short time it has taken me to walk to this pub in central London, I probably know more about her than if I had spent an hour talking to her face-to-face. She doesn't know it yet, but Louise is about to meet her new digital stalker …

Undeterred, users enjoy this application that turns real life into a game. As of June 2011, Foursquare had close to ten million users worldwide (Foursquare, 2011). Other life-games include 'Recognizer', which is an application that allows the user to point their smartphone at someone and retrieve their online profile and phone number via face recognition technology even if you don't know them (see: http://gawker.com/5478562/stalking-app-can-give-creepy-strangers-your-phone-number). Another 'game' is 'Where is Robert', which is an app to 'get location news' about (and stalk) Robert Pattinson (the lead actor in the Twilight films), with users posting sightings (see: http://itunes.apple.com/us/app/where-is--a-robert-pattinson/id379379623?mt=8). This sort of connection can be used for any celebrity or cause. In China, crowdsourcing through the 'human flesh search engine' allows users to identify and expose individuals to public denouncement on bulletin board systems, chat rooms or via instant messaging, principally out of Chinese nationalistic sentiment (Fletcher, 2008), but offers all sorts of social collaboration. Problematically, as Fletcher (2008) outlines, it can be used for both good and ill as the following scenario illustrates:

> She looks like any other disgruntled young person. Arms tightly crossed, mouth twisted in contempt, she could be letting off steam about parents, school, or boyfriends. But when 21-year-old Gao Qianhui sat down in front her webcam last month, she had far more important issues on her mind. Upset that the three-day mourning period for the 80,000 victims of the earthquake in southwest China had disrupted her television viewing schedule, she launched into a five-minute spew of vitriol and then posted the video online.
>
> 'I turn on the TV and see injured people, corpses, rotten bodies … I don't want to watch these things. I have no choice.' Ms Gao sighed: 'Come on, how many of you died? Just a few, right? There are so many people in China anyway.'
>
> Within hours, Ms Gao had become the latest victim of a human flesh search engine, where Chinese netizens become cyber-vigilantes and online communities turn into the world's largest lynch mobs. Using the vast human power behind the Chinese web, every detail of Ms Gao's

life, from her home and work address in Liaoning province, north east China, to the fact that her parents were divorced, was dug up and published on hundreds of forums and chatrooms.

'Now humiliate her,' ordered one internet user, Yang Zhiyan.

Clearly, internet use can be liberating when exposing government corruption, but terrifying, as the example above demonstrates. So why do we make so much personal information available to others online via only a couple a swift key strokes?

Social networks: Size does matter

Current research clearly indicates that youth value the community, intimacy and constant connectivity that the digital world and games like Foursquare and others provide. Socialising with peers is important (Watkins, 2010: 6) and in some cohorts internet use demonstrates increased self-esteem (Leung, 2003). Results of a study undertaken by Norris (2002: 13) found that 'online participation has the capacity to deepen linkages among those sharing similar beliefs as well as serving as a virtual community that cuts across at least some traditional social divisions'. Investigating the theme of online participation further, early research undertaken by Lampe, Ellison and Steinfield (2006) discovered that, while college students were avid Facebook users, they use it largely to learn more about people they meet offline than to use this particular site to initiate new connections. In a later study, Ellison, Steinfield and Lampe (2007) found that Facebook usage among undergraduate university students helped to promote ties with family and close friends, suggesting that the site helps to maintain largely offline relations over many years through high school, college and latter working years. Such connections, the authors argued, have pay-offs in terms of jobs, internships and other opportunities via these connections. While research such as this points to the value of the social network for connecting people, other studies indicate that the notion of 'friend' has a different understanding online, with one survey noting that a significant 46 per cent of users reported that they had neutral feelings or felt disconnected from their friends on Facebook (Vanden Boogart, 2006).

The notion of 'friendship' or being a 'friend' is seemingly not the same in the online world as it is in the offline one. Increasingly, with the widespread uptake of new social technologies, 'users no longer have to rely on an individual's self-composed emails, chat statements, or personal web pages to garner impressions about a subject. Users employ strategies unique to CMC [Computer Mediated Communication] including browsing archived transcripts of discussions and chats, surfing personal and institutional websites, or using search engines to uncover a variety of information repositories' (Tong et al., 2008: 531–2). In the offline world, before the advent of social networks, this 'creepy' sort of investigation behind a friend's back might be akin to hiring a private investigator to gather information to be used and digested for unknown purposes. Further, a sample of Facebook users at one university reported a mean of 246 friends (Walther et al., 2008). Would it be realistic to catch up for coffee, have dinner, party and send Christmas cards to this many 'friends' in the offline world? Probably not, but, again, we manage our friendships differently online than we do offline.

A further conundrum is how to treat our online 'friends' when we fall out. For example, what if you were to break up with your boyfriend? Could you realistically terminate your friendship with him when his links to all your other friends update him as to how you are feeling (via recent photos of you looking a bit sad), who you start dating (looking a bit happier), the new job you get, where you go on holiday—all without him having to contact you—again … creepy? As Tong et al. (2008: 538) explain, 'the size of one's apparent friend network on a system such as Facebook can easily become much larger than the traditional offline networks, because friendship is in some cases mostly superficial, because the technology facilitates greater connection at some level and because social norms inhibit refusals to friend requests'.

The implications for an individual's privacy, social connections and future work prospects are not, however, always considered in the documentation of important thoughts, images and events for others to review. Your friend now might be your boss in ten years' time. Some university faculties are teaching users how to 'manage' their profiles online by constructing a positive image, which includes lying about failed exams and reporting excellent final-term results instead. Research into user expectations is being undertaken (see Viégas, 2005) but only preliminary findings have, however, been reported. The greater problem is that the research cannot be generalised to the wider *global* online population because a consensus will never be achieved. The best we can hope for is local understanding/law that reflects local customs or norms.

Moreover, have you ever considered what happens to a lifetime of information about an individual when they die? A new service to emerge in the digital age is that of the *digital* undertaker. This is a service provided to collate digital information pertaining to wealth and assets or to manage one's online identity upon death. One such organisation, established in Perth, Western Australia, in April 2010, registered the domain name thedigitalundertakers.com some months ago but has just made their website live. The Digital Undertakers (2010) state that their services are necessary for the following reasons:

- Unless you have recorded the key things you do on the Internet, stored any data securely and told somebody how to access it, then like unravelling any complex problem it would take a huge amount of time for anyone to find all the relevant information.
- Any financial aspects in relation to your online assets would need to be investigated and that alone would benefit from being recorded in one place.
- It is a process that helps family and loved ones in the event of a death.

So perhaps we need not worry about how we appear in the future if we have made some mistakes we would prefer forgotten, as we might look to the services of digital PR specialists to reframe our online identity should we require it.

Certainly new means of communication engender fears that it might corrupt the vulnerable. However, the dream of independence remains. Regulation of the internet is something that has been strongly resisted by individuals such as John Perry Barlow in his *Declaration of the Independence of Cyberspace* (https://projects.eff.org/~barlow/Declaration-Final.html) and organisations such as the Electronic Frontier Foundation (EFF) defending digital rights online. As criminal justice author Peter Grabosky (1998: 7) has argued:

> The risk, or indeed, the fact, that freedom of speech will be abused by some, is insufficient justification for 'pulling the plug' on telecommunications. One must always bear in mind that excessive constraints on freedom of expression and communication may inhibit the realization of competitive advantage.

So what do we need in internet policy?

Young people raised with access to the internet and other new media technologies have developed different expectations of their media in terms of choice, access, affordability and functionality. Some key aspects that are important include: (1) a clear sense of the technical capacity of the medium;

(2) some acknowledgment that the internet content is more than mere electronic publishing and broadcasting; (3) a notion of access equity allotted at least as much value as censorship; and (4) a sense of the global audience when formulating options for access and for responsibility. In evaluating our values in the digital world, it would be reasonable to consider whether such faster-easier-better online services as shopping, banking or communication are really opportunities. At what or whose expense? Traditional institutions such as banks, the corner store and public schools are being undermined as more and more services go online. With regard to online shopping, consumers might end up using electronic businesses utilising vast warehousing space, or will complete all banking transactions online via the internet, electronic kiosks or phone services rather than taking a trip into town or going to local shopping and banking locations, where valuable human connections are often made. The middle-person in business may well become obsolete, as in the case of online shopping where distribution centres come to cater directly to clients, and customer service representatives in a limited number of central locations handle banking transactions and enquiries on a 24-hour basis replacing staff in branch sites. Overall, we might question whether people have the choice to participate in the digital world—or is it mandatory that they do so? These issues must be addressed with regard to ensuring that all users are aware of their online choices no matter where they live, and have the confidence and skills and affordable access to equipment that is necessary in order to participate should they *wish* to do so.

Summary

This chapter has provided a thumbnail sketch of the internet's early development. It noted that the internet was developed with public funding from the US Government for research projects centred on national defence. What resulted was the global networked communications we call the internet. Its use as a research tool was expanded to the wider public during the 1990s and swift commercialisation soon followed. Today there are numerous social applications being used, from Twitter, for brief messages/statements, to profile sites such as Facebook. Shopping has been revolutionised through the electronic commerce provided by the likes of Amazon, lastminute and the like. Games are now leading the way in terms of blending games with social networking. While amusing, time-saving, convenient and often free, there are negative aspects to the use of the technology, which include our personal information being collated, stored and shared by unknown entities for unknown purposes in perpetuity and the frightening aspects of cyberstalking.

Further reading

Goldsmith, J & Wu, T 2008, *Who Controls the Internet: Illusions of a Borderless World*, Oxford University Press, New York.

Watkins, S C 2009, *The Young and the Digital: What the Migration to Social-Networking Sites, Games, and Anytime, Anywhere Media Means for our Future*, Beacon, Boston.

13 Constructed Reality: What's 'Real' Nowadays?

chapter

Brad Warren

Master X and how to *not* make friends online

Master X thought the internet was a fascinating place, because everybody had something to share, and everybody wanted to be his friend. And it seemed that people were giving stuff away: *lots* of stuff, lots of *good* stuff … Except he hadn't actually won anything, not yet, anyway. But he was sure he would, very soon. It was just a matter of time. All he had to do was keep entering the competitions, and filling in the forms with all his personal details. But that was okay. Wasn't it? After all, he could spell his full name, and these days he knew his address and phone number by heart.

Last week, Master X was contacted by email by one of the people running those competitions, to say he'd made it to the final round, and was now only one step away from winning $100,000. Master X was so excited he could barely breathe. He had to provide more personal details, including his bank account number and password, but that was okay, too. Wasn't it? It was, after all, kind of like an investment in his future. An exchange of emails followed, and strangely, by some bizarre coincidence, the person running the competition lived in the same city as he did, and wanted to catch up with him in real life, not just on the computer. Another new friend! Master X couldn't wait!

Master X arrived at the arranged spot on time (in fact, he was early) but, sadly, no one showed up. He waited for three hours, and then wandered home, bitterly disappointed. But he soon had plenty to take his mind off that small misery: upon entering the house, he discovered that his computer was gone. So was his TV. So was the fridge. So was every last cent in his bank account.

What you will learn from this chapter

- Phishing emails: 'You've Already Won!!' Yeah, sure I have
- Data mining—the sneaky collection and sale of personal information
- The dangers of being too willing to just put yourself out there online
- Michel Foucault on Bentham's panopticon, and how this metaphor for society may no longer hold true, especially online
- The increasing irrelevance of the online/offline distinction in contemporary cultural environments—being online is just part of life
- Deception in social networking—a sliding scale where few are completely innocent (and a place where ethical behaviour becomes increasingly problematic)
- Types of play: Paidia and Ludus
- Denotation and connotation, and the limitations of txt-ing
- The techno-legal time gap, and why CDs are getting cheaper.

Introduction: 'You may have already won!!'

When did you last receive an email telling you …

1   that your bank had changed its something or other, and needed to reconfirm your password and account number details

2   that there were unclaimed funds waiting for you

3   that you'd been selected from a pool of over a million, and were already in the final draw

4   that beautiful women were waiting for you—just click on the link

Phishing: the practice of collecting personal details, via online means, for the purposes of fraud. The most common forms of phishing are unsolicited email, and click-through links on insecure websites.

Unsolicited email like this preys on the vulnerable, seeking people willing to hope that *maybe this one's for real, maybe I really am lucky, so what's the harm in doing as they ask?* The process of attempting to obtain personal details by fraudulent electronic means is known as **phishing**. There are several strategies used in phishing, some more obvious than others. Example 1 (above) is one of the most blatant forms, asking outright for personal banking details. Example 2 may or may not ask for your bank account number straight off. Instead, such emails tend to ask for contact addresses, full name, stuff like that—nothing that seems too harmful to give out. But it is harmful, and there are two reasons for asking such seemingly innocuous questions: either to build a profile of who you are and where you live, to be combined with other details gleaned later, or to encourage your trust, so that when the next email comes, asking for that account number, you'll be more likely to comply. Example 3 says you've already been lucky, and all you need to do is take things that one step further. This form of phishing is usually accompanied by a need for speed, along the lines of 'But this offer won't last! Please respond within five working days of receiving this email or else …' And example 4 is one of the worst. It doesn't ask for anything. But by clicking on a link, or especially opening an attachment, invisible software may be downloaded to your computer that then searches your hard drive for anything that looks like a password or a credit card number. Your details are then passed back to the source (the phisherman?) the next time you are online.

Seriously, though, who'd fall for this stuff? In the recent movie *The Bucket List* (2007), Edward Cole (Jack Nicholson) states that, among other things, he wants to kiss the most beautiful girl in the world before he dies. When Carter Chambers (Morgan Freeman) asks him how he plans to do this, Cole's response is 'Volume'. That is, if Cole kisses enough women, then he must get to kiss the most beautiful one sooner or later. For much the same reason, millions of people continue to buy lotto tickets week after week, despite the astronomical odds against a major payout. The same principle also applies to **phishing**—it's just maths, the statistical effects of sheer volume. Most of us are fully aware of the dangers of phishing emails, of what they look like, and of what not to do. But not all of us are and that's why so many of these things keep showing up in our inboxes. The reasoning runs that if phish emails are sent to enough people, sooner or later someone will fall for them.

Data mining—phishing's semi-respectable cousin

There's a fine line separating phishing from other, legal practices of collecting personal data that we're all exposed to every day. Every time you use a loyalty card to claim a discount at the chemist, or a credit card at the supermarket checkout, your personal details and the details of your purchases are collated and stored. Similarly, every time you visit a website, there's a chance that your computer's IP address (Internet Protocol address: a unique number assigned to every device in an online network) will also be recorded. Collectively, these processes are known as **data mining**. Such clandestine information collection results in mountains of raw data that is then sold to companies whose sole function is to create demographic profiles of neighbourhoods, and indeed of individuals. It is used by commercial companies in direct marketing campaigns and in ensuring that their stores are stocked with the items most likely to sell, and by governments and security agencies in personality profiling, as well as for a host of other reasons.

> Three of the biggest data-miners are ChoicePoint, Axiom and Experian. And now these companies are entering into commercial arrangements to sell data back to the US Government, the FBI and the CIA. No doubt the Australian authorities are interested. ChoicePoint collects, collates and merges data from many databases, and managing director Howard Saffir says that it is his patriotic duty to sell this information back to the US Government to help it sift out suspicious behaviour and map profiles of suspected terrorists
>
> (Hirst & Harrison, 2007: 327)

That last bit rings a bit hollow. It's Mr Saffir's patriotic duty to data mine, and then *sell* the information on in the interests of American national security? If the motivation is for love of country, why is he charging said country for it? But enough of that. The selling-on of private information is by no means a new phenomenon. Over a decade ago, Thomas Friedman wrote in *The Lexus and the Olive Tree* that:

> states such as Texas are already putting their state criminal histories online. The Texas criminal-record database is searchable for $3.15 per name … An offshore company called PublicData, based in Anguilla, British West Indies, buys public records in bulk and puts them online in a database searchable for as little as 3 cents per search.
>
> (Friedman, 1999: 409)

Data mining: companies collect and sort the information in our online user profiles and sell the results to commercial and public organisations, including governments. It also involves offline point-of-sale use of credit and loyalty cards.

And yet, here's an interesting phenomenon: one would think, given the growth in online surveillance, and in on- and offline data mining over the past ten years, that we as a population would have become more careful about what we say, do and reveal about ourselves. Strangely, though, this appears to not be the case. Consider the following:

> [in an] interactive network, not only do users often voluntarily give up their right to control their own information by providing personal information without fully considering future consequences, but ... individual users' identities become more and more exposed, while [those conducting] ... surveillance ... become less and less identifiable.
>
> (Woo & Lee, 2006: 16–17)

> In 1999, Scott McNealy, CEO of Sun Microsystems, said: 'you have no privacy ... get over it' (Sprenger, 1999). And popular notions suggest that the new millennial generation is perhaps the most cavalier about their expectations of privacy and what they are willing to disclose, particularly in online contexts
>
> (Kisselburgh, 2009: 30–1)

If all this talk of data mining is leaving you feeling a little bit worried (maybe even paranoid?), then compound it with this: spend one day, or even a couple of hours, paying close attention to how many times you're recorded on camera.

Master X and the one about PIN numbers

Somewhere along the line, Master X managed to compile enough forms of ID to get himself a bank account. He even operated it fairly reasonably, for about six or seven months. And he was so proud of his ATM card; he'd show it to anyone who'd look. So shiny! But he never told anyone the PIN number, he was very careful about that. When the letter came with his PIN in it, he memorised the number very carefully; then he ate the letter, in the interests of personal security.

But then, one day, Master X showed the card to one too many people, and almost got himself robbed at the ATM. On his way there, though, he had passed beneath the security cameras in his street and three sets of traffic cameras. He also took a short cut through the local university, and was captured twice on their security cameras, too. And then there was the camera overseeing the shopping mall, and also the one built into the ATM ...

For most of us, no one has any interest in compiling our comings and goings; we're all recorded, all the time ... but there are those who watch Master X. Ever since that thing with the cookie-dough ...

So people were watching when Master X was attacked at knife-point and money was demanded. Master X was scared, but not out of control, because he'd heard that if you entered your PIN number backwards, the police would come, just like calling 000. And he'd received this information in an email, so had no reason not to believe it (is this a meme, maybe? see Chapter 18). Perhaps stupidly, Master X explained all this to his attacker while he tried it. Punching numbers furiously, he pointed out that the would-be thief didn't know his PIN, and therefore wouldn't know if he was entering the number correctly or not. At this point, the thief wasn't sure whether to be annoyed or amused, and kind of just let events take their course. Master X kept keying in numbers, and listening for the sirens, and then the machine ate his card.

Master X's potential assailant couldn't take it anymore, and doubled over in fits of uncontrollable laughter. Upon seeing this, Master X took advantage of the situation and kneed him in the face.

Having seen the whole thing on camera, the police showed up a minute or two later, and arrested Master X for assault.

Security, naivety and life online

Building on the paranoia we've established so far in this chapter, social media websites are perfect for the combing of personal details by sexual predators, burglars and others. Have you published where you work on your Facebook page? Whether or not you're employed full-time? Who you live with? What you both do for a living? If so, you've declared to the world at large when your house is likely to be empty.

And that's not the worst of it. It appears that the 'casing' of houses by potential thieves is no longer a problem. Today, they don't need to lurk in dark alleys and around corners in order to get a good look at your place. We have Google Street View for that, and wannabe criminals can now peruse our homes from the comfort of their own computers. And if you're selling your house, and the real estate agent suggests posting a series of interior photos online, just stop and think for a moment about who might be looking at them.

Australian comedian Tim Minchin summarises this issue far more succinctly than I can. Please have a look at the following: www.youtube.com/watch?v=CZ7U3Cu4Mr4. Many of the issues covered in this section are addressed in more detail in Chapter 17, which is directly concerned with surveillance.

How worried should we be? Housebreakers, stalkers, sexual predators: all making the internet their greatest asset. Or perhaps this is a bit unfair. Maybe people—especially Gen Y, and even the younger Gen Z—are well aware of the risks, and routinely conduct themselves in a manner that ensures their safety. In the interests of fair treatment of existent literature, it must be said that there are an abundance of claims by internet users that they are fully cognisant of the potential dangers.

> There has only been one major (U.S) study of the threat of sexual predators online. Funded by the Department of Justice, the study confirmed what many kids have been saying all along: that most of them know to ignore unwanted solicitations they receive on the internet.

> (*Cutting Edge*, 2008)

In a similar vein (and post-dating the study just mentioned), Cho et al. examined awareness of, and engagement with, privacy issues in online contexts across a number of different demographics. Their findings reflect *Cutting Edge*'s assertion that today's internet-natives are very security conscious (2009: 395).

The comfort and (at least perceived sense of) security with which Gen Y navigate online environments is best conveyed through their own testimonies. Consider the following:

> [Student One:] My parents, like, they don't understand that I've spent since, like, second grade online, and that I know what to avoid and I know, pretty much, like, what can happen, and I think sometimes they forget that 'cos they didn't have, like, they didn't grow up online.

> [Student Two:] [If someone] … IMs [instant-messages] you and says, like, 'Hey, where do you live? I wanna meet you.' [laughs] It's pretty obvious, like, this person might be a predator [laughs sarcastically].

> [Student Three:] If someone asks me, like, 'Where do you live?', I'll delete them as a friend, like, why do you want to know where I live at? Like, I don't tell people where I live at.

> (*Cutting Edge*, 2008)

This seems encouraging. *But what if they're wrong?* In the end, the possibility that young people participating online might not be ideally equipped to make claims about their security/privacy is rather a moot point, since the case cannot be proven either way. Nonetheless, the processes by which personal details are harvested in such environments generally take place without the knowledge of those from whom they are taken. In itself, this is sufficient justification to at least consider the idea that social network users are not as secure as they might feel or believe.

All this talk of online security (or lack of it!) suggests a more general question about the nature of the internet, and about social networking sites in particular. Famously, **Michel Foucault** has argued that constant surveillance serves to regulate behaviour, that it keeps us on our toes and makes us (at least a bit more likely to) fly straight and do the right thing. But is that what's happening online? Are we better behaved because of the constant surveillance that the internet makes possible? The inherent security threats addressed in the preceding pages would seem to suggest otherwise. So, let's explore the idea a little further. One of Foucault's most well-known theorisations on this topic centred around Bentham's panopticon, 'an architectural plan for a prison system relatively simple in design, but socially and psychologically complex in effect' (Campbell & Carlson, 2002: 589—and discussed in greater detail in Chapter 17). In short, the panopticon consisted of:

> an annular building … at the periphery … ; at the centre, a tower; this tower is pierced with wide windows that open onto the inner side of the ring; [and] the peripheric building is divided into cells … All that is needed, then, is to place a supervisor in a central tower and to shut up in each cell a madman, a patient, a condemned man, a worker or a schoolboy.
>
> (Foucault, 1977: 200).

The reference here to 'workers' and 'schoolboys' is Foucault underlining that his use of the panopticon was as an explanation for the disciplinary power he held to operate in contemporary society more generally. The exercise of such power is, he maintains, 'one of the great inventions of bourgeois society. It has been a fundamental instrument in the constitution of industrial capitalism and of the type of society that is its accompaniment' (1980: 105). Expanding on the panopticon's nature, Foucault argues that its 'major effect … [is] to induce in the inmate a state of conscious and permanent visibility that assures the automatic functioning of power. So to arrange things that the surveillance is permanent in its effects, even if it is discontinuous in its actions; that the perfection of power should tend to render its actual exercise unnecessary' (1977: 201). Or, to rephrase, it is the *possibility* of constant surveillance, even if such surveillance is not actually present at any given moment, that causes the panopticon's prisoners/society to self-regulate, to impose disciplinary order upon themselves for fear of the reprisals that might otherwise ensue.

But what about the internet? The dangers inherent in life online are clear, so why doesn't the panopticon function effectively in cyberspace? That is, if online contexts are truly self-regulated, how could it be that the worst problems surrounding identity theft, stalking and other predatory behaviours even exist? It is probably fair to say that most internet users *do* self-regulate, that they bring to their online interactions their own 'ideals or codes of restraint on human behaviour' (Friedman, 1999: 449). If this were not so, the internet would not merely be potentially dangerous, it would be unresolvable chaos.

Just the same, there are at least two points at which Foucault's metaphor seems not to hold in contemporary online contexts. First, inside the panopticon, if transgression was observed, punishment was guaranteed. This notion is of fundamental importance to regulating behaviour. It is an entirely different thing to say that (as per today's cyberspace environments), if transgression is

---

Michel Foucault (1926–1984): a French sociologist and philosopher who wrote extensively on the nature of discourse and the functioning of power (including in the context of Bentham's panopticon—see also Chapter 17).

seen, punishment *may or may not* follow. To illustrate this point by example, if someone commits online fraud, perhaps they will be noticed. So far, this is in line with the theory of the panopticon. However, inside the prison, responses to the following two questions:

Observed by whom? and

With what consequences?

were known quantities, with the answers being 'the prison guards' and 'some form of punishment', respectively. In cyberspace, the identity/role of the potential observer(s), and whether or not they care about an instance of online fraud either way, are in no sense guaranteed. These additional variables serve to weaken the effectiveness of a society to self-regulate, as they decrease the likelihood that transgressions will meet with repercussions.

Secondly, part of the successful functioning of the panopticon lies in the fact that the guard's tower is always visible to the prison population, serving as a constant reminder that conformity to imposed regulation is the best course of action. Although somewhat of an indictment on human nature, the absence of such reminders lessens the likelihood of the desired behaviour. Campbell and Carlson point out that there are no such reminders in the contemporary milieu: that 'the agent of surveillance is not as apparent in cyberspace—neither the guard nor the central tower can be seen even though they can be assumed to be omnipresent' (2002: 603). In summary, then, Foucault's panopticon is a very small, very closed system, and hence perhaps not a completely adequate analogy for our complicated and multifaceted online existences.

Master X and early adventures in cyberspace

For his thirteenth birthday (long before the cookie-dough debacle), Master X was given a computer to help him with his homework. At first, his parents were thrilled with the difference it made: he spent hours alone in his room, working diligently away …

After a while, though, Mr and Mrs X became suspicious—the change in behaviour was just too great, and no one could be that much of a study-nerd, surely? So they made a point of walking in on him unannounced a few times, after which they decided it was probably a good idea to install NetNanny.

After that Master X actually did some homework, for a little while anyway.

But the internet was just so fascinating, and there was so much stuff out there that Mr and Mrs X (perhaps naively) hadn't set the filter to catch—virtual worlds, online games, social networking sites … the possibilities were endless. Master X started spending still more time in online environments until, after a while, the boundaries between 'online worlds' and the 'real world' (whatever that was) weren't so clear anymore …

The increasing irrelevance of the online/offline distinction

The (mis)adventures of Master X described above raise the question: what's the difference between 'real' and 'online' worlds? At a surface level, the answer seems obvious, barely worthy of consideration. The 'real' world is the one we can touch, taste, feel; the one our physical bodies move around in, where food has flavour and if you prick your finger it hurts. Online worlds are, more or less, role-play fantasy games, accessed through our computer screens.

But are things this simple? Is the separation between 'real' and 'online' really so clear?

Consider the following dialogue. It's a snippet from a 'real' conversation (please note the deliberate contradiction/irony) that took place between the author of this chapter and a friend, on Facebook:

Brad (by the way, inviting you to my birthday through Facebook wasn't my intention; it's kind of an impersonal forum … you were on my list to call in person, but I seized the opportunity)
7:19 pm

Juliet LOL That's such a Gen X thing to say
7:19 pm

Brad guilty as charged …
7:19 pm

Juliet Gen Ys don't care, Facebook is life (for better or worse)
7:20 pm

As straightforward as it may appear, this brief chat is worthy of a little further discussion.

'Facebook is life'. For many people, online forums including email, chat and social networking sites are perfectly valid places to be having conversations that have a direct outcome in the 'real' world (in this case, whether or not Juliet would attend my birthday). Perhaps the point to be emphasised here is that 'online worlds' are not only of the avatar-driven **Second Life** variety, where people assume characteristics that are not (necessarily) their own, and direct ramifications in the 'real world' are not so obvious.

Further, there is no clear distinction between the supposedly more 'real' online forums and the overtly constructed, artificial ones. As discussed in the early pages of this chapter with regard to phishing, there are some aspects of email that are thoroughly not-real (as opposed to un-real, which has other connotations entirely—more on connotation and denotation later in the chapter). Likewise, there are those for whom Second Life is very real indeed: as suggested, it is possible to buy land there, or clothes, using real money, and there are those who go there seeking to establish real relationships—personal, professional, business, whatever.

So, rather than try to categorise online environments as being of one kind or another, perhaps they are all better understood as existing on a sliding scale, where the moving variable is the potential for, and acceptability of, deception. Taken overall, there would be little argument that most of us expect our emails to be more or less honest, whereas identity-play (i.e. sanctioned and generally

Second Life: an animated-character (avatar) driven, virtual world. It is an immersive online environment where it is possible to shop, be a tourist, own land, do everything except feel real physical contact and taste real food.

accepted forms of deceit) in a forum like Second Life are pretty much the norm. Nonetheless, all online environments contain this potential for deceit, to a greater or lesser extent.[1]

And, to return again to Facebook, perhaps it exists somewhere in the middle of this email-to-Second Life continuum we've drawn. Most of us wouldn't lie about our name in an email, but secondary accounts under pseudonyms in Facebook are quite common, as are fictitious profiles and white lies about age. All of these things constitute deliberate deception—at different points on that sliding scale—but deception nonetheless.

To play or not to play: Set your 'relationship status' to stun

It is worth discussing the deception facilitated by online environments a little further, in the context of relationships and dating. Once upon a time (and not so very long ago), it used to be that finding a date, or indeed a partner, online was considered something of a last resort, a final chance for the desperate, lonely and hopelessly introverted. Increasingly, however, this is no longer the case. Today, people of all ages are shunning pubs and clubs as potential pick-up venues, and seeking to meet people over the internet. Whether through Facebook, organised dating services such as Lavalife, or wherever, online dating no longer has the stigma it once did. As argued throughout this chapter, online interaction is now just another part of everyday life.

Likewise, it is becoming increasingly true that people are conducting at least portions of their 'real-life' relationships online. For an example of the severe ramifications that even a small deception-in-dating can have in online contexts, have a look at the movie about the origins of Facebook, *The Social Network* (2010), particularly the scene where Eduardo Saverin (Andrew Garfield), one of Facebook's founders, faces the wrath of his soon-to-be-ex-girlfriend because he recorded his Facebook status as 'single'. While the potential for urban myths perhaps needs to be acknowledged here, this author has nonetheless heard many other, similar stories.

And there are also other, even greater risks if you're taking or seeking relationships online, especially if you're playing in the deep end of the pool, in places like Second Life where identity—and particularly gender—experimentation is extremely common.

Mr X's quest

Mr X had too much time on his hands. Having been recently laid off, with quite a sizeable redundancy package, he found that he was spending a disproportionate amount of time fooling around on the internet. So much so, that even Facebook was starting to become boring.

But then he discovered Second Life, and this online fantasy world was fertile ground for all kinds of new games. Mr X wandered (well, flew) around for a while, exploring cities, islands, shops and clubs, collecting stuff for his avatar, including friends. Mr X's own avatar looked a bit like himself, actually, only a little less pudgy and bald.

After a while, Mr X got the distinct impression that people were forming real relationships here on Second Life (well, sort of real—he wasn't sure exactly where that distinction actually lay) and the idea fascinated him. So he asked his wife: Mrs X, is it okay with you if I go onto Second Life to find myself a Second Wife?'

At first, Mrs X was both shocked and appalled: 'What's wrong with me, then?', she wanted to know. 'And what's this Second Life thing, anyway? Some kind of dating site? And why are you asking me, anyway? If you're so unhappy, just leave!'

It was Mr X's turn to be appalled, and he became very distressed, then went to great pains to explain to Mrs X that Second Life was a kind of virtual world, but that the people in it weren't real ... they were just playing.

'Then what do I care?' she replied. 'Play your stupid game.'

So Mr X went looking for a Second Wife. Unfortunately, though, he couldn't find one. No one was interested. After a while, he had the bright idea to change tactics and try his luck as a lesbian. He redesigned his avatar, from that previous facsimile of himself into a beautiful young woman, and pretty soon the offers came rolling in. Mr X found another young lady, fell deeply in Second Love, and was Second Married in the spring.

All in all, though, it was a good thing that Second Life was a game to Mr X. Unknown to him, his Second Life lover was a 65-year-old man with a beer gut, bad personal hygiene and a pimply bum.

Mr X is by no means the first to have experimented with gender-swapping online, nor is he the first to notice the increased attention that can result from adopting a female persona. Consider the following examples:

Steve Silberman, a writer for *Wired* magazine, posed as 'Rose' in a chat room, though he felt shamefully dishonest about it. His first lesson came as he began receiving one message after another from people who had ignored him in his male persona. Some messages were friendly, some were come-ons, and a few were [even] nasty, brutal and harassing.

(Wallace, 1999: 45)

In a similar vein, the following describes a very early case of online gender play:

A widely publicized and notorious story of online gender-swapping involved the Joan/Alex chimera, a.k.a, the 'case of the electronic lover'. Alex was a New York psychiatrist who used the nickname *Shrink, Inc.* to chat [online] ... and began having ... conversations with women who assumed he was actually a female psychiatrist. Titillated by the immediacy and intimacy of the conversations in which people thought he was a woman, he began logging on as 'Joan' and created an elaborate and detailed persona to go with his new nickname ... Women flocked to chat with Joan, and some experimented with lesbian netsex ...

(Wallace, 1999: 46)

The greatest problem with such online role-playing is that *not everyone's playing*. Some people are just in it for fun, some are looking to establish real relationships and build real fortunes, while others are somewhere in between (there's that continuum/sliding scale again). The difficulty is compounded because, especially in environments like Second Life, *no one can tell who's who!* It's not as if anyone wears a banner or a T-shirt, saying 'This is Just a Game to Me', or 'Talk to Me About a Genuine Real Estate Opportunity, and No, I'm Not Kidding', or even 'Exploit Me, I'm Naive and Stupid'. This never happens!

A brief exploration of recent publications about Second Life makes its participants' different attitudes abundantly clear. At one end of the spectrum are characters like 'Chancie' who—while she takes the game itself quite seriously indeed—insists that Second Life *is* just that, *a game*, and does not want it to encroach on her RL ('real life') existence in any way: 'Like many residents, for Chancie Second Life was not a communications tool allowing her to meet someone with shared actual-world interests. Second Life was the place where shared interests were forged and experienced, and they had no plan to meet in the actual world' (Boellstorff, 2008: 167).

For others, though, their first- and Second Life existences are closely intertwined, especially when financial interests become involved: 'Involving money in the equation of our little virtual world changed everything. Not because we were making money, but because we had invested our real lives … My work—and therefore my money—depended on my avatar' (Meadows, 2008: 61, 59). Elsewhere in the same text, Meadows appears to take a stand against deceptive role-playing experiments (at least at that point, anyway), and goes so far as to tutor readers on how to spot a man masquerading as a woman (it has something to do with nipple size, apparently) (2008: 39).

In short, identity games including 'Gender-swapping, or any deliberate demographic disconnect between your real self and your online persona, could be considered fanciful role-playing, or it could be classified as outright lying … The play within a play can cause all sorts of problems when others don't know the frame of reference in which you are operating' (Wallace, 1999: 47).

And the moral of the story is: if you're going to fool around online, as it were, exercise some caution as to where you do it. After all, on the internet, no one *really* knows if you're a woman, a man, a dog or a three-legged goat.

Types of games (or Tales of the Sandpit) …

One of the frequent criticisms of an online 'game' such as Second Life is that it *doesn't appear to have a point*. Unlike, say, World of Warcraft, one of Second Life's contemporaries, there are no clear levels to finish, tasks to complete, points to be scored or anything of that nature. You're free to just, kind of, wander around. You can buy and sell stuff if you want, but if there's any imperative to do so, it's self-imposed, not directed by the rules of the game (a lot like 'real' life, in many ways, at least until you have to start paying your own grocery bills). But do all games need to have a point, a purpose? In attempting to make sense of Second Life, it might be useful to consider the work of Roger Caillois, who has suggested that there are different kinds of play and that, no, not all games need to have a concrete objective.

Caillois argues that that there are two types of play: **Paidia** and **Ludus** (or, more accurately, these terms form opposite ends of the same **play continuum**). **Paidia** refers to the kinds of games that have no purpose per se—they're just about messing around, and making stuff up as you go along. Think, for example, about the kinds of play that five-year-olds engage in in the sandpit during recess time at school. At the other end of the scale is **Ludus**, and this is the type of game most of us are more familiar with. Quite simply, Ludus games have an objective, something that needs to be achieved (Caillois, 2001: 13). World of Warcraft was mentioned above in this context, but many much simpler games also have clear purposes. 'To win' is perhaps the most basic and concise of these. Checkers, anyone?

Considered in this light, maybe Second Life is okay, as it can be seen as existing more at the Paidia end of the scale.

But wait a second, there's still a problem with this. Let's take the sandpit analogy a step further. Even at five years of age, everyone in the sandpit *knows* they're playing games (except Master X in the corner, but he's going to have issues his whole life). They know that, when the bell rings, it's time to get up, dust off and go back to classes in the real world. And so we return to the problem outlined at the end of the previous section: Second Life isn't like that. Some people in the sandbox are playing for real, some aren't, and nobody knows if you're playing or not. So Paidia is all well and good, but only as a form of play, and Second Life isn't always a game.

Paidia and **Ludus:** different kinds of play. Paidia is the sort of free-form improvisation common among children, and Ludus refers to games with a clear purpose or objective: to win, to score points, etc.

A little more on 'Facebook is life'

Revisiting the brief Facebook chat with Juliet earlier in this chapter, Facebook was described as 'kind of an impersonal forum'. Now, although I was gently ridiculed for holding such an opinion, it is nonetheless not an uncommon one (particularly among Gen X, as Juliet rightly points out). And so the question must be asked: what is it, exactly, that might be considered impersonal about Facebook? There are (at least) a couple of answers.

The first response pertains to the open-forum nature of the Facebook 'wall'—that writing space where you, the message's recipient, and any or all of your 493 mutual Facebook friends, are free to stare at it. Surely such open publication, as it were, is enough to give this communication channel at least a touch of the impersonal.

However, this response is insufficient on its own, because not all Facebook communication needs to take place on the 'wall': there is also a 'chat' function, reminiscent of MSN Messenger. Could it be, then, that the charge of being a little impersonal is due to the fact that text-based communication has less emotional cues, such as tone and volume of voice, and deliberate pauses in conversation (other than those resulting from computer-lag)? Very possibly. And yet, this is still not an adequate explanation, because the same could also be said of old-fashioned letter writing (look it up in a history book: a pen and paper were involved).

And so we come to the heart of this matter: txt-ing. Txt-ing is sending messages in a shorthand text (txt) format, either online or via mobile phone (and these days that's increasingly the same thing), where words and sometimes whole phrases are abbreviated (i.e. text = txt, laugh out loud = LOL) and punctuation and grammar are largely absent. This form of techno-shorthand can be attributed to two causes: (1) the demands for instant reply imposed by the nature of digital communication (i.e. you're waiting for my reply *right now*, so I don't have time to spell or punctuate); and (2) in the case of mobile phones, service providers limit the number of characters per message, and charge by the message. Children and students (or anyone on a restricted income, for that matter) have adapted to these constraints, and learned to make best possible use of the available space. To be fair, it must be said that there are always emoticons to stand in for emotions (☺, ☹, etc.), but, while they're better than nothing, they're not *that* much better.

Figure 13.1 A sample from a first-year university student's Media and Communication essay, 2007

One further observation with regard to the impersonal nature of txt-ing: for some, when faced with a potentially awkward or difficult situation (say, breaking up with a girlfriend/ boyfriend), txting is just easier, as it removes the element of direct contact, and so minimises the emotional pain. In this sense, txt-ing serves the function of the old-fashioned 'Dear John' letter. Like the 'Dear John' letter, though, many would consider using txt in this manner to be extremely rude, and a form of cowardice. However, txt-ing is becoming more and more an integral part of everyday life: recent informal surveys of students reveal surprising results concerning just how many Gen Ys have dumped or been dumped via SMS (Short Message Service).

Elsewhere, this author has argued that txt-speak is a negative progression with regard to effective communication and English literacy overall (see Warren, 2008, for an extended rant on this subject), although it should also be noted that there are those who'd disagree (see, for example, Maslen, 2010). Perhaps txt abbreviations wouldn't be a problem if they remained in the contexts of online chat and SMS messaging. But unfortunately this is not the case. Consider Figure 13.1, a snapshot from a first-year Media and Communications student's final essay.

Clearly, the behaviours and conventions of 'online worlds' *are* having a definite effect in (at least some places in) the 'real world', and not always for the better!

Denotation and connotation

Examined from a slightly different perspective, perhaps the greatest casualty of the **txt-ing** phenomenon is the loss of clear connotations; that is, an increase in *mis*understanding of the suggested or implied meanings that frequently form part of language, either written or spoken. For example, many of us will have been engaged in txt conversations, and the meanings will have become just too hard to follow: 'What did you mean by that? I didn't understand your last message? Were you being sarcastic?'[2] Under such circumstances, the solution is generally to give up and call the person you were txt-ing, rendering the whole preceding txt conversation a little bit redundant.

So, connotations are suggested or implied meanings of things, while denotations are literal or generally accepted meanings. For example, a wooden spoon has a generally accepted meaning as a large-ish kitchen implement, used in the preparation of food. However, for many children of this author's generation, the sight of a wooden spoon would cause them to stop what they were doing, and possibly begin to cry—because in days past, the wooden spoon also carried a suggested, implied or *connoted* threat of violence, since it was frequently used for disciplinary purposes (today, we'd call this practice by its other name: child abuse. My, how the world has changed). Stuart Hall explored these terms in some depth in his famous 'Encoding/Decoding' essay:

> The term 'denotation' is widely equated with the literal meaning of a sign ... Connotation, on the other hand, is employed simply to refer to less fixed and therefore more conventionalized and changeable, associative meanings, which clearly vary from instance to instance.
>
> (1980: 122)

However, Hall doesn't stop at this point. Taking these matters of definition a step further, he observes that a clear-cut distinction between denoted and connoted meanings is a little too simplistic, because most of the things we encounter in the world will contain elements of both, unevenly mixed. Or, to put this another way, while denotation and connotation are useful as what he calls **analytic distinctions**, they rarely operate in such a clearly defined manner in real life:

> We do *not* use the distinction—denotation/connotation—in this [the conventionally understood] way ... [Such] analytic distinctions must not be confused with distinctions in the real world. There will be very few instances in which signs organised in a discourse signify *only* their 'literal' (that is, near-universally consensualized) meaning. In actual discourse most signs will combine both the denotative and the connotative *aspects*.
>
> (Hall, 1980: 122)

Stuart Hall (1932–): a Jamaican-born sociologist who works mostly in Britain, significantly as a member of Birmingham's CCCS (Centre for Contemporary Cultural Studies). He has written on many topics, including diaspora and spectacular youth subcultures.

Sometimes, in fact, connotative meanings can come to be even more important than their denotative, more literal counterparts. Think for a moment about the connotative and denotative meanings of flowers, and particularly of the culturally enshrined habit of giving cut flowers as gifts.

Imagine this: a young man gives his girlfriend a bunch of roses for her birthday, and she's so appreciative, because she's the romantic type, and her head is filled with visions of romance, love and so on. She runs to the kitchen for her best crystal vase, fills it with water, adds the flowers, and then puts them on top of the bookcase where they'll be easily seen.

Figure 13.2 When is a rose not a rose? (or, 'I want to watch you die')

Why is this girl so happy? Because what she's engaging with are the **connotative** meanings of the roses—love and romance. And it's a good thing that the connotations generally prevail over the denotations in this case, because otherwise it'd be a very different story:

A young man finds some plants that are beautiful in their natural setting. He cuts off their sex organs (the flowers) and presents them to his girlfriend. She's thrilled, and wastes no time putting the severed organs on life-support (the vase and water) and on display (the bookcase), whereupon she will take pleasure in watching them slowly die over the coming week.

The techno-legal time-gap

Techno-legal time-gap: the time it takes for authorities to come to terms with problems arising from new technologies. A current example is intellectual property theft inherent in internet file sharing of music and movies.

Many of the issues addressed over the course of this chapter can be attributed to what is known as the **techno-legal time-gap**, which is the difference in time between the introduction of a new technology and the capacity of authorities (e.g. the law and school bureaucracies) to deal with the problems arising from it. (Some discussion of this phenomenon can also be found in the context of surveillance in Chapter 17). Hatchen and Scotton note that 'each technological innovation seems to create new problems, but not the … will capable of resolving them' (2002: 6).

Online identity fraud and phishing are both affected by the techno-legal time-gap: both activities are clearly illegal and to legislate against crimes of this nature is not difficult; however, how to enforce such laws is an entirely different issue, especially when international jurisdictions are involved.

Data mining, while not technically illegal, is considered by many to be a breach of privacy. However, legislation against data mining is unlikely, since some of the miners' largest clients are federal intelligence agencies (Hirst & Harrison, 2007: 327 (see p 147)).

The problems raised earlier with regard to Second Life and identity experimentation were largely ethical and moral. But isn't deception, such as concealing or changing your true persona, by definition a kind of fraud?

Finally, it would be remiss not to acknowledge that, at the time of writing, we are in the middle of the largest **techno-legal time-gap** the world has ever known. The issue at stake is intellectual property rights, and how they are increasingly violated through the sale of 'pirate' copies of CDs and DVDs, and the illegal online file sharing of music and movies. The effects of file sharing, in particular, are another strong example of the breakdown of the online/offline distinction discussed earlier. As a result of piracy, the entertainment industry is losing billions of dollars in revenue every year, and the effects are tangible. Has anyone else noticed that music stores appear to be closing just about everywhere you look? Or that CDs are roughly 30 per cent cheaper than they were five years ago, in an attempt to encourage people to actually pay for music?

At present, the Australian authorities are taking a rather heavy-handed approach to video and music piracy; every week, the news reports another major arrest of such pirates, and the seizure of thousands of … you get the idea. Likewise, there are aggressive advertising campaigns on television and at the beginning of every DVD, appealing to moral integrity, threatening severe penalties and so on.

While not encouraging anyone to engage in activities that are currently against the law, it is the opinion of this author that the strategies just outlined will ultimately be unsuccessful—*the problem is just too big*. Instead, some new form of transaction model is needed for artists to receive income from their work because, put simply, the current one no longer works.

Summary

This chapter has explored the interplay between online and offline social interactions, and looked at many issues relating to identity construction on the internet. A range of topics were raised, relating to online dating, selling, deception and crime. In particular, the chapter looked at the following:

- Phishing and its semi-legitimate cousin, data mining
- The dangers of putting yourself 'out there' online, especially the publishing of personal details on social networking sites
- Foucault's theorising on Bentham's panopticon, and the ways in which that particular metaphor may no longer hold true in online contexts
- The collapse of the online/offline distinction in today's day and age—'Facebook is life'
- Deception regarding our online identities—what's acceptable, and where
- Paidia and Ludus—two different kinds of play, and their usefulness in attempting to make sense of something like Second Life
- Stuart Hall, denotation and connotation, in the context of the perils of txt-messaging
- The techno-legal time gap, and the issue of downloading music and movies for free.

Further reading

Boellstorff, T 2008, *Coming of Age in Second Life: An Anthropologist Explores the Virtually Human*, Princeton University Press, Princeton and Oxford.

Foucault, M 1977, *Discipline and Punish: The Birth of the Prison*, trans. A Sheridan, Penguin, London.

Friedman, T 1999, *The Lexus and the Olive Tree*, Farrar, Straus & Giroux, New York.

Hachten, W & Scotton, J 2002, *The World News Prism: Global Media in an Era of Terrorism*, 6th edn, Iowa State, Ames.

Hall, S 1980, 'Encoding/Decoding', in S Hall, D Hobson, A Lowe & P Willis (eds), *Culture, Media, Language: Working Papers in Cultural Studies, 1972–79*, Hutchinson, London, 128–39.

Maslen, G 2010, 'Why Short Message Plays Go a Long Way', *The Age*, 8 February, retrieved 10 April 2010, <www.theage.com.au/national/education/why-short-message-plays-go-a-long-way-20100207-nk9e.html>.

Meadows, M 2008, *I, Avatar: The Culture and Consequences of Having a Second Life*, New Riders, Berkeley.

Wallace, P 1999, *The Psychology of the Internet*, Cambridge University Press, Cambridge.

Warren, B 2008, 'There May Be a Ghost in the Machine, But it Can't Spell or Punctuate. SMS Txting as a Contributing Factor to Literary Decline (or wotz rong w my spllng? y do u care?)', *The Australian Sociological Association (TASA) Refereed Conference Proceedings*, TASA, Melbourne.

Weblinks

Google Street View: http://maps.google.com.au/help/maps/streetview/

Minchin, Tim. Google Street View (song): www.youtube.com/watch?v=CZ7U3Cu4Mr4

For revision questions, please visit www.oup.com.au/orc/chalkley.

Endnotes

1   One further note on this topic: it must be recognised that the *potential for deceit* just discussed doesn't only exist in online contexts. To one extent or another, it exists everywhere. Perhaps, then, the difference between online and offline is not one of kind, but of degree; that is, it could be argued that deception in online contexts is sometimes more tempting because it's just so much easier.

2   Here's another example of a difference in degree rather than kind, insofar as misunderstandings can also occur in more conventional writing, especially where linguistic devices such as sarcasm are concerned. Sarcasm is among the hardest things to convey in written form, but using txt compounds the problem further.

PART 3

COMMUNICATION AND CONTROL

14

Social Networking and Social Norms: 'Be Nice or I'll Delete You'

Adam Brown

Do you use social networking? 'I do!'

In the middle of winter, the Family X are invited to a wedding of some close friends in the United States. Flying over to attend the ceremony, Mr and Mrs X admire all of those things that one can find at an everyday wedding, just like back at home: beautiful flowers, elegant clothing, free-flowing tears. They've seen it all before, but they never get sick of it. The children, on the other hand, are over it before they walk into the church.

A woman and man very much in love are standing side by side, seconds away from being pronounced 'wife and husband'. The groom hastily interrupts the proceedings, but not because he's had a sudden change of heart. The man takes out his mobile phone and starts typing. Moments later, the following words appear on Twitter and the man's Facebook page:

'Standing at the altar with @Jacinta213 where just a second ago, she became my wife! Gotta go, time to kiss my bride'.

Amid much surprised laughter, the marriage celebrant pronounces the man and woman 'husband and wife', and the newly wed couple complete their union with a kiss.

Mr X is unimpressed by the unconventional proceedings. Mrs X is pleasantly surprised. The children love it.

What you will learn from this chapter

This chapter introduces you to the growing phenomenon of social networking and its effects on everyday life. You will be able to:

- Understand what implications social networking has for individuals and society
- Analyse how social networking impacts on human identity
- Debate issues of privacy and social control
- Identify and interpret the intersection of social networking and politics.

Introduction

Although the Family X couldn't attend, the above event did actually occur in New Delhi in December of 2009 ('US Man Tweets About His Wedding from the Altar', 2009), and is one of many, many examples in which new media has the potential to have an impact on our everyday lives. Similar instances involving people in the process of getting married have occurred at other times and in other places (a quick search of YouTube attests to this), revealing a merging of the virtual world with the non-virtual or so-called 'real' world. This chapter explores the crucial issue of how communicating through **social networking** programs transforms social norms.

Figure 14.1 Screenshot of newly-wed's Facebook profile with updated status (invented)

Not everybody uses social software applications such as Facebook, MySpace or Twitter on a daily, or even a weekly, basis. A large number of people do not use them at all. And for many people (both users and non-users of social networking sites), the groom described above will be perceived as 'sad', 'lonely', 'depressed', maybe even a 'loser'. In other words, the man will be thought of as what has been (stereotypically) termed a 'social media zombie'. But his wife still married him, everyone enjoyed the wedding (perhaps even more than they would have otherwise) and he's still a functioning human being. The main point here is that it does not matter whether or not you are a frequent user of social networking, or whether or not you would ever conceive of making this a part of your wedding ceremony.

It is common for people to have very negative judgments about users of social networking, particularly when it comes to situations such as the example described above. Some people will cringe at the thought of one person being in a romantic relationship with another online for several months without meeting face to face; however, there is a good chance that several of their friends and acquaintances have been in such a situation. Making judgments about the use of social networking is fine, but when studying its application in human lives, it is important to attempt to move past these judgments in order to develop a full and critical understanding of the issues involved.

Online communities: What is social networking and what is it for?

We are social beings. It's not really an issue that can be debated—we simply need to interact with each other. And when one considers that, in July 2010, Facebook was declared to have 500 million users (and is, metaphorically at least, the fourth largest country in the world), all signs are pointing to social networking playing an increasingly significant role in this interaction.

Nonetheless, what exactly can be classified as social networking is far from a clear-cut issue. Online sites such as YouTube, which primarily consist of people and organisations uploading video clips for general viewing, are not generally the first examples that spring to mind when thinking about 'social networking'. Yet YouTube includes the facility to 'subscribe' to one's favourite channels (by adding them as a 'friend'), to 'share' videos by having links sent to other people and to post messages in response to videos. Video clips themselves are used to respond to the content of other videos and, of course, any YouTube clip can be embedded in other social software, such as Facebook and Twitter.

The writers of *New Media: A Critical Introduction* (Lister et al., 2009: 12–13) point out that new media comprises not only new technological developments, but also new textual experiences, new means of representing the world, new relationships between people and technologies, among others. In this sense, social networking can be considered a *process* just as much as a *device* or series of devices. As noted above, while Facebook and Twitter are perhaps the more 'obvious' means of social networking, there are countless others. These include random chat sites such as Chatroulette, content sharing sites such as Flickr, e-commerce sites such as eBay, dating sites such as RSVP, blog sites such as Blogger, travel advice sites such as TripAdvisor, reunion sites such as OzReunion, sports sites such as BaggyGreen and celebrity fan sites such as TomCruiseFan.com.

For the purposes of this discussion, we define social networking as the building of online communities through the movement of non-virtual human relationships into the virtual world via the use of various technological devices. Of course, these relationships are not necessarily separate from the 'real' world. This facet of social networking might be related back to the earlier discussion of whether or not new media is actually *new* (see Chapter 2). Social networking is used to gain and share information, to entertain, to conduct business transactions, and to form and develop relationships.

Is the function of social networking revolutionary or does it essentially involve the same kinds of communication transposed onto new forms? Many people invite friends to a party at their house through the use of a Facebook announcement. Someone watching a football match live at a sporting ground might simultaneously contribute to a related blog via their mobile phone. Setting aside the issue of whether social networking is actually 'new', these examples signify something *different* about social networking: that relationships generally move back and forth between the virtual and the non-virtual, which also exemplifies the connections social networking has to everyday life.

The online communities created and maintained by social networking affect countless aspects of everyday life. One must not underestimate changes to business and advertising practices, with both small and large companies constructing profiles on Facebook. Furthermore, in contrast to their earlier reliance on faxed press releases, journalists now receive many—if not the majority—of their news alerts from their Twitter accounts. The impact of social networking on the political realm, a topic to which we will return, is also immense. The construction of public personas of all kinds has

Get exploring!
To develop your understanding of social networking, jump on the net and browse the many offerings available. Who are they targeted at? What are their apparent functions? What are they actually used for?

moved far beyond the need to be careful of what you say and how you look in front of television cameras. Some well-known celebrities have more contacts on Twitter or Facebook than could fit into the world's largest sports stadium.

The rise of social networking has forced Communication Studies scholars to re-evaluate the complexity of the notions of 'relationships', 'friends' and 'communication' itself. The fundamental concepts of 'identity' and 'reality' are also affected by the worldwide growth of online communities. In short, social networking involves far too many important issues than could be covered in a single chapter. While we will focus on a few of these issues here, try to keep in mind the wider context of social networking as it applies both to your life and the local, national and international communities around you.

'Identity' in everyday life: Profiling our selves

Here's a true story: A girl, let's call her Deb, is about to head off on a week-long holiday. Deb asks her boyfriend to look after her garden. The girl's boyfriend, let's call him Charles, agrees to look after her garden: 'No problem'. So far, it sounds like a fairly normal (and even boring) story. But the difference here is that the 'garden'—or more precisely, the 'farm'—that Charles is entrusted to take care of is on Farmville, a computer game application that can be accessed as an 'add-on' via Facebook. The game involves planting seeds, harvesting crops and earning enough money from the sales to buy animals and other items. Deb is aiming to buy a golden chicken, so she's been saving up! After many weeks of hard work, Deb has earned almost enough 'Farmcash'. After providing Charles with a list of 'things to do', Deb heads off on her holiday and Charles logs onto Deb's profile on Facebook twice daily and 'runs' the farm: sowing, harvesting and selling. When Deb returns from her trip and visits her farm, she is horrified to see that Charles has spent all of her Farmcash to buy petrol for a tractor so that the daily task of harvesting is four times faster! Deb and Charles don't quite break up, but there is a long period of not talking to each other.

Figure 14.2 Screenshot of *Farmville*

So, what has happened here? As mentioned earlier, if you are not an avid Farmville user, you may need to move past your instinctive judgments about Deb being a so-called 'social media zombie'. No matter what we think about Deb and Charles's relationship, this brief example can tell us some important things about ourselves. Why was Deb so upset that she could no longer afford the golden chicken? Well, it can be argued that this was because the farm she kept on Facebook was *her* farm—it belonged to her and was, by extension, a *part of her*. Think about how you would feel if someone broke one of your prized possessions. The only ostensible difference between these situations is that one object is physical while the other is virtual.

To take another example, if your partner laughs at a romantic poem you carefully wrote in a letter for him or her, is there any substantial difference between this and sending the same poem via text message, or email, or Facebook post, and receiving the reply 'LOL'? It is highly likely that the emotions elicited in any of these scenarios would be very similar, if not exactly the same, raising the question about how distinct communication in the virtual and 'real' worlds actually is. Are the virtual and non-virtual 'worlds' really all that different? And if they are, does this mean our lives and our selves have been transformed into something different, something 'new'?

Susannah Stern's research into the use(s) of new media by teenagers reveals that 'online publications can provide important opportunities for managing their complex situations and shifting self-expectations that characterize adolescence' (2008: 97). On the other hand, the highly complex nature of social networking itself means that the reverse of this is also true: the building of, and participation in, online communities might be seen to affect *how* we view ourselves and what is important to us in the first place. The above example of Deb's fascination with obtaining a golden chicken on Farmville might be a (minor, perhaps even unimportant) instance of this. In this way, social networking is implicated in the active (re)construction of selfhood or identity.

We like to think of ourselves as being constituted by one 'true' self—the 'real me'. This idea is, with some reflection, fairly simplistic, as each person's 'self' is both multifaceted and constantly changing. The poststructuralist conception of identity involves rejecting the notion of a singular, 'true' self and acknowledging that there are multiple 'selves'. As Thwaites et al. point out, one's identity is a unique conglomeration of elements, a 'social composite' (1994: 214). This 'social composite' is made up of the interactions between the roles an individual adopts, the social positions one occupies and the categories one is placed in. These factors always shift over time as our identities are reconstructed, but do they radically change just because social networking is brought into the equation? When examining many instances of people using social media, the interactions, positions and categories that constitute one's identity invariably remain the same.

Let's think about the example this chapter began with of the man 'tweeting' at his own wedding. In the case of this individual, the 'social composite' is made up of the interactions between the roles the man adopts (such as becoming a husband), the social positions he occupies (such as an adult able to get married) and the categories he is placed in (such as a male in a heterosexual relationship). Even though the man is 'tweeting' at the altar, these crucial aspects of social interaction, social position and social categories are still present. The use of new media has no substantial impact on the function of the communication or, as it happens, on the event unfolding.

It must also be stressed that the 'self-presentation' undertaken by users of social networking is not free of the constraints of the 'real' world, but develops within a complicated network of conventions, social expectations and other people's identities. In their discussion of 'identity management', Ronald Adler and George Rodman (2009: 54) distinguish between (internally) 'perceived' and (outwardly) 'presenting' selves, and emphasise the 'facework' that people use to maintain their constructed persona(s). We 'manage' our non-virtual identities every day we get dressed for university, work or a party. Likewise, considerations of our audience and the expectations (we think) they may have affect the way we present our/selves online.

If I generally consider myself to be a shy person (my *perceived* self), uploading a profile picture onto Facebook of myself dancing and dressed as a Jedi Knight (my *presenting* self) might be seen to conflict with this. On the other hand, if *Star Wars* was widely hated by my peer group of Facebook contacts, I might decide it better to dress as Spock instead. In any case, does this mean that the management of my identity on Facebook is 'fake'? Is it really 'me' interacting with other online identities? If I obtained positive online feedback regarding a characteristic of my presenting self, could that then form part of my perceived self and then be incorporated into my 'non-virtual' persona?

According to Adler and Rodman (2009: 168), the use of new media such as email and instant messaging can be considered 'contextually interpersonal', as it involves communication between two or more people. This can also be applied to other forms of social networking, such as the 'tweeting' newly-weds. Indeed, this scenario would seem to reinforce Adler and Rodman's point that 'mediated communication can *enhance*, not diminish, the quantity and quality of interpersonal communication' (2009: 168). Furthermore, conducting 'facework' online may be argued to be more conscious and intentional than in the non-virtual world. Arguably, social media users have greater opportunity to deliberately consider and censor what information they provide on their Facebook page than in non-virtual everyday conversations.

In David Buckingham's words, identity formation should be seen 'not as an inexorable process of socialization, but as a process in which individuals are active and self-aware' (2003: 159). Social networking can even offer opportunities for people to explore and experiment with aspects of themselves, which they might be more uncomfortable about doing in other venues or situations. However, while it is evident that communicating through social networking sites frequently complements more traditional forms of communication and has the potential to impact positively on everyday life, there are many ethical issues in relation to social networking that must be addressed.

Gaining or losing control: 'Get out of my face, stay out of my space!'

Our lives have become integrally intertwined with computer-generated realities—from the basic economic transactions necessary for everyday life to membership in social networking programs such as MySpace or Facebook, to the construction of identities in synthetic worlds such as Second Life or World of Warcraft. In all these spaces, given the necessity of exchanging information to make digital worlds work, concepts of privacy, free speech, and copyright are disrupted.

(Halbert, 2009)

Another true story: an Australian man, let's call him Paul, finishes his work, has dinner and goes to bed for the night. Somewhere in the Northern Hemisphere, a complete stranger hacks into Paul's Facebook account and sends a private message to several of Paul's friends in the United States asking for money. By the time Paul wakes up the following morning in Australia, one of his friends has deposited US$1000 into the stranger's bank account and Paul's Facebook account has been deleted. All of this happened within the space of eight hours. The money was never recovered and Paul was uncertain about whether he would re-join the online community he once felt to be secure, a place where he was 'in control'.

Dystopian perspective: a pessimistic worldview that, in the context of new media, stresses the negative effects and consequences of technological innovation.

Social networking applications, particularly the massively popular site Facebook, have been the subject of countless stories in the mass media in recent years. Many of these articles represent what has been termed the **dystopian perspective**, which holds that the effects of new media on individuals and society are overwhelmingly negative. Newspaper headlines such as 'Friends you can trust, and friends on the net' (2010) and 'Be careful what you reveal to your "friends"' (Farrer, 2009) are relatively commonplace in daily newspapers. In mid-2010, much international criticism was levelled at Facebook in relation to its privacy settings and the potential for identity fraud or identity theft.

Many people felt that the information they had uploaded onto their profiles was accessible by too many people and that it was difficult to limit the audience to whom personal details were shared. In response to the unease, Facebook redesigned its security settings to make them more 'user friendly', although many commentators remained sceptical.

On the other hand, it should be noted that, despite the widespread criticism, there seemed to be very little that people were prepared to do about it. Logging off and deleting one's profile (although the information would still admittedly remain in cyberspace) seemed to be an option that very few seriously considered. One protest group organised what was coined 'Quit Facebook Day', set for 31 May 2010. The protestors' website (www.quitfacebookday.com) reveals that only 37,000 people had signed up to reject the social network, a tiny proportion of Facebook's more than half a billion users. However, academic research has identified a recent trend in 18- and 19-year-old Facebook users to alter their security settings throughout the year of controversy (Boyd & Hargittai, 2010).

Noting the vested interest that Facebook and similar applications have in obtaining people's private information, Leon Gettler (2010) writes:

> The world of online privacy is unexplored territory. It raises questions for business and society. How will these shifts change social interactions? Should companies have policies? Privacy regulators will have their hands full defining the boundaries. Nobody has managed to do it yet.

A major problem highlighted here is that non-virtual legal systems are essentially unable to 'keep up' with the speed with which we adopt social networking and shift more aspects of our everyday lives into and out of virtual worlds. On the other hand, many people argue that rather than lose control, people can gain control: that there are ways in which social networking can lead to the empowerment of individuals, such as in the political realm—although this too has its problems.

Adopting new media in the public sphere: Poke a politician

An important application of social networking not often highlighted by Communication Studies scholars is its use by politicians in the public realm. It is fast becoming 'compulsory' for leading politicians in Western countries to communicate with the people they represent in more and more virtual forums. Arguably, the success of Barack Obama's 2008 presidential campaign in the United States was heavily influenced by his use of social media. The effectiveness of the Obama campaign's ability to attract donations from tens of thousands of Americans through his website (www.obama.com) gave him a massive financial advantage over his principal opponent, John McCain. More broadly, Obama's success signalled a turning point for future political campaigns around the world, with much more emphasis being placed on new media than ever before.

Former Australian Prime Minister Kevin Rudd was particularly well known for his use of Twitter, often inspiring satirical send-ups by comedians nationwide. When Julia Gillard replaced Rudd as Prime Minister, she bowed to the pressure to establish a Twitter account very quickly, declaring that she would be writing her own 'tweets' (Counihan, 2010). This highlights the important point that social networking, while always putting forward an implicit claim to being more 'informal' and 'friendly' than the more 'authoritative' and 'bland' performances in television interviews, may be just as stage-managed as any other medium. As with other users of social networking, there is seldom any way of knowing exactly who is 'communicating' with their audience. In the lead-up to the 2010 federal election in Australia, the use of social networking by politicians raised more attention than ever before. In the article 'Blogs, vlogs and tweets the order of the day as campaign hits the net', Peter Munro and Carol Nader (2010) gave a clear indication of the various outlets available to political parties early in their campaign:

Soon after announcing her first election campaign as Prime Minister, Julia Gillard found time to tweet. Her now trademark pledge 'to move Australia forward' went out especially to her Twitter followers, whose numbers grew beyond 23,000 yesterday.

Shortly after her press conference, she also filmed a short video on the Labor Party website, with a link to YouTube. There she was, wearing the same white outfit and pearls shown on national television, speaking again of 'moving forward'.

Such efforts reveal that social media, too, is on the march. Labor has dedicated a 'small but quality' team to campaigning on social networking sites such as Twitter and Facebook. Last week, the party also opened its interactive 'social network space', where voters may list events, create discussion groups or contribute to policy debates.

The Labor Connect web portal is a key component of the government's re-election strategy, says Michael Allen of Campaigns and Communications Group, which designed the site. 'The rise of social media as a political communication tool is on par with the advent of television and telephone', he says.

The place of social networking in contemporary politics is crucial, and its importance is bound only to increase; nonetheless, new media is not the *only* way that politicians need to deliver their message, as traditional radio interviews, press conferences and televised debates still persist. The current social climate demands that politicians make themselves, and their message, available across a number of different forums, 'new' and 'old'. Social networking renders the construction of a public persona by public figures a more complex task than ever. As social networking applications are generally thought to appeal more widely to younger audiences, they may also require a different mode of **representation** than a politician would construct for a news or current affairs program. Yet social networking is not only used by politicians.

> **Representation:** the ways in which images and language are used to create meaning (see also Chapter 3). It follows from this that knowledge about everyday life and 'reality' is constructed.

Social networking applications arguably give 'ordinary' people the opportunity to play a greater role in the 'democratic process', and even, according to some commentators, enhance the practice of democracy in general. The interactive nature of Twitter and Facebook enables user-generated content from all directions, allowing potential voters to respond to the remarks and policy proposals made by political figures. Such activities also allow political parties to gauge public opinion using means other than the traditional opinion polls, and potentially take views expressed by the public into account when campaigning or serving in office.

Another example often cited as evidence that social networking enhances democracy is the filming of mass protests and the violent reactions to them by government forces during the Iranian presidential election in mid-2009. The video footage was generally captured on mobile phones and sent overseas to be uploaded onto social networking sites such as Facebook and YouTube. From here, the videos were released on more traditional television news programs all around the world, ensuring the violence became a major international talking point throughout the election process.

The increasing use of digitised technologies by the mass media continues to shape the political domain. The perceived need for 'instant', 'up-to-the-minute' reportage, made possible through social networking sites such as Twitter, provides political figures with less planning time to respond to breaking news. Channel 24, the ABC's twenty-four hour news channel, for example, was launched during the 2010 election campaign. Another significant intersection between politics and social media in July of that year, this time in the United States, involved the controversy surrounding Shirley Sherrod, an official in the US Department of Agriculture.

The furore began immediately after a conservative blogger, Andrew Breitbart, posted video clips of Sherrod, an African-American woman, making apparently racist remarks during a speech to the National Association for the Advancement of Colored People (NAACP) in March 2010. Sherrod was swiftly forced to resign by her superiors in the government, amid widespread condemnation from all sides of the political spectrum. In the days that followed, it was discovered that the several minutes of video footage, part of a much longer address, had been taken out of context and actually opposed racism. US President Barack Obama's administration then came under fire for its mismanagement of the issue, apologised to Sherrod and offered her a new position (Cornwell, 2010).

These tumultuous events occurred within the space of less than a week and inspired a vigorous debate over what many believed to be the negative consequences of an overly hasty news cycle. Indeed, Obama himself had explained the incident as partly the result of the fact that 'we now live in this media culture where something goes up on YouTube or a blog and everybody scrambles' (Zengerle, 2010). Thus, the rise of social media does not necessarily guarantee the enhancement of the democratic process. The overall failure of the pro-democracy movement following the aforementioned protests in Iran is another case in point.

The future of social networking: Calling it qwitts and blogging off?

So where to from here? Social networking is far from a stagnant phenomenon. New variations on social networking formats are constantly appearing and it's difficult, if not impossible, to know what will be the new 'flavour of the month' (or the week). The rapid (and always increasing) rate of change makes any prediction of the future direction of human interaction in the virtual world 'educated' at best. This chapter has revealed that social networking has had and will continue to have a considerable impact on everyday life, on both an individual and a societal level.

When this chapter was first drafted, this section included a discussion of the social networking site Google Wave, a collaborative project-building application that was primarily designed to allow a group of people—whether this be a group of friends, students or work colleagues—to upload and edit information in various forms. However, before this book went to the printer, Google Wave was cancelled, and so we wave goodbye to what was widely perceived to be a promising form of new media. Who knows what will be next?

One setting in which the adoption of new media has not been discussed yet in this chapter is the educational context. The use of social networking in schools and universities remains a complex issue and how students of various ages can (and should) be engaged through interactive communication technologies as part of their learning experience is still being debated. The aforementioned dystopian perceptions of new media lead many teachers to doubt its effectiveness—and even suspect its negative implications for student literacy (see Chapter 4). Nonetheless, the ways in which social media now saturate youth culture in particular arguably make any outright rejection of its use difficult, if not problematic.

The software package called Moodle has been widely used in the preparation, delivery and assessment of curriculum material in high schools for a number of years. Moodle stands for 'Modular

Object-Oriented Dynamic Learning Environment' and comprises numerous facets of e-learning, such as discussion forums and instant messaging, that can be used to facilitate fully online course delivery or complement existing face-to-face teaching. Many institutions, particularly universities that have a large number of distance education students, develop their own interactive e-learning sites. Deakin University in Australia has recently upgraded its former Deakin Studies Online Blackboard-based platform and developed D2L, which comprises interactive features such as a customisable profile (not unlike, some might think, Facebook). Some universities have built entire virtual campuses through Second Life. It is interesting to reflect on what kind of premise this development is founded on and what kind of implications this might have (if any?) for student learning.

The widespread use of social networking also gives rise to many ethical issues. For example, how can teachers manage cyberbullying in the virtual realm? Is it appropriate for tutors and students to be 'friends' on Facebook (see Chapter 17)? These are the kinds of questions that will need to be constantly (re-)negotiated in the future.

The emphasis on multimedia, interactivity, speed and open access, along with other perceived benefits of new media, is bound to shape social networking for years to come. At the same time, the process of convergence can also be seen in the continuation of social networking programs such as Facebook, which frequently adds new applications (often created by users) to its long list of possibilities. In a sense, one can witness a perpetual evolutionary cycle in the world(s) of social networking—a development of the 'new within the new'. It is impossible and frustrating—but equally fascinating—to predict where technological developments will take us next. In the meantime, go have a play on Farmville (if it's still there!) and try to earn enough 'cash' to buy a golden chicken before you read the next chapter, on yet another type of social networking: computer games.

Summary

This chapter has demonstrated that:

- Due to the very broad area of social networking, it is difficult to grasp its ever-increasing impact on our everyday lives (or even define it).
- It is nonetheless crucial for us to understand the effects of new media on the formation of individual and group identities.
- The role(s) of social networking in contemporary politics in the public sphere is complex.
- While concerns over privacy, identity fraud and social control will remain hotly contested issues, the merging of the virtual world and the non-virtual world is bound to continue into the future.

Further reading

Adler, R B & Rodman, G 2009, *Understanding Human Communication*, Oxford University Press, New York.

Boyd, D & Hargittai, E 2010, 'Facebook Privacy Settings: Who Cares?', *First Monday*, vol. 15, no. 8.

Buckingham, D (ed.) 2008, *Youth, Identity, and Digital Media*, MIT, Cambridge & London.

Halbert, D J 2009, 'Public Lives and Private Communities: The Terms of Service Agreement and Lives in Virtual Worlds', *First Monday*, vol. 14, no. 12.

Lister, M, Dovey, J, Giddings, S, Grant, I & Kelly, K 2009, *New Media: A Critical Introduction*, 2nd edn, Routledge, New York.

Stewart, C & Kowaltzke, A 2007, *Media: New Ways and Meanings*, 3rd edn, John Wiley & Sons, Milton.

Thwaites, T, Davis, L & Mules, W 1994, *Tools for Cultural Studies: An Introduction*, Macmillan Education, South Melbourne.

Weblinks

Bebo: www.bebo.com

Facebook: www.facebook.com

MySpace: www.myspace.com

Second Life: www.secondlife.com

Wikipedia's list of social networking sites: http://en.wikipedia.org/wiki/List_of_social_networking_websites

For revision questions, please visit www.oup.com.au/orc/chalkley.

15

Games: The Serious Business of Play

Mark Finn

Do you speak gamer?

Like many of their generation, the X children increasingly prefer interactive entertainment to traditional forms of entertainment such as television and DVDs. Both devote considerable amounts of their leisure time to both online and offline gaming and, as a consequence, have begun to adopt many of the words and phrases that characterise gamer culture. Master X even dreams of one day working in the games industry, so that he can correct many of the problems he sees with current generation titles. Below is a transcript of a recent conversation, recorded during a two-player *Tekken 6* battle. Importantly, the conversation took place both through text chat and voice as the siblings used the game as a medium through which to communicate.

Player One: Pwned! You should know Nina's special moves are a waste of time!
Player Two: Whatever! If our WLAN wasn't so laggy you would have been the one pwned
Player One: Whatever! Now you been pwned in both this and *COD2*. I've seen NPCs that have more skillz
Player Two: That's not fair. The way you set up the controller makes everyone play like an artard. If this was my game I'd fix that so the setup wasn't so important.
Player One: Sif. What company is going to hire you?
Player One: Don't need to. The indie scene is going to be where it's at.
Player Two: Whatever. Hey, you hear Capcom is going to release new DLC. Sweeeet!
Player One: Srsly? For The Win!!!
Player Two: Loser. Only losers use that kind of l33tspeak
Player One: Sif! Anyway, outta here. Mac and cheese for lunch!
Player Two: Win!

What you will learn from this chapter

This chapter introduces you to games and the culture that is evolving around gaming:

- The division of the industry into three distinct sections: the core, the casual, the independent
- The advantages and disadvantages each of these divisions have for consumers and developers
- The issues around games, effects and representation, including how gaming can affect gamers, and how they can reinforce or subvert stereotypes
- What the evolution of gaming technology might mean for the future of interactive entertainment.

Introduction: Mapping the terrain

If each generation is defined by the media they produce and consume, it could be argued that gaming represents the key media form of the current generation. Just as previous generations looked to forms such as radio, cinema and television for entertainment, many of today's consumers seek to entertain themselves through more interactive media like games. This trend has resulted in the status of games changing from niche product ('just for **geeks**') to mainstream entertainment form, with this being clearly indicated in the sales figures. In 1979, US sales of computer game software and hardware totalled approximately US$400 million (McGill, 1989: A1), but by 1996 sales had risen to US$2.6 billion (Entertainment Software Association, 2008: 11). By the end of 2008, sales of games software and hardware in the US topped US$11.7 billion (Entertainment Software Association, 2009), making it one of the fastest growing sectors in the American economy.

The rapid rise in sales can be attributed to a variety of factors, including the gradual reduction in the cost of entry to consumers as well as the increase in exposure to computing technology in general. Whereas the 1970s saw the gradual introduction of computers into the workplace, the 1980s and beyond have been characterised by the rapid adoption of computers in the domestic environment. This trend essentially began with the arrival of relatively inexpensive machines from Commodore and Atari in the early 1980s, and has continued to accelerate, due primarily to falling hardware costs. Most significantly, even though most of the early computers were designed primarily to run business and/or educational applications, most either shipped with one or two games, or had games available for them. This meant that, even from the very early days, computers were seen as having an entertainment function, and many of today's players had their first experience of computer games on these types of units.

It is important to note that, contrary to popular belief, many of these early players did not 'grow out' of their computer gaming phase, and have continued to play games as they have grown older, attained jobs and had families. Demographic data suggests that in the US the average age of players is 35, and that they have been playing games for 12 years (Entertainment Software Association, 2009). Similarly, a recent Australian study found the average age of players to be 30, while a 2006 survey found that the average age of Chinese gamers was 23.6 (Wang & Mainwaring, 2008: 2). The slightly younger average age for Chinese gamers can perhaps be attributed to the relative recency of

Geeks: a term used to refer to someone with a strong interest in computers or technology. Originally a derogatory term, but now possessing more positive connotations especially among computing and gaming enthusiasts.

computers becoming readily available in the domestic environment in that country, meaning that older consumers had less exposure to the technology as a business or entertainment device.

While the ageing of the gamer demographic might account for a steady growth in sales over time, the explosive growth we see can only be explained if this existing group is supplemented with a fresh new group of consumers on a regular basis. It is here that games become especially interesting, in that while games have been a part of our entertainment universe since machines like the Atari 2600 in the late 1970s, it has only been in the last decade that they have become part of the mainstream entertainment milieu. This period has seen enormous growth in the games industry, to the extent that by 2004 sales of game hardware and software surpassed cinema box office receipts (Holson, 2004). Perhaps more importantly, it has resulted in a radical restructuring of the industry itself, as existing hardware and software producers seek to adjust to changing consumer desires, and new producers appear, attempting to capitalise on emerging market segments. In this respect, understanding games becomes a case of understanding the interaction between a rapidly evolving consumer culture, and the industry that is trying to keep pace with that evolution.

The three industries

While producers of computer games are frequently grouped together under the general term 'games industry', it is in fact possible to identify several distinct modes of production depending on which criteria you choose to employ. If, for instance, you want to look at the industry from a platform perspective, it is still possible to differentiate between those companies that design games primarily for personal computers (PC), and those who design for **games consoles** such as the PlayStation or Xbox platforms. Indeed, one of the greatest shifts in game production over the past decade has been the shifting balance between PC and console games, with sales of PC software accounting for US$10.5 billion in 2008, compared with US$19.66 billion for console hardware and software (NPD, 2010). While it is difficult to make a direct comparison, because PC sales figures generally exclude hardware (since few PCs are sold exclusively as gaming machines), the fact remains that PC gaming revenues have continued to decline as consoles have increased in popularity.

In addition to the gradual shift in dominance from PC to console games, the last decade has also witnessed the steady rise of portable gaming devices. These take the form of either dedicated gaming devices such as the PlayStation Portable (PSP) and the Nintendo DS, or software developed for non-gaming devices such as mobile phones. These devices appeal more to those commonly called **casual gamers**, who do not wish to spend the money needed to purchase a console or high-end gaming computer, but still want a gaming experience. Importantly, portable game players also tend to have shorter play sessions than their console and PC counterparts, frequently fitting their gaming sessions around other activities (Bell et al., 2006: 417–21). Given the relatively low cost of entry, and the lower demand on time, portable gaming has become one of the fastest growing segments in the market, with figures indicating that, in the US market alone, publisher revenue from mobile games rose from $382 million in 2006 to $540 million in 2009 (Dredge, 2010).

Since the focus of this chapter is on the cultural aspects of gaming, perhaps a more appropriate way of looking at the games industry is to focus on how people actually play games, as in the way they engage with the hardware. In some respects this is perhaps the most accurate way to approach the industry, as in many ways the key changes that have taken place over the last decade have been in response to the changing consumer culture around games. When looked at from this perspective, it is possible to identify three main industry formations, though it must be noted that there is often considerable overlap between them. For the purposes of this chapter, we will refer to them as the 'core', the 'casual' and the 'independent'.

Games consoles: a piece of computer hardware dedicated primarily to playing games. Current examples include the Xbox 360 and PlayStation 3.

Casual gamers: a subcategory of player for whom gaming is just another pastime, to be consumed in much the same way as other media such as music and television.

The core

The core games industry refers to the developers producing mainstream (often referred to as 'AAA') titles for both PCs and consoles, and is responsible for generating a majority of the revenue. Companies operating in this category are often large organisations employing hundreds of people, and frequently are either subsidiaries of, or have close working relations with, hardware manufacturers. This kind of arrangement is particularly beneficial to the hardware companies, like Sony and Microsoft, as it guarantees them a high degree of control over the software, and is also beneficial for the developers, who have a more guaranteed income stream than would otherwise be the case. In this respect the core games industry closely resembles the film, music and book industries, in that there is often tight vertical integration between publishing, production and distribution.

The economics of the core industry are strongly biased towards the publishers, who fund the majority of the mainstream titles. While the development cycle actually begins within the production studio with pre-production, real work on the title usually only starts once a publishing/distribution deal has been signed with a publisher. In many cases publishers will demand to see a technical **proof-of-concept** demonstration before agreeing to fund a project (Rutter & Bryce, 2006: 41–2), which can be a costly exercise for the developers if the project is not subsequently picked up. Again, developers with a pre-existing relationship with hardware manufacturers and/or publishers have a clear advantage over what is commonly referred to as third-party developers, in that the latter usually have to overcome more hurdles to prove they are capable of delivering the final product.

The growing power of the publishers has had an interesting effect on the types of titles being produced over the last two decades, and has arguably resulted in a decline in the variety of titles being released. As with the film industry, the rising costs of production have made games publishers more reluctant to fund unknown properties, and this has led to an increasing emphasis on funding products with a proven track record. This is evidenced by sales charts, which show that in 2009 eight of the top ten best-selling titles were either sequels such as *Call of Duty: Modern Warfare 2* (see Figure 15.1),

or variations on an existing franchise such as *Mario Kart Wii* (NPD, 2010).

Another side effect of the power of the publishers has been an increasing reliance on established intellectual property from outside the games industry itself, especially in the form of film and television tie-ins. While gamers themselves often feel the quality of gameplay is sacrificed in favour of a timely release, for publishers it means that their product will benefit from the publicity surrounding the text on which the game is based. Perhaps more importantly, producing games based on well-known film or

Proof-of-concept: an early technical demonstration of a game, often with low-quality graphics and sound effects. Designed primarily to convince a funding source that the final game is worth financing.

Figure 15.1 *Call of Duty: Modern Warfare 2*

On the day of its launch, the game sold 4.7 million copies, generating US$310 million. This made it the highest entertainment launch in history, surpassing previous record holders *Grand Theft Auto 4* and the film *Dark Knight* (Silverman, 2009).

Source: Activision

television products has the potential of attracting consumers who might not consider themselves gamers at all. The idea seems to be that if a Harry Potter fan reads the books and sees the film then they might also consider buying a game so they can experience the franchise in an interactive way. Although there is no conclusive evidence to support this assumption, the rising number of tie-ins between games and other media clearly indicates that publishers believe this behaviour is occurring.

The casual

As noted above, one of the greatest changes to have occurred in games in the last ten years has been the rapid rise in the number of people playing, partly due to the gradual rise in the numbers of people playing mainstream titles, but mostly due to the emergence of a new category of gamer: the casual. Unlike many consumers of mainstream games, the casual gamer does not really see gaming as a key part of their entertainment diet, still preferring to entertain themselves with non-interactive media such as music, television and films. For them, games are often seen as something to fill the time between other activities rather than a key activity in itself. Indeed, some have argued that one of the key factors in a casual game's success is the ease with which it can be integrated into the player's everyday life (Bell et al., 2006). For this reason, casual gamers tend to invest in cheaper and more portable gaming hardware, often adding games to existing devices such as mobile phones.

To capitalise on and indeed expand this growing market, a whole new sub-industry has emerged. While some of the members of this group are also core developers, many are smaller operations with only a few staff, some of whom might be part-time or even volunteer. Since games for portable platforms tend to be less sophisticated in terms of their audio and graphical requirements, development time for casual games is much shorter than for mainstream titles, and this also translates to significantly lower production costs. The result of this is that the barriers to entry for this segment of the industry are much lower than for the core, meaning that many developers are now beginning their careers in this sector.

Another key difference between core and casual games development is the distribution mechanism. As noted above, the core games industry is still largely dominated by the publishers, who effectively control both production and distribution of mainstream titles. While this is also the case with some casual games, the smaller dimension of the **code** required for casual games means that developers have many more options for getting their product to consumers, frequently bypassing publishers entirely. This is especially true for games developed for mobile phones, where the small file sizes often allow developers to distribute from their own websites. While this is efficient in that it means all profits go to the developers themselves, cutting out the publishers also removes the promotional services publishers provide, so that smaller casual games developers often struggle to get their titles known in the increasingly crowded market.

An interesting recent trend in this sphere is the move towards content aggregation, where the work of many developers is distributed together through the same online outlet. In some cases, the software repository is established by enthusiasts who collect titles they perceive to be especially good, while in other cases the repository is hosted by hardware manufacturers such as Nokia or Motorola as a way of adding value to their products. Perhaps the most successful example of this practice has been Apple's App Store, which serves as a repository for a variety of games and other software in exchange for a small percentage of sales made through it. By leveraging the rapidly growing user-base of the iPhone and iPad, the App Store gives developers high-profile access to hundreds of thousands of potential customers, as well as providing a well-established download and payment system.

The independent

Independent game producers are not so much a third category of developers as a sub-category of both core and casual games industries, as independents can be found in both. They are, however, important to distinguish because their status as independent often affords them the flexibility needed to develop truly innovative content. Whereas many major developers are locked into the increasingly franchise-based projects, independents are free to create and explore their own intellectual property.

Code: the computer language used to create a game. Often based on established languages such as C++ but there are many variations depending on the platform the game is to be delivered on.

This is especially true of casual game development, where the lower production costs mean the company's finances will not be heavily damaged if a project does not succeed as planned.

This freedom often presents itself in the aesthetic approach to game design. Whereas mainstream developers are often focused on pushing the boundaries of current hardware with spectacular graphics and sound effects, independent developers often turn to more simplistic or stylised effects to achieve their gameplay goals. Games such as *FlOw* and *Darwinia* utilise technology that is often two or three generations behind the current standards, but do so in such a way as to foreground **playability** over flashy presentation. Perhaps more importantly, these games are often distributed free of charge or at a minimal price by their developers, in an attempt to build as large a fan base as possible.

Independent games developers are also important because their lack of constraints from either hardware manufacturers or publishers allows them to explore themes that would usually be too contentious for mainstream studios. For example, *Timothy and Titus* takes the standard imagery of a role playing game and overlays it with Christian values, so that players are rewarded for carrying out good deeds rather than killing and maiming (Jahn-Sudmann, 2008: 9). Similarly, Gonzalo Frasca's *September 12* (see Figure 15.2) places players in the familiar role of dropping missiles onto 'terrorists', only to subvert this by demonstrating that the more terrorists that are killed, the more that are created. Games such as these are exploiting the storytelling potential of games in ways that the core industry is only just beginning to explore, while also demonstrating the potential of games to investigate moral and political dilemmas.

Playability: the subjective assessment of the ease with which players can engage with a game. A game can be challenging but playable, but issues like software bugs degrade playability.

Cut-scene: Studying gamer culture

This chapter began with a fictional exchange between two gamers, and was designed to emphasise the point that those who play games are often perceived as belonging to a distinct sub-culture, complete with their own syntax and vocabulary. While both television and cinema have fans (usually

Figure 15.2 *September 12*

While many games feature militaristic themes, Frasca's *September 12* uses easily recognisable imagery to deliver an anti-war message.

Source: Gonzalo Frascal Powerful Robot

of particular texts), neither medium has produced 'televisioners' or 'filmers', which points to a significant cultural difference between games and these more established media.

The distinctive nature of gamer culture has certainly caught the attention of academics, who have generally focused on the relationship between games and wider society. Psychologists in particular have focused on games as potentially dangerous, and there have been numerous studies that try to establish a link between playing video games and antisocial behaviour, especially violence. In this respect, scholars such as Craig Anderson and Karen Dill have been especially prolific, compiling a large body of literature based primarily on experimental research. While the actual methodology varies from study to study, the general form this research takes is to expose selected subjects to video game content and then measure their reaction, either through their verbal or observed responses, or in some cases through physiological measures (for an example of this approach, see Rajava et al.,

2005). The results are then extrapolated to make predictions about the possible effects of playing video games.

This research is actually an extension of earlier work done in relation to films and television, which similarly attempted to find a correlation between media use and behavioural change, an area of research commonly referred to as **media effects theory**. As with these earlier studies, effects researchers have struggled to find a clear link between gameplay and changes in behaviour, most likely due to the complexity of the influences at work. While it might be possible to suggest a connection between gameplay and behaviour change under controlled test conditions, the tests themselves are necessarily artificial, thereby making it almost impossible to apply the findings to real-life instances of game-playing. Perhaps most importantly, research conducted in this manner deliberately attempts to isolate the activity of game-playing in order to reduce the number of variables, when in reality players experience games as part of a rich mix of social and cultural influences, including other media.

Media effects theory: a paradigm of media studies that seeks to find a connection between exposure to particular types of media and behavioural or attitudinal change.

Looking for effects

Though many academic researchers have turned away from the idea of direct media effects, the mainstream media still pursue the idea with some enthusiasm, primarily because bad news seems to sell more newspapers than good news. A classic example of this occurred in 2004, when the Rockstar game *Manhunt* was implicated in the murder of a 14-year-old schoolboy by his 17-year-old friend. The ensuing media frenzy focused on the violent content of the game, claiming that the murder was a result of the 17-year-old copying the behaviour he had seen in the game. Police subsequently revealed that the murder was in fact a robbery gone wrong, publicly stating that they found no connection between the murder and the game in question.

A related area of research seeks to explore how the practice of playing games might influence a player's perception of the world outside the game. Whereas traditional effects research often focuses on behaviour, this body of research focuses more on attitudes, and is based on the premise that our media usage has the potential of affecting the way we view the world. At the centre of this research is the practice of representation, and it is argued that how people, places and actions are represented in games and other media embody the ideology of the society in which they were created and consumed.

In this respect, representations of gender and/or ethnicity are regarded as being of particular importance, as these constitute two of the most common social identifiers. The depiction of women in video games has been of particular concern to many feminist scholars, who point to the exaggerated female attributes of many female game characters as a sign that games are perpetuating patriarchal ideas of women as sex objects. Dill, for example, argues that

> [t]he vision of masculinity video game characters project is that men should be powerful, dominant, and aggressive. The story video game characters tell about femininity is that women should be extreme physical specimens, visions of beauty, objects of men's heterosexual fantasies, and less important than men.

(Dill, 2005: 861)

Others, however, have noted that representations of gender are open to multiple interpretations, with Schleiner, for example, arguing that the image of Lara Croft from *Tomb Raider* (perhaps the most famous female game character to date) can also be read as drag queen, dominatrix, femme fatale, positive role model and vehicle for queer female gaze (Schleiner, 2001).

The situation is equally complex in terms of ethnicity, with some researchers expressing great concern regarding what they perceive as dangerous stereotyping. Barrett, for example, is extremely critical of the depiction of African-American characters in *Grand Theft Auto: San Andreas* (see Figure 15.3), arguing that the ability of players to control a black character and make them perpetrate acts of violence against other black characters works to reinforce negative racial stereotypes. For Barrett, games such as *Grand Theft Auto: San Andreas* can be seen as part of a wider social agenda that seeks to normalise discrimination and further what the author terms 'neoliberal fantasies' (Barrett, 2006).

By contrast, Annandale (2006) proposes a very different reading of the same game, arguing that players themselves understand that the representation of African-American characters in the game are meant to be read ironically. Annandale postulates that the excessive stereotyping apparent in the game actually works to undermine the stereotypes themselves, so that players are forced to consider the social implications of the stereotyped characters even as they embody them. For this writer, a game like *Grand Theft Auto: San Andreas* can be read not as an ideological tool for perpetuating racial stereotypes, but as a parody aimed at critiquing them.

Figure 15.3 *Grand Theft Auto: San Andreas*

Like most of the recent instalments in the franchise, *Grand Theft Auto: San Andreas* combined driving, shooting and role-playing games, framed by a free-roaming '*sandbox*' environment. The decision to give the game's violent protagonist an African-American appearance attracted many allegations of racial stereotyping.

Source: AAP Image/AP Photo/Paul Sakuma

Sandbox games: a subgenre of games in which players are given a large (but bounded) open world to explore as part of the game's narrative (e.g. *Grand Theft Auto*).

Avatar: a digitally constructed image that represents a person in a game. Can be human or not, and allows the player to interact with the game world as well as other players.

Whereas the games *Tomb Raider* and *Grand Theft Auto* present players with pre-constructed characters to inhabit, other games offer players much greater flexibility, both in terms of how their characters look and what they do with them. This has resulted in the emergence of another large area of research focusing on the way in which the player interacts with the virtual world through their **avatar**. To some extent, this research has its origins in the cyber-studies of the 1980s and 1990s and seeks to understand how virtual worlds can be seen as a useful metaphor with which to explore the complexity of postmodern society. As Turkle explains, virtual environments:

> imply difference, multiplicity, heterogeneity, and fragmentation. Such an experience of identity contradicts the Latin root of the word, idem, meaning 'the same.' But this contradiction increasingly defines the conditions of our lives beyond the virtual world. [Virtual worlds] thus become objects-to-think-with for thinking about postmodern selves. Indeed, the unfolding of all [virtual world] action takes place in a resolutely postmodern context.

(Turkle, 1995: 185)

When viewed in this context, the act of taking on an avatar identity in a game world is less about escaping from the real world, and more a case of extending the range of identities available to the individual. Importantly, this implies that there should be no prioritising of 'real' world experiences over virtual ones, because the avatar identity is seen as simply another expression of an already fragmented postmodern subjectivity.

While all media (and indeed most social interaction) provide opportunities for identity exploration, the range of identities available in game worlds, and the ease with which players can inhabit and the leave those identities, is significant. In a game such as *Aliens Versus Predator,* for instance, players can choose to experience the narrative as one of three species (humans, aliens or predators), each with their own specific strengths and weaknesses. In fact, to complete the game, players must actively switch between the different identities, as each one articulates the narrative from its own unique perspective.

From a sociological perspective, the ability to play as aliens or predators is perhaps less interesting than the ability to switch genders or ethnicity, as this points to games providing a space in which to experiment with key social identifiers. Much of the research in this area focuses on Massively Multiplayer Online Role Playing Games (**MMORPG**) such as *World of Warcraft*, which bring thousands of players together in a persistent virtual world. Ducheneaut et al. (2009), for example, studied avatar creation in three virtual worlds, and found that 34 per cent of players chose to create avatars with a different gender to their own, with this being most common among male players (Ducheneaut et al., 2009: 1153). Similarly, Hussain and Griffiths' study of players in five online games found that 57 per cent of players had engaged in gender swapping, although in this case female players were more likely to engage in the practice than males (Hussain & Griffiths, 2007: 50).

Other studies in this area focus on the ability of players to modify the physical appearance of their characters, an act which it is argued says much about how the players perceive physical appearance outside the game. According to Kafai et al. (2010), avatar creation in games operates in a similar way to identity construction in the real world, with players choosing elements they would like to emphasise while ignoring elements they would rather downplay. Drawing on Goffman's work on identity construction, the authors argue that game worlds can be seen as stages where individuals represent themselves and perform via their avatar creations (Kafai et al., 2010: 26). It is, however, important to remember that while MMORPGs do offer players more freedom in designing their characters than many other game forms, it is not total freedom, and the constraints are themselves socially important. As Pace and Houssian explain, the limitations placed on avatar creation in games such as *World of Warcraft* are based partially on established cultural ideas of gender and ethnicity, and partially on ideas drawn from other media. While as noted above some areas of research seek to isolate games in order to study them, Pace and Houssian remind us that many games essentially 'remediate' the imagery and ideology that is prevalent in other media forms (2009: 194). Thus, while it is possible to adopt a range of personas in a fantasy quest game like *World of Warcraft*, it is not possible to play as a punk skater or Marine sniper.

MMORPG: an abbreviation for Massively Multiplayer Online Role Playing Games. These games allow thousands of players to simultaneously inhabit the same virtual universe and interact with one another.

Taking the character out of the game

While many games now offer players the chance to customise their characters to resemble their real-world (or imagined real-world) appearance, gamers themselves are also taking things in the other direction. 'Cosplay' (short for costume play) involves players dressing up as their favourite game or animation characters, usually in the context of a convention or similar event. Although originally focused on Japanese anime characters, the last five years has seen the Cosplay community expand dramatically to include characters based on a range of popular video game characters.

Emerging trends in games and games research

As the preceding discussion indicates, the study of computer games is extremely complex. Not only is the industry itself experiencing massive change as it tries to both capture and respond to new audiences, the role of games in society is also the focus of much academic debate. For every study that claims to have identified a link between games and antisocial behaviour, another is produced that casts doubt on that link, and this has been a pattern that has repeated for at least the past fifteen years. The result is that the only thing we can say for certain about games is that we still don't know very much, and that as gaming continues to become more and more mainstream more research will be needed.

Further complicating the issues is the fact that gaming itself is rapidly evolving, throwing up a host of new challenges for researchers working in the area. Like most forms of media, gaming is essentially a technology-driven enterprise and, as such, changes in technology have the potential to radically alter the relationship between games and players. A good example of this is the notion of **photorealism**, which for some in the games industry has been the holy grail of game design. As game playing computers have become increasingly powerful, the ability to render graphics that simulate photographic images has become more possible, to the extent that, in some recent games, still images of game environments may be mistaken for photographs of real places. Not surprisingly, this is of particular concern to those worried about the possible negative impacts of gaming on players, who fear that players are going to find it increasingly difficult to differentiate between actions that are permissible in the game world and those in the real world.

At the same time, there is a growing body of research that argues photorealism is actually counterproductive in terms of gameplay, and may actually serve as an obstacle that impedes enjoyment of a game. As Tinwell explains, while developers strive to produce more and more realistic character models, there comes a point where players begin to resist the simulation. Derived from robotics, this point is commonly referred to as the **uncanny valley**, and describes a phenomenon whereby audiences' acceptance of virtual characters increases up to a point of near-realism, but then suddenly decreases as the simulation fails to conform to expectations of the real, sometimes reaching revulsion (Tinwell, 2009). Importantly, a perfect simulation does not suffer from this decline, but since even the best of the current character models are at best approximations of photo-realism, the uncanny valley effect may well be impacting on the current generation of gamers.

In this respect, the casual and independent games sectors may actually fare better than their core industry counterparts, since their relatively lower budgets mean that they don't have access to the technology required to produce photorealistic characters. Instead, these developers tend to focus more on refining gameplay than creating realistic graphics, with the result often being a game that is not as visually impressive as a mainstream title, but which offers a more enjoyable experience. Indeed, even though Nintendo is clearly a part of the core games industry, its decision to not push the boundaries of available technology with its Wii console has seemingly been a wise one, as it has enabled the company to price its console lower than the competitors and maintain significant market share. While not showing the same level of graphical sophistication as the latest Xbox or PlayStation, the Wii has attracted legions of gamers with its emphasis on intuitive gameplay, perhaps indicating that the future of games is not solely about realistic graphics.

The Nintendo Wii also illustrates another key trend in games: new ways of interacting with the software (see Figure 15.4). For most of their existence, players have interacted with games through keyboards or simple control pads, which seek to map complex actions onto keys or buttons. While the Wii still uses a game controller, the controller itself is a sensitive motion-sensing device, which

Photorealism: a subjective assessment of a constructed object's resemblance to a real-world object. In game development, producing graphics that resemble photographs is sometimes seen as a desirable goal for designers.

Uncanny valley: a term derived from robotics that describes the unease many people feel when they encounter an *almost* human simulation.

Figure 15.4 The Nintendo Wii

One of Nintendo's most successful consoles to date, the Wii uses motion detection hardware and software to allow players to control their avatars with body movements. In addition to generating significant revenue for Nintendo, the physicality of the game control has meant that Wiis have become popular in hospitals for injury rehabilitation.

Source: Edmonton Journal/Ed Kaiser

allows players to interact with games by imitating actions they would perform in real life. Whereas most tennis games, for instance, require players to use a thumbstick to move their avatar around the court and a well-timed button press to strike the ball, Wii tennis requires them to simulate a racquet swing to make a shot. This works to make the experience a much more immersive one, despite the fact that the graphical presentation might be considered inferior to that of more powerful games machines.

To date, the Wii has been the most successful of devices employing motion sensing for gameplay, but both Sony and Microsoft have been quick to develop their own systems. Similarly, many of the games available for Apple's iPhone and iPad platform have also been designed to make use of motion-sensing capabilities, and other device manufacturers seem set to follow suit with their own variations on motion-sensing technology. Although some computer science research into the technical implications of this has been conducted, media researchers have yet to really begin exploring the social implications of these new modes of interaction.

Increasing graphical sophistication and changing modes of interaction are but two of the technical changes that are rippling through the games industry, but the industrial and cultural changes are perhaps even more significant. The rising cost of producing mainstream titles has made it much more difficult for companies to make a profit, to the extent that many of the major developers and publishers are forecasting dire times ahead (Richtel, 2009). At the same time, gaming has quickly moved from a niche pastime to a mainstream activity, with the casual games market in particular growing exponentially. Thus, while it is likely that more people will be playing more games in the future, who will be making them, what they will look like and even how they will be played is open to question.

Summary

This chapter has provided an overview of games as a form of media, focusing on:
- The history of computer games as entertainment media
- Different ways of imagining the games industry, such as the 'core', the 'casual' and the 'independent'
- The rise of gamer culture, and the variety of ways it has been studied
- The problematic nature of 'media effects' as they apply to games
- The importance of representation in games
- Emerging trends, in both games and games studies.

Further reading

Bogost, I 2007, *Persuasive Games: The Expressive Power of Videogames,* MIT Press, Cambridge, Massachusetts.

Carr, D, Buckingham, D, Burn, A & Schott, G 2006, *Computer Games: Text, Narrative and Play,* Polity Press, Cambridge.

Fenty, S 2008, 'Why Old School is "Cool": A Brief Analysis of Classic Video Game Nostalgia', in Z Whalen & L N Taylor (eds), *Playing the Past: History and Nostalgia in Video Games,* Vanderbilt University Press, Nashville, 19–31.

Grossman, A 2003, *Post Mortems from Game Developer,* CMP Books, San Francisco.

Hjorth, L 2008, *Games of Locality: Gaming Cultures in Asia-Pacific,* Routledge, London.

Juul, J 2006, *Half-real: Video Games between Real Rules and Fictional Worlds,* MIT Press, Cambridge, Massachusetts.

King, G & Krzywinska, T 2006, *Tomb Raiders & Space Invaders: Videogame Forms and Contexts,* Tauris, London.

Krzywinska, T & Atkins, B 2007, *Videogame, Player, Text,* Wallflower, London.

Nitsche, M 2008, *Video Game Spaces: Image, Play, and Structure in 3D Game Worlds,* MIT Press, Cambridge, Massachusetts.

Rutter, J & Bryce, J 2006, *Understanding Video Games,* Sage, London.

Salen, K & Zimmerman, E 2004, *Rules of Play: Game Design Fundamentals,* MIT Press, Cambridge, Massachusetts.

Wolf, M 2002, *The Medium of the Video Game,* University of Texas Press, Dallas.

Wolf, M & Perron, B 2003, *The Video Game Theory Reader,* Routledge, New York.

Zimmerman, E 2006, 'Narrative, interactivity, play and games: Four naughty concepts in need of discipline', retrieved 12 April 2011, <www.anabiosispress.org/VM606/1stPerson_ezimmerman.pdf>.

Weblinks

Gamasutra: www.gamasutra.com

Games Industry Business: www.gamesindustry.biz

Games Industry News: www.gameindustry.com

Gamestudies.org: http://gamestudies.org

Kotaku: www.kotaku.com.au

Microsoft Xbox: www.xbox.com

Nintendo: www.nintendo.com.au

Sony PlayStation: http://au.playstation.com

Video Game History: www.thegameconsole.com

For revision questions, please visit www.oup.com.au/orc/chalkley.

16

Has Captain Jack Sparrow got an iPod? Technology, Piracy, Creativity and Ownership

Tony Chalkley

Can the digital pirate evoke the 'right to parlay'?

Mr X is a keen online shopper and has just received a rather large parcel: it is a USB turntable that connects to his laptop and allows him to play his old records, store them on his computer and then burn them to a CD (or load them on to his iPod). After installing his new software, he asked his daughter to help him make it all work. As they slowly load what she calls his 'old people music', Mr X's daughter teases him about the fact that his records are so old, she are out of copyright. This joke gets them thinking about the piles of copied 'stuff' around the house, and to fill in the hours it takes to load the music they scribble a list of all the pirated things in the house. Here's a short (but not exhaustive) list of what they found:

Mrs X:
Fake Jimmy Choo shoes (3 pairs)
1 fake Jimmy Choo 'Mini Sky' handbag
Many CDs purchased in South-East Asia
A 'China phone'—an iPhone copy (faulty)

Mr X:
Pirate copy of Microsoft Office
Many copied DVDs

Ten $3 Nike shirts from Bali Night Market

30 copied ebooks on his iPad

Master X:

24 pirated PlayStation 2 games

7 pirated Xbox games

Mixed T-shirts: including Tintin, WWF, AC/DC and many others

Almost 40 copied DVDs

One gold 'Rolex' (broken)

1000 shared tracks on his iPod

Ms X:

A fake Eames 'Danish Design' armchair

13 pirated PSP games

230 hours of mostly new release movies on a portable hard drive (from friends)

Faux Chanel perfumes (mixed)

1200 shared tracks on her iPod

2000-word essay (more on that later in this chapter)

Family X has 'accidentally' collected quite a volume of pirated material, some purchased in countries with little or no copyright compliance, some received as presents and the rest copied from friends at university and school. The Family X didn't intentionally set out to deprive the original producers of income, they don't see themselves as 'pirates' and, if the truth be known, they probably don't think they are breaking the law; well, not that much. As you read this chapter, you will learn how (and why) we now 'burn, share and swap', and you will discover how the move from 'fixed and protected' to 'digital and mobile' has challenged the concept of 'ownership'.

What you will learn from this chapter

This chapter explores the history of recording from wax paper to digital file and why this journey is important. In this chapter:

- You will discover that three important developments have altered (and continue to alter) the landscape of media communication: mechanical invention, software development and social change.
- You will read about the issues created by new media, especially around ownership and copyright, and how these issues play out in our everyday life.
- You will explore how piracy has been redefined by the young and not-so-young, and read how our lifelong indoctrination that 'it's good to share with others' has had a dramatic impact on the entertainment industry.
- Finally, you will find that the night before an assignment due date and the internet are not a good combination. Here you will read about an old problem with a new twist: plagiarism and the university/academic world.

Introduction

**Piracy/pirated/
pirating:** the act of
copying material that
we have not paid for.
It can be for personal
use or, in some cases,
commercial gain.

Most of us take for granted mobile, inexpensive (or free) and readily available music; small, portable DVD players; ready access to YouTube; discrete storage for many thousands of digital photographs; and, more recently, e-books. What most of us don't really know, or care about, is how we got to this point, how we came to live in a time where speed, size and convenience are (for most, not all) just part of everyday life. This chapter will explain how this occurred, how we started with the printing press and just a few hundred years later are beginning to see the traditional printed word as a digital signal: mobile, free and increasingly redundant.

With this background as a framework, the focus will move to more recent history and examine how the production of text, image, and sound has been revolutionised by inexpensive and powerful technology. This chapter explains why file sharing is commonly perceived to be 'OK' (even though, really, it's not) and will describe how traditional industries have struggled (and continue to struggle) with **piracy**, free expression, artistic freedom, ownership and profit.

Digital natives: those
born after the invention
of inexpensive, fast and
effective computing.
They have always had
access to computers,
digital files and online
communities.

You will also examine recent research into what 'sort' of person is likely to be actively (or passively) involved in the rapidly growing world of piracy. The reasons why we (particularly young **digital natives** (Palfrey & Gasser, 2008)) have embraced piracy are very simple and yet quite persuasive. After reading this chapter you might feel compelled to examine your own collections and evaluate to what degree you are involved in this social phenomenon.

Finally, this chapter will take the reader to a difficult and contentious place: the world of wikis, 'cutting and pasting' and, eventually, plagiarism. The freeing up of text from its origins has been fantastic! The definition of 'library' has changed, e-books are cheap and environmentally friendly, little-known musicians and performers have new audiences online, and hard to find and little-published research is quickly and easily accessed. Information and knowledge are now easily located, downloaded and digested. Like most new developments, with the good comes the bad. As a result of this 'freeing-up', it is now very easy and exceptionally tempting to highlight, cut and then paste large chunks of work and attempt to pass it off as your own. This enticement to plagiarise intensifies when combined with another global phenomenon. University students are increasingly time poor—research shows that over the past decade the average university student has been forced to work long hours simply to 'pay the bills' (James et al., 2007). Around the world, educational institutions have scrambled to react to this new version of an old problem, working to produce a solution, only to find that, in the meantime, the technology, software and plagiarism techniques have changed once again.

Genealogy: A simple metaphor

Before you read this chapter, it is important to understand the complex and elaborate process that produced the cheap, powerful and portable media device you have in your pocket today. The iPhone, laptop and MP3 player didn't simply 'appear' in our lives (although sometimes it feels like they did!). A really useful approach to understanding how this happened is to adapt an idea from Foucault; in this case, his theory about 'genealogy'. He had this to say:

> Genealogy is not the search for origins, and is not the construction of a linear development. Instead it seeks to show the plural and sometimes contradictory past that reveals traces of the influence that power has had on truth.

(Rabinow(ed.), 1997–9)

Of course, Foucault wasn't talking about the development of new media, but his concept of genealogy is useful here because it captures the non-linear, sometimes nonsensical nature of the way communication and media have developed. Think of your own family tree—with many branches and groups, some running for generations, some finishing after only one iteration. The way new media develops was/is the same, with many branches, many sudden and unexpected deaths and, in some cases, a long and highly successful lineage. It's worth remembering that the telegraph was 'invented' twice (the first time

Figure 16.1 On the left, the Newton; on the right, its offspring
Source: Blake Patterson

it was neither popular nor accepted!) and in 1987, when Apple released the Newton hand-held personal organiser, very few people knew what to do with it. As a result, by 2002, the Newton had all but disappeared. But the knowledge gained through the invention of the innovative little Newton was not wasted because some years later we see the 'offspring' of the Newton—anything with an 'i' at the start of its name!

Three seemingly unrelated and yet very important historical events have allowed us to own these things with 'i' before their names: mechanical invention, software development and social change. The following section will deal with each in turn, but it's important to remember that these events didn't really occur in the chronological order presented here; the process was haphazard and sometimes circuitous—just like Foucault's genealogy.

Mechanical invention: The printing press, books and the PC

Bearing in mind the genealogy of new media, this chapter starts at a very early and important stage in the family tree: the invention of the Gutenberg printing press (1450–55). Although forms of print production existed before Gutenberg (the Chinese invented a form of printing press centuries earlier), they were slow, labour intensive and did not produce text in meaningful quantities (Palfrey & Gasser, 2008). Gutenberg's new printing press was fast (up to 240 page prints per hour) and relatively cheap. This development meant that the days of expensive, hand-made literature for the upper classes were over. Theoretically, the 'man in the street' could now own a book (that is, if they could read) and the knowledge previously landlocked in one class or country could now cross centuries-old social divides, transported around the globe and enjoyed by the masses. Suddenly, knowledge, ideas and stories were no longer trapped in the brains of great thinkers or in the pages of rare and expensive books, and by the late 1500s book production had increased to such a level that the 'man in the street' could have access to his own copy of the Bible.

The invention of the printing press was an important stage in the development of new media and, in the five hundred years or so that followed, there would be many more. In 1822, Babbage 'reinvented' Mueller's mechanical mathematics device known as a 'Difference Machine'. (You might be interested to know that Ada Lovelace is thought to be the first computer programmer given that she was writing programs: she spent her days manipulating symbols according to Babbage's rules.) During the Second World War, a scientist named Konrad Zuse invented a machine he called the Z1. The Z1 is considered to be one of the first real operational, binary computers (in fact, it was more like a very large calculator). Zuse used the Z1 to investigate several groundbreaking technologies in calculator development: his machine could undertake floating-point arithmetic, high-capacity memory and modules or relays operating on the yes/no principle. An inexpensive modern calculator purchased from your local supermarket would be several thousand times more powerful than the Z1!

The first 'real' electronic computer (that is, one that is able to store its own programs) was produced in 1948 by staff at Manchester University. It was nicknamed 'The baby' and is widely considered to be the forerunner of the modern computer. It's hard for us to imagine how a machine with so little memory and such limited function could be considered groundbreaking. But it was.

The emergence of the common, popular and sometimes temperamental personal computer, familiar to the one we see today, really started in August 1981. Prior to this, a number of PC-type devices, mostly constructed from components purchased by the home handy-person, were available for the very keen computer 'nerd' (the author owned an expensive Sinclair ZX80, which performed functions so limited and dull that they are not worth mentioning here!). Early personal comput-

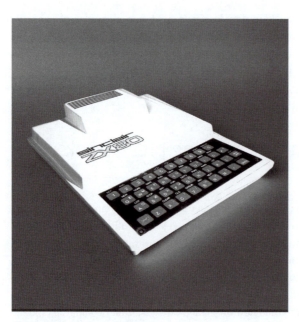

Figure 16.2 The Sinclair ZX80

Source: Photolibrary/Christian Darkin

ers were comparatively expensive. In 1983, a time when salaries were considerably lower than today, a typical PC cost $1500, and the groundbreaking Compaq two-disc portable cost just over US$3500. Not surprisingly, in these early years, take-up was relatively slow. But the arrival of 'clones', cheaper components and attractive functions such as games and chat resulted in a change in attitude and the computer emerged as a domestic device, a little like owning a refrigerator or kettle—we all suddenly 'needed' one (recognising that the 'digital divide' means that not everyone had/has equal access to this technology).

By the late 1990s the rate of change was so fast that your newly purchased computer was superseded by the time you had carried it from the store to your car. This is an exaggeration, but the rate of change was (and continues to be) quite staggering. This rapid change and development was made possible by one important thing: the discovery of a fast, compressed and reliable way to store, record and transmit data. The digital revolution had begun.

Software development: From analogue to digital

First, what exactly do the terms analogue (or 'analog') and digital mean? The *Australian Concise Oxford Dictionary* defines them as follows:

Analogue:

relating to or using signals or information represented by a continuously variable physical quantity such as spatial position, voltage, etc.

Digital:

1   Relating to or using signals or information represented by discrete values of polarisation.

2   (of a clock, watch, etc.) that gives a reading by means of displayed digits instead of hands.

The distinction between these two terms is very well expressed on the 'difference between' website.

There are two types of signals that carry information—analog and digital signals. The difference between analog and digital signals is that analog is a continuous electrical signal, whereas digital is a non-continuous electrical signal.

Analog signals vary in time, and the variations follow that of the non-electric signal. When compared to analog signals, digital signals change in individual steps and consist of pulses or digits. Analog signals are a model of the real quantity and the voice intensification that causes electric current variations. Digital signals have discrete levels, and the specified value of the pulse remains constant until the change in the next digit. There are two amplitude levels, which are called nodes that are based on 1 or 0, true or false, and high or low.

(www.differencebetween.net)

The simplest way to understand the difference between analogue and digital data is to imagine two clocks, one old-fashioned with hands, the other modern with a numeric display. Although the old analogue clock has markings and gradations (hours, minutes, seconds), the hands never stop; they seem to never be at a distinct place, sweeping past one second on their way to the next. This is analogue.

The newer, digital clock is different. The hours, minutes and seconds are discrete and can be observed as distinct units. This is digital.

Why was digitisation so important? Because this discovery enabled engineers to condense files, easily and quickly move them, and reproduce them with great accuracy. It allowed tiny devices to hold information so enormous that in the past it would fill a room and, most importantly for this chapter, it allowed for easy copying and simple **file sharing**.

The inclusion of a brief history of computing may seem out of place here, but the mechanical inventions and software developments over the past five hundred years provide an important backdrop for the concepts in the next section of this chapter. New machinery, mass production, digitalisation

File sharing: the process of allowing access to your digital files (especially music and film) in order to have similar access to the files of others.

and inexpensive components played an important role in the exponential growth of computers in our everyday life. Another really important factor in this process is not the staggering development of machinery, but the way we have accepted and adopted new media (and technology) into the fabric of our daily life and changed society as a result.

Social change: Adoption, adaptation, and then dependence

Once we had access (albeit very limited for some) to personal computing, individuals, governments, organisations and businesses set out to find new uses for this technology. In the late 1970s and early 1980s, 'Usenets', bulletin boards and electronic interpersonal posting began, and was, in the main, the domain of 'hard-core' early adopters. Things change quickly in the world of computers: by the latter half of the 1980s email had become increasingly popular, and the arrival of the World Wide Web in 1991 signalled a revolution in the way we used our PCs. Search engines, browsers, online sales and web pages were no longer just for computer programmers and electrical engineers. With a PC and a phone line, you could now surf the web from the comfort of your home (albeit very slowly—early dial-up was all about being patient!).

In 2000, a new phenomenon came along and it was called social networking. Here's how Palfrey and Gasser explain what this meant for those born into a digital landscape:

Digital immigrants: often your mother and father. They were born before the proliferation of computing and the digitisation of data.

> Digital natives are constantly connected. They have plenty of friends, in real space and in the virtual worlds—indeed, a growing collection of friends they keep a count of, often for the world to see, in their social network sights. In the course of this relentless connectivity, the very nature of relationships is changing.
>
> (Palfrey & Gasser, 2008: 5)

But it's not just the idea of what makes a relationship that has been reconceptualised: the idea of ownership, sharing and copyright has also changed. Palfrey and Gasser on music and the digital native:

> And they still share a lot of music. But the experience is far less likely than before to take place in a physical space, with friend hanging out to listen to a stereo system. The network lets them share music that they each, then, can hear through headphones, walking down the street or in their dorm rooms, mediated by an iPod or the iTunes Music System on their hard drive.
>
> (Palfrey & Gasser, 2008: 5–6)

And as a result of this hyper-mobility:

> [a] generation has come to expect music to be digitally formatted, often free for the taking, and endlessly shareable and portable.
>
> (Palfrey & Gasser, 2008: 6)

The mass production of inexpensive technology, simple and efficient software, a breathtaking capacity to store 'stuff' and a whole generation that has no experience of the pre-digital world means that the rules have changed. The following section looks at two implications of these rules: piracy and plagiarism.

The motivation to pirate

'I didn't do it, nobody saw me do it, there's no way you can prove anything!'

(Bart Simpson)

At the start of this chapter you read how the Family X compiled a significant list of pirated material: they have iPods with copied music, fake DVDs, downloaded new release films and cheap copies of expensive products. It's quite possible, to a greater or lesser degree, that your house is the same. And like Bart Simpson, we like to think that 'I didn't do it, nobody saw me do it, there's no way you can prove anything'. In part, this is true, but the inventors of Napster and LimeWire might disagree! Most of us have at least one burnt album or a copy of a film that we wouldn't normally pay to see at the cinema and the research used in this chapter suggests that this is not about to change.

The discussion here is not about the legality of piracy or the application of complex copyright legislation. It's much simpler than that: it's about why we do it.

The first reason is the most obvious, and really needs no explanation—it is free (or close to).

The second reason is that we do it because everyone else is. Palfrey and Gasser's research found that:

> The vast majority of digital natives are currently breaking copyright laws on a regular basis. By and large, many young people don't pay for music. Sometimes, they watch television shows or movies illegally. Often they use the systems created by other digital natives in order to copy or watch the files … the practice is pervasive. And an entire generation is thwarting the copyright law as they grow up.

(Palfrey & Gasser, 2008: 132)

The digital native's belief that piracy is a normal, socially acceptable everyday event is a big challenge for producers of portable and compact digitised files. The longer a behaviour goes 'unpunished' the more **normalised** it becomes and, as a result, we do it more often and for more things.

It's a **vicious circle**. Palfrey and Gasser also discovered something really interesting: part of this acceptance comes from the fact that, from a very young age, we are socialised 'to share'. They suspect that the strongly held and deeply entrenched social norm that 'sharing is good' is far more persuasive that the threat of punishment, effectively overwriting the rules and norms set out in copyright law (Palfrey & Gasser, 2008).

Another potent reason for the popularity of piracy is that it is acceptable because of a perception that it causes no harm to those who own the source material. In other words, if your friend has, say, a Metallica album you like, they can copy it for you and they still have their copy. Sharing an album in a digital form is not like stealing a CD from the artist or a store. On the whole, digital natives see no link between (or crime in) burning a copy and causing a loss to the artist (Palfrey & Gasser, 2008). Further compounding this problem is the fact that we find it hard to perceive a successful and rich band or artist as a 'victim' of crime. It's hard to think of Lady Gaga or Katy Perry as victims—they are rich and powerful, and we think 'Surely downloading one album can't do them any harm?'

There is another element to the many problems with pirates: the presence of commercial products (that is, music and film) in an environment that promotes an anti-commercial culture (that is, the internet) is also a problem. The insubstantial nature of 'things' on the internet means that we don't tend to treat them as 'property'. In digitised form, music and film relies on the protection offered by global intellectual property rights laws and this is also a problem because when it comes to property we make a fundamental distinction between, say, a leather jacket and a digital file. We can see and touch the leather jacket; it has a physical form and is entirely visible to the human eye. Possibly you know the

Normalised: the process by which an action is repeated so often that it comes to be considered an acceptable part of everyday life.

Vicious circle: a process by which an action (usually to solve a problem) causes a reaction that results in a return to the initial problem.

owner of the jacket. The digital file, on the other hand, is invisible, has no real physical form and is very easy to steal (and yet simultaneously leave in its original place). I doubt that you know Lady Gaga, so it's easy to steal her invisible, digitised music file. It's not the right thing to do, but it's easy!

So, it would seem that, for your average 'pirate', there is a disconnect between 'file sharing' and 'theft', but the act of 'softlifting' (software piracy by individuals) is a little different. When we set out to 'softlift' we face a different ethical decision and it's one that we have to make a much more conscious decision to undertake. Thong and Yap, media researchers, found that when it comes to software piracy we are influenced by two evaluations: deontological and teleological. The first, deontological, starts with a simple question: *what are the rules with this activity—is it ethical or not?* Once we have made a decision about the 'ethicality' of our actions, we undertake a teleological evaluation: *what are the consequences of this action?* With these two evaluations complete, we then check our decision with the situation around us: are all our friends doing it without consequence? People do make deontological and teleological evaluations before copying and sharing software, but the practice seems less common and perhaps that's because the size and complexity of the software seems more substantial, more valuable: perhaps more like 'property'.

One of the most significant obstacles facing those charged with protection of the intellectual property rights of the artist and producer is the intangible nature of what they protect. Material objects are limited by their nature as to their use. If one person is using an object, this means that others cannot. For example, an old-fashioned record could only be played by one person at a time. Because the tangible object (the record) can only be at one place at a time, is limited by geography and is very hard to reproduce, it is more easily protected (Yar, 2008). This is not so easy for the intangible digital file.

In their paper 'Digital Piracy: Factors that Influence Attitude forward Behavior', Al-Rafee and Cronan (2006) identified seven factors that influence the decision to pirate (or not) (see Figure 16.3).

If you look closely, you will realise that the seven influential factors described in the figure are not exclusive to the decision to engage in piracy; they are really the way in which we make most everyday

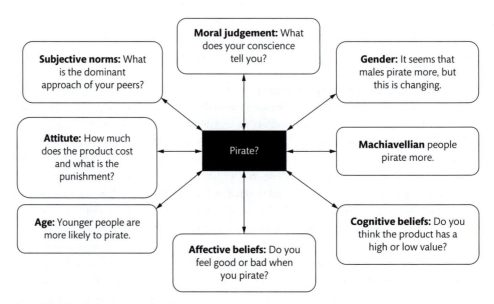

Figure 16.3 To pirate or not to pirate?

Source: Al-Rafee & Cronan, 2006

decisions. The difference between deciding to shoplift and file sharing is a good example because, using the factors in Figure 16.3, shoplifting is not often a dominant social behaviour, we can see the shopkeeper and they can see us, material goods have an easily identified value and the likelihood of detection and resultant legal action is liable to deter us. File sharing is a less complex decision. Why? Because the files are invisible, as is their owner; most of our friends file-share; and the music files have no easily identifiable monetary value.

That still doesn't make it right.

To conclude this section, it's worth revisiting the work of Palfrey and Gasser, especially their theory about how society is changing. Here's what they had to say about digital natives:

> When it comes to media, digital natives seem like a completely different species from their parents and grandparents. Digital natives don't remember photographs captured on a roll of film that had to be sent to the drugstore [chemist] to be printed out; they think in digital images, instantly viewable, 'deletable' and shareable with friends on the internet. Digital natives don't think of news and information as something that arrives in a mass of pulp on the doorstep in the morning … they don't think in terms of recorded music in the form of LPs, eight-tracks, cassette tapes or even CDs, purchased at a record store; music for them exists in a digital format they can download from the internet, move around and share.
>
> (Palfrey & Gasser, 2008: 131)

So, perhaps the simplest reason we behave like pirates is because we can.

Plagiarism: Ease, speed and pressure

> After a hard day at university, followed by a really busy shift at work, Ms X returned home to face the nasty realisation that she had a relatively major essay due the next morning. It was too late for an extension (and she really didn't have a legitimate reason); she was just paying for a few weeks of procrastination. At 11pm she finally sat down with her laptop open and Google at the ready (and Wikipedia as well, though she knew that most professors had banned the use of Wikipedia). As she started to research her topic she came across a website that had many, many sample essays on the topic. As they were Word documents, with a little re-writing and a few 'find and change alls', in an hour (tops) she would have the essay completed.
>
> With a full day of classes the next day and four weekend shifts lined up at work, she knew that it was now or never and decided (using a similar decision-making model to that in Figure 16.3) that, because the chance of being caught was slim and she really had no other option, she would plagiarise the essay and hope it worked.

All universities (and most schools) have a policy and procedure for dealing with plagiarism and, generally, these procedures evolve at a rate that simply cannot match technological change. It's tempting to plagiarise, digitisation has made it easy to do so and it's always possible to justify why 'it was the only option'. Here is what one of the most prestigious universities in the world has to say:

The Challenge of Original Work

You must always distinguish your own words and ideas from the words and ideas of others—including the authors of print or electronic sources, faculty members, classmates, and friends. Making those distinctions isn't always easy and can be made even more difficult by less-than-careful research habits or the time pressure of submission deadlines … Such a failure can lead to the accusation of plagiarism—defined as the use of any source, published or unpublished, without proper acknowledgment. Plagiarism is a very serious charge at Princeton, which can result in disciplinary probation, suspension, or expulsion.

(Princeton University, 2008)

The 'Academic Integrity at Princeton' booklet is very similar to most other universities, but their well written policy is not new, nor is it groundbreaking. Plagiarism has existed for as long as formal assessment—where there is one, you will find the other! What is new is the ease by which students can cut, paste and print the work of others and attempt to pass it off as their own (the early part of this chapter explained how digitalisation unlocked data from its origins, freed text from the page and allowed knowledge to migrate uninhibited by geography—these developments also had a profound impact on plagiarism).

Sadly, when under-the-pump, Ms X decided to cut and paste the work of others, pass it off as her own and email it to the assignment team, she didn't know that her university would use a software package to scan her work, check it against the billions of words found on the internet and send it on to the university's discipline committee. This works for writing where the primary source is found and is easily identified, but what about a web-based custom-written essay?

The rapid development in media technology presents a real challenge to educational institutions: it provides attractive shortcuts for increasingly busy students and now it presents a number of new opportunities for the enterprising e-business person. Here's what one Australian essay service has for sale:

Affordable Essay Writing Services.

Don't fail your assignments, get help! We provide the needed assistance to many Australian students who are stressed out with their essay assignments. See for yourself how our knowledge and experience can work for you. Let our trusted team of professional essay writers create an essay directly from your instructions. Stop worrying about how you will write your essay and let a professional writer give you the advantage you need. We can save you hours of time when it comes to researching and writing an original essay. When you need help writing your essays, just remember that the professional essay writers of BestEssays.com.au can meet any deadline guaranteed. What are you waiting for? Stop stressing out and order a custom written essay today!

(Best Essays, 2011)

For A$106.36 and a seven-day wait, Ms X could email her essay question to the service and receive a well-written and polished 'original' essay that would fool both her tutor and the plagiarism software. Once again, essay writing for money is not new, but services such as these are very attractive: they make use of the ease with which data can be moved, they actively work to foil university systems and provide a targeted service to a cohort of people already under pressure. Ms X's custom essay would cost her less than she makes from one shift at work!

Here's what an employee of a US essay writing service had to say about the average work day for him:

The request came in by e-mail around 2 in the afternoon. It was from a previous customer, and she had urgent business. I quote her message here verbatim (if I had to put up with it, so should you): 'You did me business ethics propsal for me I need propsal got approved pls can you will write me paper?'

I've gotten pretty good at interpreting this kind of correspondence. The client had attached a document from her professor with details about the paper. She needed the first section in a week. Seventy-five pages.

I told her no problem.

It truly was no problem. In the past year, I've written roughly 5,000 pages of scholarly literature, most on very tight deadlines. But you won't find my name on a single paper.

(Dante, 2010)

This new phenomenon is genuinely disturbing for those who work in education, but, to some degree, the digital revolution made it inevitable. When a service such as this is made available to busy digital natives, who 'seem like a completely different species from their parents and grandparents' (Palfrey & Gasser, 2008) but are expected to follow the same rules, of course some of them take it up. But how popular might these services become, and how will universities respond?

Conclusion

First, piracy is theft. Not theft like robbing a house, or shoplifting or stealing from a friend, but theft nonetheless. The intangible nature of digital material and the invisibility of the owner or producer make us think of piracy as a 'victimless crime': how can a binary series of '0s' and '1s' be someone's property?

One thing is certain: pirates don't necessarily look like Jack Sparrow, but they will have a burnt copy of his movies!

Summary

In this chapter you discovered that:
* The world of file sharing has grown exponentially: as one file share site is shut down, many others spring up to take its place.
* Digital natives increasingly come to view file sharing as an acceptable, everyday practice. This is a challenge for artists, producers, lawyers and professors alike.
* The 'victimlessness' of piracy allows us to disconnect from the idea that we are stealing from anyone in particular.
* The freeing up of text from its creator has not just produced problems for the music and film industries; universities and schools now face challenges in ascertaining whose work is original and whose isn't!

Further reading

Al-Rafee, S & Cronan, T 2006, 'Digital Piracy: Factors that Influence Attitude toward Behavior', *Journal of Business Ethics*, vol. 63, no. 1, 237–59.

Best Essays 2011, 'Custom Essay Writing', retrieved 19 May 2011, <www.bestessays.com.au/doc_essay.php>.

Dante, E 2010, 'The Shadow Scholar', *Chronicle of Higher Education*, November 12, retrieved 19 May 2011, <http://chronicle.com/article/article-content/125329>.

James, R, Bexley, E, Devlin, M & Marginson, S 2007, *Australian University Student Finances 2006: A Summary of Finding from a National Survey of Students in Public Universities*, University of Melbourne, Melbourne, retrieved 6 February 2011, <http://www.universitiesaustralia.edu.au/resources/136/AUSF%20Report%202006.pdf>.

Palfrey, J & Gasser, U 2008, *Born Digital: Understanding the First Generation of Digital Natives*, Basic, New York.

Princeton University 2008, 'Academic Integrity at Princeton', retrieved 19 May 2011, <www.princeton.edu/pr/pub/integrity/08/academic_integrity_2008.pdf>.

Rabinow, P (ed.) 1997–9, *Essential Works of Foucault, 1954–1984*, The New Press, New York.

Yar, M 2008, 'The Rhetorics and Myths of Anti-piracy Campaigns: Criminalization, Moral Pedagogy and Capitalist Property Relations in the Classroom', *New Media and Society*, vol. 10, no. 4, 605–23.

Weblinks

Best Essays ('providing students with help since 1997'): www.bestessays.com.au

Difference Between Similar Terms and Objects: www.differencebetween.net

For revision questions, please visit www.oup.com.au/orc/chalkley.

Surveillance: Why is Everybody Staring?

Tony Chalkley

Family X returns from their Bali holiday

When they touch down in Melbourne, they are photographed and their passports are scanned on arrival. Tired and scruffy, they have their hand luggage scanned and checked by customs, and they politely answer questions about their holiday in the sun. Mr X travels often for his work, and by a strange twist of fate has now sequentially visited four countries that are considered to 'be of interest' and his records are more closely checked: his bag and passport are removed to a secure room for close scrutiny. Details of the flight and all other travel information are recorded on the immigration travel database.

Finally the family exit the airport and use their credit card to buy tickets for the car park shuttle. The family are recorded by airport security cameras and on the shuttle bus, which drops them at their car, all of which is covered by closed circuit television (CCTV). When they departed, they accidentally left their car lights on and, as a result, the car battery has gone flat. They make a quick call to their Roadside Assistance and, after giving their registration and membership details, the car starts and they are on their way home.

As the family drives out of the airport, they switch on their sat-nav system, which guides them home, but also alerts them to speed and traffic-light cameras on the way (these cameras record their progress, but also capture the fact that Mr X is going 8 kilometres an hour over the speed limit). Master X uses his mobile to call a friend and check his voicemail; this is logged by the telephone company and could be used by police to locate where the phone was at the time.

On the way back they stop at an out-of-town shopping centre and race into (Safeway) to buy bread, milk and other items. CCTV records them in the car park and entering the supermarket. All details of their shopping are recorded when they pay using a loyalty card.

This will be used to build up a customer profile. This data is often sold on to others and, as a result, Ms X has noticed that she seems to get more junk mail than her brothers!

The money they spend on credit cards is also monitored to check for any unusual spending patterns and a large purchase of 312 DVDs in the central Javanese city of Bandung results in an email to Mr X: his bank needs conformation that he authorised such a purchase. The amounts spent and whether the family keep within agreed credit levels are also monitored and used to build a credit profile.

On the way home, they use (CityLink), and, as the (e-tag) is in their other car, Mrs X calls the toll company and pays via her mobile. All details, including photographs of them entering central (Melbourne), are recorded. Even though they are all tired, they decide to collect the family dog from the boarding kennel, a quick process because the manager simply scans the dog's microchip to ensure they have the right pooch!

At home in (Seddon), they unload under the watchful eye of a neighbour's private CCTV system and laugh as the Google Street View van photographs their pile of suitcases and the dog peeing in the lawn. Waiting at home is a pile of personally addressed junk mail.

Master X goes to his room to read a letter telling him his police check is clear and that he has a place on a voluntary scheme with the (Red Cross). While he reads the letter, he (tweets) to his soccer mates that he is 'too shagged to play tomorrow'. His sister quickly checks her email and uploads her swimming photos to her (Facebook) page. Her IP and clickstream are recorded and her photograph titled 'too hot for a wetsuit' is secretly phished and uploaded to a dedicated server in a little-regulated country in central Europe.

Master X orders the family some takeaway. His address, card details and previous orders are already held by the pizza chain and he simply orders 'the usual'. As they suspended their cable television for the month they were away, no one can remember the password, but a brief call to the cable company and three identity questions later, the family sits down to watch, argue about and SMS vote on (*So You Think You Can Dance*). (Based on a story that appeared in *The Age* newspaper, September 2008.)

What you will learn from this chapter

- This chapter introduces you to the 'panopticon', a 1785 prison design that is a useful concept for examining modern surveillance.
- (How) Do we live in a surveillance society?
- The problems with power, watching and being watched
- The emergence of micro-surveillance in everyday life
- Cases studies: Facebook, the school canteen and cameras
- How consumption and cards are surveilled
- Surveillance, terrorism, moral panic and the rights of the individual.

Introduction

When we hear the word 'surveillance', often our first instinct is to think of an all-knowing, all-seeing authority tracking, recording and storing our private conversations and massing volumes of data for later scrutiny. Chances are, your instinctive definition of this word is likely to be drawn from science fiction/thriller films, jam-packed with hidden cameras and evil agents who are either 'out to get you' or 'out to save you'. Surveillance is more complex than this, and the aim of this chapter is to describe and explain how surveillance is more than simply 'Big Brother' watching over us; in the pages that follow, you will discover how (and why) surveillance is actually an elaborate process of control, compliance and resistance. This chapter uses **social construction** theory to explain the consequences of living in a **surveillance society**, the 'problems with watching', the power of the viewer and the emergence of 'Little Brothers' as part of our everyday lives (Hirst & Harrison, 2007).

If you type the word 'surveillance' into any popular internet search engine, you are guaranteed more than 45,200,000 hits, many definitions, many thousands of citizen protest sites and even links to companies keen to sell you devices so small, so discreet that 'your friends and family will never know they are there'. For eighty dollars and seven days delivery, you could have this 'Little Brother' on your desk, bedside table or mantel (see Figure 17.1).

The ready availability of this hidden camera clock makes me wonder: 'Why would you want a camera hidden in a clock?' and 'What would you do with the images you record?' In order to better understand the motivation (and problems) associated with the use of these (and other) 'Little Brothers' we need to explore some of the theories and key concepts that underpin our assumptions and beliefs around why we have come to so readily embrace and tolerate surveillance as a component of our everyday lives. To do this, we need to review some of the 'big ideas' about the theories and concepts captured in the expression 'social construction'.

Social construction: When we say that something is 'socially constructed' we are saying that its existence is dependence on contingent aspects of our social selves.

Surveillance society: living in a community that promotes, accepts and embraces increasing levels of surveillance (physical, electronic and anonymous) as an important component of everyday life.

Figure 17.1 Clock radio with hidden pinhole camera set

'This surveillance system is a great looking old fashioned clock, but with a well hidden full color mini wireless camera. The wireless camera CCTV transmitter is completely invisible to the human eye, and this covert system can be used in almost any situation, from serious security to just plain fun situations'.

Source: Chinavision.com

The panopticon: Sounds like a carnival ride (but it's not)

Jeremy Bentham (1748–1832) designed a 'panopticon' style of prison in order to overcome the chaos of older, overcrowded and labour-intensive prisons typical at the time. The architectural design of Bentham's panoptic prison enabled one-way viewing of prisoners at all times, the separation of inmates and an immediate reduction in the number of guards required to supervise prisoners (Thornton, 2009). The real significance of Bentham's design was not so much the economic benefit of reduced staffing, nor the architectural simplicity of his clever design or even the separation of inmates: it was the potential manner by which prisoners could now be 'watched' and controlled. Bentham's design enabled a single guard to very effectively monitor a significant number of prisoners, without them knowing when (or if) they were being watched.

Until his release in 1955, Fidel Castro was held in the **Presidio Modelo**, a prison of panopticon design, built by the dictator Gerardo Machado on the former Isla de Pinos (Isla de la Juventud) in Cuba.

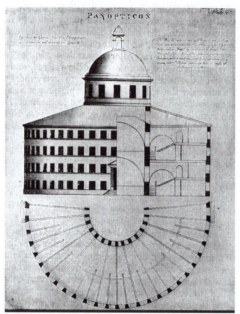

Figure 17.2 The panopticon: Crime and punishment in 18th- and 19th-century England

Source: Getty Images/Time & Life Pictures

Bentham's panopticon was of immense interest to Michel Foucault, the philosopher, sociologist and historian discussed in Chapters 11 and 13. Foucault argued that the visibility of the prisoners and invisibility of the guards results in entrenched prisoner subordination, total social control and the demolition of a basic human right: privacy. Each prisoner is seen but cannot communicate with the guards or other prisoners. The mob is eliminated and the individual isolated. The panopticon induces a sense of permanent visibility and ensures the functioning of power, the management of behaviour and the promise of punishment for infringement of prison law. Foucault argued that Bentham's prison was a useful metaphor to help us understand how governments and other public bodies work to ensure that power is visible yet unverifiable in our everyday lives. In Bentham's panopticon, the prisoner can always see the tower but never knows from where (or even if) he is being observed.

By looking at the rather extreme model of the panoptic prison, one develops a better understanding of how the processes of observation and examination might operate in our everyday lives. Foucault theorised that surveillance has three important social functions (you will note that this diagram has four elements—the new one 'to feel/be safe' is discussed later in this chapter): see Figure 17.3.

This system is effective because, according to Foucault, it allows individuals to be scrutinised, described and studied, and, most significantly, punitive, remedial action may be taken if they are seen to deviate from 'socially acceptable' behaviour (Foucault, 1977). The sign at my local sports ground is a good example of a life in a surveillance society: 'This area is covered by CCTV and all unacceptable behaviour will be actioned'. Anonymous security personnel watch the fans, record and classify their actions, assess them against the club's code of conduct and report breaches (including CCTV footage) to the local police force for action.

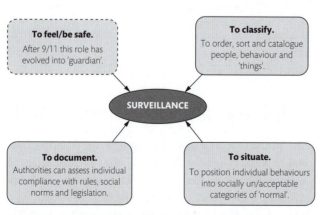

Figure 17.3 Foucault's surveillance system

(How) Do we live in a surveillance society?

Before discussing how we live in a surveillance society, it's worth revisiting the Family X to see how surveillance might be part of everyday life. In the opening section of this chapter, you read about the Family X holiday to Bali, their return through customs and the data-trail they scattered as they made their way home. As you read their account, you quickly realise that the family are frequently and habitually surveilled, as are we all. But why do we tolerate (and even encourage) surveillance as an everyday practice? Foucault's explanation is very simple: we embrace surveillance because it promises a society in which discipline is based on observation and examination; a surveillance society offers convenience and reward (for example, closed circuit television is often justified by increased public safety at night). Surveillance discourse tells us that visibility ensures moral and social order and, to paraphrase the founder of Second Life: 'If people know they are being watched, fundamentally, they will be good!' Assuming that this rather simplistic explanation is accurate—that is, knowing we are being panoptically observed will ensure compliance with social rules and public law—what are the 'panopticons' of our everyday life? What types of panoptic devices and strategies do modern governments (and corporations) employ to ensure economic, legal, moral and social order?

Consider the following two newspaper articles.

LOOK is a 2008 film that uses the concept of panoptic vision to create a suspense-filled horror story. It is shot entirely from the point of view of the security cameras. See: www. look-themovie.com.

Cops watch Twitter, Facebook for muck-up day

By Emily Power | Herald Sun | October 16, 2009 02:00am

Police will check social networking websites Facebook, MySpace and Twitter to detect plans for antisocial or illegal stunts when year 12s finish classes.

The traditional 'muck-up day' moniker, still used by many students, has been rebranded as 'celebration day' by principals and police to discourage misbehaviour.

Security will be stepped up at secondary schools across Victoria with about 50,000 VCE students set to let off steam after 13 years of study.

Sen-Sgt Tim Hardiman, of the police youth unit, said social networking sites were another tool for authorities.

'We are always interested in, and we are always aware of, the mediums the kids use, whether it is SMS messages, or whatever technology they are using,' he said.

'Facebook, MySpace, Twitter—there are occasions when police use these mediums to find out a little bit more about what is going on in the community.'

Sen-Sgt Hardiman said students risked being charged if celebrations got out of control and police were called.

'The top of the range worst result for a student is they end up with a criminal record, and it may affect their job opportunities, affect a passport application, a placement or overseas holiday,' he said.

The promise/threat of surveillance in this newspaper 'e-clipping' would probably disturb and amuse Foucault. In his book *Discipline and Punish: The Birth of the Prison,* he states that 'Knowledge is an organized collection of facts about a subject or individual, obtained by specific technical means'

Figure 17.4 Who's watching who?

Source: http://interneteyes.co.uk

and this means that 'the individual is caught up in a complicated relationship between disciplinary power and the knowledge that it creates' (Foucault, 1977). This story has all the elements of the panopticon: the presence of the ubiquitous, but invisible guard 'detecting plans for antisocial or illegal stunts' and the threat of punishment as a result, with misbehaving students risking 'a criminal record, reduced job opportunities, affect a passport application, a work placement or overseas holiday'. The police make it very clear to the partying school leaver that 'we are watching; you don't know when or who, but we are watching'. The everyday use of panoptic vision is not just limited to the 'Big Brothers' of police and government. An innovative company in the UK, Internet Eyes, plans to turn individual citizens into Little Brothers. See Figure 17.4 for an excerpt from their web page.

This second example is a good illustration of how new media panopticons are evolving: the person in the street becomes the powerful yet invisible guard in Bentham's model prison, and now we can simultaneously watch and be watched (so maybe those sci-fi films weren't so far-fetched after all?). There are a number of reasons for the rapid evolution and increasing acceptance of this type of surveillance: first, the modern panopticon is dispersed and is now more likely to be a series of Little Brothers, citizens are now the observers and the observed, and the internet has removed the physical and geographical boundaries that have in the past restricted surveillance activity. Second, the threat of terrorism has resulted in a paradigmatic shift in the way we understand and value our 'privacy'.

Not really 'Big Brother' anymore: More like 'Little Brothers' (or Sisters)

A quick reflection on your own 'everyday life' should easily uncover at least one interaction with a 'Little Brother'. Have you sent a text, used an ATM, updated an online profile, used a tollway or logged on to e-banking to see if your pay has gone in? In the last three hours, I have done all three, and with each activity a Little Brother silently watched, cached and archived my activities as data. Citizens such as myself produce an enormous quantity of data, from the mundane (using loyalty cards at the local store) to the globally significant (such as the trade of international currency to support terrorism). The collection of data isn't really new: my own grandparents had an account at the butcher's, a telephone account for betting on horse races, a hardware store account, a licence to drive and a card for the local library. Dispersed through the small town in which they lived was an artefactual record of the meat they purchased, their prescriptions and what books they liked to read. This data was tough to retrieve, written in hard copy on paper and 'guarded' by personal relationships with traders and store owners. Moreover, it was difficult and time-consuming to access. However, in the last decade the manner by which organisations and governments can efficiently and silently employ Little Brothers to help mine this personal data has grown at a rate that is hard to ascertain.

Following 9/11 the US Government developed a program known as Total Information Awareness, using five different data mining packages to 'find links between terrorism suspects and previously unknown people; track the international flow of money, operatives and materials; and search for clues in the worldwide communications over phone lines, wireless connections and Internet links' (Kelley, 2006). The ever-declining cost of digital storage teamed with new, highly efficient software has allowed the US Government to collect, archive and mine an enormous volume of data about its citizens. The collection and processing of data is a global growth phenomenon, heralding a new age in manufacturing; the production and mining of data that is primarily gathered by way of surveillance. I doubt that my grandfather's hardware store account would be of much interest or value to data miners, but this might change if he purchased a significant volume of fertiliser in this post-9/11 world.

Depending on individual beliefs, experience and opinion, each of us will tend to frame the growing use of surveillance (especially the use of Little Brothers) in one of three ways: as either a *utopian* development (largely positive and optimistic; life in an ideal community or society) or a *dystopian* development (largely negative and distrusting, a negative utopia; life in a totalitarian and repressive world), and some of us will be *ambivalent* (a little of both, but mostly we don't have sufficient knowledge or motivation to form an opinion). In the popular television series *The Simpsons*, Marge takes a utopian view of surveillance: 'You know, the courts might not work anymore, but as long as everybody is videotaping everyone else, justice will be done' (Season 6, episode: 'Homer: Bad Man').

Below are two more examples of utopian and dystopian perceptions around Little Brothers as surveillance.

Little Brother: A utopian view

Most of us have a camera in our mobile phone; some of us have quite good cameras with high resolution and MP4/video capacity. I use mine often and mostly to record pretty tedious stuff. Proponents of a utopian view would argue that the increased ability of citizens to record everyday life has been overwhelmingly positive. For example, in the past twelve months, the local paper has reported that citizens have assisted police in arresting felons for the following: an attempted abduction at a school, an armed hold-up at a service station and the illegal dumping of toxic waste. Over the same period, the Google Street View team recorded a robbery in progress and captured images of historic buildings (prior to a fire), thus allowing architects to use these images to replicate and repair the building. I myself recorded the licence plate of a car that, after smashing into a parked car, attempted to drive off. I used my Bluetooth to send the image to the other driver, allowing them to pursue a damages claim for the repair of their car. These are all positive effects of the proliferation of Little Brothers in our everyday life.

A more dystopian example

Most people carry a mobile phone (or even two or three) and give little thought to its function beyond texting, browsing, calling and playing with widgets to waste time and procrastinate. The convenience and functionality of this small, powerful machine are perceived to offset the dystopian surveillance function embedded in the device. We understand that mobile phones can be used to surveil us, but they are so dispersed and embedded in our everyday life, their functions and services so essential

China's mobile network: A Big Brother surveillance tool?

Posted Mon Jan 28, 2008 8:32am AEDT

Serious concerns were raised at the World Economic Forum (WEF) in Davos last week about the ability of the Chinese Government to spy on the country's 500 million mobile phone users.

The head of China's biggest mobile phone company, which has more than 300 million subscribers, stunned delegates by revealing that the company had unlimited access to the personal data of its customers and handed it over to Chinese security officials when demanded.

The admission, described as 'bone-chilling' by US Congressman Ed Markey, sent shivers through an audience of telecom experts at WEF who immediately saw the potential for misuse and surveillance.

'We know who you are, but also where you are,' said the CEO of China Mobile Communications Corporation, Wang Jianzhou, whose company adds six million new customers to its network each month and is already the biggest mobile group in the world by users.

He was explaining how the company could use the personal data of its customers to sell advertising and services to them based on knowledge of where they were and what they were doing.

When pressed about the privacy and security implications of this, he added: 'We can access the information and see where someone is, but we never give this information away ... only if the security authorities ask for it.'

The movement of mobile phone users can be tracked because they connect to local base stations, giving a trail that can only be accessed in most democratic countries by security officials under strict conditions.

Mobile phones can also be easily tapped.

(AFP)

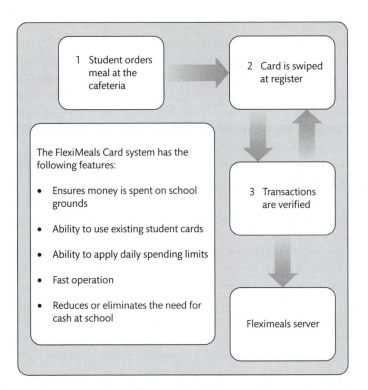

Figure 17.5 Some of the functions you might find in a 'cashless canteen'

Source: Flexischools.com.au

to our social well-being that, for some of us, we are almost powerless without them. As a result of our dependence on, and infatuation with, mobile telephony, we end up in a state of self-imposed powerlessness: *I know my phone can be used for evil, I know that it's a potential little spy, but I love it and couldn't possibly live without it*. One of the great conflicts of new media in everyday life is the way technological advances have both utopian and dystopian consequences. You will recall that Chapter 11 discussed the way we both determine and are determined by new media. The mobile telephone is an excellent example of the complexity of digital determination.

But surveillance isn't just limited to protecting us, ensuring national safety, spying on our phone use or constructing our consumer profile for marketers: it can be much more mundane, much closer to home. As a parent, I can survey and control my children's eating, from the comfort of my desk! A growing number of schools are moving to 'cashless canteens' and in the US a significant number have operated this way for years. There are a number of software and hardware providers of an Australian example from the FlexiSchools company (see Figure 17.5).

The FlexiSchools company was selected for three reasons: first, they promote their product to Australian schools and in Australia few canteens have moved to swipe cards; second, their web page was well designed; and finally, their product outline was simple, well-written and easy to follow. Other software providers (mostly in the US) promote the next generation of cashless canteens as allowing parents to limit the product range available to their children, allowing parents to remote lock the student account on days when a home lunch is provided and one 'premium' package even offered SMS alerts when a child attempts to purchase a 'banned' product. The Australian FlexiSchools system for tracking student expenditure in the canteen seems a much more benign form of surveillance and a cashless canteen makes a lot of sense, but recently, when I spoke to a group of first-year university students about this system, they became agitated, argumentative and quite vocal: 'This makes me mad—at high school you should be old enough and independent enough to pick what you buy and choose what you eat. This is just 'Big Mother' at work!' (I do need to point out that none of this group had attended a school with a cashless canteen!) It would appear that, for this cohort of mobile phone carrying, Facebook updating, online shopping with a tweeters, the fact that your parents can spy on (and control) your eating habits at school is far more offensive, far more intrusive and more an invasion of privacy than panoptic surveillance from government and business.

Foucault's theorisation around the problems with power and watching provides some insight into why we might accept/tolerate Big Brother (and his siblings) watching us, gathering data, recording our actions and tracking our phone calls, but are horrified at the thought that our parents might discover that we have fries for lunch five days a week, and that they can prevent this with a click of their mouse. Working backwards, the first reason we might dislike the cashless canteen is very simple and it relates to power and action: parents manipulating your canteen habits with a click of their mouse is about the elimination of choice and the reduction of independence, and no one likes to have their actions controlled and limited in such a personal, powerful and domestic way. The second insight into why we might more readily tolerate surveillance by anonymous Big/Little Brothers is related to the central idea in Bentham's panoptic prison: like the prisoner who can always see the tower but never knows from where (or even, if) they are being observed, we find ourselves aware that we are being watched (or not) and are powerless to do anything about it. Over time, you come to expect and accept Big Brother surveillance as a natural and normal part of everyday life.

Prisons, CCTV, data mining, cashless canteens and now Facebook

Sometimes, we accidentally (yet purposefully) set out to engage in a cycle of surveillance! MySpace, LinkedIn, Facebook and Twitter are only four of many social networking services available, and

How to Lose a Job via Facebook in 140 Characters or Less

Posted by Mark in Career, News, Social Media on 08 9th, 2009 | 236 responses

These days, social media and job search go hand in hand. Of course the age old knock on the door and 'are you hiring?' scenario is still out there but many people favour job search via networking and making use of online job search sites. Over the years networking platforms such as Twitter, Facebook and LinkedIn have become a must for job seekers. If you aren't on the web, at times it's almost impossible to secure a job. However, some people seem to keep forgetting that social media if not utilized properly can hurt your job search and can lead to job loss. We came across one and had to share it.

Please take a look at the image below.

The image above clearly shows the implications if you use social media platforms the wrong way. Of course, when you have a Facebook account it's your personal account. However, it depends how you are using it. Are you using it to simply connect with your friends and family or are you using it to connect with professionals? Before you go ahead and utilize the power of free speech on Facebook or any other social media platforms make sure you watch what you are saying. Social media has given us tremendous amount of power in terms of job search but it has also made everything we do much more vulnerable. The saying 'choose your words carefully' might be true now than ever before.

Just make sure before you publish anything on twitter, Facebook, LinkedIn or anywhere else, you haven't friended one of your colleagues or bosses before you make a rude remark about them. And even if they are not your friends, there are still ways things can get out, so at times it's best to keep it yourself. Just cause social media is about transparency doesn't mean you have to be transparent in everything you do. Transparency comes with a cost, in some cases it's you giving away your own privacy and in some cases losing a job, just like the one above.

Source: http://applicant.com/how-to-lose-a-job-via-facebook-in-140-characaters-or-less [sic]

poking, tweeting and 'thinking out loud' are now part of everyday life. Surveillance in social software is different from the anonymous watching of CCTV and the spying Little Brothers in our pockets. The nature of web services like Facebook results in a blurring of the boundary between the public and private selves, allowing those in/with authority to observe and react to our sometimes very personal interactions and postings. Take, for example, the story above from a popular UK job application blog.

It's not just employment and relationships that can be detrimentally affected by the 'omnopticonical' nature of Facebook. As a university teacher, myself and my colleagues receive many requests for extensions for assessment—here's an example from late last year:

Two related concepts are the **synopticon** (everyone watching the few, especially watching 'the famous') and the **omnopticon** (everybody watching everybody!).

Kate (not her real name): Dear Professor, I am writing to request an extension for the assignment due next Monday the 23rd. I have been unwell and today (Friday) I am worse than ever and want to spend the weekend in bed and recover properly, screw up the writing I have done while I was sick and start again. As a result, would it be possible to get a week's extension, sorry I have been too sick to go to the Dr. Thanx, Kate

Tony Hi Kate, sorry to hear that you have been unwell, the constant talk of swine flu makes us all nervous, I hope you get well soon. Please take an extra seven days to get well, and then work up a good assignment. Please note this email on your coversheet. Next time you get ill, please obtain a Drs Certificate (for free) from the campus medical centre. Get well soon, Tony.

This is just one of many hundreds of thousands of requests going from student to teacher and this story of 'request and extension' was boring and mundane until the following Monday, when I logged unto my Facebook account. Earlier in the year, Kate and many other Media and Communication students joined a growing cohort of students and staff who were 'media/comm friends'. As a result, I was one of Kate's 300+ Facebook 'friends' and she was one of mine. Here's what Kate posted as her status as of 11am on Monday (the day the assignment was due):

STATUS UPDATE:

Kate: MINE WAS THE BEST 18th EVER!!! Thanx guys for coming, awesome fotos posted soon. Still pissed from sat ;-) After party at ##### this arvo!

How to respond? Is it even appropriate to respond? Kate had clearly 'scammed' an extension, had a great party and completely forgotten the fact that I was her Facebook friend. Because social media blurs the boundaries between public and private life, I found myself in a very difficult situation, 'accidentally' using social software to spy on students. In the end, I did nothing, but now I tell this story as a cautionary tale for all new communication students. But what does this mean for the members of a society (especially mid- to late-teens) who live in the public sphere, online and unmediated?

The book *Facebook Marketing for Dummies* (2009) suggests we need a number of rules for 'using social software whilst keeping your job'. These rules seem both restrictive and yet sensible. Here is what one of the authors, Richard Krueger, suggests:

1 Thou Shall Not Reveal—embarrassing details in your status update (or Twitter, or anywhere else for that matter!)

2 Thou Shall Not Post Photos—that in any way could be construed as being credibility damaging in any way.

3 Thou Shall Not Be Negative—overly negative/hateful sentiments towards any issue, no matter how strongly you feel about it, will certainly rub someone in the wrong way.

4   Thou Shall Not Think You Are Protected—under the first amendment you have the right to say what you believe via blogs and social networks, but your employer is free to fire you for just about any reason.

5   Thou Shall Not Think They Are Not Listening—big brother is most likely watching you, as 66% of bosses monitor employees' Internet connections.

(Dunay & Krueger, 2009)

Most readers would find these guidelines quite difficult to follow. Facebook, MySpace, Twitter and other social networking platforms are deeply embedded in our everyday lives and, for most of us, posting, chatting and poking on these online forums is an important and normal component of what we do each day. The idea that this part of our social lives can be stored, recovered and surveyed is personally challenging: should a comment made online 'live forever' and one day cost us our career, relationship or public office?

Has surveillance been normalised?

One of the central questions in this chapter is: why have we come to so readily embrace and tolerate surveillance as a component of our everyday lives? The first reason is very simple: surveillance makes us (feel) safe; local governments attempt to manage inner city violence with CCTV (some with loudspeakers!), shopkeepers have cameras to reduce theft, universities use them to make 24-hour PC labs safer, public transport employs cameras to reduce violence and vandalism, and government agencies track our travel and use key loggers to detect and prevent acts of terrorism. The media reinforces this perception: each and every night on television a crime is solved with GPS trackers, credit card purchases and phone records. On the news, police show grainy, black-and-white images of crimes in progress, law-breakers and missing people. Public swimming pools have cameras trained on change-room entrances so as to deter sex offenders and, soon, you will be able to use 'Internet Eyes' to help protect a store on the other side of the globe. This sense of security and safety comes from the way in which surveillance is used to collect data and manufacture knowledge about how we act in the world. Remember, from earlier in this chapter: 'Knowledge is an organized collection of facts about a subject or individual, obtained by specific technical means' (Foucault, 1977). The 'organised collection of facts' makes us feel safe(r) in the same way giving a child a mobile phone makes a parent feel better about the welfare of their offspring. Some would argue that they are no safer, but the perception of safety is strong enough to justify the purchase.

Finally, the emergence/acceptance of a surveillance society is easiest understood as the 'normalisation' of surveillance. Normalisation is a social process by which ideas and behaviours come to be seen as 'normalised' and are accepted as a natural part of everyday life. Foucault understood this process as the development of socially acceptable ideals (norms), using surveillance tools to observe citizen behaviour and, finally, to reward or punish individuals for conforming to or deviating from these ideals. Why would we want a pinhole camera in a bedside clock? Mostly because it exists, but also because the concept of privacy is a slippery construction in a surveillance society and the acceptance of covert surveillance has changed since 9/11. And it's not a bad-looking clock for the money.

Summary

- This chapter introduced you to a 1785 prison design, the 'panopticon', as a useful concept for examining the role and impact of modern surveillance such as CCTV and other 'crowd control' devices.
- This chapter explored how we now live (happily?) in a surveillance society.
- You read how Foucault explained and understood the many problems with power, watching and being watched.
- Here you discovered the emergence of micro-surveillance in everyday life, reading how things like hidden cameras and global positioning systems can be used to observe and plot our 'private' movements.
- You read case studies about how Facebook and even the school canteen can be now used to surveil citizens, and how consumption and credit cards provide a compact and valued record of our spending habits.
- You discovered that global events, such as terrorism, have resulted in a moral panic that has changed forever the rights of the individual.

Further reading

Dunay, P & Krueger, R 2009, *Facebook Marketing for Dummies*, Wiley, New Jersey.

Foucault, M 1977, *Discipline and Punish: The Birth of the Prison*, trans. A Sheridan, Penguin, London.

Hirst, M & Harrison, J 2007, *Communication and New Media: From Broadcast to Narrowcast*, Oxford University Press, South Melbourne.

Kelley, M 2006, 'Feds Sharpen Secret Tools for Data Mining', *USA Today*, Gannett Co. Inc., Washington, 2.

Smith, J 2008, 'China's Mobile Network: A Big Brother Surveillance Tool?' *ABC News Online* retrieved 6 February 2011, <www.abc.net.au/news/stories/2008/01/28/2147712.htm>.

Thornton, K 2009, 'Crime and Punishment in 18th & 19th Century England', retrieved 11 October 2009, <www.deakin.edu.au/alfreddeakin/spc/exhibitions/candp/candp.php>.

Weblinks

For revision questions, please visit www.oup.com.au/orc/chalkley.)

18 Reality TV and Constructed Reality: What Would Foucault Think of Big Brother?

Brad Warren

Master X and early engagements with *Big Brother*

Sometime after his release from prison following the hyperreality debacle (see Chapter 9), Master X discovered reality television. It had been around for a while, actually, but he had always steered clear because he didn't know what to make of it. Master X thought reality television sounded like a contradiction in terms: he mostly switched on the set to *escape* from reality, to kick back and zone out for a while, not to get another dose of it (again, hijacking-lessons notwithstanding).

It soon occurred to Master X that there were secret codes to be learned if he wanted to work this stuff out: his early viewings of *Big Brother* just left him wondering why he bothered. Wasn't this just normal television, except with no scripting and fake actors? In what he considered to be one of his cleverer moments, Master X actually wondered if the television networks had stumbled upon a way to make lots of money for doing very little at all.

But then he rebuked himself: maybe he just needed to look at things differently. After all, hadn't television *always* featured normal, relatively untalented people embarrassing themselves? Home-video programs? Most game shows? Was *Big Brother* perhaps a next-generation game show, rather than a drama or a situation comedy? When looked at from this perspective, *Big Brother* made a little more sense.

(Although he might have struggled to explain this shift in thinking, the idea Master X is engaging with here is discourse—in this case, the different discourses that might be brought to bear in order to understand/appreciate reality television. This theoretical concept is explored in more depth later in this chapter.)

What you will learn from this chapter

- All about reality television, and just how real it really is (or isn't)
- Different flavours of reality television, including 'docusoaps', game shows and talk shows
- All about discourse, and how it's not just academic jargon (including the discourse/paradigm distinction)
- Foucault, and more on discourse and postmodernism
- Memes. What does it all meme? What's in a meme? (Information soundbites examined)
- Cultural hegemony, the maintenance of power, and what Marxism has got to do with anything
- Engaging with media on your own terms: Stuart Hall's dominant, negotiated and oppositional readings
- Revisiting the pitfalls of Bentham's panopticon in making sense of new media.

Introduction: Reality television

Reality television:
programs that claim to be 'a window on the world', providing viewers with a glimpse into how (mostly) ordinary people behave, albeit in some quite constructed, unordinary situations.

The original premise of **reality television** was to tap into the attraction of watching *real* people do *real* things—it was a kind of socially acceptable voyeurism, because it was screened in prime time.[1] Early experiments with the medium brought us *Big Brother (Australia)* in 2001—a phenomenal success that would go on to run for eight seasons—and at the time of writing the first season of *Junior MasterChef* has just finished screening. Other popular reality programs have included *Farmer Wants a Wife*, *The Biggest Loser*, *Extreme Makeover*, *Survivor*, *Queer Eye for the Straight Guy*, *The Osbournes* and many others.

When did reality become TV? …

And when did Ozzy become an actor?

(Bowling for Soup, 2004)

This quotation is a song lyric. It's better if you listen to it: www.youtube.com/watch?v=k38xNqZvBJI. So, when did Ozzy Osbourne become an actor, indeed? Some would say never, and yet *The Osbournes*, a reality television show based on the life of rock star Ozzy and family, with no apparent plot or purpose except to highlight their dysfunctionality and highly accomplished use of bad language, ran successfully for four seasons. Ozzy's own

Figure 18.1 Publicity shot from popular 'docusoap' *The Osbournes*

Source: The Kobal Collection/MTV

reflections on the popularity and eventual demise of the program cut to the core of a problem that has plagued reality television from the beginning:

> By 2005 the show was over … It started to feel a bit fake, which was the exact opposite of what *The Osbournes* was all about … and the crew moved out.

> (Osbourne, 2009: 373)

The problem is this:

Just how *real* is reality television, really?

Clearly, Ozzy's own opinion is that reality television should reflect true life as far as possible, and when this seemed to no longer be the case then it was time to cancel the show. However, in this instance it's possible that Ozzy was being a tiny bit idealistic. The act of being watched, and of knowing that you're watched, can have marked effects on the behaviour of the 'actors' involved, with the result that the 'reality' captured may not be the same as if the cameras had not been present. Likewise, the creation of a documentary (or 'docusoap', the subset of reality television into which *The Osbournes* most closely fits) is not arbitrary or accidental. Such shows are all produced and edited: decisions are made about which bits to include and how long they should run, how the footage is to be segmented into scenes and arranged in a deliberate order, and so on.

> The relationship between documentary television formats and 'the real' has been the subject of a long debate that has taken many forms. These have primarily been concerned with the documentary aesthetic, the codes and conventions associated with documentary, and the subversion of its privileged status as a form that purports to reflect reality (see Corner, 1996; Fiske, 1990; Kilborn & Izod, 1998; Nichols, 1991; Paget, 1998; Roscoe & Hight, 2001; Winston, 2000).

> (Jones, 2003: 401)

Further, Sparks (2007) adds that 'a further dimension of "realism" is added [to docusoaps such as *The Osbournes*] by the fact that the contestants are usually not professional actors and they are usually seen in unscripted and mundane situations. [Nonetheless, it is then reiterated that] … what we see is a highly-constructed artefact rather than a slice of "real life"'.

This is a recurrent theme—perhaps *the* recurrent theme—in the emerging body of literature pertaining to reality television. A few more examples are indicative:

> The growth of reality TV or 'factual entertainment' has created a hybrid in which the codes of reality and appearance are blurred.

> (Lewis, 2004: 288)

> Television producers also partly stage-manage the settings and scenes to ensure that reactions among the family members are interesting and dramatic.

> (Iwabuchi, 2004: 32)

> In short, what is considered most important in … reality television is the subtle stage-managing of 'reality'.

> (Iwabuchi, 2004: 26)

So, *The Osbournes* might be a kind of (distorted) window into a particular reality, or an indication of a particular reality, but the show in itself is not reality *per se*. (This stuff can get confusing: *The Osbournes* is reality insofar as it exists, and it's a real show, but it's not an exact—real—rendering of the family that are the focus of the show.)

Similar debates about what's real in reality television can also be found in other subsets of the genre. Take, for example, constructed game shows like *Big Brother*, in which a group of people live together in a locked house and try to avoid eviction. The 'Big Brother house' is under constant video surveillance, and choices for eviction are generally determined by viewer polls. The 'game' is complicated through the inclusion of prescribed tasks or requirements being given to the housemates, and sometimes not all housemates are aware of the roles that others have been assigned. Here, many of the same ideas emerge: obviously, *Big Brother* is at least as constructed as docusoaps such as *The Osbournes* (arguably more so), and in addition there is the attraction for viewers of 'identify[ing] with the ordinary people who are chosen as participants and then become famous' (Balkin, 2004: 10). (*The Osbournes* is clearly an exception in this regard—Ozzy and family can be described as many things, but not ordinary.) And, again, 'viewers are titillated by the voyeuristic thrill they get from "peeking in"' (Balkin, 2004: 10–11).

Figure 18.2 Kyle Sandilands, host of the Australian version of *Big Brother*

Source: AAP Image/Channel 10

One further point that must be stressed in any consideration of *Big Brother* is the degree to which the program has only been made possible by (relatively) recent technological advances. Even more so than docusoaps and other reality television formats, the interactive nature of *Big Brother* is dependent on the instantaneous nature of digital media for its success.

> As a result of the transformation in communications technology we are now living in an increasingly 'wired' world in which we have access to a vast range of interlinked informational and entertainment-based services. These services are rapidly merging and amalgamating, to the extent that there is now increasing convergence between once separate media forms.
>
> (Kilborn, 2003: 17)

And it's not all about *The Osbournes* and *Big Brother*. Talk shows also constitute a kind of reality television—a fact that is sometimes overlooked because this particular format has a much longer history. Nonetheless, these shows—*Tonight Live*, *Oprah*, etc.—are frequently as constructed as any of the others considered so far, and sometimes this is true even when the show at hand makes overt claims to the contrary. Chu (2004: 100) notes that subtle factors, including the personalities of a show's panel members, and the amount of time allocated for guests to speak, can all contribute to a program's final shape, and may not be an entirely unbiased or accurate reflection of the issue under discussion.

An excellent deconstruction of the talk-show form can be found in Theobold's (2006) 'Mystification in the Media: From "Ritual Murder" to the "War on Terrorism"', the latter part of which analyses a BBC *Panorama* 'clash-of-cultures' confrontation between Western/civilised anti-Muslim and Muslim people (2006: 61). Although the show purports to provide fair and impartial current affairs, Theobald's analysis finds its overall construction to be decidedly pro-Western. Perhaps the greatest indication of this bias lies in the framing of the entire debate, insofar as 'Western' is overtly and (apparently) unproblematically linked with 'civilized', thereby implying that Muslims necessarily are not. In addition to such framing, Theobold also notes[2]:

- the overt linking, using visuals, of Islam with Osama Bin Laden in the show's opening sequence
- the choice of panel experts on the show containing a gender bias, with an aggressive male on the Western side and a passive female on the East, resulting in a situation akin to bullying
- disproportionate time allocations for speaking, answering questions and so on, strongly favouring the Western side (2006: 63–4).

Reality television (2): Learning to discourse

On 12 September 2010, the first episode of *Junior MasterChef* aired on Australian television. On blogs and in the news, opinions varied widely about the appropriateness of the show, about whether or not the children taking part (aged 8–12) should be exposed to the high levels of competitiveness necessarily involved. It's a contentious issue, although there can be no doubt that the kids were feeling the pressure.

In a telling statement, one young contestant claimed: 'I'm cooking for my life!'

We're used to hearing pronouncements of this kind. The competitors in the show's grown-up version are frequently hoping to use *MasterChef* to springboard a career change or improve their current financial situation, for example, and such claims don't seem like too much of an exaggeration. But was the child in question cooking for her life? One would hope not (and if she was, someone should probably give the Department of Children's Services a quick call).

But this begs the question: *why* would she say such a thing? The answer is that she's learned from watching the best model at her disposal—the show's adult version—and the patterns of speech and behaviour picked up, in this case, were almost suited to her own situation, but not quite. It is the slight mismatch between the learned schemas of *MasterChef* and its Junior counterpart that make this example interesting, by highlighting that so-called reality programs have peculiar languages that are all their own. What we are discussing here is the *discourse* of *MasterChef*. This is another way in which reality television and reality itself are strangely related, and yet not the same.

If you look up 'discourse' in a dictionary, you'll likely find a straightforward definition that equates the word with conversation, talking or communication in more general terms. And that's fine, except that in academic/university contexts it also means something more: discourses, quite simply, are ways of thinking and speaking about stuff. But what does that mean, exactly? The following vignette further illustrates the point.

Discourses: ways of thinking and speaking about stuff. They can address small matters or large (although in the latter case they sometimes go by the name of paradigms), and can change over time.

Mr Y, and why he never made it to the 1980s

One day, after a particularly challenging discussion with a very smart person online, Master X asked his dad what a 'discourse' was. In response, Mr X had a story to tell.

'I'd like to tell you about my great great grand-uncle Mr Y', Mr. X said.

'The year is 1932 (and this is important, wait and see). Mr Y's feeling very stressed. He doesn't quite know what's wrong, except that everything is. He has a nice wife, a mid-level office job and a house with a picket fence and a dog, but somehow everything's too hard, and just not worth the effort.

'So Mr Y goes to visit his doctor, to lay out all his problems. It wasn't an easy decision to make, because nobody really knew what depression was, not back then, and there was a general feeling that Mr Y should just suck his gut in, puff his chest out, grow up and be a man. But nonetheless he went, and his doctor was a sincere and caring gentleman, but unfortunately he was also a product of his time.

'When Mr Y opened his heart and mind to his doctor, the doctor's reaction was to prescribe that he take up smoking cigarettes, because it would help calm his nerves.

'So much for Mr Y,' said Mr X, sadly. 'History doesn't tell us whether the cigarettes did much good for his initial illness, but we do know he died of a smoking-related chest infection in 1979.'

At this point, Master X was just sitting there, flabbergasted. *Prescribe smoking? Surely that's insane!*

By today's standards, and with today's advances in medical knowledge, yes, it's insane. But that's the point: the discourse—ways of thinking and speaking about stuff—has changed between 1932 and the present day.

And **discourses** don't just change over time. As noted above, they also change based on context (such as *MasterChef*); and on variables such as location, the task at hand, and the wide range of background experiences and attitudes that might be in play at any given moment. To provide one further example, the discourse surrounding how-many-beers-is-too-many-beers will vary greatly between, say, what is said during your yearly health check with the local doctor, compared with the prevailing attitudes when you're having a couple with your mates at the footy on a Friday night.

This academic understanding of discourse is widely associated with the work of French theorist Michel Foucault. He discussed the concept at length in his *The Order of Things* (1966) and *The Archaeology of Knowledge* (1969) (Abercrombie et al., 1994: 172), and then again in *Power/Knowledge* (1980).

> According to [Foucault's understanding of the term 'discourse'] … in any given historical period
> we can write, speak or think about a given social object or practice (madness, for example) only
> in certain specific ways and not others. '*A discourse*' would then be *whatever* constrains—but
> also enables—writing, speaking and thinking within such specific historical limits.
>
> (McHoul & Grace, 1993: 31)

It must be emphasised here that *discourses have real, concrete effects*. We have seen this already in the language used by the *Junior MasterChef* contestant, and in the unfortunate outcome for Mr Y. To take one further example, consider the above passage, and its mention of madness/insanity. Over the years, there have been many discourses surrounding this controversial topic, tending towards the criminalisation of those suffering from mental illness at one extreme, to treating them more humanely as patients in need at the other.

But so what, you ask? Aren't we just talking? After all, isn't discourse just ways of thinking and speaking about stuff? Where are the real effects? To see them, we need to go a step further: for example, in the early 1990s in Victoria, the prevailing thought of governing bodies tended towards the first of the positions just outlined, with the direct effect being the closure of several mental institutions in Melbourne. In the years since, this has meant that many of those suffering from mental conditions have unfortunately found their way into Victorian prisons. At the time of writing, this issue was making headlines in the context of the impending state election, because in some quarters it appears that the prevailing discourse is changing, and hopefully we will see concrete effects that attempt to remedy the situation.

How and why Master X never made it beyond the first audition for *MasterChef*

After Master X realised that *Big Brother* was okay if you could just get your perspective right, he spent a joyous six months watching as many back-episodes as he could, as well as several series of *The Osbournes* and *MasterChef*. For a while, this made him extremely happy (if perhaps a little antisocial). But then Master X realised that something still wasn't right. It had to do with that *discourse* thing, and also with that title, *reality television*.

Here was the problem: Master X was starting to see patterns. That is, to take *MasterChef* as an example, Master X was starting to notice that the 'players' were behaving in some common and predictable ways. There was generally good sportsmanship, some 'good judge/bad judge' stuff and a whole range of anxieties arising from the fact that more time was spent eliminating people than actually cooking. And there were always lots of tears and hugs …

Was this reality? Or TV? Or, as the name suggested, a strange new mix of the two that was developing its own set of rules? Discourses, Master X was realising, weren't just about ways of thinking (perspectives: ways of 'looking at things'), they were ways of speaking about them (ways of behaving) too (see Abercrombie et al., 1994: 119). For Master X, this was a moment of realisation! *He* could be on *MasterChef*, if he just got his behaviour, his mannerisms right. Real culinary skill might help but surely he could learn what he needed as he went along … now if he just knew who to call …

Master X didn't make it past the first round of auditions, but not because he couldn't walk the walk and talk the talk—he'd done his homework well, so far as that went. The problem was his recipe for cookie-dough (**sigh**) … (see Chapter 9).

Nothing exists outside of discourse: Beware postmodern negativity

Famously, Foucault has written that 'History has no "meaning"' (1980: 114), and there is a danger here that we might be straying perilously close to that postmodern futility and collapse of meaning discussed in Chapter 9 (in the context of Jameson's pastiche and Baudrillardean hyperreality). However, please note Foucault's disclaimer in the passage that follows: 'History has no "meaning", *though this is not to say that it is absurd or incoherent*' (1980: 114, my emphasis). Interpreting this phrase, rather than dashing headlong toward the end of everything, Foucault's observation can probably be more properly understood as recognition that we understand everything we see from within *some* frame of reference, some discursive position—to not do so is completely impossible. Even for the simplest things, discourse—remember, again, ways of thinking and speaking about stuff—comes into play. Take a kitchen table, for example. For most of us, we would look and our frame of reference would cause us to see a functional tool, something to eat and prepare food at, or if it's a particularly nice one then perhaps an investment piece. Hypothetically, however, if we could transport one of our cave-dwelling ancestors to our dining rooms, perhaps all they'd see would be firewood. So, this is not the end of everything—real things exist, and I don't think Foucault was disputing that—but we can only appreciate them, make meaning of them, through discourse.

The discourse/paradigm distinction

There isn't one, not really. Or at least no distinction worth becoming overly worried about. Paradigms, in broad terms, can be described in terms of worldviews, over-arching conceptual schema that can affect the way we see things—the functionalist paradigm, a feminist paradigm, and so on. But hold on, isn't this remarkably close to the ways of thinking and speaking that characterise discourses? Well, yes, it is, and the reason for the similarity may well be that one was strongly influenced by the other. Consider further the following definition of paradigm:

> In its sociological use, this term [paradigm] derives from the work of T. S. Kuhn (1970) on
> the nature of scientific change. For Kuhn scientists work within paradigms, which are general

ways of seeing the world and which dictate what kind of scientific work should be done and what kinds of theory are acceptable.

(Abercrombie et al., 1994: 301)

Thus, a paradigm/discourse distinction is becoming harder and harder to trace. Further, in Kuhn's own words, he maintains that '... the emergence of a paradigm affects the structure of the group that practices the field' (1970: 18). It was argued a little earlier that one of the important aspects of discourses was that they had concrete, tangible effects in the real world, as it were. Here, again, we can see that paradigms are held to behave similarly. This strong resemblance between Foucault's understanding of discourse and Kuhn's paradigms has also been noted elsewhere:

Foucault stresses that certain forms of knowledge (about the human mind and body, about biology, politics or language), after periods of stability in which the fundamental processes of a discourse remain largely unquestioned, undergo rapid transformations. During these transformations (which sound uncannily like Thomas Kuhn's 'paradigm shifts') there is not only a change in the content of a discourse, but also a fundamental change in what might count as knowledge itself.

(Sim, 1998: 246)

If there is any distinction to be made between the two terms it could be that, in conventional usage at least, paradigms are generally held to be bigger. That is, while paradigms are more likely to be those over-arching 'isms' that organise our lives (see Chapter 9), discourses can be more particular, such as the kinds of language used on *MasterChef*, as per the discussion earlier. Or put another way (and again, in general usage), paradigms are always forms of discourses, but given the size differential this isn't necessarily so the other way around.

What do you meme?

Memes (mimesis):
Memes are small units of information, bite-sized ideas taken up and spread by popular/ mainstream culture and other media. They seem to have the capacity to replicate independently, so are often likened to viruses.

There is more than one way of understanding culture and media. This section looks at an alternative (or perhaps parallel is a better word?) idea to discourse: **memes**. According to Hirst and Harrison, a meme is:

[a] small but powerful chunk of ideological 'DNA' that carries ideas, meanings, trends, and fashions through both time and space via the process of mimetic (imitative) transfer. Memes can be generated by hegemonic[3] or subversive social forces and are usually transported via the various communication vectors of the mass media, narrowcasting and popular culture.

(2007: 22)

To stress a point, you shouldn't become overly concerned trying to tell the difference between a meme, a discourse, and even a paradigm although, as discussed in the previous section, by most popular accounts these days paradigms tend to be bigger. Memes, by contrast, are a bit like soundbites, and they're also a bit like viruses. As the above passage suggests, they're small, bite-sized (byte-sized?) pieces of information that have the capacity to reproduce, seemingly independently, although in reality their dissemination through media has a good deal to do with their abilities in this regard. Their reproductive nature is, in fact, contained in their name: the term mimesis (of which meme is the base-word) literally means 'to copy'. Also like viruses, if they catch on strongly enough, memes have the ability to change the world. And they don't even have to be true. Consider the following example (which may not be world-altering, but it will certainly resonate with the day-to-day experiences of many of us).

Here is the meme: 'Talking on your phone while driving is dangerous'. Imagine, for a moment, that you're driving down Burwood Highway, talking on your phone, because you accidentally left your Bluetooth headset in your other jacket. There's a pretty good chance, if someone catches you at it, that a flurry of abuse will follow, hurled from the next car, along the lines of 'Get off your %&#$*phone!! How dare you be so reckless/thoughtless/stupid?!' (other descriptive terms may also apply).

However, there are many other activities in which you might also engage while driving, any one of which is potentially (at least) as distracting as talking on your poor, unfairly abused telephone. For example, while driving you could be juggling scalding coffee, smoking/lighting a cigarette, arguing with your partner in the seat next to you, cleaning up the cheeseburger you just dropped in your lap, changing a CD, adjusting a seat belt, re-routing a GPS … you get the idea. You could even be doing several of these things, all at the same time.

Let's be really clear: this author is *not* suggesting that using your phone while driving isn't dangerous. To think that would be to miss the point: the point is that none of the *other* dangerous activities just listed will incite the rage of your nosey fellow motorists the way that using a phone will, *and this is precisely because of the power of the meme*; the effectiveness/success with which it has been marketed is testament to just how completely this little soundbite of information has been accepted as truth[4] and embraced as a part of our everyday lives. Or, to put this another way, the success of the meme can be seen through the disproportionate reactions that phoning-while-you-drive can elicit, relative to the seriousness of this particular misdemeanour.

To take this argument a step further, consider another, related meme: 'Advertising to drivers is okay'. But wait a moment. The sole function of advertising, its fundamental purpose, is to attract your attention—to distract you from what you are otherwise doing, which in this case is driving. It is truly ironic that that huge billboard on the Princes Highway is there for no other reason than to make you look at its graphic anti-txting message (well, maybe one other reason: there's often a police car parked directly behind it). And just when you thought things couldn't get any weirder, consider this: when I was taught to drive (some time ago now) I was instructed that, when caught behind a large van or a bus, a good safety strategy was to look right through the bigger vehicle's windows, to get at least a sense of what traffic was like further ahead. You can't do that anymore. Advertising to drivers is more important, apparently, so much so that a special surface has been developed upon which ads can be plastered. The bus/van driver can still see out, but other drivers can't see in or through the bus windows. Instead, we have to look at the ad for the latest Stephen King[5] novel or dietary supplement, in full colour and filling up our field of vision. How can it be that one form of driver-distraction is both sanctioned and legal, while another will earn you a $300 fine if you're caught … it's all about *the power of memes*, and the more you dwell on this, the more your head is likely to hurt.

So, you know that world we live in, the one we sort of assumed was so rational and reasonable? Well, maybe it's not really like that after all. Maybe a better description would be mostly profit- and media-driven, and often quite silly.

(Cultural) Hegemony

No discussion of discourse, memes or any other strategies for understanding culture and the pervasive effects of media would be complete without giving a name to the discourse-in-dominance, to the ideas/memes/paradigms that are generally assumed to be correct, by virtue of an apparently logical assumption that 'that's just the way things are'. The name for this concept is hegemony. Originally a

Marxist term, outlined by **Antonio Gramsci** in his *Prison Notebooks* (1997 [1971]), a collection of his writings while he was incarcerated, hegemony is attained:

> when the power of the dominant groups in a society appears natural. It is a form of power or rule not limited to direct political control but one where those who have power maintain their position through the creation of a particular world view, one that *seems to be based on common sense*. Newspapers, TV and radio can be used to communicate the viewpoint of the ruling elites …[and] hegemony doesn't confine itself to intellectual matters or ideas. It works within everyday culture and seems to provide a frame for understanding experience.

> (Steven, 2003: 52–3, my emphasis)

In its initial formulation, hegemony referred to the domination of one social class over another (i.e. the classical Marxist formulation of the ruling class/working class, or bourgeoisie/proletariat dichotomy). In more recent usage, hegemony, and particularly **cultural hegemony**, has come to refer to the ideological domination of one cultural group over another in more general terms. The coupling of ideas such as 'Americanisation' and globalisation provides a good example—that is, there has long been a hegemonic assumption that a Western (read American, in this case) way of life/point of view is somehow necessarily and inherently better than any other, and social and political commentators have debated whether or not American culture will take over the world, at the expense of myriad indigenous cultures elsewhere. Like memes and discourses more generally, cultural hegemonic positions such as 'Americanisation' have largely been propagated by the mass media (as noted in the above citation, and see also Loader, 2007: 5). In recent literature, however, questions have been raised about the 'relative decline of American cultural hegemony' (Iwabuchi, 2004: 23). Could it be we're headed for another paradigm shift?

Antonio Gramsci (1891–1937): renowned for coining the term 'cultural hegemony', Gramsci was a Marxist academic and political activist. His most famous work is generally referred to as *The Prison Notebooks* (1971).

Cultural hegemony: Hegemony was a term used to explain the subordination of one social class to another, through the control of ideology. 'Cultural hegemony' is generally applied to explain the domination of one culture's position over others.

Do not go quietly: Stuart Hall and encoding/decoding

In any given context, just because a dominant hegemonic position or reading of a cultural text[6] exists, that doesn't mean we have to accept it. Receivers/viewers/readers of media have the capacity to resist, albeit sometimes in limited ways depending on circumstance, but the possibility of not accepting the primary meanings of things (the **dominant ideologies**—see Chapter 10) is always inherent to at least some degree. One of the best articles on this topic is Stuart Hall's 'Encoding/Decoding', which explores the notions of dominant/preferred, negotiated and oppositional readings in some depth.

A dominant/preferred reading is one that accepts its creators' intended meaning[7] and/or the dominant ideology at face value. In Hall's words, such a reading is explained as follows:

> The domains of [dominant or] 'preferred meanings' have the whole social order embedded in them as a set of meanings, practices and beliefs: the everyday knowledge of social structures, of 'how things work for all practical purposes in this culture'.

> (1980: 134)

Or, to rephrase from the previous sub-section on cultural hegemony, dominant/preferred readings carry within them an implicit assumption of *that's just the way things are*. To disrupt the preferred reading, or to question the status quo, if you like, requires a conscious act of will. Such deliberate action brings us then to negotiated and oppositional readings. Simply put, negotiated readings rock the boat a little bit; oppositional readings rock the boat a lot. A negotiated reading contains:

> a mixture of adaptive and oppositional elements: it acknowledges the legitimacy of the hegemonic definitions to make the grand significations (abstract), while, at a more restricted, situational (situated) level, it makes its own ground rules—it operates with exceptions to the rule. It accords the privileged position to the dominant definitions of events while reserving the right to make a more negotiated application to 'local conditions' … This negotiated version of the dominant ideology is thus shot through with contradictions, though these are only on certain occasions brought to full visibility. Negotiated codes operate through what we might call particular or situated logics: and these logics are sustained by their differential and unequal relation to the discourses and logics of power.
>
> (Hall, 1980: 137)

And if we progress further along the same lines, oppositional readings are those in which the viewer/reader

> detotalizes the message in the preferred code in order to retotalize the message within some alternative framework of reference. This is the case of the viewer who listens to a debate on the need to limit wages but 'reads' every mention of the 'national interest' as 'class interest'. He/she is operating with what we must call an *oppositional code*.
>
> (Hall, 1980: 138)

That is, oppositional readings of cultural texts tend to be along the lines of: 'I understand exactly what it is you're trying to say, I just happen to think you're completely wrong'. Finally, to restate, an individual's capacity to resist a dominant/preferred interpretation will largely be a result of their particular background and experience; that is, the cultural context they bring with them to their 'reading' in the first place.

Revisiting the prison …

There's a little more to be said about Foucault: we originally encountered his theorisation of Bentham's panopticon in Chapter 13, in relation to constructed reality, and then again with regard to surveillance in Chapter 17, and there seems no benefit in going there again in too much detail. Nonetheless, it is worth drawing attention to the fact that some of the ideas raised earlier, especially pertaining to the panopticon's increasingly limited power for explaining virtual online worlds such as Second Life, are also relevant to this chapter's exploration of reality television. In particular, the panopticon idea holds that if surveillance is constant, then order is maintained, society will self-regulate and people will behave themselves. Clearly, from a brief perusal of any given episode of *Big Brother* or *The Osbournes*, this is not the case. In fact, frequently the opposite is true, and instead of playing nice, reality television contestants/participants appear to play up to the cameras. And so, the key point again: reality television is not reality, or even television seeking to reliably portray reality. It's something else, and a new explanatory metaphor is needed.

Summary

Over the course of this chapter, we have examined:

*   Reality television, its various manifestations, and just how real it really isn't
*   How discourses are ways of thinking and speaking about stuff, and the (apparent lack of a) distinction between discourses and paradigms
*   Foucault's interpretation of the notion of discourse
*   Memes, tenacious little soundbites of information that don't even have to be true
*   Gramsci and cultural hegemony, which concerns how those in superior cultural positions maintain those positions by convincing the rest that 'that's just the way it is'
*   Stuart Hall's dominant, negotiated and oppositional readings of cultural texts
*   Further questions surrounding the ongoing usefulness of Foucault's/Bentham's panopticon as an explanatory metaphor for the functioning of contemporary society, this time in the context of reality TV.

Further reading

Abercrombie, N, Hill, S & Turner, B 1994, *Dictionary of Sociology*, Penguin, London.

Babbie, E 2008, *The Basics of Social Research*, 4th edn, Thomson Wadsworth, United States.

Balkin, K (ed.) 2004, *Reality TV*, Greenhaven, San Diego.

Foucault, M 1980, *Power/Knowledge: Selected Interviews and Other Writings, 1972–1977*, C Gordon (ed.), Pantheon, New York.

Gramsci, A 1997 [1971], *Selections from the Prison Notebooks*, International, New York.

Hall, S 1980, 'Encoding/Decoding', in S Hall, D Hobson, A Lowe & P Willis (eds), *Culture, Media, Language: Working Papers in Cultural Studies, 1972–79*, Hutchinson, London, 128–39.

Kilborn, R 2003, *Staging the Real: Factual TV Programming in the Age of* Big Brother, Manchester University Press, Manchester & New York.

Kuhn, T 1970, *The Structure of Scientific Revolutions*, University of Chicago Press, Chicago & London.

Lewis, J 2004, 'The Meaning of Real Life', in S Murray & L Ouellette (eds), *Reality TV: Remaking Television Culture*, New York University Press, New York & London, 288–302.

McHoul, A & Grace, W 1993, *A Foucault Primer: Discourse, Power and the Subject*, Melbourne University Press, Melbourne.

Osbourne, O 2009, *I Am Ozzy*, Sphere, London.

Theobold, J 2006, 'Mystification in the Media: From "Ritual Murder" to the "War On Terrorism"', in J H Brinks, S Rock & E Timms (eds), *Nationalist Myths and Modern Media: Contested Identities in the Age of Globalization*, Tauris Academic Studies, London, 55–67.

Weblinks

Bowling for Soup *1985*: www.youtube.com/watch?v=kvAjdDOshbs

Sparks, C 2007 'Reality TV: The *Big Brother* phenomenon', *International Socialism* (online journal), issue 114, posted 9 April: www.isj.org.uk/index.php4?id=314&issue=114

For revision questions, please visit www.oup.com.au/orc/chalkley.

Endnotes

1   Exceptions such as the late night *Big Brother (Uncut)* notwithstanding.

2   Among other factors. Only an indicative selection is provided here.

3   Further discussion of hegemony, particularly as it pertains to culture, is included in the following sub-section.

4   A further note on the nature of truth (or, 'lies, damn lies and statistics'): there have indeed been studies done on the risks of phone usage while driving, with the high percentages of danger reported in specific, numerical terms. However, without identifying any particular report, a critical reader may pause to ask a range of questions, including: 'Who commissioned such research?' 'What kinds of questions were asked?' 'What were the analytical procedures used (for example, mean, median or mode, for nominal, ordinal or interval level data)?' This is not the place to even begin explaining such terms (for those interested, Babbie (2008) provides an accessible and comprehensive introduction to research methods). What needs to be emphasised here is that (1) without actually lying, data can be manipulated, and frequently is, and (2) despite the best intentions of most private sector (i.e. non-university) research firms, a constant tension exists between research integrity and the client's expectations/demands. The author of this chapter has had need of working in such contexts from time to time, and also teaches research methods, including statistical analysis.

5   No offence intended to Mr King. It just happens that an ad for his *Lisey's Story* was one of the first ads of this kind I happened to see.

6   Please note here that a 'text' doesn't merely mean a book or a journal. In the context of cultural analyses, the scope encompassed by 'text' is very broad; it could be a T-shirt, a piece of music, a building or literally anything that conveys meaning.

7   Assuming that said creator is operating within the dominant hegemonic framework—if the cultural text in question is itself predominantly negotiated or oppositional, then things start getting messy (i.e. if you have an oppositional stance to a text that was essentially oppositional in the first place, are you operating within a dominant/preferred mode in so doing? Or perhaps a negotiated one?) Food for thought, but the scope of the chapter does not allow us to pursue this further right now.

19

Conclusion: Do We Communicate 'Less' or 'More' in the Digital Age?

Tony Chalkley

These final pages serve as a signpost to where you might go next. The great challenge for communication theorists and commentators is in which direction to point the signpost. In some areas, finding a clear direction is relatively easy because the vast majority of the concepts and theories are well established: narratives have been around for as long as cave painting and repetitive utterances; we have long used non-verbal cues to send messages to each other; and men and women have, for generations, used different styles of communication. Likewise, the signs and symbols of semiotics have always played a key role in our everyday life, films have long told us stories about ourselves and who we want to be, and the frameworks of modernity and postmodernity are often disputed, but on the whole, the principles and arguments are fairly stable. For most of these topics, the authors have been able to point you in a direction that has a clear and well-illuminated path!

Not all topics are so stable, straightforward to describe and relatively easy to understand. You may recall that, in the introduction, the file-sharing service LimeWire got a mention as a good example of how quickly things change in the world of new media. When the writers started to formulate the content of this book, LimeWire was an incredibly popular way to share files (in particular, music) but legal action in 2010 meant that, by the time this book went to press, it was gone. Chances are that by the time you read this, some of you will not remember what LimeWire was and some will have never heard the name. Change is fast and constant.

Even though the framework of personal communication continues to be built around people being 'geographically co-located' and 'offline' and 'physically intimate', new innovations are starting to sneak in. It is now common to 'LOL'; poke people; and tweet, text or IM your friends and family. Facebook has even given us a new form of relationship ('it's complicated'), a status that simultaneously suggests that we are in a relationship and, at the same time, open to proposals! It would appear that the communication matrix that drives society and socialisation is undergoing a process of gradual and irreversible restructure. At the same time, it might be argued that new media has just made pre-existing aspects of everyday life more explicit or 'obvious'. Is a teenager or young adult who is undertaking a lot of 'facework' via social media sites doing something essentially different from one who throws aside their shyness and 'puts on a show' in the playground? Yet there is something *different* about the way(s) in which technology has 'intruded' into our everyday lives.

As a result, communication is at an interesting crossroad: at some stage innovation stopped being all about changing technology and became more about changing culture. It is very easy to focus on the 'hardware' of new communication media—the pods, pads and phones. However, the next wave of innovation isn't going to be better Photoshop, faster data speeds, smaller and more powerful phones, or even new forms of online shopping. The next change is likely to be in the fabric and construction of what we call 'friends', 'lovers', 'community' and 'society' more generally. These exciting (or, as some would argue, frightening) changes are already well under way and are not without their challenges and problems. How do the proponents of this world of new media (especially those in positions of governmental power) make sure they are creating environments in which everone is a participant? How do we offset the positives of online social networking against the risk of bullying that never stops and is no longer geographically restricted to the school yard? How do we balance the positives of virtual worlds and social groups with the adult users who assume a teenage identity in order to exploit and abuse young members? And, for the big, broad question: does new media enhance our agency or diminish our freedoms by 'controlling' our lives? The next few years will represent a period in time where the old devices of control (for example, the law and internet filters) seem to no longer work as well is they did in the past.

These are some of the challenges of new media; but it's worth remembering that problems caused by change are not exclusive to modern society. The invention of street lights in the late nineteenth century resulted in a lack of sleep for the fine citizens of London, the printing press posed a significant risk to those in positions of power and the invention of the tape-to-tape cassette recorder was blamed (by record companies) for the loss of many hundreds of thousands of dollars of artist income. When the VHS recorder arrived (after the BETA recorder died!) the cinema industry in Australia claimed that the act of 'going to the movies' was over. Some commentators are now suggesting the same with the hasty growth of home cinema systems in the form of 54-inch (now too small?) televisions, Blu-ray players and surround-sound speakers. After lining up at my local, newly constructed cinema to see a movie, it would seem that these assertions have been proven very wrong.

The contents of this text are by no means comprehensive and, as a result, you might find the lack of discussion of some issues frustrating. This is a good thing! Now that you've been introduced to a diverse range of topics and issues, you might like to spend some time exploring the concepts we could not include: watch how the development of 3D technology changes how we are 'entertained' (and consider whether this is 'new'); keep up to date with WikiLeaks and the way 'ownership', 'security' and 'secrets' are redefined; or discover the latest changes made to the 'home', as the functions of this safe 'refuge' of everyday life become more and more automated. The role of new media technology, particularly in the areas of robotics, cyberculture and artificial intelligence, has led to questions— and will lead to further questions—about what 'life' is, who or what should have 'rights', and what, indeed, makes us *human*. Science fiction and other films continue to highlight the (positive and negative) possibilities of technological innovation, so keep your eye out for the different discourses about new media that you are exposed to. And, of course, you could always research the history of pornography—not the content, but the way this industry has long been a leader in technological innovation, production and distribution!

The three main ideas or 'subjects' this book has been concerned with are (as noted in its title) communication, new media and everyday life. We have been particularly concerned with how these three things intersect with one another, and have revealed that all three are both (1) completely new and different, and (2) the same as before.

So, after reading these chapters, return to the suggestion in the introduction to this book and think about whether you should re-write 'new' over the word you initially crossed out. Many of the previous chapters have, directly or indirectly, pointed out that the 'reality' of everyday life is and always has been constructed, and this will continue to be the case. But something has changed. Something is *different*. What this is, in the end, is up to you!

Glossary

Advertisers
Regional national or transnational corporations and businesses that seek to market their goods and services through national and/or regional media.

Advertising agencies
Central to the production of advertising and the purchase of communications space, acting as intermediaries between 'clients' (regional and national advertisers) and the media. Although some advertisers create their own advertisements, the agencies produce the vast majority of Australia's national advertising for well-known national and transnational brands. Traditionally, advertising agencies have two streams of income: (1) they receive a service fee for the production of an advertisement or a marketing strategy (from an advertiser); and (2) they often receive 'sales commissions' from different media organisations, in recognition of the airtime or page space that they purchase on behalf of their client.

Advertising Claims Board
Responsible for investigating and ruling on complaints made by advertisers about each other, so as to ensure competitive, fair and truthful conduct.

Advertising Standards Board
Responsible for investigating and ruling on complaints made by members of the community regarding advertisements that might be misleading or offensive. If an advertiser refuses to comply with a determination of the Standards Board, then the matter can be referred to the relevant government body (such as ACMA), which can then take action to have the advertisement modified, removed or discontinued.

Agenda setting
Is arguably undertaken by the media on behalf of dominant elite groups in society by selecting, shaping and restricting the types of information that we are exposed to, thus controlling the range of opinions that appear.

Audience identification
The process by which viewers are positioned or encouraged to sympathise with a character or group of characters within a film's narrative.

Australian Communications and Media Authority (ACMA)
A federal 'statutory authority' (or government agency) responsible for the regulation of: (1) broadcasting (including television and radio); (2) the internet; (3) radio communications; and (4) telecommunications. ACMA works with relevant industries to promote their self-regulation, while ensuring that they comply with relevant licence conditions, codes and standards.

Avatar
A digitally constructed image that represents a person in a game. Can be human or not, and allows the player to interact with the game world as well as other players.

Baudrillard, Jean (1929–2007)
One of the major theorists associated with **postmodernism**, Baudrillard was a French intellectual/sociologist. He is credited with developing the concepts of **hyperreality** and **simulacra**. Some of his best known works include *America* (1988) and *Cool Memories* (1990). These texts make for interesting reading, but they are not particularly accessible; the language used is not difficult, but their style is very unorthodox and sometimes hard to follow.

Behaviouralism or empiricism
This is a psychological method that focuses on human behaviours, actions or acts rather than the characteristics of industries.

Binary oppositions

The construction of a clear-cut distinction between two concepts that are perceived to be opposites, with one concept dominant over the other.

Bricolage

Bricolage is all about making the best out of whatever you've got on hand, combining and re-combining elements (of whatever) to best suit your needs. The practice of bricolage carries within it connotations of a do-it-yourself ethos. Bricolage is **pastiche**-with-purpose, and it is this positive intent/inherent meaning that keeps **Lévi-Strauss**, who coined the term, at arm's length from **postmodernism**. Those who engage in bricolage are referred to as 'bricoleurs'.

Casual gamers

A subcategory of player for whom gaming is just another pastime, to be consumed in much the same way as other media such as music and television. Casual gamers are often defined against 'hard-core' gamers, especially in terms of the amount of time they devote to gaming.

Closure

The degree to which a **narrative** offers a resolution to the tensions within it.

Code

The assembly of computer language used to create a game. Often based on established languages such as C++ but there are many variations depending on the platform the game is to be delivered on.

Codes

Frameworks of meaning that define how we interpret a **sign**. For example, a language is a code that defines the meanings of its verbal and symbolic units for those fluent in its use. Likewise, a **genre** is a type of code that frames the meaning of signs that appear in certain films and television programs.

Complementary schismogenesis

'Complementary' means 'forming a satisfactory or balanced whole' and 'schismogenesis' means the 'creation of division'. These two words, when combined, describe a situation where two parts (often people) work with and against each other to behave, and then respond, in a predictable, often destructive, manner.

Connotation

A secondary latent meaning of a sign, which operates at the 'second-order of signification', building upon the **denotative** features of a text to convey a **mythic** message. For instance, a photograph of Nike sneakers **denotes** merely footwear, while simultaneously connoting messages of wealth and athletic prowess (at least to those individuals familiar with the company's preferred interpretative code).

Convention

An established practice or constructed device that is understood by a wide audience through its repeated use over time.

Convergence

The term can be used to describe how the previously separate businesses of (1) media, (2) telecommunications and (3) computing/information technology have come together, or converged, to offer interdependent services via digital networks.

Cultural hegemony

Hegemony was originally a Marxist term, coined to explain the subordination of one social class to another, not by violence but through the control of ideology, whereby subordinate classes became convinced that their lesser position was somehow natural, an effect of 'just the way things are'. In latter usages, hegemony (and particularly 'cultural hegemony') have been more generally used to explain the domination of one culture's position over another, such as the common assumption that 'Western' culture must somehow necessarily be better/superior.

Data mining

The process of analysing public and private data produced by citizens, groups and organisations, looking for meaningful patterns, signs or repetition (also referred to as 'knowledge discovery in databases' or 'KDD'). 'When doing our online business, we scatter snippets of personal information around. Data mining companies aggregate the information in user profiles and sell those to commercial and public organizations ... Most Internet users are not aware of the spyware that tracks their behavior and collects personal information' (van der Geest, 2005: 151). Data mining also has an offline component, whereby personal details and purchasing preferences are collected from the point-of-sale use of credit and loyalty cards.

Denotation
The term used to describe the first order meaning of a sign. It is the blatant, standard, primary meaning of the sign—its primary signification. As such, it refers to the obvious elements or features that are signified by the signifier. For example, a photograph of a shoe denotes a clear referent (in this case, footwear).

Digital divide
The situation in which some groups in society are advantaged over others in not only the tools that some have access to, but in education, skills base and knowledge. It occurs not only between nations but *within* nations as well.

Digital immigrants
Often your mother and father. They were born before the proliferation of computing and the digitisation of data.

Digital natives
Those born after the invention of inexpensive, fast and effective computing. They have always had access to computers, digital files and online communities.

Digitisation
Digitisation is the process of converting information (usually analogue) into a digital format or a series of zero and one digits (called binary code).

Discourse
Discourses are ways of thinking and speaking about stuff. They can address small matters or large (although in the latter case they sometimes go by the name of paradigms). Discourses typically arise out of the situations in which they occur, as a result of specific cultural and historical conditions. That is, they do not just change over time, but can also vary depending on context. Importantly, ways of thinking and speaking can have real, tangible effects in the larger world in which they occur.

Dominant ideology
A construction of ideas about people and the world that privileges more powerful social groups while marginalising other groups.

Dominant, negotiated and oppositional readings
In Stuart Hall's famous 'Encoding/Decoding' article (1980), he discusses the possibility of dominant, negotiated and oppositional readings of cultural forms. Although the hegemonic status quo may encourage the uptake of dominant readings (i.e. those which the producers of cultural texts generally intended), Hall insists that individuals have the capacity to resist, either in whole or in part—to disagree with dominant or intended meanings and thus produce negotiated or oppositional interpretations.

Dystopian perspective
A pessimistic worldview that, in the context of new media, stresses the negative effects and consequences of technological innovation.

File sharing
The process of allowing access to your digital files (especially music and film) in order to have similar access to the files of others.

Film analysis
The critical engagement with film **narratives** that investigates the ideological messages within films and how these are constructed through **film techniques**.

Film techniques
The various devices utilised by filmmakers to construct meaning through moving images and sound.

Focaliser

The subject position or character through which a viewer is positioned to understand a **narrative**.

Foucault, Michel (1926–1984)

Michel Foucault was a French sociologist and philosopher. Over the course of his relatively short life, he produced a large body of work, some of which has not surfaced to this day (due to legal restrictions on his estate). He wrote extensively on the nature of **discourse** and on the functioning of power (including in the context of Bentham's panopticon—there is more on this in Chapters 13 and 17). His best known works include *The Birth of the Clinic* (1963), *Discipline and Punish* (1975) and *The History of Sexuality* (published in three volumes between 1976 and 1984).

Fourth estate

This is the ideal by which audiences of democratic nations are meant to get accountability and the truth from their media reportage.

Frame

The visual contents of a particular camera shot.

FTP

File Transfer Protocol.

Games consoles

A piece of computer hardware dedicated primarily to playing games. Current examples include the Xbox 360 and PlayStation 3.

Geeks

A term commonly used to refer to someone with a strong interest in computers or technology. Originally a derogatory term, it has now taken on positive connotations as computing and gaming have become more mainstream pursuits.

Gender

While the appropriate definition of this term is still contested by theorists, gender is defined here as a socially constructed performance determined by cultural assumptions and expectations. People are exposed to these assumptions and expectations throughout their entire lives (think about what blue and pink blankets have come to imply about babies in hospitals). Importantly, gender is different from biological sex (whether one is 'male' or 'female') and sexuality (based on sexual desire and preferences).

Genre

A 'type' of **narrative** consisting of a set of **conventions** that has been established over time.

Globalisation

A process whereby industries are operating increasingly on an international basis as a result of the deregulation of communications industries and improved communications technologies.

Gramsci, Antonio (1891–1937)

The theorist reknowned for coining the term '**cultural hegemony**' (see above), Gramsci was a Marxist academic and political activist, with strong links to the Italian Communist Party. He died at an early age (only 47), largely an effect of having spent much of his later life in prison (for political dissent). Gramsci's most famous work is generally referred to as *The Prison Notebooks* (1971), a collection of writings he made while incarcerated, and it is here that his original formulations on hegemony can be found.

Hall, Stuart (1932–)

Stuart Hall is a Jamaican-born sociologist who has spent most of his working life in Britain, significantly as a member of Birmingham's CCCS (Centre for Contemporary Cultural Studies) group, with others including Raymond Williams, Richard Hoggart, Paul Willis and Dick Hebdige. He left this position in 1979 to become a Professor of Sociology at the Open University. He has written extensively on many topics, although some of the work for which he is best known concerns diaspora, and also spectacular youth subcultures.

HTML

Hyper Text Mark-up Language.

Hyperreality

Reality imitating media imitating reality. Hyperreality is more than just exaggerated media images. Hyperreality is best understood as *a process*, whereby emphasised or accentuated media is accepted by those engaging with it as a true reflection of reality, and their behaviours are affected as a result. Giving the concept a negative inflection, **Jean Baudrillard** (the theorist with whom hyperreality is most frequently associated) describes it as the corruption of meaning by media. See, for example, *The Evil Demon of Images* (1987: 29, 50-1).

i Lecture

A digitally recorded lecture that is available as a media file, live steam or podcast.

Identity

A much-debated term, though scholars generally agree that the (ongoing) construction of one's sense of self is not concrete or static, but fluid, multiple and constantly changing.

Ideology

A collection or system of views and values shared by a certain group of people.

Intertextuality

The inherently interrelated or interconnected nature of all **texts** and **conventions**. This suggests that the meaning of a text is often interpreted and understood in relation to other texts.

Jameson, Fredric (1934–)

Another important postmodern theorist, Jameson is an American Marxist critic who is probably best known for his *Postmodernism, or, the Cultural Logic of Late Capitalism* (1991), which echoes and considerably expands the content of an article (of the same name) published in *New Left Review* in 1984. Both works contain consideration of the concept of **pastiche**, for which he is well known. Jameson's engagement with **postmodernism** covers a range of areas including, famously, architecture, through his discussion of the Los Angeles Bonaventure Hotel.

Kinetics

The study of body movements, gesture and posture.

Lévi-Strauss, Claude (1908–2009)

Lévi-Strauss is more firmly associated with anthropology than **postmodernism**, and his work has also been instrumental in the fields of sociology, philosophy, social theory and, particularly, **structuralism**. Famously, Lévi-Strauss applied structuralist analysis to the study of **myth**. His best known publication is probably *The Savage Mind* (translated into English in 1966), which is renowned for its discussion of **bricolage** (see below).

Marketing

In the most common usage of the term, refers to the processes used by companies to create and communicate a branded message to a desired consumer group. As such, advertising should be thought of as a central technique within a broader marketing campaign/strategy (which can include other forms of production promotion).

Mass media

Mass media is media for a large group of individuals engaging in similar activities such as watching a particular television show during prime time (7:00pm to 9:00pm) or reading the Saturday edition of a newspaper.

Media effects theory

A paradigm of media studies that seeks to find a connection between exposure to particular types of media and behavioural or attitudinal change. It has been applied to most forms of media, including cinema and television, and has experienced a resurgence in recent times in relation to games.

Media industries

Media industries are involved in developing, producing and disseminating content through a wide variety of formats including the press, electronic publishing, telecommunications, radio, music, cinema and television.

Mediation

Mediation is a process whereby the sender relays versions of issues or events to the receiver that he or she cannot directly observe for him/herself by way of the media.

Memes (mimesis)

Memes are small units of information, bite-sized ideas taken up and spread by popular/mainstream culture and other media. They seem to have the capacity to replicate independently, and as a result are often likened to viruses, although in reality it is their promotion through media that makes this possible. In fact, the term 'mimesis', of which meme is the base, literally means 'to copy'. Although they often appear so, memes do not have to be true.

Meta-message

These are the 'hidden' meanings behind (and among) the words we hear.

Metaphor

A common figure of speech where an object, concept or action is used through language to refer to another object, concept or action generally used to mean something else.

MMORPG

An abbreviation for Massively Multiplayer Online Role Playing Games. These games allow thousands of players to simultaneously inhabit the same virtual universe and interact with one another. Examples include *World of Warcraft* and *Lord of the Rings Online*.

Modernism

The period of high modernism is generally agreed to fall between 1890 and 1930. It was characterised by a belief in reason, and in (primarily Western-capitalist) notions of progress. Through progress, it was felt that perfection was possible—all the big questions could be answered, definitively, once and for all. Many ideas associated with modernism are still evident today (despite that we are now supposedly in the *post*-modern era), in a variety of fields, including but not limited to science, business, and so on. One of the best texts to explore modernism in all its forms was written by Bradbury and McFarlane (1976)—everything you need is there ... but be warned, it's heavy reading.

Mise-en-scène

The overall shot composition of what is visually depicted on film.

Myths

The common discourses (or ways of thinking) of a particular culture. Thus myths can define how we perceive certain events, objects or ideas. As such, myth has an ideological quality that shapes how we perceive and value its referents.

Narrative

A story that is constructed using various **genres** and other **conventions** in order for people to make sense of the world.

Narrative perspective

The point(s) of view from which a **narrative** is told.

New age

A philosophy, originating in the late 1980s, characterised by a belief in alternative medicine, astrology, spiritualism, etc.

New media

Includes content that is created, stored or retrieved in digital form. New media includes digital forms of text, still pictures, audio and video.

Noise

A disturbance in a communications system that interferes with or prevents reception of a signal or of information. Noise involves a cognitive (knowledge) gap between the sender and the receiver of the message, and can be categorised as auditory (such as talking in a nightclub), physical (the person whispers or the listener is hard of hearing) or cogitative (the listener does not understand the words used).

Normalised

The process by which an action is repeated so often that it comes to be considered an acceptable part of everyday life.

Packet switching

The basic languages used in packet switching are a combination of Transmission Control Protocol (a language for sending data) and Internet Protocol (a language for addressing data). **TCP/IP** forms the basis of the internet communications applications.

Paidia and Ludus

Paidia and Ludus are two different kinds of play. The first, Paidia, is the sort of free-form improvisation that children do, before they're old enough to really get that most games (grown-up games, anyway) have rules. Ludus, then, refers to games with a clear purpose or objective: to win, to score points, whatever. Further, Paidia and Ludus aren't entirely separate categories so much as two ends of the same continuum, insofar as many games contain elements of both.

Passive ideologies

Implicit messages that are present 'underneath' the **surface ideology** of a **narrative**.

Pastiche

Jameson's concept of pastiche is not too dissimilar from **Lévi-Strauss's bricolage**, or even the more common notion of collage: bring together a more-or-less random collection of stuff, and stick them together to make something new. The difference with regard to pastiche is that, at least according to Jameson, pastiche is also stamped with that characteristic negativity that inflects (infects?) **Baudrillard's hyperreality**. Jameson maintains that pastiche is 'blank parody', that the new ensembles are without intent, without motive or meaning. This text suggests strongly that to create anything completely devoid of meaning is impossible—another interesting postmodern idea has been pushed a little too far.

Patterned behaviour

Any action(s) repeated over and over. Typically, it 1) feels like it's beyond our control, 2) is cyclical and very hard to change, 3) is a response to a familiar, long-standing problem.

Photorealism

A subjective assessment of a constructed object's resemblance to a real-world object. In game development, producing graphics that resemble photographs is sometimes seen as a desirable goal for designers.

Pirate/pirated/pirating

The act of copying material that we have not paid for. It can be for personal use or, in some cases, commercial gain.

Playability

The subjective assessment of the ease with which players can engage with a game. A game can be challenging but playable, but a game that contains serious software bugs or imprecise controls is usually regarded as having poor playability.

Political economy

This is an empirical approach to understanding the economic structures and dynamics of media industries and the ideological content of media.

Polysemy

The capacity of a sign or signs to be interpreted differently by different readers of a text. As such, signs can signify 'multiple meanings', as defined by the social and cultural context of the audience.

Postmodernism

First and foremost, **postmodernism** should be understood as a lack of faith in the modernist project. Postmodernists claim that modernism's search for answers is fundamentally flawed, because there are no final answers to any questions, large or small, just ever-shifting, multiple and transient meanings. Some postmodern theorists push this idea to an extreme, and argue that, because meaning is not fixed, then nothing means anything at all. Beginning dates for postmodernism vary widely, depending on where you look and who you ask. Among the most well-known postmodern theorists are **Jean Baudrillard**, **Fredric Jameson** and **Michel Foucault**, although there are many others. One of the best general introductions to postmodernism is Appignanesi et al.'s *Postmodernism for Beginners* (1995)—it's a very accessible overview.

Post-structuralism

A broad theoretical perspective that emerged from, and in response to, the **structuralist** theory of scholars such as Ferdinand de Saussure and that of the French anthropologist, **Claude Lévi-Strauss** (both of whom looked for universal rules governing cultural phenomena such as language and mythology). Post-structuralism is most often associated with the writings of Jacques Derrida, and the later publications of Roland Barthes, **Michel Foucault** and **Jean Baudrillard**. Most post-structuralist thinkers are not disputing the existence of social structures that shape how we see and experience the world. However, they argue that our understandings of 'reality' are often problematic as language is a flawed medium for the interpretation and communication of the physical and social world. In relation to the practice of semiotics, post-structural theory reminds researchers to avoid making generalisations about the universal meanings of signs or the structures of languages. Instead, researchers must consider the contextual basis of meaning.

Presidio Modelo

Until his release from prison on 15 May 1955, in a general amnesty, Fidel Castro was held in the Presidio Modelo, a 'model prison' of panopticon design, built by the dictator Gerardo Machado on the former Isla de Pinos (Isla de la Juventud) in Cuba.

Process of naturalisation

The ways in which certain messages are portrayed over time and in numerous texts as 'normal' or 'commonsense'. Similar to the process where something becomes normalised.

Proof-of-concept

An early technical demonstration of a game, often with low-quality graphics and sound effects. Designed primarily to convince a funding source that the final game is worth financing.

Propaganda

This term describes the situation of print or broadcasting being used to strictly influence the hearts and minds of citizens.

Public broadcasting

A government-funded (at arm's length) form of broadcasting charged with the responsibility of contributing a sense of national identity as well as informing and entertaining audiences.

Public sphere

Habermas' theory of the public sphere holds the tenet for liberal democracy (here liberal denotes social and political views favouring progress and reform): that of rationalising public authority under the established practice of informed discussion and reasoned—open, free and equal—agreement. That is, power relationships can be neutralised as political authority is transformed into rational authority when dealing with the needs of civil society.

Radical pessimism

The theory that print and radio/television programs are provided according to what audiences want rather than what might afford a 'public benefit'; for example, information or opinions that might add to or challenge an audience member's personal beliefs.

Reality television

Reality TV programs are those that claim to be 'a window on the world', providing viewers with a glimpse into how (mostly) ordinary people behave, albeit in some quite constructed, unordinary situations. Recent popular examples include *Big Brother* and *MasterChef*. A common question, however, concerns just how real such programs really are.

Representation

The ways in which images and language are used to create meaning. It follows from this that knowledge about everyday life and 'reality' is constructed.

Resistant reading

A process by which a reader or viewer rejects the ideological messages a text encourages its audience to accept.

Rhetorical device

A **convention** or technique that is used with the intention of persuading an audience to adopt a certain idea.

Rough consensus

A phrase that indicates the general feeling of a group, usually concerning a particular matter, issue or problem. It is sometimes called the 'dominant view' of a group.

Sandbox games

A subgenre of games in which players are given a large (but bounded) open world to explore as part of the game's narrative. Exemplified by games such as the *Grand Theft Auto* series of games, in which players can spend many hours exploring the virtual environment.

Second Life

Second Life is an animated-character (avatar) driven, virtual world, created in stages by Linden Labs over the first few years of the twenty-first century. It is an immersive online environment where it is possible to do pretty much everything you might want to do in your 'first life': shop, be a tourist, own land—everything except feel real physical contact and taste the virtual food you're supposedly eating.

Self-regulation

Adopted by many industries seeking to avoid direct government regulation, which they consider to be interference in the workings of the marketplace. The **Advertising Standards Bureau (ASB)** is responsible for coordinating the system of self-regulation governing the practices of the Australian advertising industry.

'Semiology' or 'semiotics'

Stemming from the work of Ferdinand de Saussure, 'semiology' has often been used by European scholars to describe their method of analysing signs. In contrast, Anglophone academics (those from English-speaking countries) tend to use the term 'semiotics' to describe their methodological approach. Although both terms refer to the same method, at present 'semiotics' is the more common of the two labels.

Semiosis

Refers to the interpretative process that occurs as we decode the meaning of a **sign**. It is often used interchangeably with its synonym 'signification' (which originates from the Saussurean tradition of semiology).

Semiotic device

An action of or pertaining to **signs**.

Signs

Meaningful units that represent concepts, objects or things. A sign can be a word, sound, image or object, and serves as a vehicle for the communication of meaning. Yet the meaning of a sign is not intrinsic within its form, as it is the interpreter of the sign that 'makes meaning' through the decoding of its message.

Simulacra

Copies of copies of copies. Simulacra are closely related to **Baudrillard's hyperreality**, and are also generally associated with him. Simulacra, as a concept, is one of Baudrillard's more negative ideas—he argued that media re-report events and/or re-broadcast images that are covered by other media, on and on in a never-ending cycle. In the process, meaning is held to become lost. This text maintains that simulacra is an interesting notion, pushed to an illogical extreme. Nonetheless, those interested can explore Baudrillard's argument further in *Cool Memories* (1990—see, for example, 8, 22, 23, 26).

Social construction

When we say that something is 'socially constructed' we are saying that its existence is dependent on contingent aspects of our social selves. For example: hunger and poverty exist on a number of levels. The first is medical/scientific/economic: if you consume less than X grams of food, less than X dollars per annum. The second definition is socially constructed: poverty is relative—it's an emotional feeling and it's negotiated through dialogue with others. Students are poor, but do they live in poverty? Possibly they do, depending on how you understand 'poverty'.

Social networking

The building of online communities through the movement of non-virtual human relationships into the virtual world via the use of various technological devices.

Stereotypes

Simplistic, generalised versions or representations of a particular group of people.

Structuralism and semiology
The study of **signs** whereby the focus is on media systems and organisations, and their relationship to the wider society (McQuail, 2005).

Subversive ideology
A set of ideas that challenge, contradict or undermine a **dominant ideology**.

Surface ideologies
Explicit messages that seem to be consciously communicated through a **narrative**.

Surveillance society
Living in a community that promotes, accepts and embraces increasing levels of surveillance (physical, electronic and anonymous) as an important component of everyday life.

TCP/IP
Transmission Control Protocol (a language for sending data) and Internet Protocol (a language for addressing data). TCP/IP forms the basis of the internet communications applications.

Techno-legal time-gap
The techno-legal time-gap is the time it takes for authorities to come to terms with the problems arising from new technologies. One of the strongest current examples of this time-gap concerns the intellectual property theft inherent in the internet file sharing of music and movies.

Texts
Documents, objects or things that comprise one or more **signs**. All media industries produce texts that are a collection of still or moving images and/or sounds functioning as a group to create meaning. Anything that generates meaning through signifying practices can be called a text. We 'read' texts, such as newspapers and clothing, for their meaning.

Uncanny valley
A term derived from robotics that describes the unease many people feel when they encounter an *almost* human simulation.

Vicious circle
A process by which an action (usually to solve a problem) causes a reaction that results in a return to the initial problem.

Viral distribution
Spread by distribution, from person to person.

Virtual learning
A mode of computer-based education whereby the teacher interacts with students either via videoconferencing, internet broadcast or email (or combination of the above).

WWW
World Wide Web.

Bibliography

Abercrombie, N, Hill, S & Turner, B 1994, *Dictionary of Sociology*, Penguin, London.

Adler, R B & Rodman, G 2009, *Understanding Human Communication*, Oxford University Press, New York.

Adorno, T W & Horkheimer, M 1973 (1947), *Dialectic of Enlightenment*, trans. J Cumming, Allen Lane, London.

Advertising Standards Bureau 2009, 'Case Report 450/09: GASP Jeans', Canberra, 28 October.

Alexander, J 1981, 'The Mass Media in Systematic, Historical and Comparative Perspective', in E Katz & T Szescho (eds), *Mass Media and Social Change*, Sage, Beverly Hills, 17–52.

Al-Rafee, S & Cronan, T 2006, 'Digital Piracy: Factors that Influence Attitude toward Behavior', *Journal of Business Ethics*, vol. 63, no. 1, 237–59.

American Civil Liberties Union v Reno 1997, 929 F. Supp. 824, 830–849 (E.D. pa 1996), *aff'd* 521 US 844, 117 SCt 2329, 138 L Ed2d 874.

Annandale, D 2006, 'The Subversive Carnival of *Grand Theft Auto: San Andreas*', in N Garrelts (ed.), *Meaning and Culture of* Grand Theft Auto: *Critical Essays*, McFarland & Company, Jefferson, 88–103.

Appignanesi, R & Garrett, C with Sardar, Z & Curry, P 1995, *Postmodernism for Beginners*, Icon, Cambridge.

Appignanesi, R & Garrett, C with Sardar, Z & Curry, P 2004, *Introducing Postmodernism*, Icon, Cambridge.

Arlington, K 2004, 'Children Overboard the Most Despicable of Lies: Hawke', *The Age*, 24 August retrieved 27 January 2011, <www.theage.com.au/articles/2004/08/24/1093246520431.html?from=storylhs>.

Artcollecting.co.uk 2010, retrieved 6 February 2011, <www.artcollecting.co.uk/Modernism.html>.

Australian Communications and Media Authority (ACMA) 2010, *Television Program Standard for Australian Content in Advertising (TPS 23)*, retrieved 6 February 2011, <www.acma.gov.au/WEB/STANDARD/pc=PC_91808>.

Babbie, E 2008, *The Basics of Social Research*, 4th edn, Thomson Wadsworth, Belmont.

Bal, M (ed.) 2004, *Narrative Theory: Critical Concepts in Literary and Cultural Studies*, Routledge, London & New York.

Baldick, C 1990, *The Concise Oxford Dictionary of Literary Terms*, Oxford University Press, New York & Oxford.

Balkin, K (ed.) 2004, *Reality TV*, Greenhaven, San Diego.

Balnaves, M S, Donald, S H & Shoesmith, B 2009, *Media Theories & Approaches: A Global Perspective*, Palgrave Macmillan, Basingstoke.

Baran, S J 2010, *Introduction to Mass Communication: Media Literacy and Culture*, 6th edn, McGraw-Hill, New York.

Barnwell, N & Robbins, S 2006, *Organisation Theory: Concepts and Cases*, Pearson Educational Australia, Frenchs Forest.

Barr, T 2000, *Newmedia.com.au: The Changing Face of Australia's Media and Communications*, Allen & Unwin, Sydney.

Barrett, P 2006, 'White Thumbs, Black Bodies: Race, Violence, and Neoliberal Fantasies in *Grand Theft Auto: San Andreas*', *The Review of Education, Pedagogy, and Cultural Studies*, vol. 28, no. 1, 95–119.

Barthes, R 1964, *Elements of Semiology*, Hill and Wang, New York.

Barthes, R 1973 [1957], *Mythologies*, trans. A Lavers, HarperCollins, London.

Barthes, R 1983, *The Fashion System*, Hill and Wang, New York.

Barthes, R 1989, *Empire of Signs*, Noonday Press, New York.

Barthes, R 2006, 'The Death of the Author', in C Janaway (ed.), *Reading Aesthetics and the Philosophy of Art*, Blackwell, Malden, 188–92.

Baudrillard, J 1983, *Simulations*, Semiotext(e), New York.

Baudrillard, J 1987, *The Evil Demon of Images*, Power Institute of Fine Arts, University of Sydney, Sydney.

Baudrillard, J 1988a, *America*, trans. C Turner, Verso, London & New York.

Baudrillard, J 1988b, *The Ecstasy of Communication*, Semiotext(e), New York.

Baudrillard, J 1990, *Cool Memories*, trans. C Turner, Verso, London & New York.

Baudrillard, J 1996, *The System of Objects*, Verso, New York.

Baudrillard, J 1998, *The Consumer Society: Myths and Structures*, Sage, London.

Beckford, M 2010, 'Internet Words Form the Language of 2moro', *The Age*, 3 January, retrieved 13 August 2010, <www.theage.com.au/world/internet-words-form-the-language-of-2moro-20100102-lmic.html>.

Belbin, M 2010, 'Home to Belbin Team Roles', retrieved 1 September 2010, <www.belbin.com>.

Bell, M, Chalmers, M, Barkhuss, L, Hall, M, Sherwood, S, Tennant, P, Brown, B, Rowland, D, Bemford, S, Capra, M & Hamshire, A 2006, 'Interweaving Mobile Games with Everyday Life', paper presented at CHI, Montreal, Canada, 2006.

Bennett, A 1999, 'Subcultures or Neo-Tribes? Rethinking the Relationship between Youth, Style and Musical Taste', *Sociology*, vol. 33, no. 3, 599–617.

Benson, A L (ed.) 2000, *I Shop, Therefore I Am: Compulsive Buying and the Search for Self*, Jason Aronson Inc., London.

Best Essays 2011, 'Custom Essay Writing', retrieved 19 May 2011, <www. bestessays.com.au/doc_essay.php>.

Bignell, J 1997, *Media Semiotics: An Introduction*, Manchester University Press, Manchester.

Birch, D, Schirato, T & Srivastava, S 2001, 'Modernity, Postmodernity and Postcoloniality', in D Birch, T Schirato & S Srivastava (eds), *Asia: Cultural Politics in the Global Age*, Allen & Unwin, Crows Nest, 25–53.

Blum, K 1999, 'Gender Differences in Asynchronous Learning in Higher Education: Learning Styles, Participation Barriers and Communication Patterns', *Journal of Asynchronous Learning Networks*, vol. 3, no. 1, 46–66.

Blumler, J G & Hoffmann-Reim, W 1992, 'Toward Renewed Public Accountability in Broadcasting', in J G Blumler (ed.), *Television and the Public Interest: Vulnerable Values in West European Broadcasting*, Sage, London, 218–28.

Boellstorff, T 2008, *Coming of Age in Second Life: An Anthropologist Explores the Virtually Human*, Princeton University Press, Princeton & Oxford.

Bonney, B & Wilson, H 1983, *Australia's Commercial Media*, Macmillan, Melbourne.

Bourdieu, P 1986, *Distinction: A Social Critique of the Judgement of Taste*, trans. R Nice, Routledge, London.

Bowling for Soup 2004, '1985', from *A Hangover You Don't Deserve*, FFROE/Jive/Zomba, United States.

Boyd, D & Ellison, N 2007, 'Social Networking Sites: Definition, History, and Scholarship', *Journal of Computer-Mediated Communication*, vol. 13, no. 1, 210–30.

Boyd, D & Hargittai, E 2010, 'Facebook Privacy Settings: Who Cares?', *First Monday*, vol. 15, no. 8.

Boyne, R 2000, 'Structuralism', in B S Turner (ed.), *The Blackwell Companion to Social Theory*, 2nd edn, Blackwell, Oxford, 160–91.

Bradbury, M & Mcfarlane, J (eds) 1976, *Modernism 1890–1930*, Penguin, London.

Briggs, A 1961, *The History of Broadcasting in the United Kingdom, Vol. 1: The Birth of Broadcasting*, Oxford University Press, London.

Brown, D 1997, *Cybertrends: Chaos, Power, and Accountability in the Information Age*, Viking, London.

Bruns, A 2007, 'Introduction', in A Bruns and J Jacobs (eds), *Uses of Blogs*, Peter Lang, New York, 1–6.

The Bucket List 2007, Warner Bros.

Buckingham, D 2003, *Media Education: Literacy, Learning and Contemporary Culture*, Polity, Cambridge.

Buckingham, D (ed.) 2008, *Youth, Identity, and Digital Media*, MIT, Cambridge & London.

Burns, T 1977, *The BBC: Public Institution and Private World*, Macmillan, London.

Caillois, R 2001 [1958], *Man, Play and Games*, trans. M Barash, University of Illinois Press, Urbana & Chicago.

Campbell, J & Carlson M 2002, 'Panopticon.com: Online Surveillance and the Commodification of Privacy', *Journal of Broadcasting & Electronic Media*, vol. 46, no. 4, 586–606.

Cantril, H, Gaudet, H & Herzog, H 1940, *The Invasion from Mars: A Study in the Psychology of Panic*, Princeton University Press, Princeton.

Carew, S 2009, 'France Telecom CFO blames email for staff stress', *Reuters*, 24 September, retrieved 24 May 2011, <www.reuters.com/article/2009/09/24/us-francetelecom-stress-idUSTRE58N6ES20090924>.

Caro, A 1981, 'Advertising—An Introduction', in K Fowles & N Mills (eds), *Understanding Advertising: An Australian Guide*, TAFE Educational, Sydney, 5–17.

Castells, M 1996, *The Rise of the Network Society: The Information Age—Economy, Society and Culture*, vol. 1, Blackwell, Massachusetts.

The Castle 1997, Working Dog and Village Roadshow Entertainment.

Centre d'études sur les medias (Centre for Media Studies) 2002, *Public Broadcasting: Why? How?* A report compiled in cooperation with the Canadian Broadcasting Corporation at the behest of the World Radio Television Council, retrieved 7 February 2010, <www.cmrtv.org/documents/radio-publique-en.htm>.

Chandler, D 2007, *Semiotics: The Basics*, 2nd edn, Routledge, New York.

Chang, Y 2003, '"Glocalisation" of Television: Programming Strategies of Global Television Broadcasters in Asia', *Asian Journal of Communication*, vol. 13, no. 1, 1–36.

Chenault, B G 1998, 'Developing Personal and Emotional Relationships via Computer-mediated Communication', *Computer-Mediated Communication Magazine*, May, retrieved 19 July 2011, <www.december.com/cmc/mag/1998/may/chenault.html>.

Cho, H, Rivera-Sanchez, M & Lim, S 2009, 'A Multinational Study on Online Privacy: Global Concerns and Local Responses', *New Media & Society*, vol. 11, no. 3, 395–416.

Chu, A 2004, 'Taiwan's Mass-Mediated Crisis Discourse: Pop Politics in an Era of Political TV Call-In Shows', in D K Jordan, A D Morris & M L Moskowitz (eds), *The Minor Arts of Daily Life: Popular Culture in Taiwan*, University of Hawaii Press, Honolulu, 89–108.

Cinque, T 2009, 'A New Screen Face for Public Service Broadcasting', peer reviewed article for the Australian and New Zealand Communication Association Conference, *Communication, Creativity and Global Citizenship*, 8–10 July 2009, Brisbane, <www.anzca09.org>.

Cornwell, R 2010, 'Shirley Sherrod: Proof That a Week is a Long Time in Politics', *The Independent*, 23 July, retrieved 25 July 2010, <www.independent.co.uk/news/people/news/shirley-sherrod-the-woman-who-proves-a-week-is-a-long-time-in-politics-2033400.html>.

Counihan, B 2010, 'Gillard is No Twit', *The Age*, 7 July, retrieved 23 July 2010, <www.theage.com.au/opinion/contributors/gillard-is-no-twit-20100707-1003l.html>.

Crawford, R 2006, 'Truth in Advertising: The Impossible Dream?', *Media International Australia: Incorporating Culture & Policy*, no. 119, 124–37.

Creeber, G & Royston, M 2009, *Digital Cultures: Understanding New Media*, McGraw-Hill, Maidenhead.

Crisell, A 1998, 'Radio: Public Service, Commercialism and the Paradox of Choice', in A Briggs & P Cobley (eds), *The Media: An Introduction*, Addison Wesley Longman Limited, New York, 114–26.

Culler, J 2000, *Literary Theory: A Very Short Introduction*, Oxford University Press, Oxford.

Cunningham, S & Turner, G (eds) 1997, *The Media in Australia: Industries, Texts, Audiences*, 2nd edn, Allen & Unwin, St Leonards.

Cunningham, S & Turner, G (eds) 2010, *The Media and Communications in Australia*, 3rd edn, Allen & Unwin, Crows Nest.

Curran, J 1998, 'Newspapers and the Press', in A Briggs & P Cobley (eds), *The Media: An Introduction*, Addison Wesley Longman Limited, New York, 81–96.

Cutting Edge 2008, 'Growing Up Online', 1 April, SBS Television.

Dahlberg, L 2001. 'The Internet and Democratic Discourse: Exploring the Prospects of Online Deliberative Forums Extending the Public Sphere', *Information, Communication and Society*, vol. 4, no. 4, 615–33.

Dante, E 2010, 'The Shadow Scholar', *Chronicle of Higher Education*, November 12, retrieved 19 May 2011, <http://chronicle.com/article/article-content/125329>.

Dennis, A R, Kinney S T & Hung, Y C 1999, 'Gender Differences in the Effects of Media Richness', *Small Group Research*, vol. 30, no. 4, 405–37.

Dennis, E E & DeFleur, M L 2010, *Understanding Media in the Digital Age: Connections for Communications, Society, and Culture*, Allyn & Bacon, New York.

Dennis, E E & Merrill J C 2002, *Media Debates: Great Issues for the Digital Age*, 3rd edn, Wadsworth/ Thomson Learning, Melbourne.

Derrida, J 1976, *Of Grammatology*, Johns Hopkins University Press, Baltimore.

DeSarbo, W S & Edwards, E A 1996, 'Typologies of Compulsive Buying Behavior: A Constrained Clusterwise Regression Approach', *Journal of Consumer Psychology*, vol. 5, no. 3, 231–62.

The Digital Undertakers 2010, retrieved 8 November 2010, <www.thedigitalundertakers.com/FAQRetrieve. aspx?ID=43736>.

Dill, K E, Gentile, D A, Richter, W A & Dill, J C 2005, 'Violence, Sex, Race and Age in Popular Video Games: A Content Analysis', in E Cole & J Henderson (eds), *Featuring Females: Feminist Analyses of the Media*, American Psychological Association, Washington.

Dittmar, H 2004, 'Understanding and Diagnosing Compulsive Buying', in R H Coombs (ed.), *Handbook of Addictive Disorders: A Practical Guide to Diagnosis and Treatment*, John Wiley & Sons, New Jersey, 411–48.

Dredge, S 2010, '2009 US Mobile Games Market Worth $540m Claims Report', retrieved 6 February 2011, <www.casualgaming.biz/news/29755/2009-US-mobile-games-market-worth-540m-claims-report>.

Ducheneaut, N, Wen, M, Yee, N & Wadley, G 2009, 'Body and Mind: A Study of Avatar Personalization in Three Virtual Worlds', paper presented at CHI, Boston, 7 April 2009.

Dunay, P & Krueger R 2009, *Facebook Marketing for Dummies*, Wiley, New Jersey.

Eco, U 1976, *A Theory of Semiotics*, Indiana University Press, Ontario.

Ellison, N B, Steinfield, C & Lampe C 2007, 'The Benefits of Facebook "Friends": Social Capital and College Students' Use of Online Social Network Sites', *Journal of Computer-Mediated Communication*, no. 12, 1143–68.

Entertainment Software Association 2008, '2008: Essential Facts', retrieved 6 February 2011, <www.theesa.com/facts/pdfs/ESA_EF_2008.pdf>.

Entertainment Software Association 2009, 'Industry Facts', retrieved 6 February 2011, <www.theesa.com/facts/index.asp>.

Enzensberger, H M 1974, *The Consciousness Industry: On Literature, Politics and the Media*, trans. M Roloff, Continuum & Seabury, New York.

Errington, W & Miragliotta, N 2007, *Media & Politics: An Introduction*, Oxford University Press, South Melbourne.

Family Guy 2002, 20th Century Fox.

Farrer, G 2009, 'Be Careful What You Reveal to Your "Friends"', *The Age*, 10 October, Insight, 3.

Featherstone, M 1991, *Consumer Culture and Postmodernism*, Sage, London.

Fletcher, H 2008, 'Human Flesh Search Engines: Chinese Vigilantes that Hunt Victims on the Web', *Times Online*, retrieved 25 January 2011, <http://technology.timesonline.co.uk./tol/news/tech_and_web/article4213681.ece>.

Flew, T 2008, *New Media: An Introduction*, 3rd edn, Oxford University Press, South Melbourne.

Flexischools 2009, 'Canteen Solutions from FlexiSchools', retrieved 22 September 2009, <www.flexischools.com.au/Home/tabid/167/Default.aspx>.

Foster, D 1994, '*The Lion King* Falls Prey to Howls of Sexism, Racism', *Chicago Tribune*, 26 July, 3.

Foucault, M 1977, *Discipline and Punish: The Birth of the Prison*, trans. A Sheridan, Penguin, London.

Foucault, M 1980, *Power/Knowledge: Selected Interviews and Other Writings, 1972–1977*, C Gordon (ed.), Pantheon, New York.

Foursquare 2010, retrieved 8 November 2010, <http://foursquare.com/about>.

Foursquare 2011, retrieved 19 July 2011, <http://foursquare.com/2011/06/20/holysmokes10millionpeople>.

Freiberger, P & Swaine, M 2000, *Fire in the Valley: The Making of the Personal Computer*, McGraw-Hill, Sydney.

Friedman, T 1999, *The Lexus and the Olive Tree*, Farrar, Straus & Giroux, New York.

'Friends You Can Trust, and Friends on the Net' 2010, *The Age*, 29 May, retrieved 23 July 2010, <www.theage.com.au/opinion/editorial/friends-you-can-trust-and-friends-on-the-net-20100528-wlby.html>.

Frontline 2001, *The Merchants of Cool: A Report of the Creators and Marketers of Popular Culture for Teenagers*, retrieved 6 February 2011, <www.pbs.org/wgbh/pages/frontline/shows/cool>.

Fulton, H, Huisman, R, Murphet, J & Dunn, A (eds) 2005, *Narrative and Media*, Cambridge University Press, Port Melbourne.

Gantz, J & Rochester, J 2005, *Pirates of the Digital Millennium*, Prentice Hall, New Jersey.

Garnham, N 1998, 'Media Policy', in A Briggs & P Cobley (eds), *The Media: An Introduction*, Addison Wesley Longman Limited, New York, 210–23.

Gettler, L 2010, 'How Secure is That Site?' *The Age*, 27 May, retrieved 3 June 2010, <www.theage.com.au/business/how-secure-is-that-site-20100526-we9p.html>.

Gibb, J 1961, 'Defensive Communication', *Journal of Communication*, vol. 11, 141–8.

Giddens, A 1993, *Sociology*, 2nd edn, Polity, Cambridge.

Gitlin, T 1998, 'Public Sphere or Public Sphericules', in T Liebes and J Curran (eds), *Media, Ritual and Identity*, Routledge, London, 168–174.

Given, J 1998, *The Death of Broadcasting*, Griffin Press, Adelaide.

Goldsmith, J & Wu, T 2008, *Who Controls the Internet: Illusions of a Borderless World*, Oxford University Press, New York.

Gordon, R 2003, 'The Meanings and Implications of Convergence', in K Kawamoto (ed.), *Digital Journalism: Emerging Media and the Changing Horizons of Journalism*, Rowman & Littlefield, New York, 57–73.

Gorman, L & McLean, D 2009, *Media and Society into the 21st Century: A Historical Introduction*, 2nd edn, Wiley-Blackwell, Malden & Oxford.

Gottdiener, M 1995, *Postmodern Semiotics*, Blackwell Publishers, Massachusetts.

Grabosky, P 1998, 'Crime and Technology in the Global Village', paper presented at the Internet Crime Conference, 16–17 February, retrieved 4 November 2010, <www.aic.gov.au/crime_types/cybercrime/illegalcontent/~/media/conferences/internet/grabosky.ashx>.

Gramsci, A 1997 [1971], *Selections from the Prison Notebooks*, International, New York.

Gray, J 1993, *Men Are from Mars, Women Are from Venus. (A Practical Guide for Improving Communication and Getting What You Want in Your Relationships.)*, Harper Collins, Hammersmith.

Green, L 2001, *Technoculture: From Alphabet to Cybersex*, Allen & Unwin, Crows Nest.

Habermas, J 1989, *The Structural Transformation of the Public Sphere: An Inquiry into a Category of Bourgeois Society*, trans. T Burger with F Lawrence, MIT, Cambridge.

Hachten, W & Scotton, J 2002, *The World News Prism: Global Media in an Era of Terrorism*, 6th edn, Iowa State, Ames.

Halbert, D J 2009, 'Public Lives and Private Communities: The Terms of Service Agreement and Lives in Virtual Worlds,' *First Monday*, vol. 14, no. 12.

Hall, C 1994, *Tourism and Politics: Policy, Power and Place*, John Wiley & Sons, New York.

Hall, S 1980, 'Encoding/Decoding', in S Hall, D Hobson, A Lowe & P Willis (eds), *Culture, Media, Language: Working Papers in Cultural Studies, 1972–79*, Hutchinson, London, 128–39.

Hall, S 1997a, 'The Work of Representation', in S Hall (ed.), *Representation: Cultural Representations and Signifying Practice*, Sage, London, 13–75.

Hall, S 1997b, 'Race, Culture and Communications: Looking Backward and Forward at Cultural Studies', in J Storey (ed.), *What is Cultural Studies? A Reader*, Arnold, London, 336–43.

Hamilton, C & Denniss, R 2005, *Affluenza: When Too Much Is Never Enough*, Allen & Unwin, Sydney.

Hartley, J 2009, 'From the Consciousness Industry to the Creative Industries: Consumer-created Content, Social Network Markets and the Growth of Knowledge', in J Holt and A Perren (eds), *Media Industries: History, Theory and Methods*, Oxford, Blackwell, 231–44.

Hayward, S 2007, *Cinema Studies: The Key Concepts*, 3rd edn, Routledge, London & New York.

Hebdige, D 1979, *Subculture: The Meaning of Style*, Routledge, London.

Hendry, A 2008, 'Connected Aussies Spend More Time Online Than Watching TV but Australians Lead the Charge in High-Def TV and Home Theatre Adoption', *Computerworld*, retrieved 24 December 2008, <www.computerworld.com.au/index.php/id;614216176;fp;;fpid;;pf;1;>.

Herald Sun 2010, 'New Victoria Police uniform 'to give cops harder edge', *Herald Sun*, March 23, retrieved 17 May 2011, <www.heraldsun.com.au/news/national/new-victoria-police-uniform-to-give-cops-harder-edge/story-e6frf7l6-1225844064981>.

Herman, E S & Chomsky, N 1994, *Manufacturing Consent: The Political Economy of the Mass Media*, Vintage, London.

Hickman, L 2010, 'How I Became a Foursquare Cyberstalker', *The Age*, 27 July, retrieved 27 October 2010, <www.theage.com.au/digital-life/mobiles/how-i-became-a-foursquare-cyberstalker-20100727-10t3e.html>.

Hirst, M & Harrison, J 2007, *Communication and New Media: From Broadcast to Narrowcast*, Oxford University Press, South Melbourne.

Hoffmann-Reim, W 1992, 'Protecting Vulnerable Values in the German Broadcasting Order', in J G Blumler (ed.), *Television and the Public Interest: Vulnerable Values in West European Broadcasting*, Sage, London, 43–60.

Holson, L 2004, 'Out of Hollywood, Rising Fascination with Video Games', *New York Times*, 10 April, retrieved 6 February 2011, <http://ruby.fgcu.edu/courses/tdugas/IDS3301/acrobat/hollywoodgames.pdf>.

Howells, R & Matson, R (eds) 2009, *Using Visual Evidence*, McGraw-Hill (Open University Press), Maidenhead.

Huijser, H 2008, 'Exploring the Educational Potential of Social Networking Sites: The Fine Line Between Exploiting Opportunities and Unwelcome Opposition', *Studies in Learning, Evaluation, Innovation and Development*, vol. 5, no. 3, 45–54.

Inglis, K S 1983, *This is the ABC: The Australian Broadcasting Commission 1932–1983*, Melbourne University Press, Melbourne.

Iwabuchi, I 2004, 'Feeling Glocal: Japan in the Global Television Format Business', in A Moran & M Keane (eds), *Television Across Asia: Television Industries, Programme Formats and Globalisation*, Routledge Curzon, London, 21–35.

Jahn-Sudmann, A 2008, 'Innovation NOT Opposition: The Logic of Distinction of Independent Games', *Eludamos: Journal for Computer Game Culture*, vol. 2, no. 1, 5–10.

James, R, Bexley E, Devlin, M & Marginson S 2007, *Australian University Student Finances 2006: A Summary of Finding from a National Survey of Students in Public Universities*, University of Melbourne, Melbourne, retrieved 6 February 2011, <www.universitiesaustralia.edu.au/resources/136/AUSF%20Report%202006.pdf>.

Jameson, F 1984, 'Postmodernism, or the Cultural Logic of Late Capitalism', *New Left Review*, no. 146, 53–92.

Jameson, F 1988, 'Postmodernism and Consumer Society', in E Kaplan (ed.), *Postmodernism and its Discontents: Theories, Practices*, Verso, London, 13–29.

Jameson, F 1991, *Postmodernism, or, the Cultural Logic of Late Capitalism*, Verso, London.

Jenkins, H 2006, *Convergence Culture: Where Old and New Media Collide*, New York University Press, New York.

Jolly, F 2006, 'Jeans ad not inappropriate', media release, Advertising Standards Bureau, Canberra, 6 October.

Jolly, F 2009, 'Most complained about ads in 2009', media release, Advertising Standards Bureau, Canberra, 15 December.

Jones, J 2003, 'Show Your Real Face: A Fan Study of the UK *Big Brother* Transmissions (2000, 2001, 2002): Investigating the Boundaries between Notions of Consumers and Producers of Factual Television', *New Media and Society*, vol. 5, no. 3, 400–21.

Jung, C 1968, *The Archetypes and the Collective Unconscious*, 2nd edn, Routledge & Kegan Paul, London.

Kafai, Y, Fields, D & Cook, M 2010, 'Your Second Selves: Player-designed Avatars', *Games and Culture*, vol. 5, no. 1, 23–42.

Karim, K H 2001, 'Cyber-Utopia and the Myth of Paradise: Using Jacques Ellul's Work on Propaganda to Analyse Information Society Rhetoric', *Information, Communication and Society*, vol. 4, no. 1, 113–34.

Kelley, M 2006, 'Feds Sharpen Secret Tools for Data Mining', *USA Today*, 19 July, 2.

Kemp, B 2006, *Ancient Egypt: Anatomy of a Civilisation*, Routledge, Oxford.

Kilborn, R 2003, *Staging the Real: Factual TV Programming in the Age of* Big Brother, Manchester University Press, Manchester & New York.

Kisselburgh, L 2009, 'The Social Structure of Privacy in Sociotechnological Realms' (draft paper), International Communication Association, Chicago, 1–50.

Knapp, M & Hall J 2010, *Nonverbal Communication in Human Interaction*, Cengage Learning, Boston.

Kornblum, J 2006, 'With Cellphone Video, Little Brother is Always Watching', *USA Today*, 6 December, 1.

Krone, K, Garrett, M & Chen, L 1992, 'Managerial Communication Practices in Chinese Factories: A Preliminary Investigation', *Journal of Business Communication*, vol. 29, no. 3, 229–52.

Krotz, F & von Hasebrink, U 1998, 'The Analysis of People-Meter Data: Individual Patterns of Viewing Behaviour and Viewers' Cultural Background', *The European Journal of Communication Research*, vol. 23, no. 2, 151–74.

Kuhn, T 1970, *The Structure of Scientific Revolutions*, University of Chicago Press, Chicago & London.

Lampe, C, Ellison, N & Steinfield, C 2006, 'A Face(book) in the Crowd: Social Searching vs. Social Browsing', paper presented at Conference '06, 9–11 November, 2004, Banff, Vancouver, Canada.

Lange v Australian Broadcasting Corporation 1997, 189 CLR 520, 574 (Austl H C), retrieved 25 January 2011, <www.austlii.edu.au/au/cases/cth/HCA/1997/25.html>.

Lash, S & Urry, J 1987, 'The Semiotics of Everyday Life', in S Lash & J Urry (eds), *The End of Organised Capitalism*, Polity Press, Cambridge, 288–376.

Laswell, H D 1948, 'The Structure and Function of Communication in Society', in L Bryson (ed.), *The Communication of Ideas*, Harper, New York, 117.

Lévi-Strauss, C 1966, *The Savage Mind*, University of Chicago Press, Chicago.

Lévi-Strauss, C 1972, *Structural Anthropology, Vol. 1*, Penguin, Harmondsworth.

Leung, L 2003, 'Impacts of Net-Generation Attributes, Seductive Properties of the Internet, and Gratifications Obtained on Internet Use', *Telematics and Informatics*, no. 20, 107–29.

Levinson, P 2009, *New, New Media*, Pearson, Sydney.

Lewis, J 2004, 'The Meaning of Real Life', in S Murray & L Ouellette (eds), *Reality TV: Remaking Television Culture*, New York University Press, New York & London, 288–302.

Lister, M, Dovey, J, Giddings, S, Grant I & Kelly K 2009, *New Media: A Critical Introduction*, 2nd edn, Routledge, New York.

Livingstone, S 1999, 'New Media, New Audiences', *New Media and Society*, vol. 1, no. 1, 59–68.

Livingstone, S & Lunt, P 1994, *Talk on Television: Audience Participation and Public Debate*, London, Routledge.

Loader, B 2007, 'Introduction: Young Citizens in the Digital Age: Disaffected or Displaced?', in B D Loader (ed.), *Young Citizens in the Digital Age: Political Engagement, Young People and New Media*, Routledge, London, 1–17.

Lopez-Escobar, E 1992, 'Vulnerable Values in Spanish Multichannel Television', in G Blumler (ed.), *Television and the Public Interest: Vulnerable Values in West European Broadcasting*, Sage, London, 161–72.

Lowery, S A & DeFleur, M L 1995, *Milestones in Mass Communication Research: Media Effects*, 3rd edn, Longman, White Plains.

Lyotard, J 1979, *The Postmodern Condition: A Report on Knowledge*, trans. G Bennington & B Massumi, University of Minnesota Press, Minneapolis.

McGill, D 1989, 'A Nintendo Labyrinth Filled With Lawyers, Not Dragons', *New York Times*, 9 March.

McHoul, A & Grace, W 1993, *A Foucault Primer: Discourse, Power and the Subject*, Melbourne University Press, Melbourne.

McPherson, T (ed.) 2008, *Digital Youth, Innovation, and the Unexpected*, MIT, Massachusetts.

MacRury, I 2009, *Advertising*, Routledge, London.

McQuail, D 1987, *Mass Communication Theory*, Sage, Newbury Park.

McQuail, D 2005, *McQuail's Mass Communication Theory*, 5th edn, Sage, London.

Marcus, G 1989, *Lipstick Traces: A Secret History of the Twentieth Century*, Harvard University Press, Cambridge.

Marcuse, H 1968 [1964], *One Dimensional Man*, Sphere, London.

'Mark' 2009, 'How to Lose a Job Via Facebook in 140 Characters or Less', retrieved 20 October 2009, <http://applicant.com/how-to-lose-a-job-via-facebook-in-140-characaters-or-less>.

Marr, D 2006, 'Truth Overboard: The Story That Won't Go Away', *The Sydney Morning Herald*, 28 February, retrieved 27 January 2011, <www.smh.com.au/news/national/truth-overboard--the-story-that-wont-go-away/2006/02/27/1141020023654.html?page=fullpage#contentSwap1>.

Marsen, S 2006, *Communication Studies*, Palgrave Macmillan, Houndmills.

Marx, K 1959 [1844], *Economic and Philosophical Manuscripts of 1844*, Lawrence & Wishart, London.

Marx, K 1973 [1857], *Grundisse: Foundations of the Critique of Political Economy*, trans. M Nicolaus, Pelican, London.

Marx, K 1990 [1867], *Capital: A Critique of Political Economy*, vol. 1, trans. B Fowkes, Penguin, London.

Marx, K & Engels, F 2002 [1848], *The Communist Manifesto*, trans. S Moore, Penguin, London.

Maslen, G 2010, 'Why Short Message Plays Go a Long Way', *The Age*, 8 February, retrieved 10 April 2010, <www.theage.com.au/national/education/why-short-message-plays-go-a-long-way-20100207-nk9e.html>.

Mawhood, J & Tysver, D 2000, 'Law and the Internet', in D Langford (ed.) *Internet Ethics*, Macmillan, London, 96–126.

Meadows, M 2008, *I, Avatar: The Culture and Consequences of Having a Second Life*, New Riders, Berkeley.

Miller, D 2010, *Stuff*, Polity Press, Cambridge.

Milner, A 1996, *Literature, Culture & Society*, Allen & Unwin, St Leonards.

Moon, B 2001, *Literary Terms: A Practical Glossary*, 2nd edn, Chalkface, Cottesloe.

Mortensen, E 2007, *Communication Theory*, Transaction, New Brunswick.

Morton, D 2010, 'Recording History: The History of Recording Technology', retrieved 20 September, <www.recording-history.org/index.php>.

Munro, P & Nader, C 2010, 'Blogs, Vlogs and Tweets the Order of the Day as Campaign Hits the Net', *The Age*, 18 July, retrieved 20 July 2010, <www.theage.com.au/federal-election/blogs-vlogs-and-tweets-the-order-of-the-day-as-campaign-hits-the-net-20100717-10fe3.html>.

Murphy, H, Hildebrandt, H & Thomas, P 1997, *Effective Business Communications*, 7th edn, McGraw-Hill, New York.

Nielsen Online, 'Aussie Internet Usage Takes Over TV Viewing for the First Time', news release, March, retrieved 24 May 2008, <www.nielsennetratings.com/press.jsp?Section=new_pr&theyear=2008&country=Australia&themonth=2/>.

Noam, E 1991, *Television in Europe*, Oxford University Press, Oxford.

Norris, P 2002, 'The Bridging and Bonding Role of Online Communities', *The Harvard International Journal of Press/Politics*, vol. 7, no. 3, 3–13.

NPD 2010, '2009 U.S. Video Game Industry and PC Game Software Retail Sales Reach $20.2 Billion', retrieved 6 February 2011, <www.npd.com/press/releases/press_100114.html>.

O'Loughlin, B 2001, 'The Political Implications of Digital Innovations', *Information, Communication and Society*, vol. 4, no. 4, 595–614.

O'Reilly, T 2006, 'Web 2.0 Compact Definition: Trying Again', retrieved 30 November 2009, <http://radar.oreilly.com/2006/12/web-20-compact-definition-tryi.html>.

Osbourne, O 2009, *I Am Ozzy*, Sphere, London.

O'Shaughnessy, M & Stadler, J 2006, *Media and Society: An Introduction*, 3rd edn, Oxford University Press, Melbourne.

O'Shaughnessy, M & Stadler, J 2008, *Media and Society: An Introduction*, 4th edn, Oxford University Press, Melbourne.

Oxford University Press 2008, *Compact Oxford English Dictionary of Current English*, Oxford University Press, Melbourne.

Oxford University Press 2009, *Australian Concise Oxford Dictionary*, 5th edn, Oxford University Press, Melbourne.

Pace, T & Houssian, A 2009, 'Are Socially Exclusive Values Embedded in the Avatar Creation Interfaces of MMORPGS?', *Journal of Information, Communication & Ethics in Society*, vol. 7, no. 2/3, 192–210.

Palfrey, J & Gasser, U 2008, *Born Digital: Understanding the First Generation of Digital Natives*, Basic, New York.

Paterson, M 2006, *Consumption and Everyday Life*, Routledge, London.

Pease, A 1985, *Body Language: How To Read Others' Thoughts By Their Gestures*, Camel, North Sydney.

Pease, A & Pease, B 2003, *Why Men Can Only Do One Thing at a Time and Women Never Stop Talking*, Camel, Boston.

Peirce, C S 1960, *Collected Papers of C S Peirce*, Harvard University Press, Cambridge.

Phelan, J & Rabinowitz, P J (eds) 2005, *A Companion to Narrative Theory*, Blackwell, Oxford.

Phillips, P 2007, 'Spectator, Audience and Response', in J Nelmes (ed.), *Introduction to Film Studies*, 4th edn, Routledge, London & New York, 143–71.

Pingree, G & Gitelman, L 2003, 'Introduction: What's New About New Media?', in L Gitelman & G B Pingree (eds), *New Media 1740–1915*, MIT Press, Cambridge, xi–xxii.

Pool, I 1983, *Technologies of Freedom*, Belknap, Cambridge.

Poster, M 1997, 'Cyberdemocracy: The Internet and The Public Sphere', in D Holmes (ed), *Virtual Politics: Identity and Community in Cyberspace*, Sage, London, 212–42.

Pramaggiore, M & Wallis, T 2008, *Film: A Critical Introduction*, 2nd edn, Laurence King, London.

Princeton University 2008, 'Academic Integrity at Princeton', retrieved 19 May 2011, <www.princeton. edu/pr/pub/integrity/08/academic_integrity_2008.pdf>.

Rabinow, P (ed.) 1997–9, *Essential Works of Foucault, 1954–1984*, The New Press, New York.

Raboy, M 1990, *Missed Opportunities: The Story of Canada's Broadcasting Policy*, McGill-Queen's University Press, Montreal & Kingston.

Rajava, N, Saari, T, Laarni, J, Kallinen, K & Salminen, M 2005, 'The Psychophysiology of Video Gaming: Phasic Emotional Responses to Game Events', in *The Changing Views: Worlds in Play*, Proceedings of DiGRA 2005 Conference.

Redding, W C 1985, 'Stumbling Toward Identity: The Emergence of Organizational Communication as a Field of Study', in R D McPhee & P K Tompkins (eds.), *Organizational Communication: Traditional Themes and New Directions*, Sage, Thousand Oaks, 15–54.

Rheingold, H 1993, *Virtual Communities,* Addison-Wesley, Reading.

Richtel, M 2009, 'Video Game Makers Challenged by the Next Wave of Media', *New York Times*, 29 March, retrieved 6 February 2011, <www.nytimes.com/2009/03/30/technology/30game.html>.

Richter, D H 1996, *Narrative/Theory*, White Plains, Longman.

Robins, K 1999, 'Against Virtual Community', *Angelaki: Journal of the Theoretical Humanities,* vol. 4. no. 2, 163–9.

Robbins, S & Barnwell, N 2006, *Organisation Theory: Concepts and Cases*, Prentice Hall, Frenchs Forest.

Rutter, J & Bryce, J 2006, *Understanding Video Games*, Sage, London.

Saussure, F 1983, *Course in General Linguistics*, Owen, London.

Scharlott, B & Christ, W 1995, 'Overcoming Relationship-initiation Barriers: The Impact of a Computer-dating System on Sex Role, Shyness, and Appearance Inhibitions', *Computers in Human Behavior*, vol. 11, no. 2, 191–204.

Schleiner, A 2001, 'Does Lara Croft Wear Fake Polygons? Gender and Gender-Role Subversion in Computer Adventure Games', *Leonardo*, vol. 34, no. 3, 221–26.

Schultz, J 1998, *Reviving the Fourth Estate: Democracy, Accountability and the Media*, Cambridge University Press, Melbourne.

Sex in the City 2002, Home Box Office, Star, D (prod.).

Shakespeare, W 1999, *As You Like It*, in *The Complete Works of Shakespeare, Volume II*, Wordsworth, Hertfordshire, 611–40.

Shawcross, W 1993, *Rupert Murdoch: Ringmaster of the Information Circus*, Pan, London.

Silverman, T 2009, '*Modern Warfare 2* Breaks Day-one Entertainment Sales Record', retrieved 6 February 2011, <http://videogames.yahoo.com/events/plugged-in/-modern-warfare-2-breaks-day-one-entertainment-sales-record/1372471>.

Sim, S (ed.) 1998, *The Icon Critical Dictionary of Postmodern Thought*, Icon, Cambridge.

Simmel, G 1997 [1903], 'The Metropolis and Mental Life', trans. E Shils, in N Leach (ed.), *Rethinking Architecture: A Reader in Cultural Theory*, Routledge, London, 69–79.

Sinclair, J 2006, 'Globalisation Trends in Australia's Advertising Industry', *Media International Australia: Incorporating Culture & Policy*, no. 119, 112–23.

Sinclair, J 2010a, 'Advertising', in S Cunningham & G Turner (eds), *The Media and Communications in Australia*, 3rd edn, Allen & Unwin, Crows Nest, 189–206.

Sinclair, J 2010b, 'The Media and Communications: Theoretical Traditions', in S Cunningham & G Turner (eds), *The Media & Communications in Australia*, 3rd edn, Allen & Unwin, Crows Nest, 23–34.

Smith, J 2008, 'China's Mobile Network: A Big Brother Surveillance Tool?' *ABC News Online*, retrieved 6 February 2011, <www.abc.net.au/news/stories/2008/01/28/2147712.htm>.

Smythe, D W 1977, 'Communications: Blindspot of Western Marxism', *Canadian Journal of Political and Society Theory*, vol. 1, no. 3, 1–28.

The Social Network 2010, Columbia Pictures.

Sparks, C 2007, 'Reality TV: The *Big Brother* Phenomenon', *International Socialism*, no. 114, retrieved 23 November 2010, <www.isj.org.uk/index.php4?id=314&issue=114>.

Stephens, J 1992, *Language and Ideology in Children's Fiction*, Longman, London.

Stern, S 2008, 'Producing Sites, Exploring Identities: Youth Online Authorship', in D Buckingham (ed.), *Youth, Identity, and Digital Media*, MIT, Cambridge & London, 95–117.

Steven, P 2003, *The No-Nonsense Guide to Global Media*, New Internationalist, Oxford.

Stewart, C & Kowaltzke, A 2007, *Media: New Ways and Meanings*, 3rd edn, John Wiley & Sons, Milton.

Straubhaar, J & LaRose, R 2004, *Media Now: Understanding Media, Culture and Technology*, 4th edn, Wadsworth, Belmont.

Sturken, M & Cartwright, L 2001, *Practices of Looking: An Introduction to Visual Culture*, Oxford University Press, Oxford & New York.

Tannen, D 1991, *You Just Don't Understand: Women and Men in Conversation*, Random House, Milson's Point.

Tannen, D 1992, *That's Not What I Meant! How Conversation Style Makes or Breaks Relationships*, Ballantine, New York.

Tannen, D 1993, *Gender and Conversational Interaction*, Oxford University Press, New York.

Tannen, D 2005, *Talking From 9 to 5: How Women's and Men's Conversation Styles Affect Who Gets Heard, Who Gets Credit, and What Gets Done at Work*, Virago, London.

Tannen, D 2006, *You're Wearing That? Understanding Mothers and Daughters in Conversation*, Random House, Westminster.

Tapscott, D 1995, *The Digital Economy: Promise and Peril in the Age of Networked Intelligence*, McGraw-Hill, New York.

Tapscott, D 2009, *Grown Up Digital*, McGraw-Hill, New York.

Taylor, F 1947, *The Principles of Scientific Management*, Harper & Brothers, New York.

Taylor, J & Cooren, F 1997, 'What Makes Communication "Organizational"? How the Many Voices of a Collectivity Become the One Voice of an Organization', *Journal of Pragmatics*, vol. 27, 409–38.

Theobold, J 2006, 'Mystification in the Media: From "Ritual Murder" to the "War On Terrorism"', in J H Brinks, S Rock & E Timms (eds), *Nationalist Myths and Modern Media: Contested Identities in the Age of Globalization*, Tauris Academic Studies, London, 55–67.

Thornton, K 2009, 'Crime and Punishment in 18th & 19th Century England', retrieved 11 October 2009, <www.deakin.edu.au/alfreddeakin/spc/exhibitions/candp/candp.php>.

Thwaites, T, Davis, L & Mules, W 1994, *Tools for Cultural Studies: An Introduction*, Macmillan Education, South Melbourne.

Tinwell, A 2009, 'Uncanny as Usability Obstacle', in A A Ozok & P Zaphiris (eds), *Online Communities and Social Computing*, Proceeding of Third International Conference, OCSC 2009, 622–31.

Toffler, A 1970, *Future Shock*, Random House, New York.

Tolbert, P & Zucker, L 1997, 'The institutionalization of institutional theory', in S Clegg & C Hardy (eds), *Studying Organization: Theory and Method*, 2nd edn, Sage Publications, London.

Tong, S T, Van Der Heide, B, Langwell, L & Walther, J B 2008, 'Too Much of a Good Thing? The Relationship Between Number of Friends and Interpersonal Impressions on Facebook', *Journal of Computer-Mediated Communication*, vol. 13, no. 3, 531–49.

Tuleja, E 2009, *Intercultural Communication for Business*, Cengage, Mason.

Tumber, H 2001, 'Democracy in the Information Age: The Role of the Fourth Estate in Cyberspace', *Information, Communication and Society*, vol. 4, no. 1, 95–112.

Turkle, S 1995, *Life on the Screen: Identity in the Age of the Internet*, New York, Touchstone.

Unknown 2010a, 'Humanoid Robot', retrieved 9 March 2010, <http://en.wikipedia.org/wiki/Humanoid_robot>.

Unknown 2010b, 'Technological Convergence', retrieved 9 March 2010, <http://en.wikipedia.org/wiki/Technological_convergence>.

'US Man Tweets about His Wedding from the Altar' 2009, *IBN Live*, 7 December, retrieved 17 June 2010, <http://ibnlive.in.com/news/us-man-tweets-about-his-wedding-at-the-altar/106618-13.html>.

van der Geest, T 2005, 'Big Business, Big Brother: User Profiling on the Internet', *Information Design Journal + Document Design*, vol. 13, no. 2, 151–4.

Vanden Boogart, M R 2006, 'Uncovering the Social Impact of Facebook on a College Campus', unpublished thesis, retrieved 25 January 2011, <http://hdl.handle.net/2097/181/>.

Veblen, T 1994 [1899], *The Theory of the Leisure Class*, Penguin, Harmondsworth.

Viégas, F B 2005, 'Bloggers' Expectations of Privacy and Accountability: An Initial Survey', *Journal of Computer-Mediated Communication*, vol. 10, no. 3.

Vivian, J 2009, *The Media of Mass Communication*, Allyn and Bacon, Boston.

von Hasebrink, U 1997, 'In Search of Patterns of Individual Media Use', in U Carlsson (ed.), *Beyond Media Uses and Effects*, University of Göteborg, Göteborg, Nordicom, 99–112.

Wallace, P 1999, *The Psychology of the Internet*, Cambridge University Press, Cambridge.

Walter, J 1998, 'Citizen, Consumer, Culture: The Establishment of Television in Public Consciousness', *Journal of Australian Studies*, no. 58, 107–15.

Walther, J B, Van Der Heide, B, Kim, S, Westerman, D & Tong, S T 2008, 'The Role of Friends' Behaviour on Evaluation of Individuals' Facebook Profiles: Are We Known by the Company We Keep?', *Human Communication Research*, no. 34, 28–49.

Wang, Y & Mainwaring, S 2008 'Ethnography at Play: An Exploratory Case Study of Chinese Users' Experience in and around Online Games', *Proceedings of the CHI08 Workshop on Evaluating User Experiences in Games*, Florence, Italy.

Warren, B 2000, 'Subculture: Reassessing the Meanings of Style', unpublished thesis, Deakin University, Melbourne.

Warren, B 2008, 'There May Be a Ghost in the Machine, but It Can't Spell or Punctuate: SMS Txting as a Contributing Factor to Literary Decline (or wotz rong w my spllng? y do u care?)', *The Australian Sociological Association (TASA) Refereed Conference Proceedings*, TASA, Melbourne.

Watkins, S C 2009, *The Young and the Digital: What the Migration to Social-Networking Sites, Games, and Anytime, Anywhere Media Means for our Future*, Beacon, Boston.

Weber, M 1947, *Max Weber: The Theory of Social and Economic Organization*, Free Press, New York.

Weber, M 1968, *Economy and Society*, Bedminister Press, New York.

Wilson, K 2006, 'Fashion or Porn? Provocative "Lolita" Jeans Adverts Spark Outrage', *The Sunday Mail* (Melbourne), 10 September, 24.

Windschuttle, K 1985, *The Media: A New Analysis of the Press, Television, Radio and Advertising in Australia*, Penguin, Ringwood.

Woo, J & Lee, J 2006, 'The Limitations of Information Privacy in the Network Environment', *University of Pittsburgh Journal of Technology Law & Policy*, vol. 11, no. 1, 1–21.

World Bank 2011, 'Data: Internet Users', retrieved 26 January 2011, <http://data.worldbank.org/indicator/IT.NET.USER/countries/1W?cid=GPD_58&display=graph>.

Yar, M 2008, 'The Rhetorics and Myths of Anti-piracy Campaigns: Criminalization, Moral Pedagogy and Capitalist Property Relations in the Classroom', *New Media and Society*, vol. 10, no. 4, 605–23.

Young, A 1981, *Dada and After: Extremist Modernism and English Literature*, Manchester University Press, Manchester.

YouTube 2010, 'Bowling for Soup—1985', retrieved 15 August 2010, <www.youtube.com/watch?v=kvAjdDOshbs>.

Zengerle, P 2010, 'Obama Says USDA "Jumped the Gun" on Sherrod Ouster', Reuters, 22 July, retrieved 25 July 2010, <www.reuters.com/article/idUSTRE66L3G520100723>.

Index